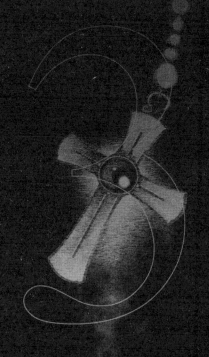

ROSARIO + VAMPIRE
Season II

AKIHISA IKEDA

Horror Story Thus Far

Tsukune Aono accidentally enrolls in Yokai Academy, a high school for monsters! After befriending the school's cutest girl, Moka Akashiya, he decides to stay...even though Yokai has a zero-tolerance policy toward humans. (A *fatal* policy.) Tsukune has to hide his true identity while fending off attacks by monster gangs. He survives with the help of his News Club friends—Moka, Kurumu, Yukari and Mizore.

But then a student riot nearly destroys the school, and classes are canceled for half a year for "remodeling." It's already spring by the time the gang (now sophomores) return... and meet Moka's rowdy little sister, Koko, who has enrolled as a freshman.

Suddenly a band of violent thieves terrorize the school, and Tsukune and his friends—joined by Koko—battle them in the school's ancient underground dungeons!

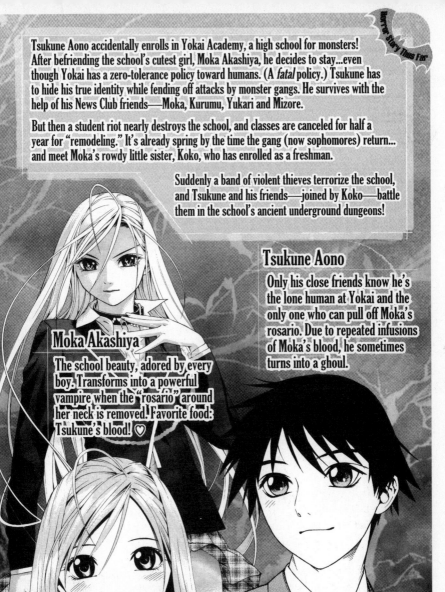

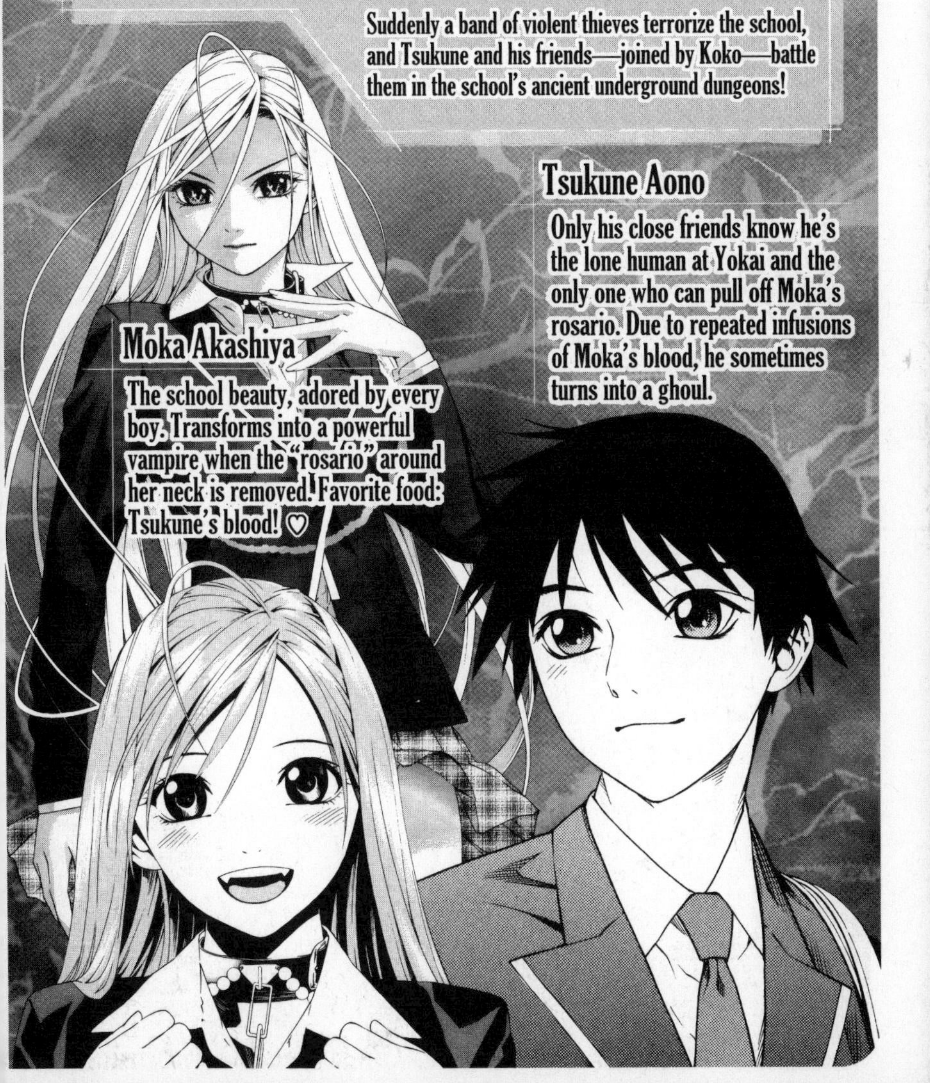
Tsukune Aono
Only his close friends know he's the lone human at Yokai and the only one who can pull off Moka's rosario. Due to repeated infusions of Moka's blood, he sometimes turns into a ghoul.
Moka Akashiya
The school beauty, adored by every boy. Transforms into a powerful vampire when the "rosario" around her neck is removed. Favorite food: Tsukune's blood! ♡

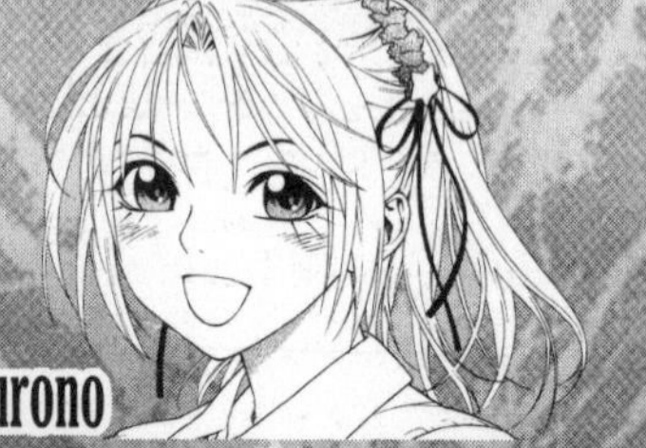

Kurumu Kurono

A succubus. Also adored by all the boys—for two obvious reasons. Fights with Moka over Tsukune.

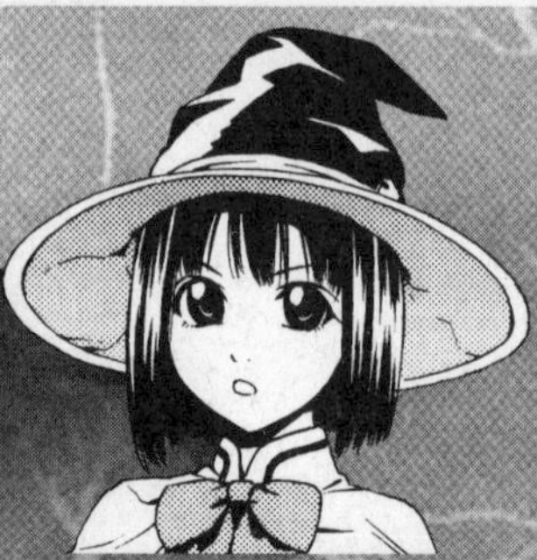

Yukari Sendo

A mischievous witch. Much younger than the others. A genius who skipped several grades.

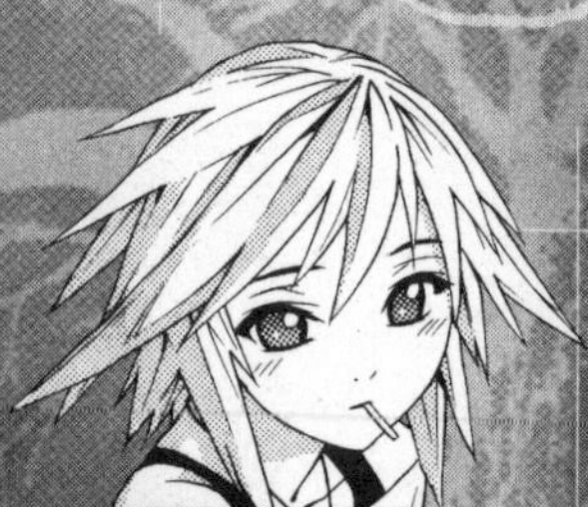

Mizore Shirayuki

A snow fairy who manipulates ice. She fell in love with Tsukune after reading his newspaper articles.

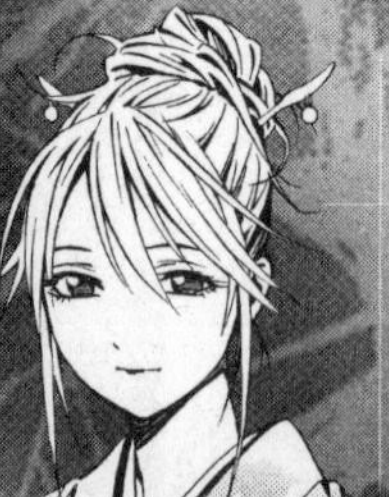

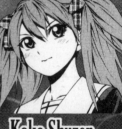

Tsurara Shirayuki

Mizore's mother. She dreams of the day that Tsukune will wake up to her daughter's charms and give her some grandchildren.

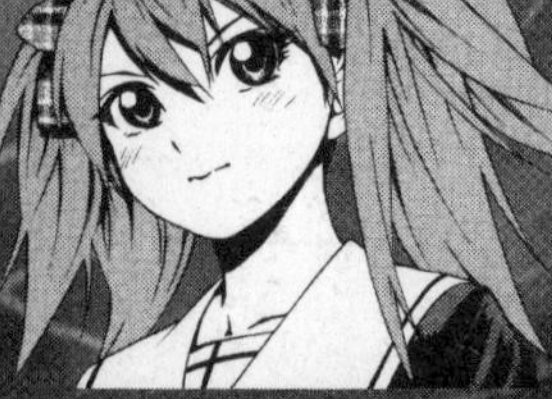

Koko Shuzen

Moka's stubborn little sister. Koko worships Moka's inner vampiric self but hates her sweet exterior. Koko's pet bat transforms into a weapon.

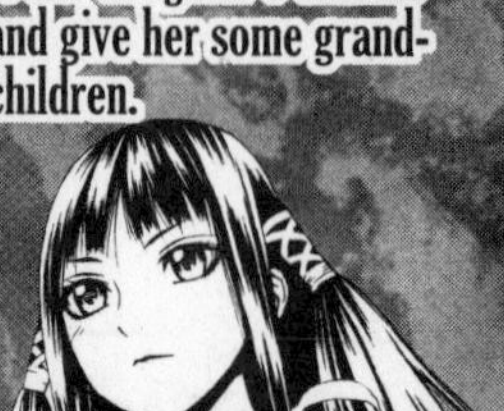

Ruby Tojo

A witch who only learned to trust humans after meeting Tsukune. Now employed as Yokai's headmaster's assistant.

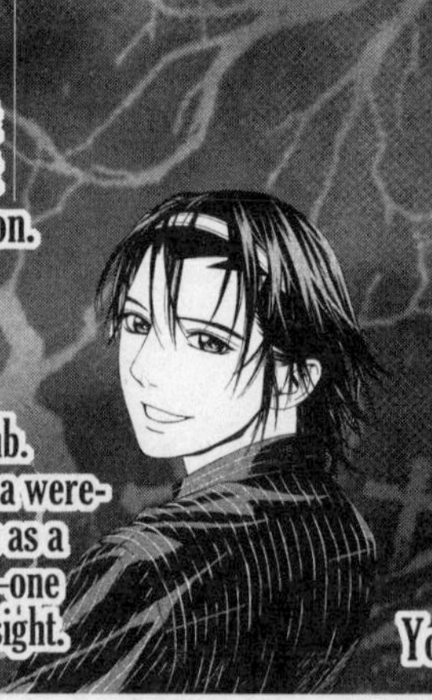

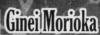

Ginei Morioka

President of the News Club. Although his true form is a werewolf, he's more notorious as a wolf of a different kind—one who chases every girl in sight.

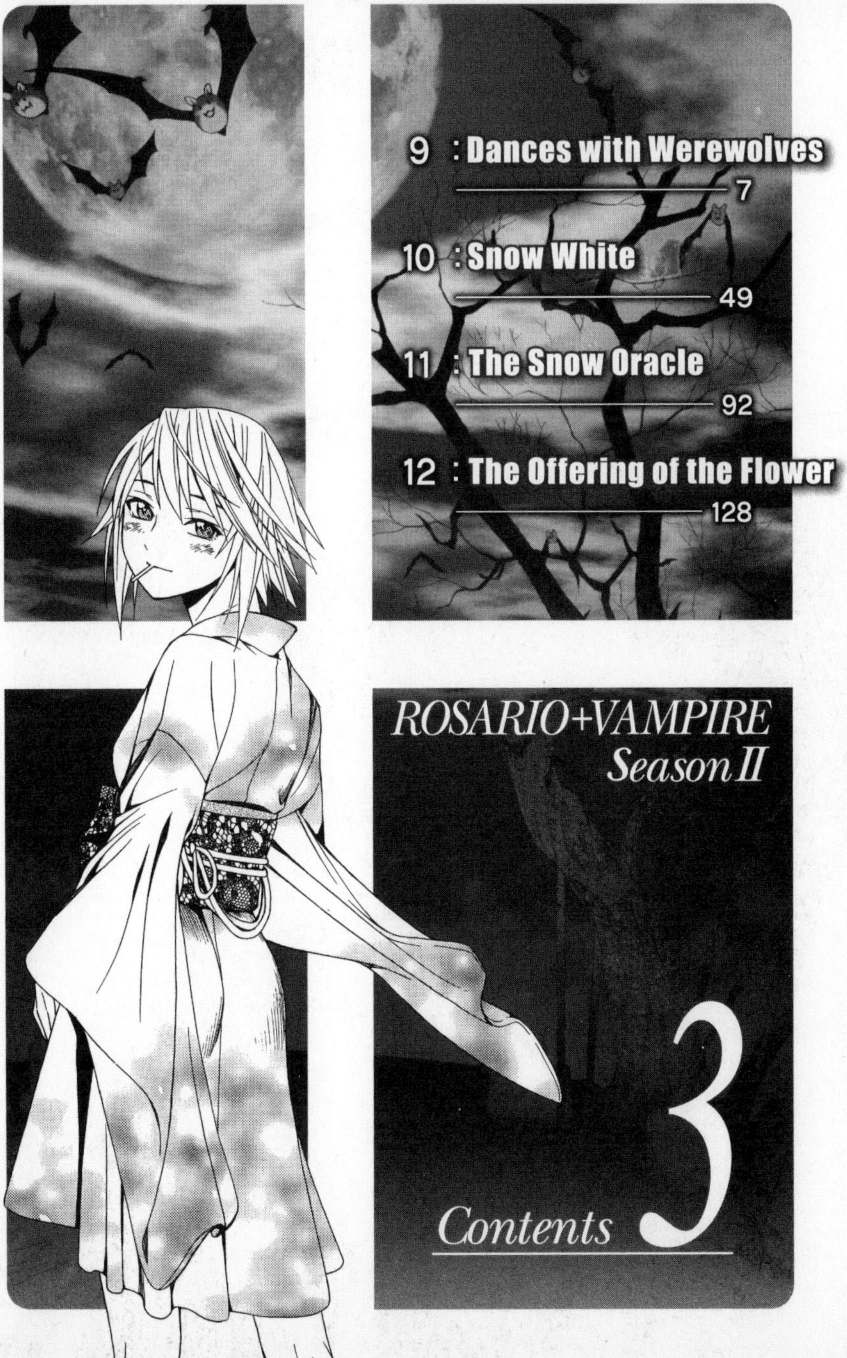

ROSARIO+VAMPIRE
Season II

Contents 3

9: Dances with Werewolves

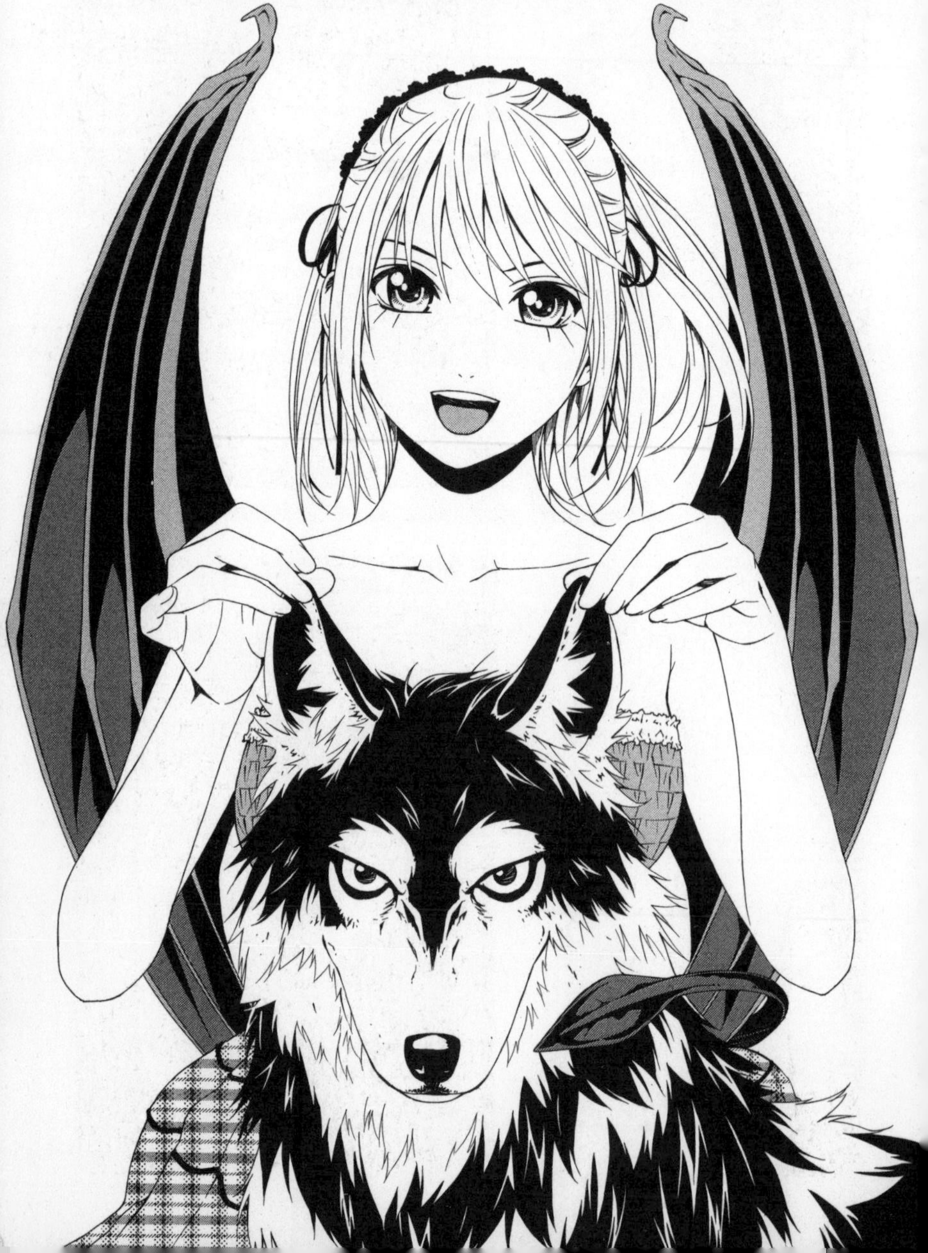

DRIP
DRIP
GR
RRRRR
OWOOOOO
!
TWIK
...
A HOWLING WOLF...?
OWOOOOO

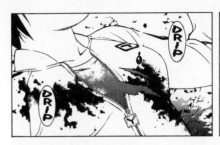

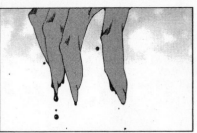

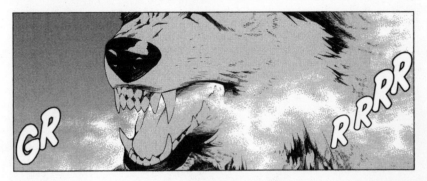

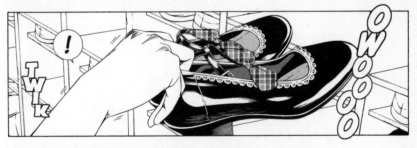

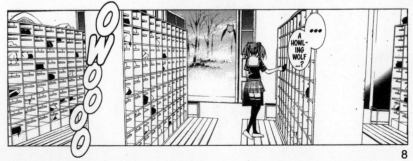

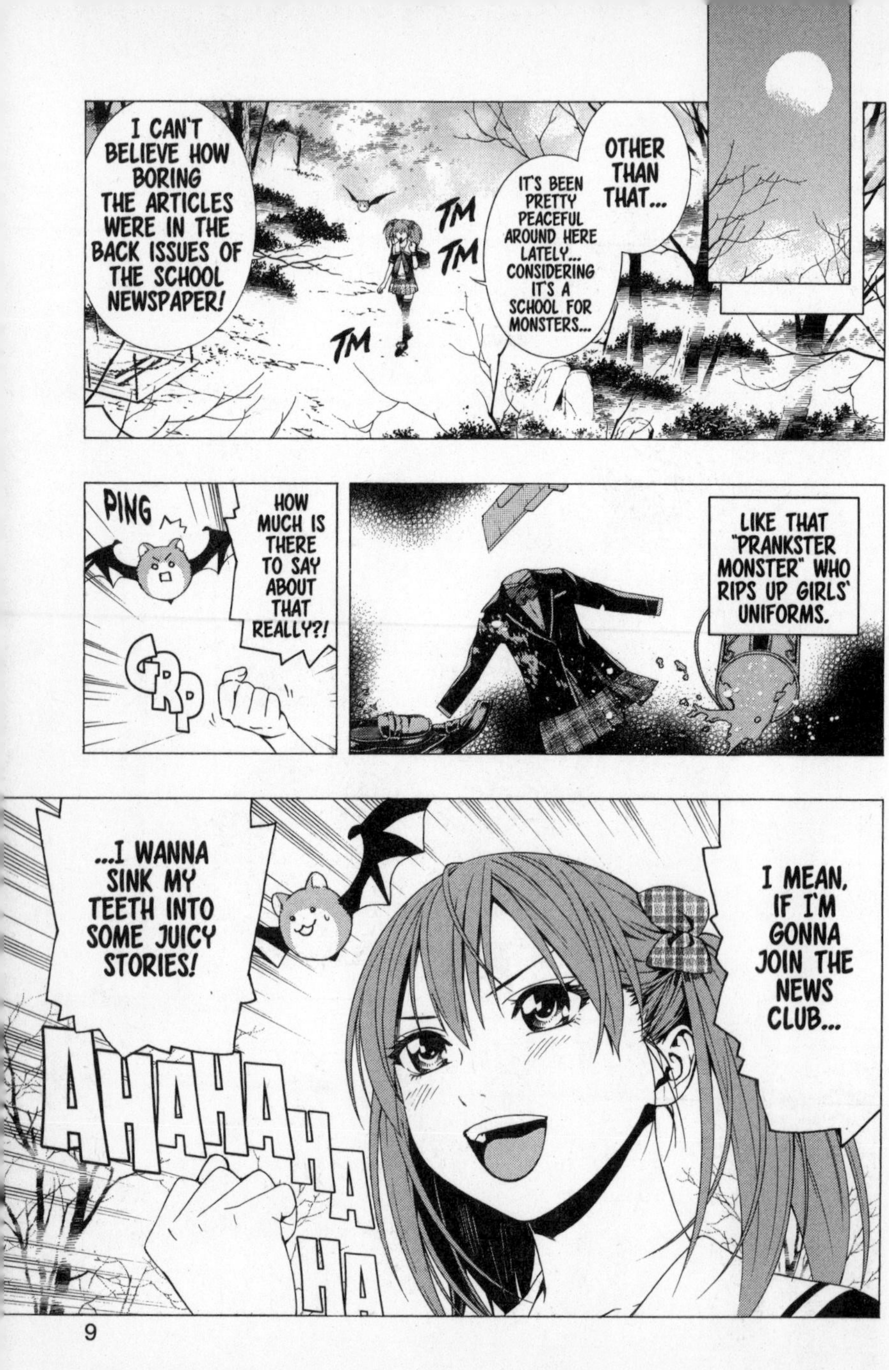
OTHER THAN THAT...
IT'S BEEN PRETTY PEACEFUL AROUND HERE LATELY... CONSIDERING IT'S A SCHOOL FOR MONSTERS...
TM
TM
TM
I CAN'T BELIEVE HOW BORING THE ARTICLES WERE IN THE BACK ISSUES OF THE SCHOOL NEWSPAPER!
LIKE THAT "PRANKSTER MONSTER" WHO RIPS UP GIRLS' UNIFORMS.
PING
HOW MUCH IS THERE TO SAY ABOUT THAT REALLY?!
GRP
I MEAN, IF I'M GONNA JOIN THE NEWS CLUB...
...I WANNA SINK MY TEETH INTO SOME JUICY STORIES!
AHAHAHAHA
HA

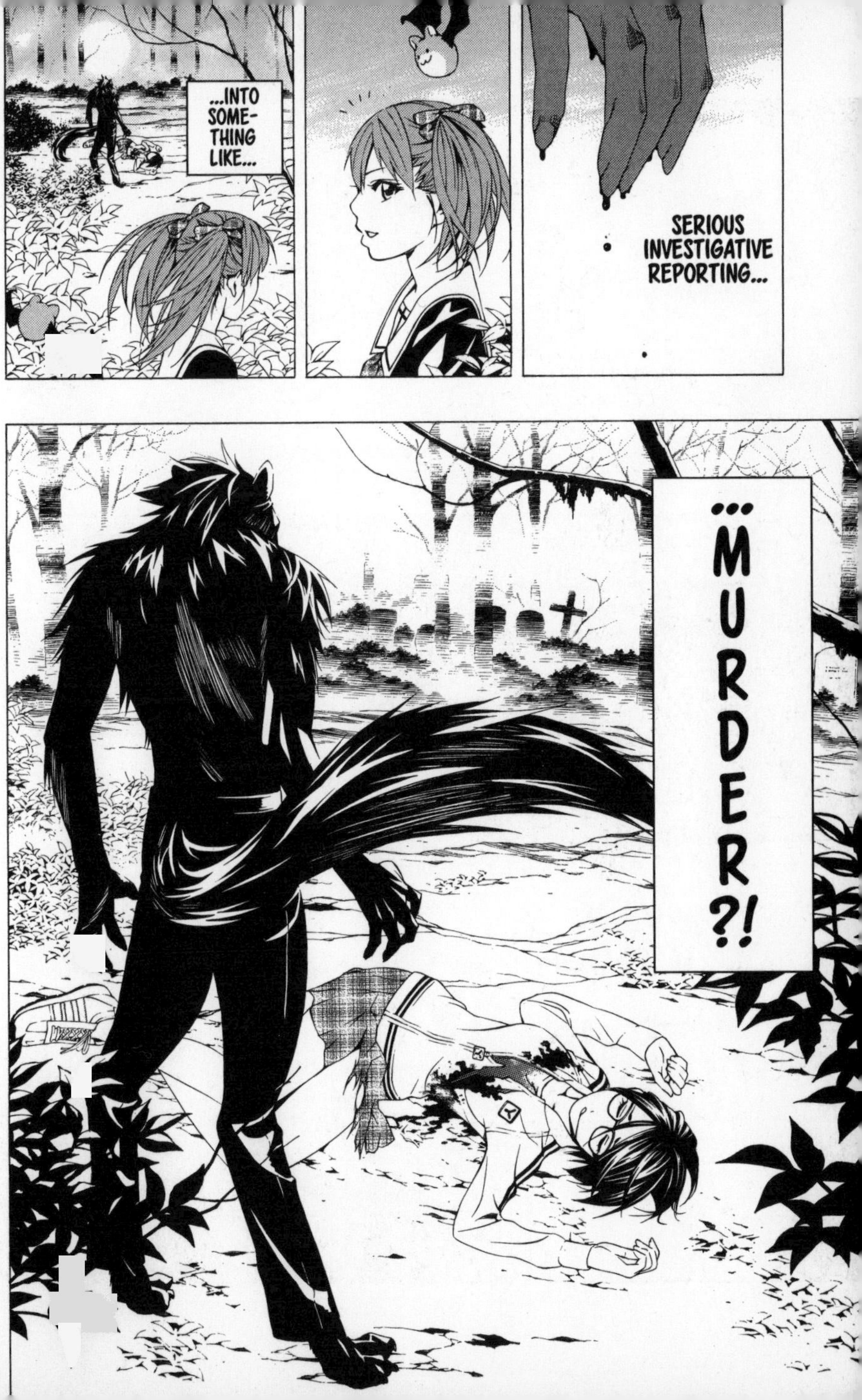
SERIOUS INVESTIGATIVE REPORTING...
...INTO SOMETHING LIKE...
...MURDER?!

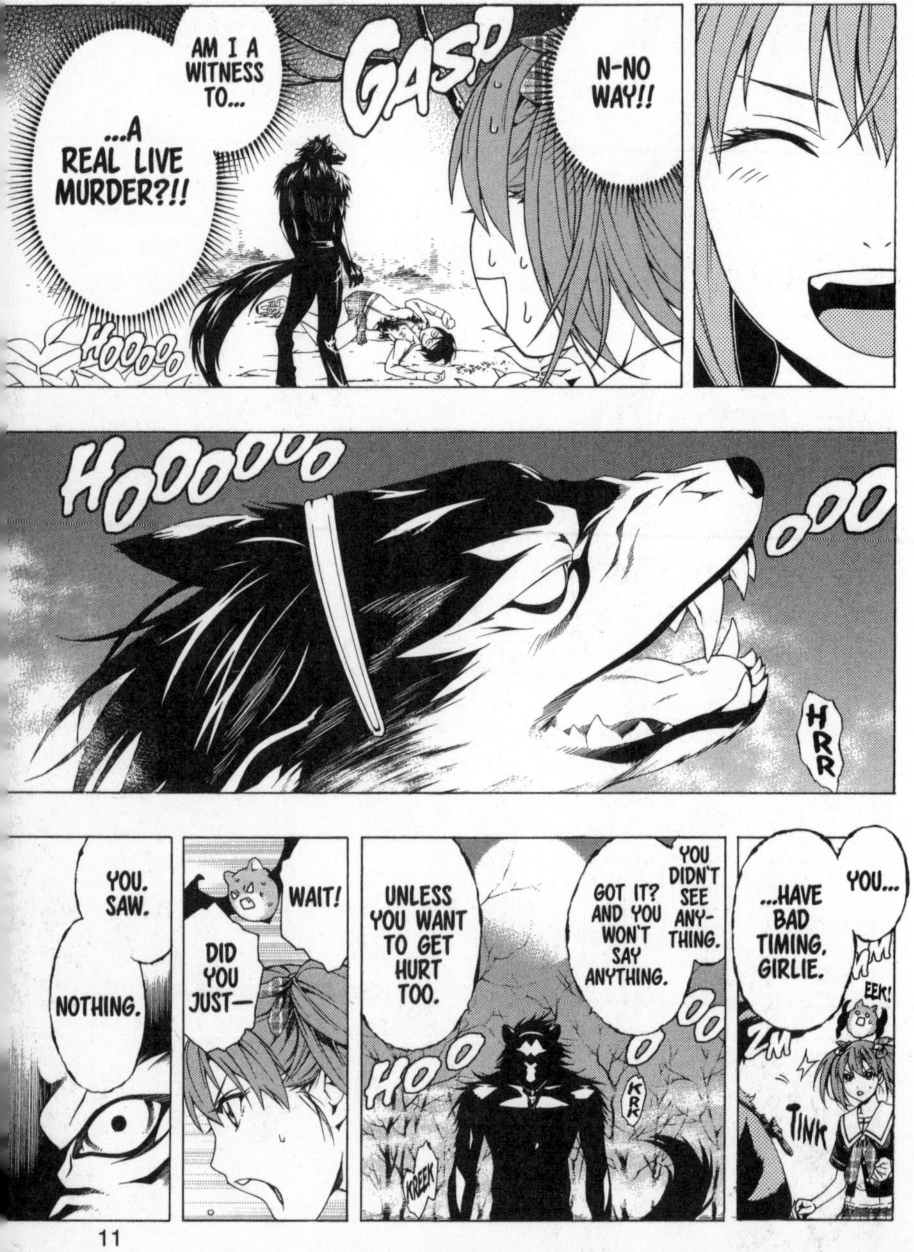
N-NO WAY!!
GASP
AM I A WITNESS TO...
...A REAL LIVE MURDER?!!
HOOOOO
HOOOOOO
OOO
HRR
YOU...
...HAVE BAD TIMING, GIRLIE.
ZM
EEK!
ZM
TINK
YOU DIDN'T SEE ANYTHING.
GOT IT? AND YOU WON'T SAY ANYTHING.
UNLESS YOU WANT TO GET HURT TOO.
OOO
KRK
HOO
KREEK
WAIT!
DID YOU JUST—
YOU. SAW.
NOTHING.

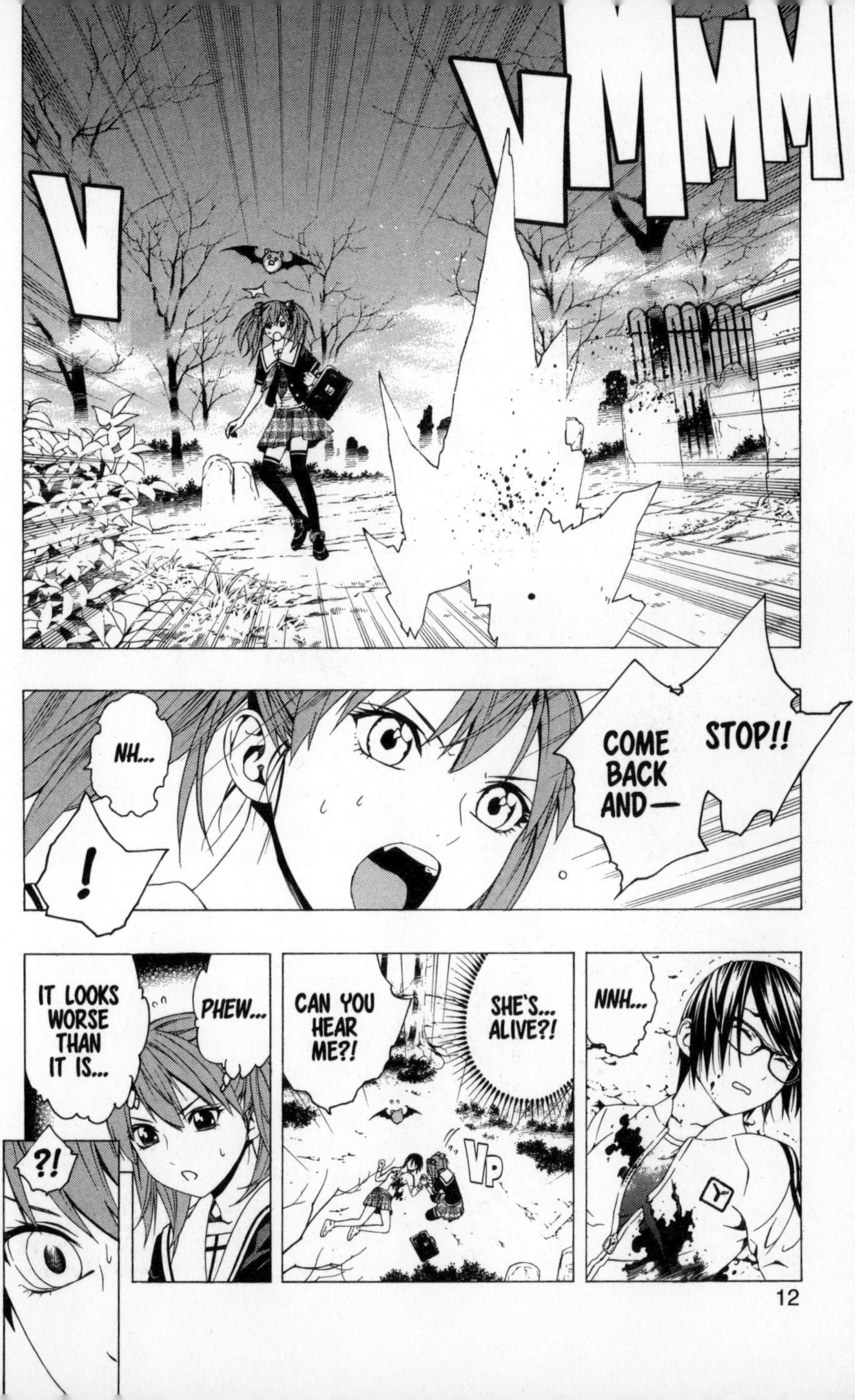
VVMMM
COME BACK AND—
STOP!!
NH...
!
NNH...
SHE'S... ALIVE?!
CAN YOU HEAR ME?!
VP
PHEW...
IT LOOKS WORSE THAN IT IS...
?!

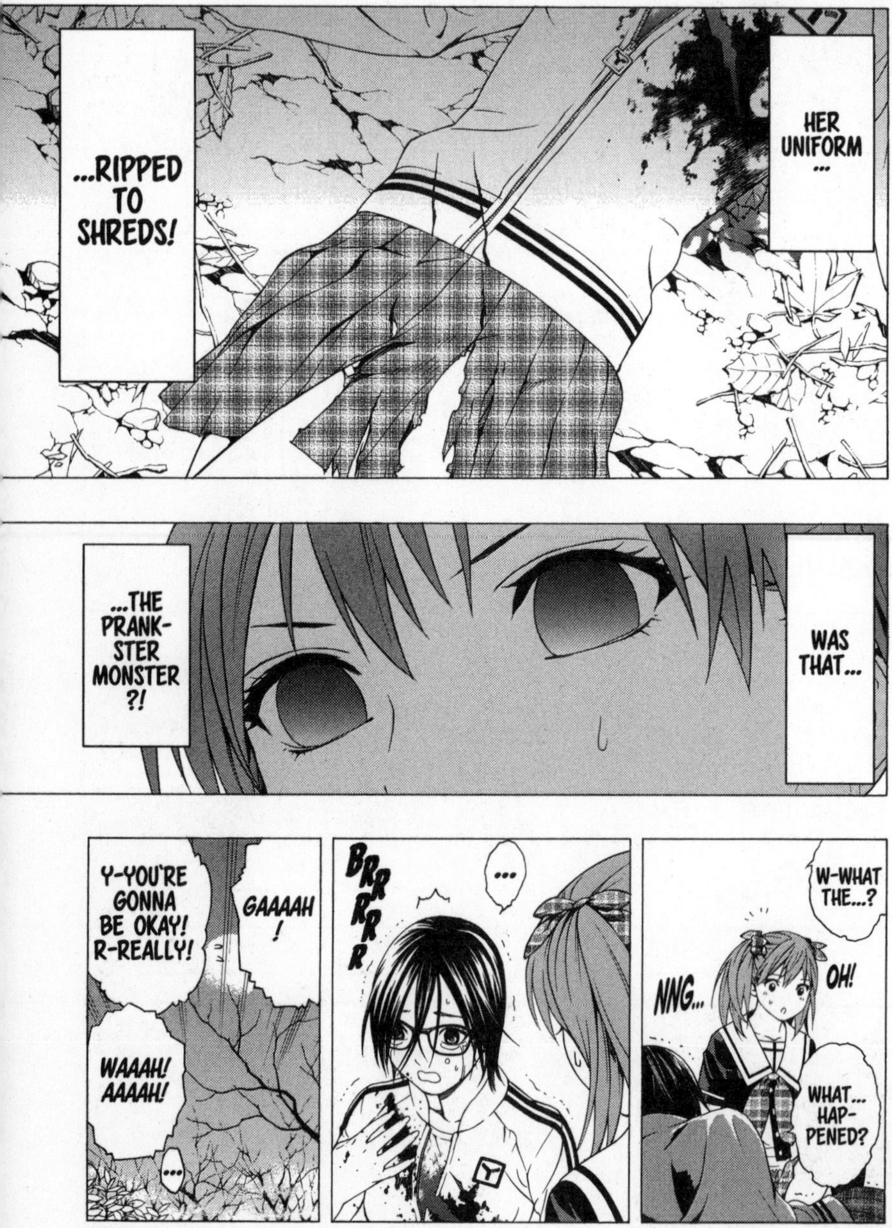
HER UNIFORM ...
...RIPPED TO SHREDS!
WAS THAT...
...THE PRANK-STER MONSTER ?!
W-WHAT THE...?
OH!
NNG...
WHAT... HAP-PENED?
...
BRRRRR
GAAAAH!
Y-YOU'RE GONNA BE OKAY! R-REALLY!
WAAAH! AAAAH!
...

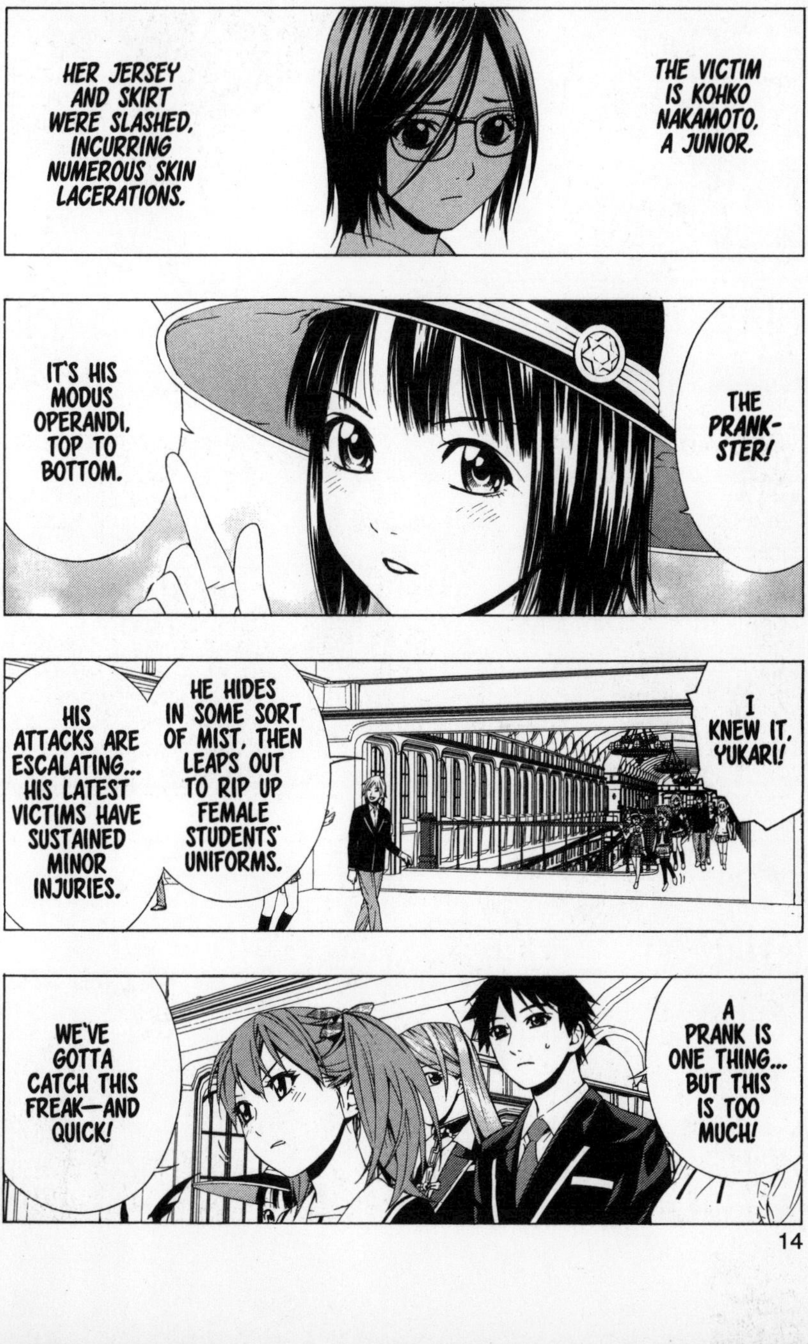
THE VICTIM IS KOHKO NAKAMOTO, A JUNIOR.
HER JERSEY AND SKIRT WERE SLASHED, INCURRING NUMEROUS SKIN LACERATIONS.
THE PRANK-STER!
IT'S HIS MODUS OPERANDI, TOP TO BOTTOM.
I KNEW IT, YUKARI!
HE HIDES IN SOME SORT OF MIST, THEN LEAPS OUT TO RIP UP FEMALE STUDENTS' UNIFORMS.
HIS ATTACKS ARE ESCALATING... HIS LATEST VICTIMS HAVE SUSTAINED MINOR INJURIES.
A PRANK IS ONE THING... BUT THIS IS TOO MUCH!
WE'VE GOTTA CATCH THIS FREAK—AND QUICK!

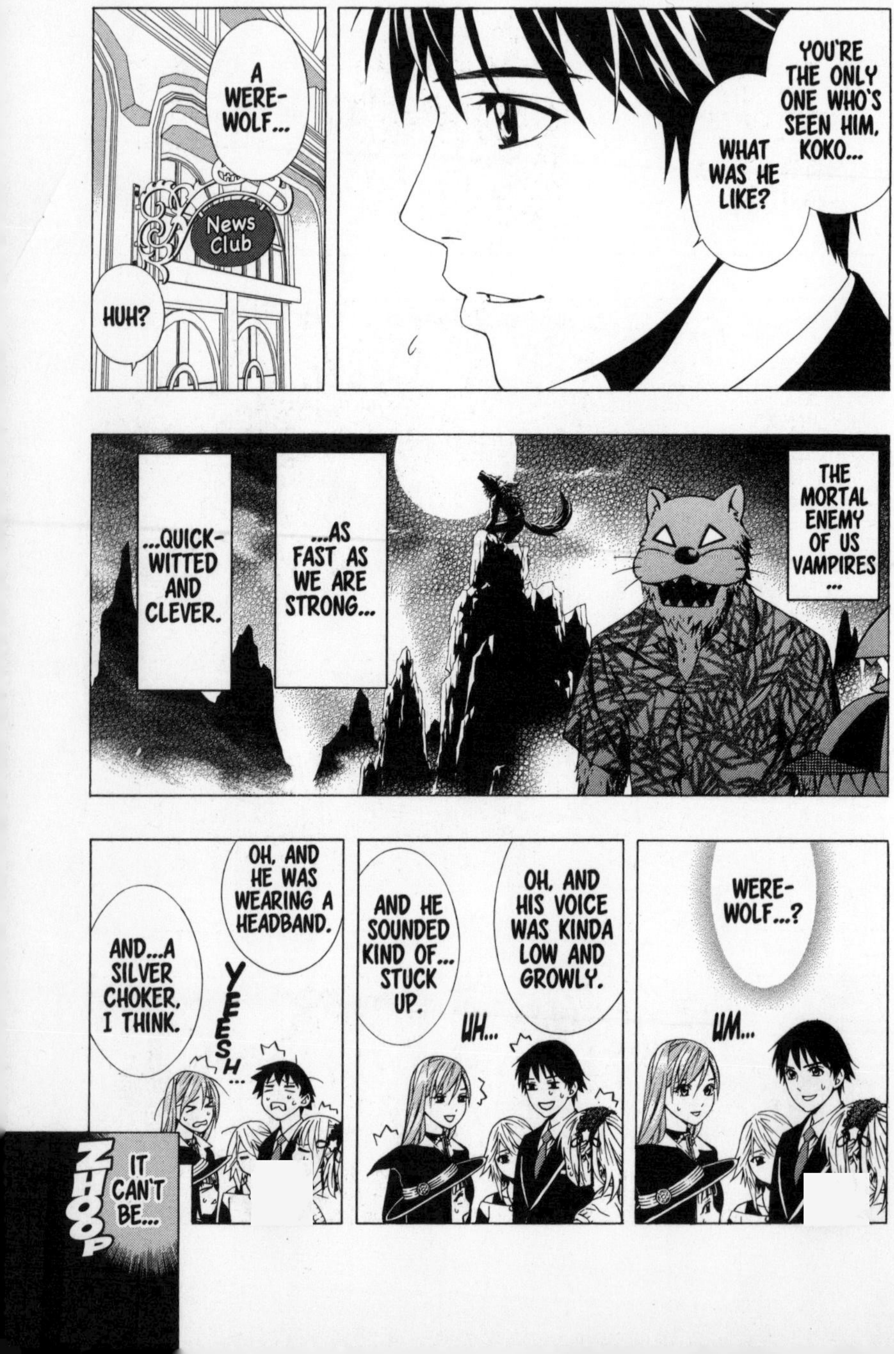
YOU'RE THE ONLY ONE WHO'S SEEN HIM, KOKO...
WHAT WAS HE LIKE?
A WERE-WOLF...
News Club
HUH?
THE MORTAL ENEMY OF US VAMPIRES...
...AS FAST AS WE ARE STRONG...
...QUICK-WITTED AND CLEVER.
WERE-WOLF...?
UM...
OH, AND HIS VOICE WAS KINDA LOW AND GROWLY.
AND HE SOUNDED KIND OF... STUCK UP.
UH...
OH, AND HE WAS WEARING A HEADBAND.
AND...A SILVER CHOKER, I THINK.
YEESH...
IT CAN'T BE...
ZHOOP

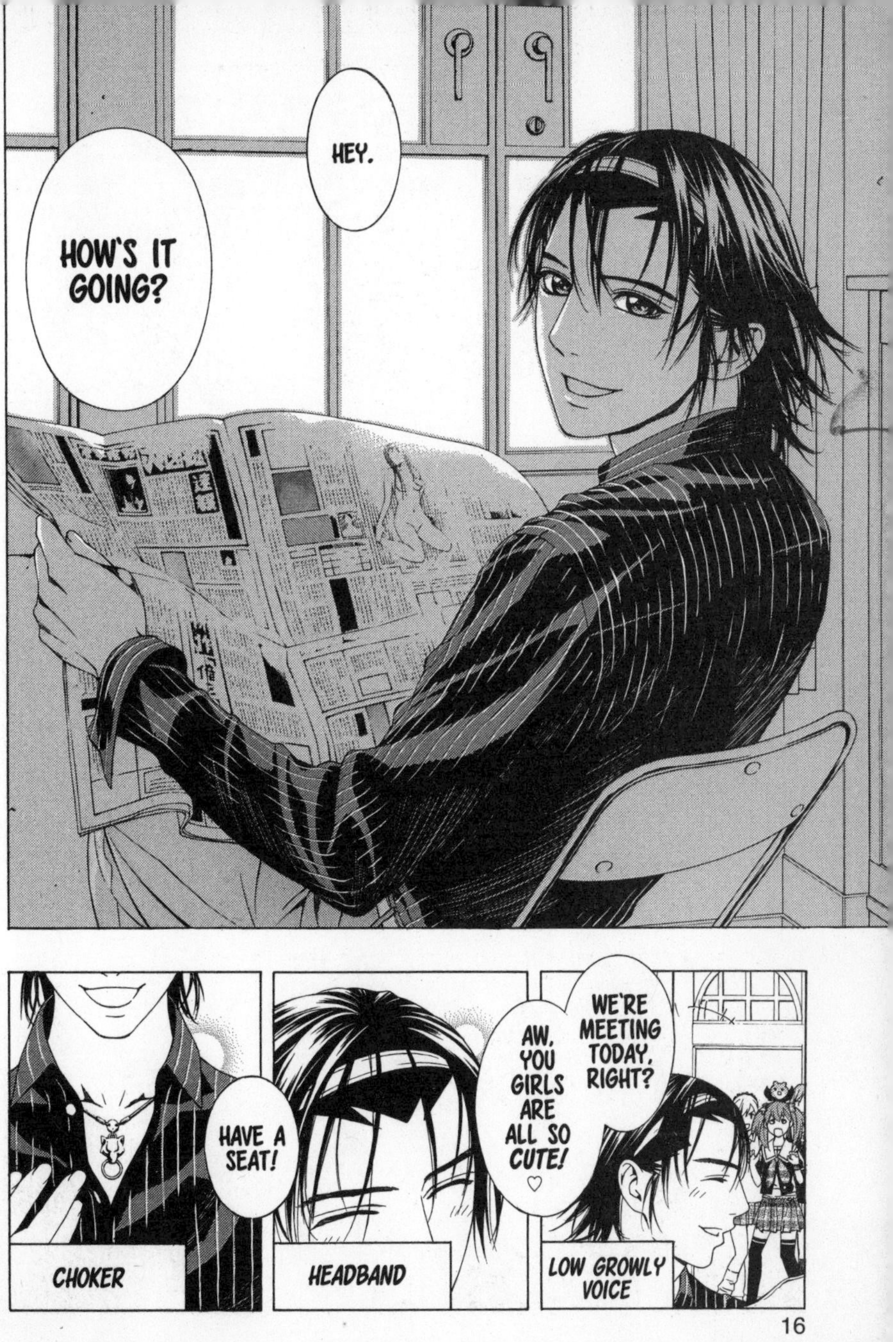
HEY.
HOW'S IT GOING?
WE'RE MEETING TODAY, RIGHT?
AW, YOU GIRLS ARE ALL SO CUTE! ♡
LOW GROWLY VOICE
HAVE A SEAT!
HEADBAND
CHOKER

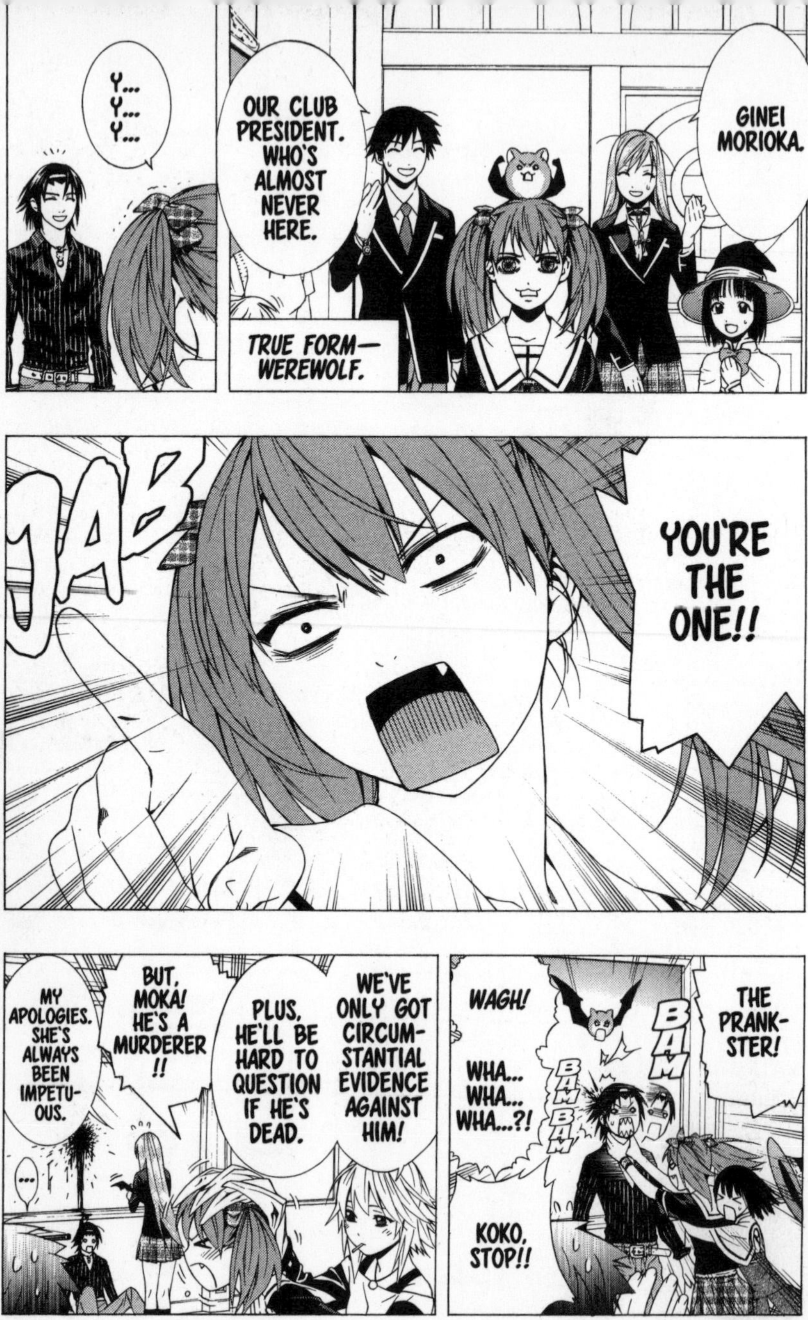
GINEI MORIOKA.
OUR CLUB PRESIDENT. WHO'S ALMOST NEVER HERE.
TRUE FORM— WEREWOLF.
Y... Y... Y...
YOU'RE THE ONE!!
JAB
THE PRANK-STER!
BAM
BAM BAM
WAGH!
WHA... WHA... WHA...?!
KOKO, STOP!!
WE'VE ONLY GOT CIRCUM-STANTIAL EVIDENCE AGAINST HIM!
PLUS, HE'LL BE HARD TO QUESTION IF HE'S DEAD.
BUT, MOKA! HE'S A MURDERER!!
MY APOLOGIES. SHE'S ALWAYS BEEN IMPETUOUS.
...

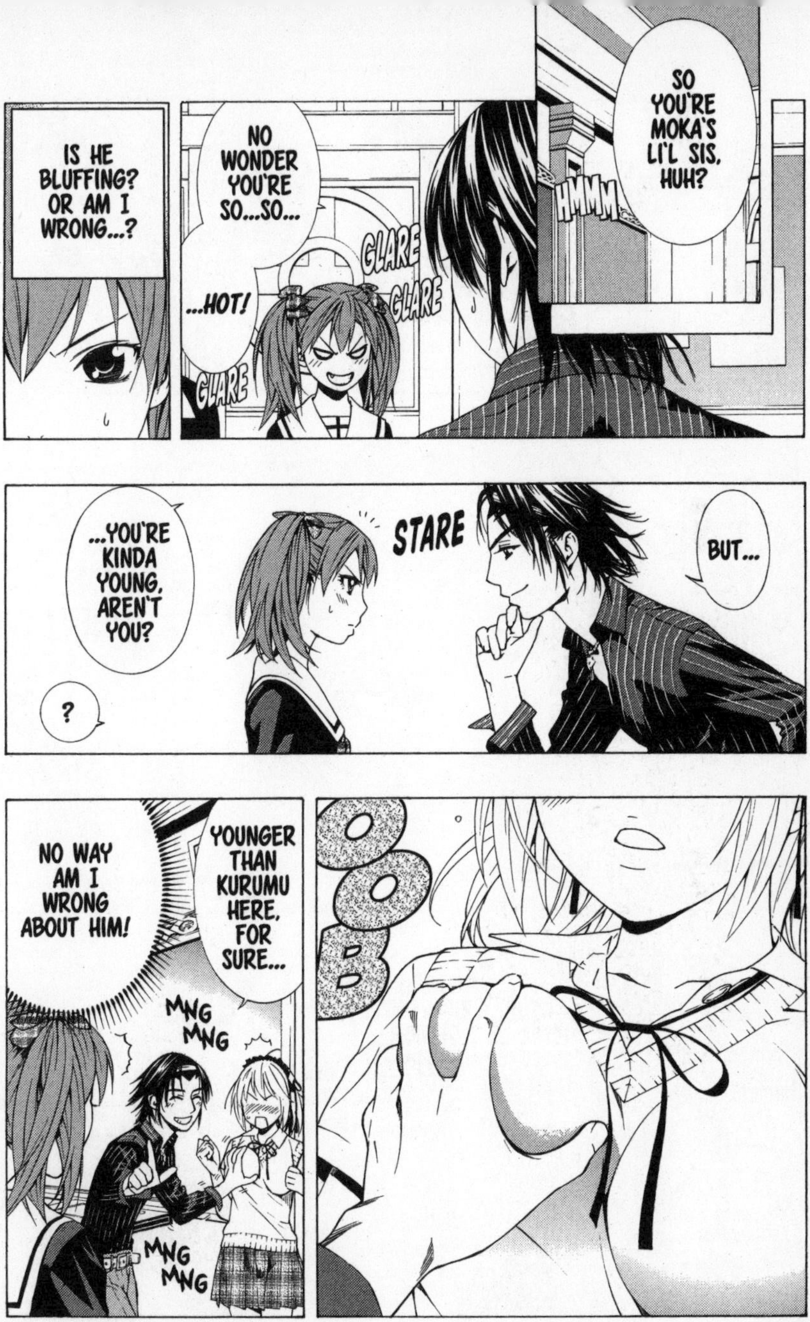
SO YOU'RE MOKA'S LI'L SIS, HUH?
HMMM
NO WONDER YOU'RE SO...SO...
...HOT!
GLARE
GLARE
GLARE
IS HE BLUFFING? OR AM I WRONG...?
BUT...
STARE
...YOU'RE KINDA YOUNG, AREN'T YOU?
?
OOOB
YOUNGER THAN KURUMU HERE, FOR SURE...
NO WAY AM I WRONG ABOUT HIM!
MNG MNG
MNG MNG

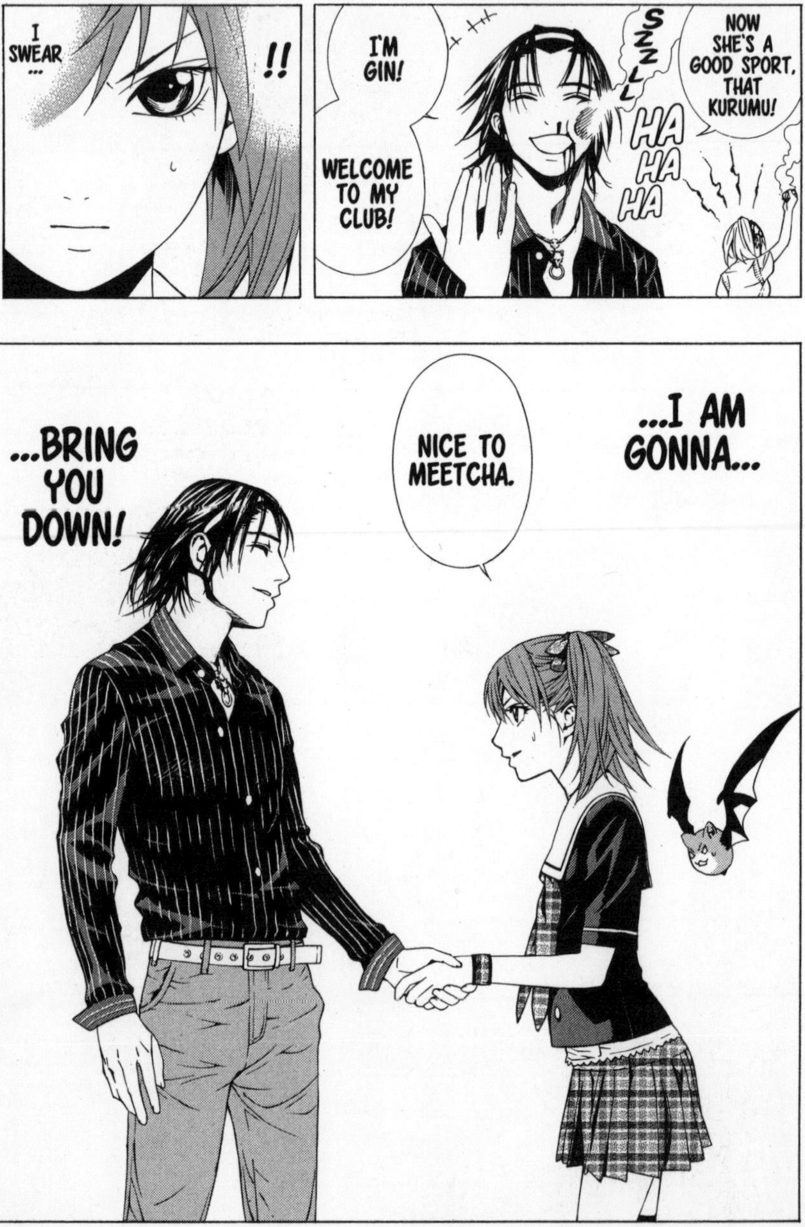
NOW SHE'S A GOOD SPORT, THAT KURUMU!
SZZL
HA HA HA
I'M GIN!
WELCOME TO MY CLUB!
!!
I SWEAR ...
...I AM GONNA...
NICE TO MEETCHA.
...BRING YOU DOWN!

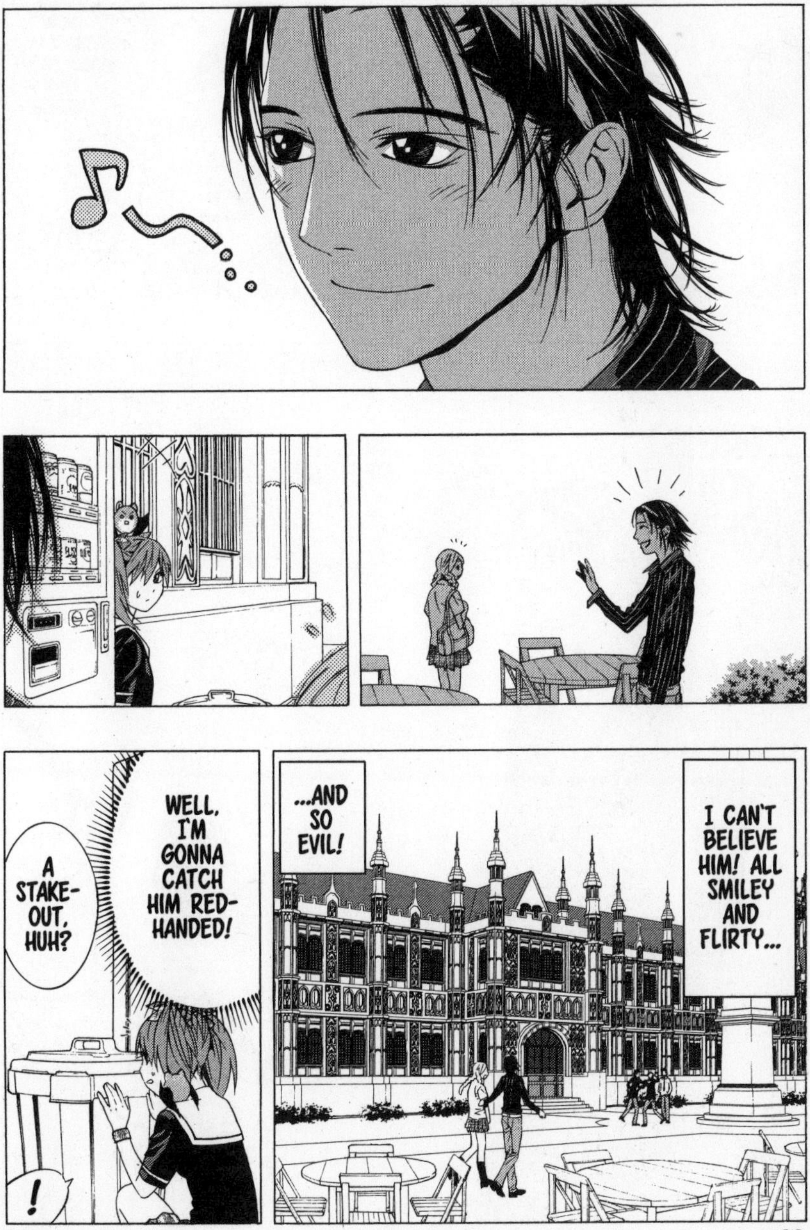
I CAN'T BELIEVE HIM! ALL SMILEY AND FLIRTY...
...AND SO EVIL!
WELL, I'M GONNA CATCH HIM RED-HANDED!
A STAKE-OUT, HUH?
!

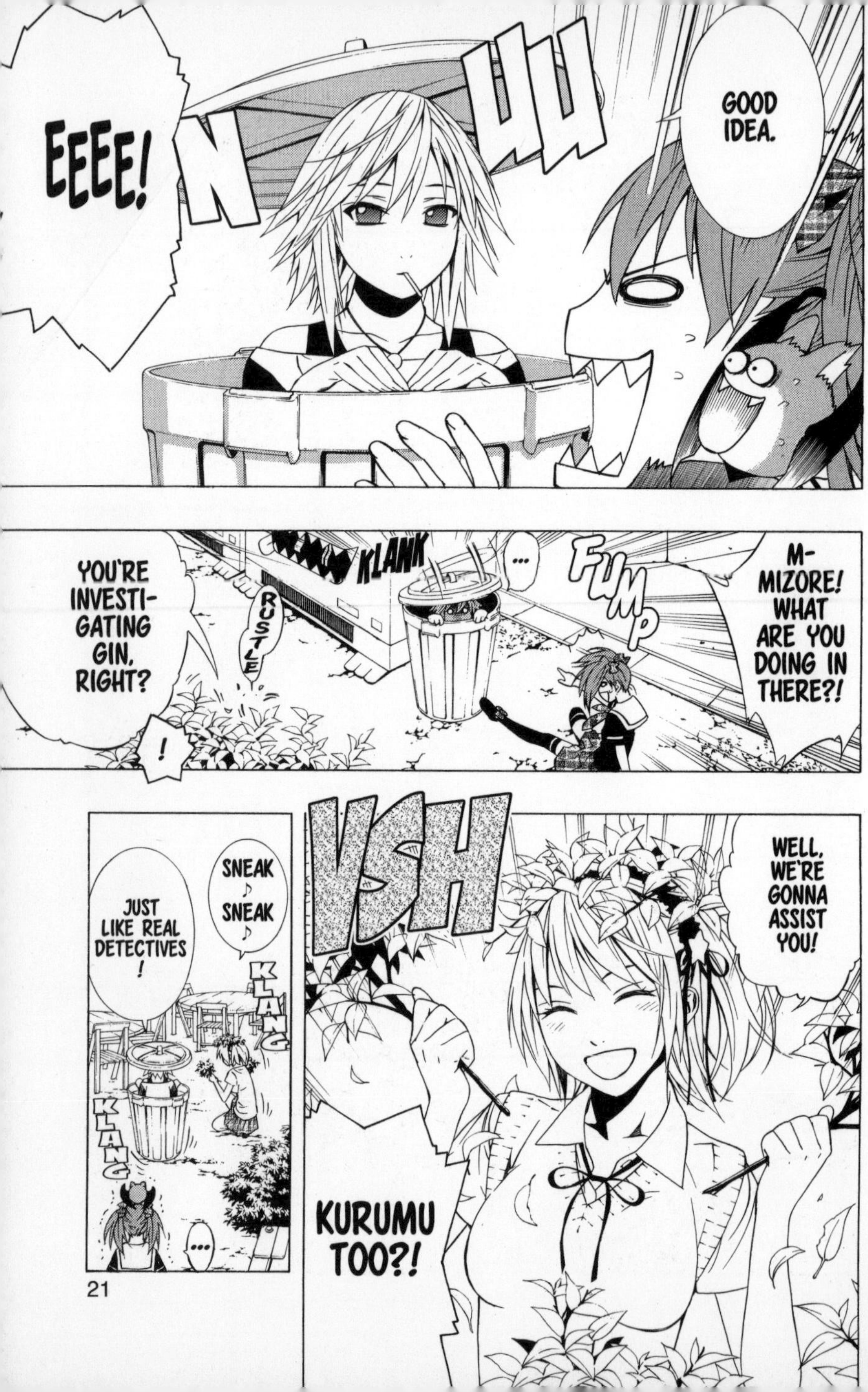
GOOD IDEA.
UUN
EEEE!
M-MIZORE! WHAT ARE YOU DOING IN THERE?!
FUMP
...
KLANK
RUSTLE
YOU'RE INVESTI-GATING GIN, RIGHT?
!
WELL, WE'RE GONNA ASSIST YOU!
VSH
KURUMU TOO?!
SNEAK ♪ SNEAK ♪
JUST LIKE REAL DETECTIVES!
KLANG
KLANG
...

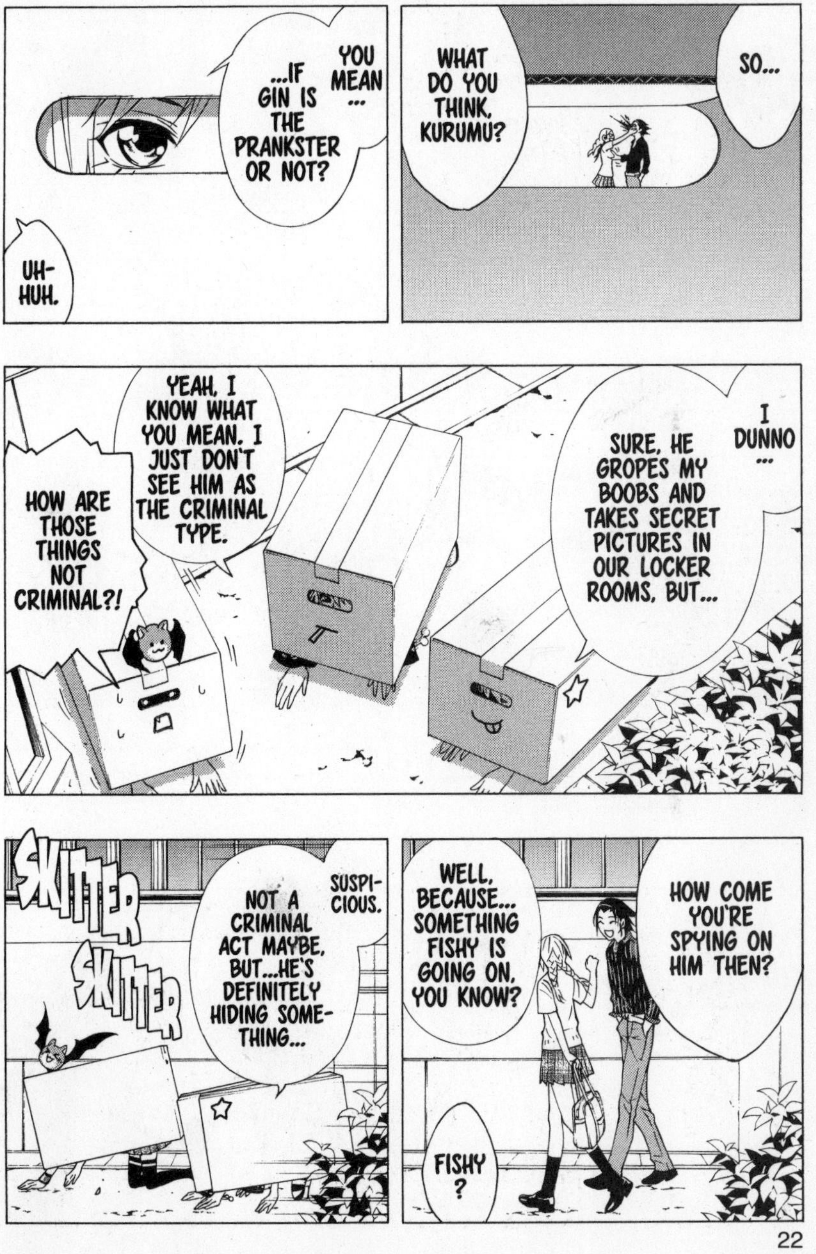

SO...
WHAT DO YOU THINK, KURUMU?
YOU MEAN...
...IF GIN IS THE PRANKSTER OR NOT?
UH-HUH.
I DUNNO...
SURE, HE GROPES MY BOOBS AND TAKES SECRET PICTURES IN OUR LOCKER ROOMS, BUT...
YEAH, I KNOW WHAT YOU MEAN. I JUST DON'T SEE HIM AS THE CRIMINAL TYPE.
HOW ARE THOSE THINGS NOT CRIMINAL?!
HOW COME YOU'RE SPYING ON HIM THEN?
WELL, BECAUSE... SOMETHING FISHY IS GOING ON, YOU KNOW?
FISHY?
SUSPICIOUS.
NOT A CRIMINAL ACT MAYBE, BUT...HE'S DEFINITELY HIDING SOMETHING...
SKITTER SKITTER

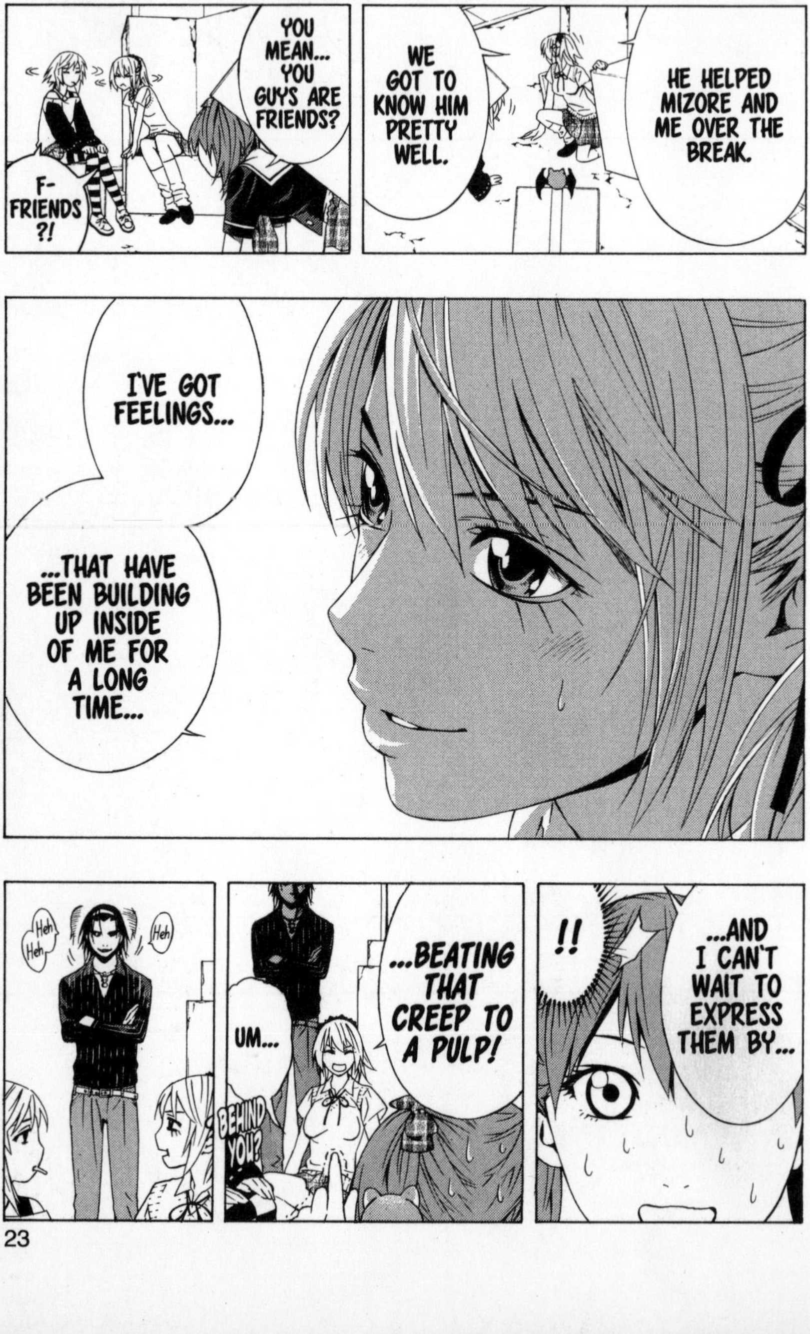
HE HELPED MIZORE AND ME OVER THE BREAK.
WE GOT TO KNOW HIM PRETTY WELL.
YOU MEAN... YOU GUYS ARE FRIENDS?
F-FRIENDS?!
I'VE GOT FEELINGS...
...THAT HAVE BEEN BUILDING UP INSIDE OF ME FOR A LONG TIME...
...AND I CAN'T WAIT TO EXPRESS THEM BY...
!!
...BEATING THAT CREEP TO A PULP!
UM...
BEHIND YOU?
Heh
Heh Heh

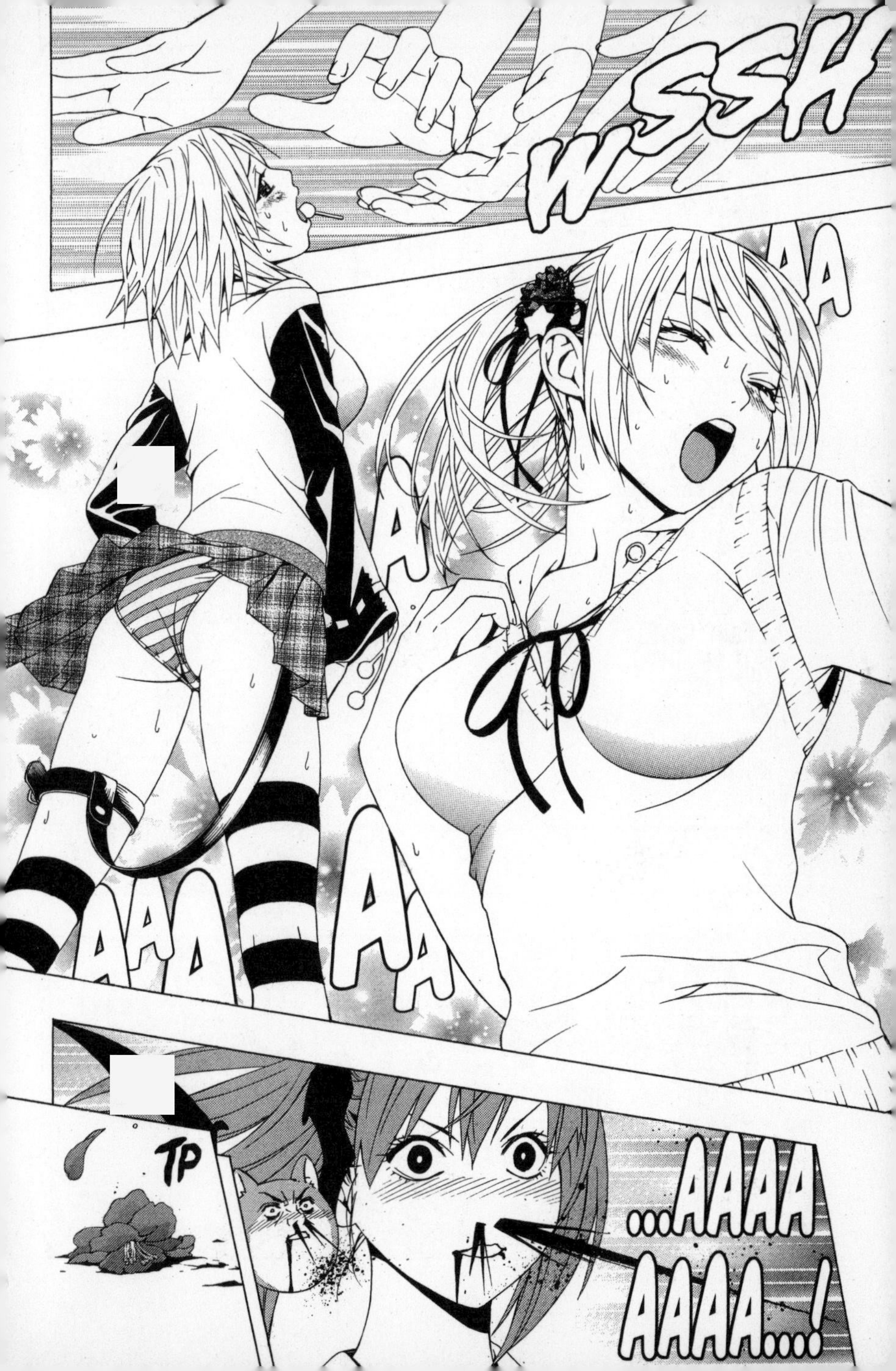
WISSH
AA
AA
AAA
AAA
...AAAA
AAAA...!
TP

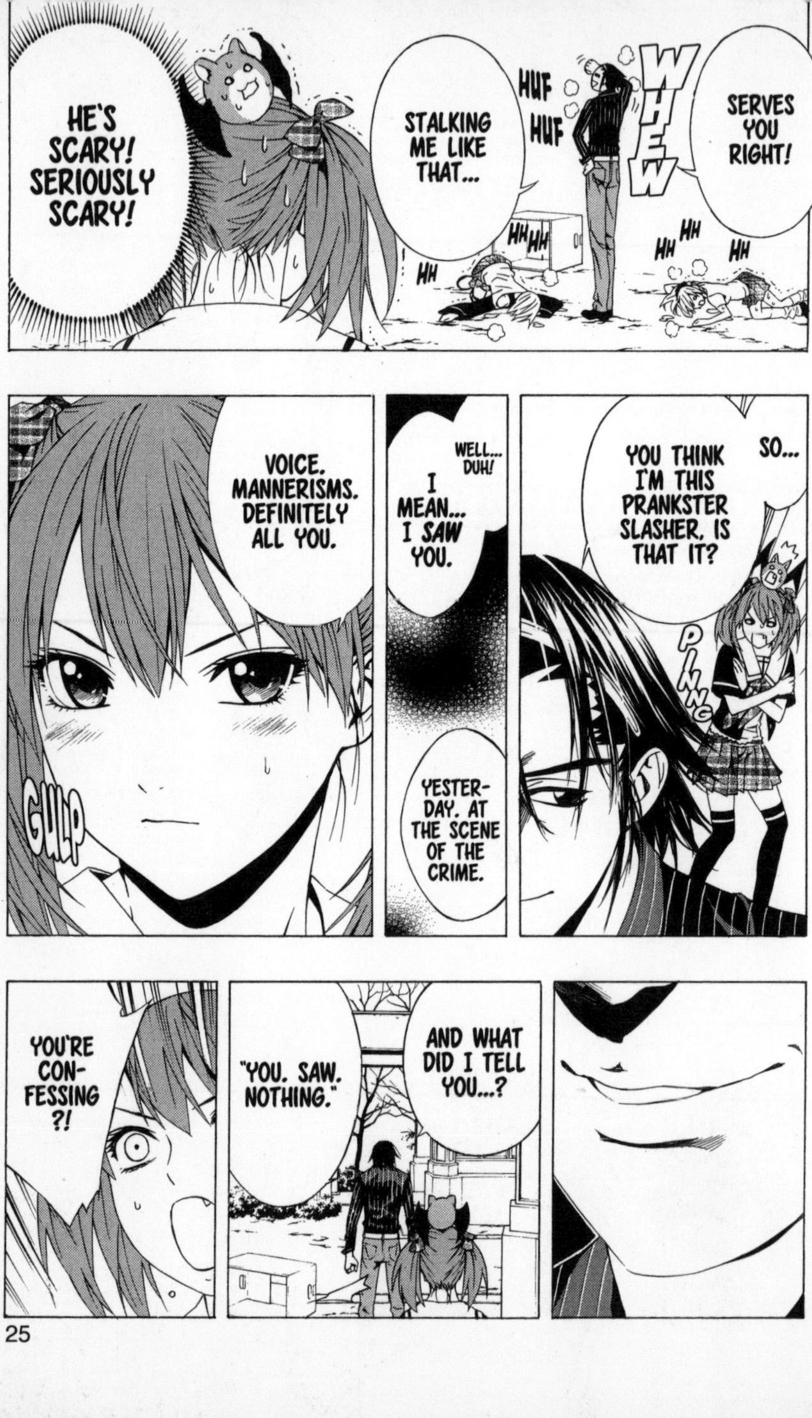
SERVES YOU RIGHT!
WHEW
HH HH HH
HUF HUF
STALKING ME LIKE THAT...
HH HH HH
HE'S SCARY! SERIOUSLY SCARY!
SO...
YOU THINK I'M THIS PRANKSTER SLASHER, IS THAT IT?
PING
WELL... DUH!
I MEAN... I SAW YOU.
YESTERDAY. AT THE SCENE OF THE CRIME.
VOICE. MANNERISMS. DEFINITELY ALL YOU.
GULP
AND WHAT DID I TELL YOU...?
"YOU. SAW. NOTHING."
YOU'RE CON-FESSING ?!

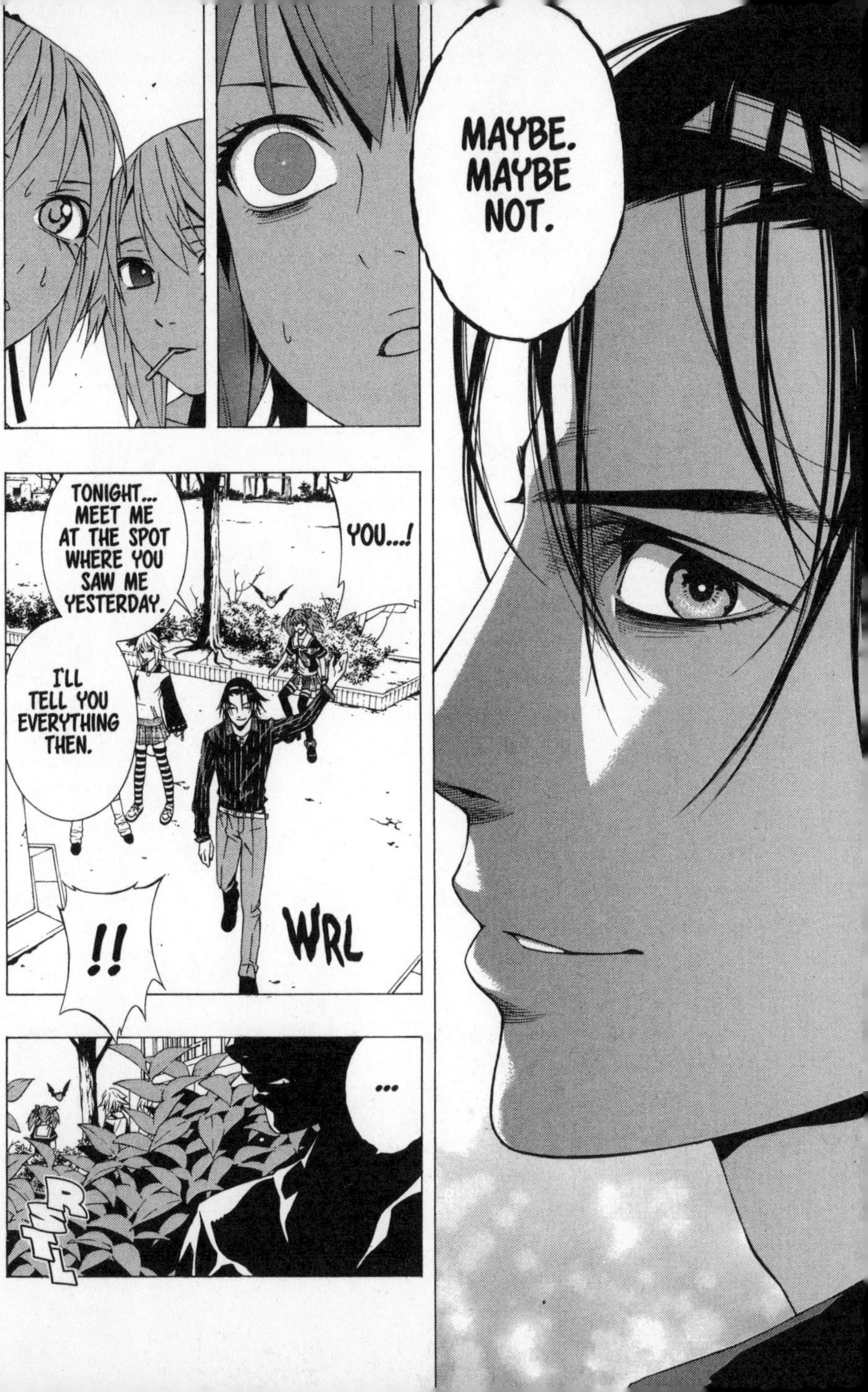
MAYBE. MAYBE NOT.
YOU...!
TONIGHT... MEET ME AT THE SPOT WHERE YOU SAW ME YESTERDAY.
I'LL TELL YOU EVERYTHING THEN.
WRL
!!
...
RSTL

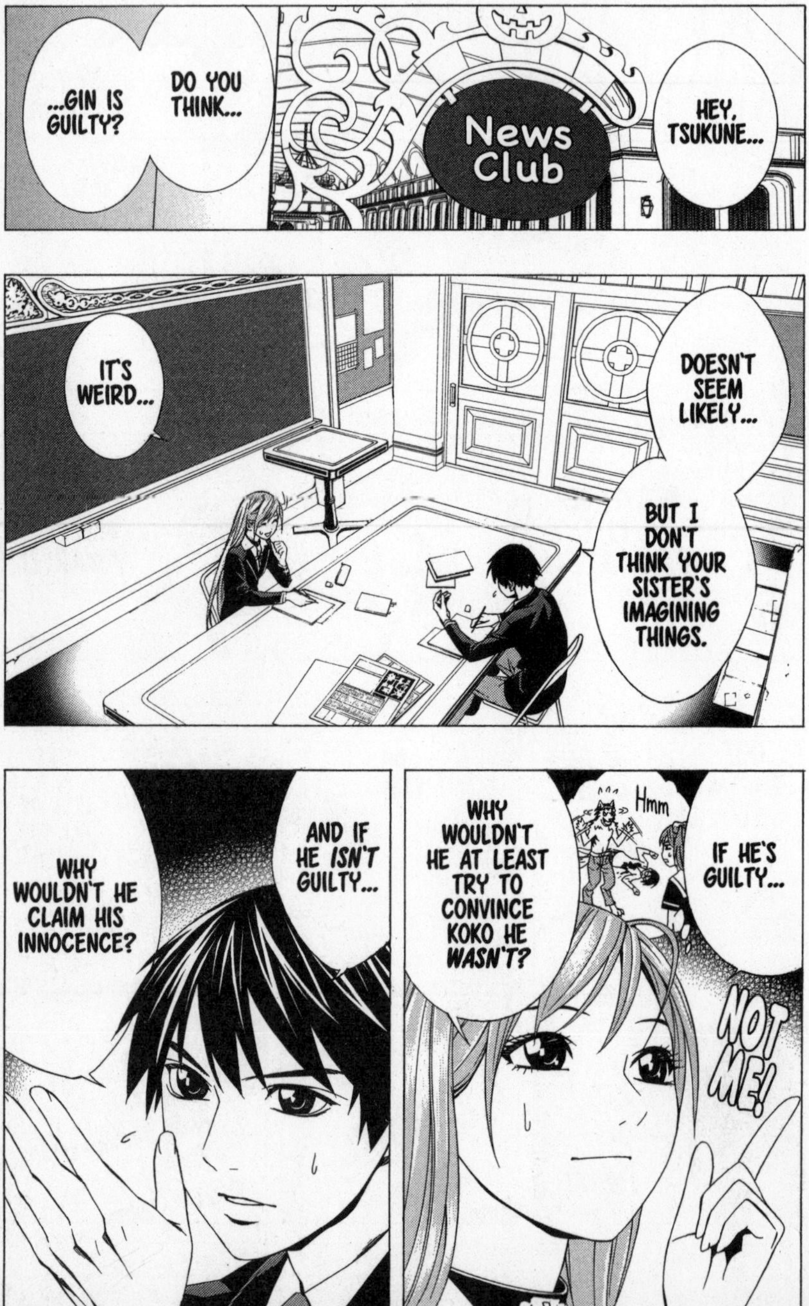
HEY, TSUKUNE...
News Club
DO YOU THINK...
...GIN IS GUILTY?
DOESN'T SEEM LIKELY...
BUT I DON'T THINK YOUR SISTER'S IMAGINING THINGS.
IT'S WEIRD...
IF HE'S GUILTY...
NOT ME!
Hmm
WHY WOULDN'T HE AT LEAST TRY TO CONVINCE KOKO HE WASN'T?
AND IF HE ISN'T GUILTY...
WHY WOULDN'T HE CLAIM HIS INNOCENCE?

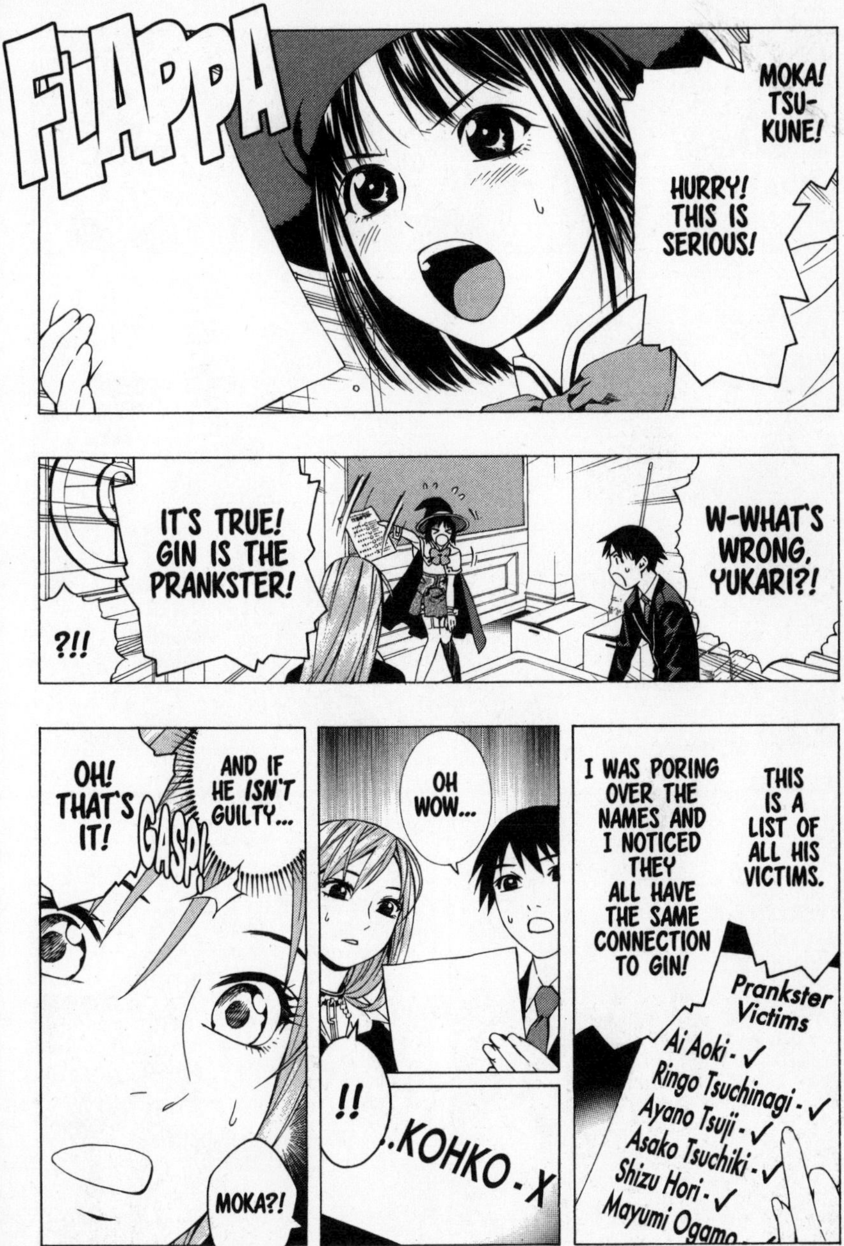

MOKA! TSU-KUNE!
HURRY! THIS IS SERIOUS!
FLAPPA
W-WHAT'S WRONG, YUKARI?!
IT'S TRUE! GIN IS THE PRANKSTER!
?!!
THIS IS A LIST OF ALL HIS VICTIMS.
I WAS PORING OVER THE NAMES AND I NOTICED THEY ALL HAVE THE SAME CONNECTION TO GIN!
Prankster Victims
Ai Aoki - ✓
Ringo Tsuchinagi - ✓
Ayano Tsuji - ✓
Asako Tsuchiki - ✓
Shizu Hori - ✓
Mayumi Ogamo...
OH WOW...
!!
..KOHKO - X
AND IF HE *ISN'T* GUILTY...
OH! THAT'S IT!
GASP!
MOKA?!

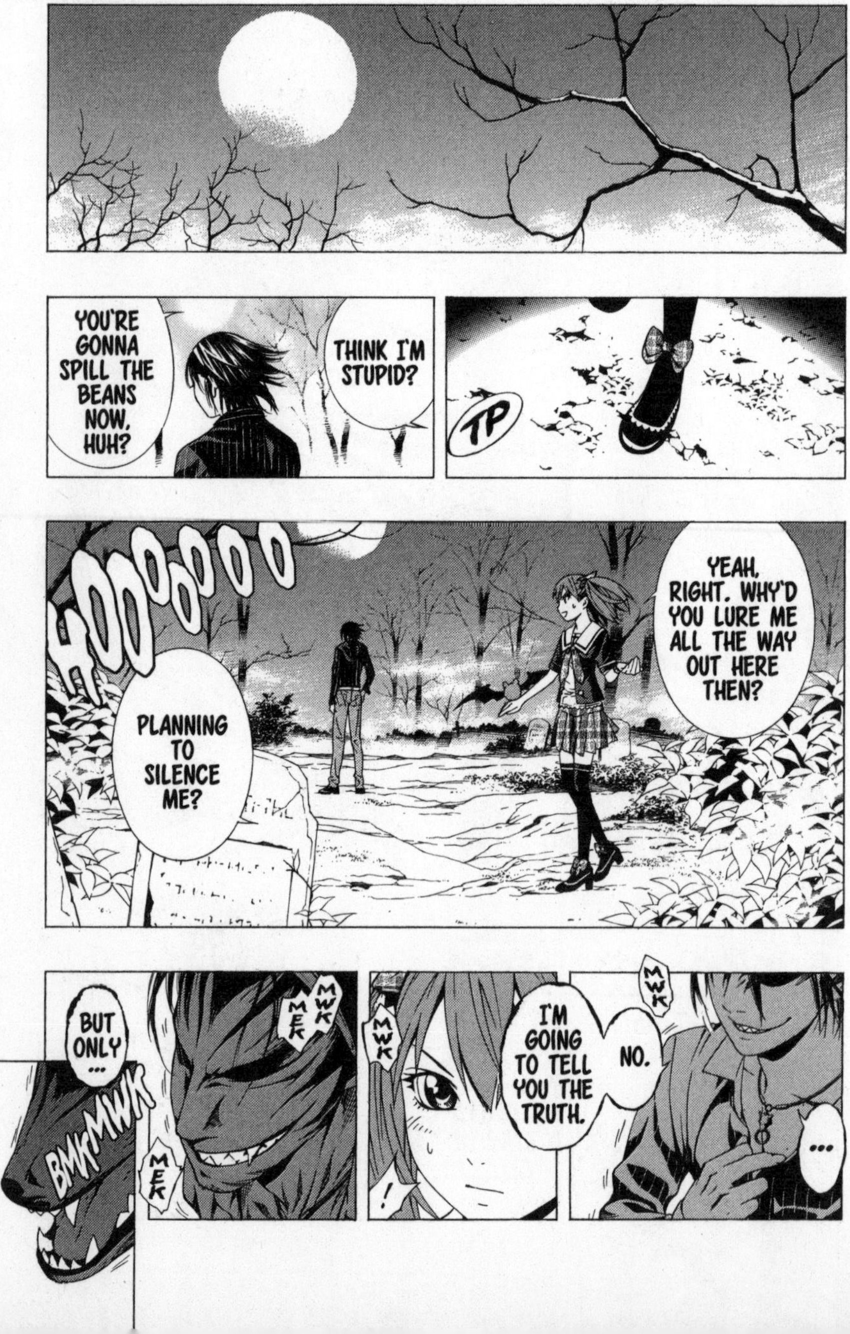
TP
THINK I'M STUPID?
YOU'RE GONNA SPILL THE BEANS NOW, HUH?
YEAH, RIGHT. WHY'D YOU LURE ME ALL THE WAY OUT HERE THEN?
PLANNING TO SILENCE ME?
HOOOOOOO
MWK
NO.
...
I'M GOING TO TELL YOU THE TRUTH.
MWK
!
MWK MEK
BUT ONLY ...
MEK
BMKMWK

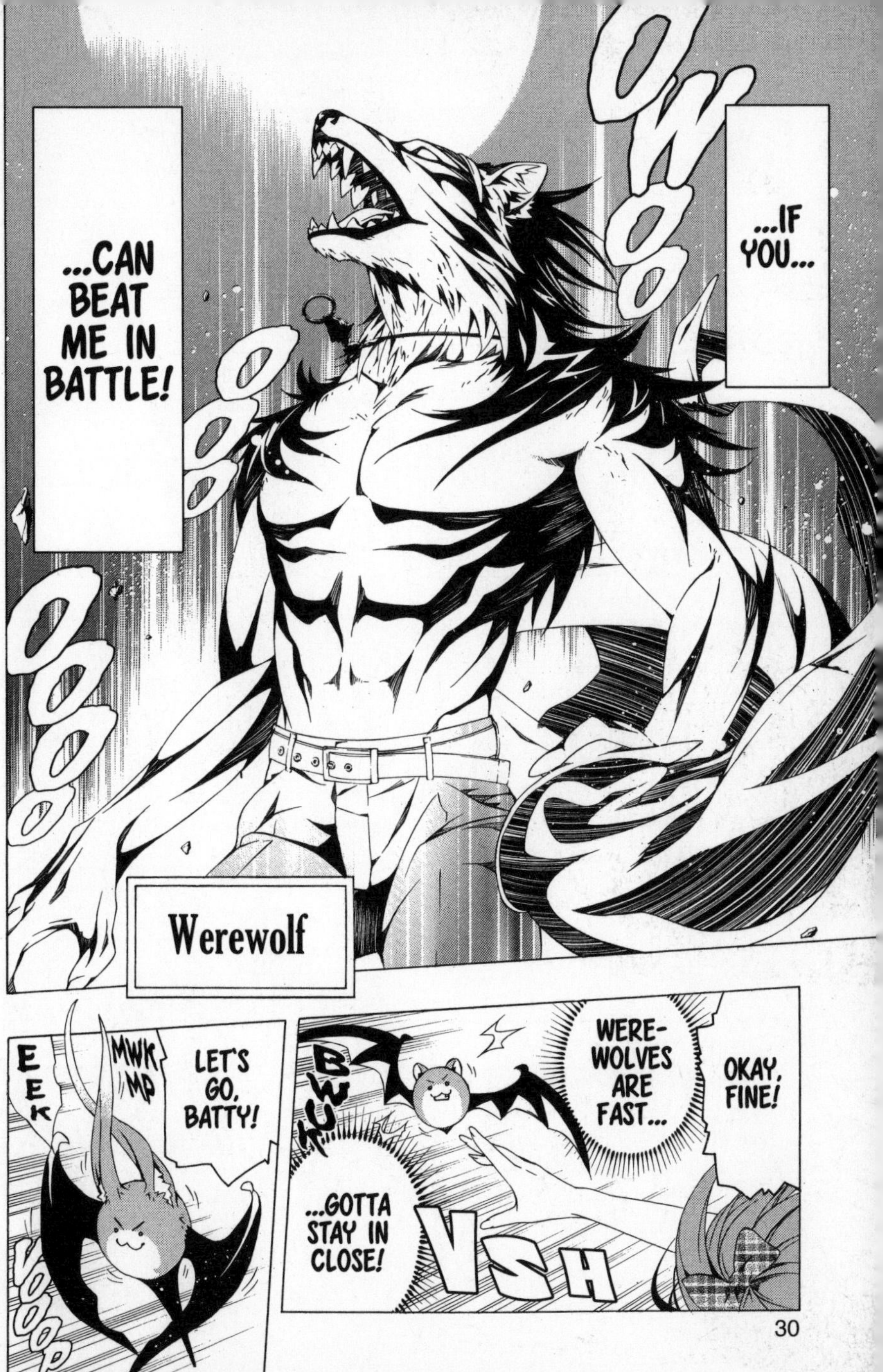

OWOOOO
...IF YOU...
...CAN BEAT ME IN BATTLE!
OOOO
OOOOOO
Werewolf
OKAY, FINE!
WERE-WOLVES ARE FAST...
BWUK
...GOTTA STAY IN CLOSE!
VSH
LET'S GO, BATTY!
MWK MP
EEK
VOOOP

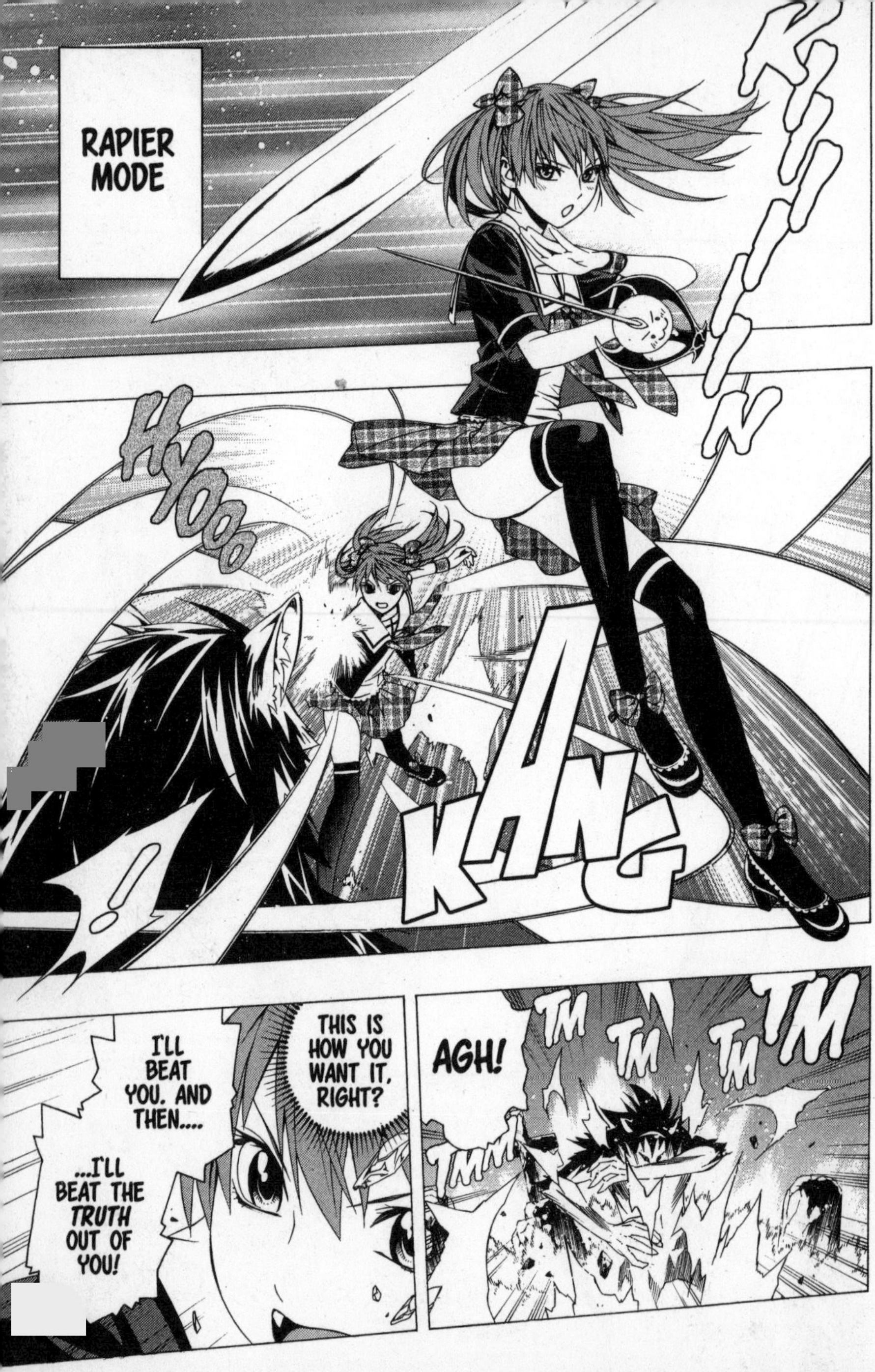
RAPIER MODE
KIIIIIN
HYOOO
KANG
!
TM TM TM TM
TMMM
AGH!
THIS IS HOW YOU WANT IT, RIGHT?
I'LL BEAT YOU. AND THEN....
...I'LL BEAT THE *TRUTH* OUT OF YOU!

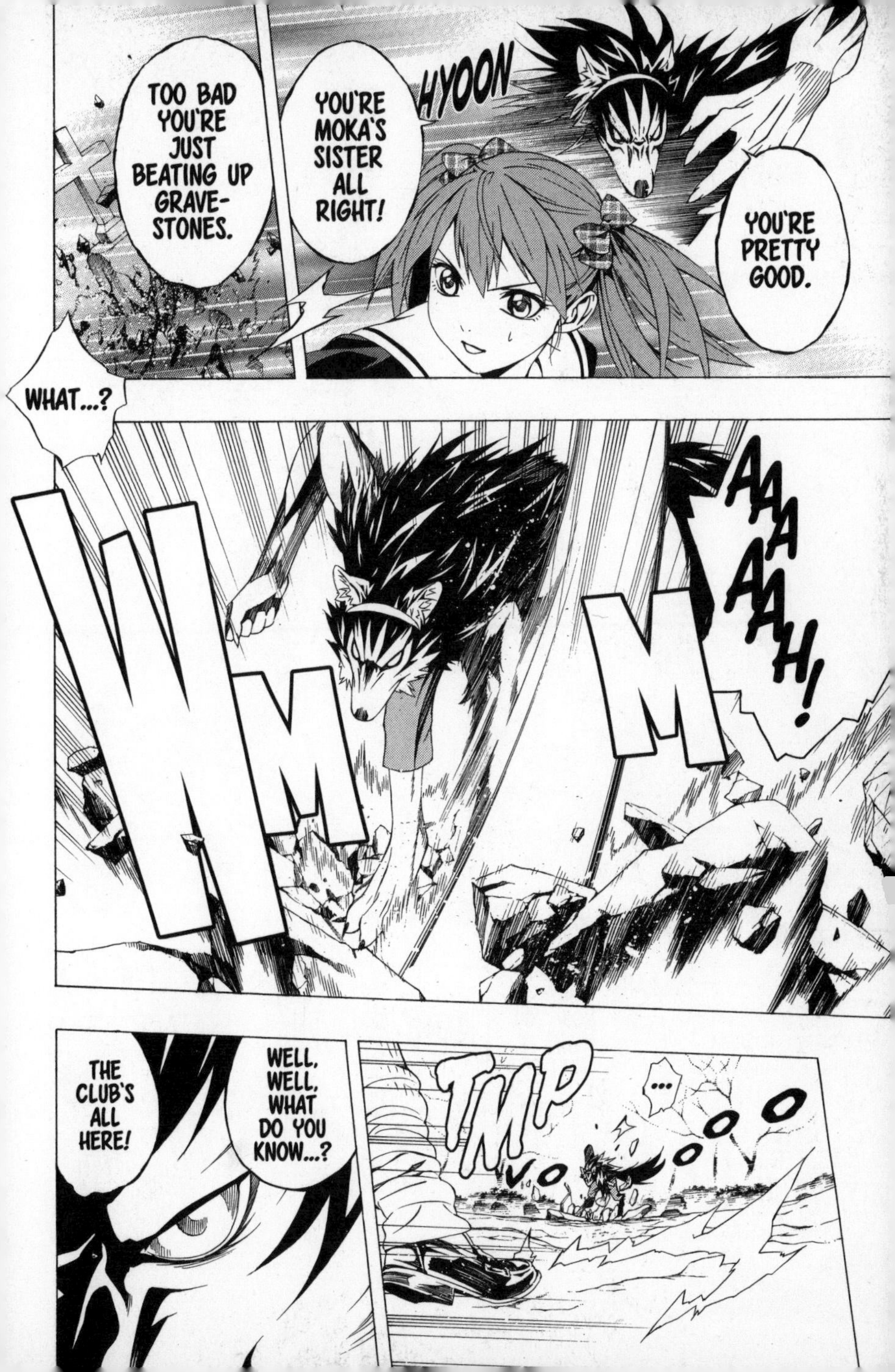
YOU'RE PRETTY GOOD.
HYOON
YOU'RE MOKA'S SISTER ALL RIGHT!
TOO BAD YOU'RE JUST BEATING UP GRAVE-STONES.
WHAT...?
AAAAAH!
WHMM
TMP
...
VOOOOO
WELL, WELL, WHAT DO YOU KNOW...?
THE CLUB'S ALL HERE!

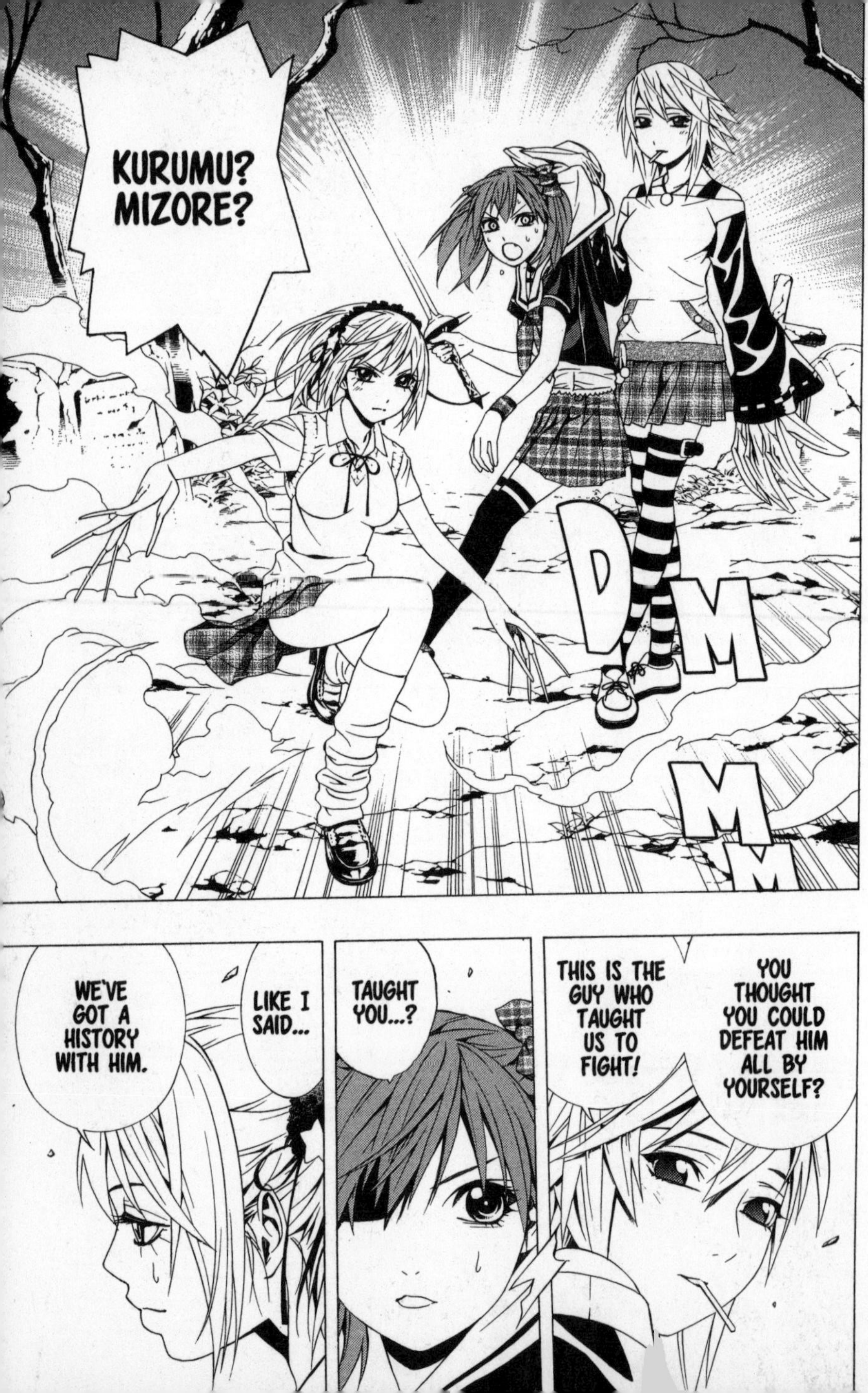
KURUMU? MIZORE?
DMMM
YOU THOUGHT YOU COULD DEFEAT HIM ALL BY YOURSELF?
THIS IS THE GUY WHO TAUGHT US TO FIGHT!
TAUGHT YOU...?
LIKE I SAID...
WE'VE GOT A HISTORY WITH HIM.

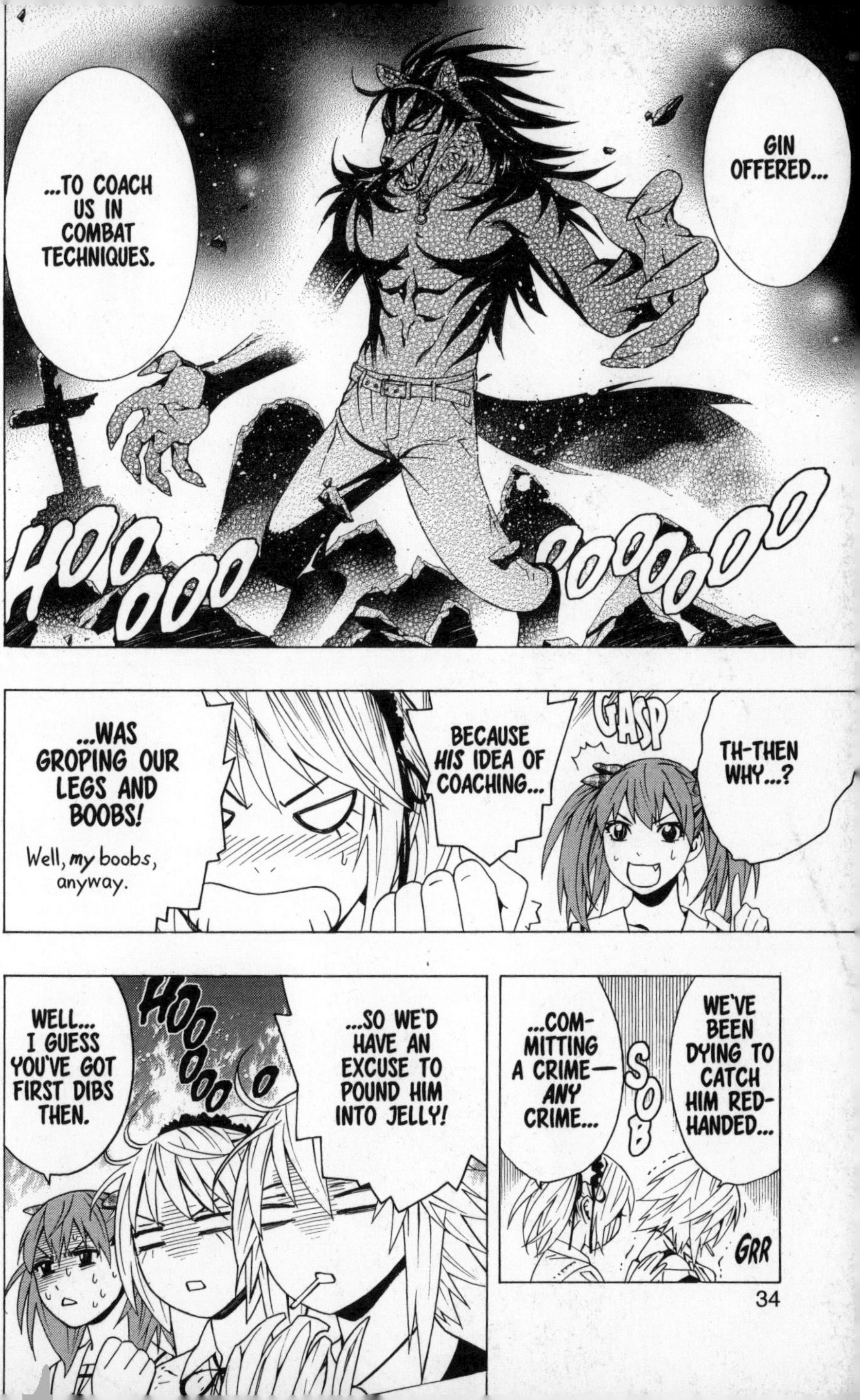
GIN OFFERED...
...TO COACH US IN COMBAT TECHNIQUES.
HOOOOOOOOOOOOOOOO
TH-THEN WHY...?
GASP
BECAUSE *HIS* IDEA OF COACHING...
...WAS GROPING OUR LEGS AND BOOBS!
Well, *my* boobs, anyway.
WE'VE BEEN DYING TO CATCH HIM RED-HANDED...
SOB
...COM-MITTING A CRIME—*ANY* CRIME...
GRR
...SO WE'D HAVE AN EXCUSE TO POUND HIM INTO JELLY!
HOOOOOO
WELL... I GUESS YOU'VE GOT FIRST DIBS THEN.

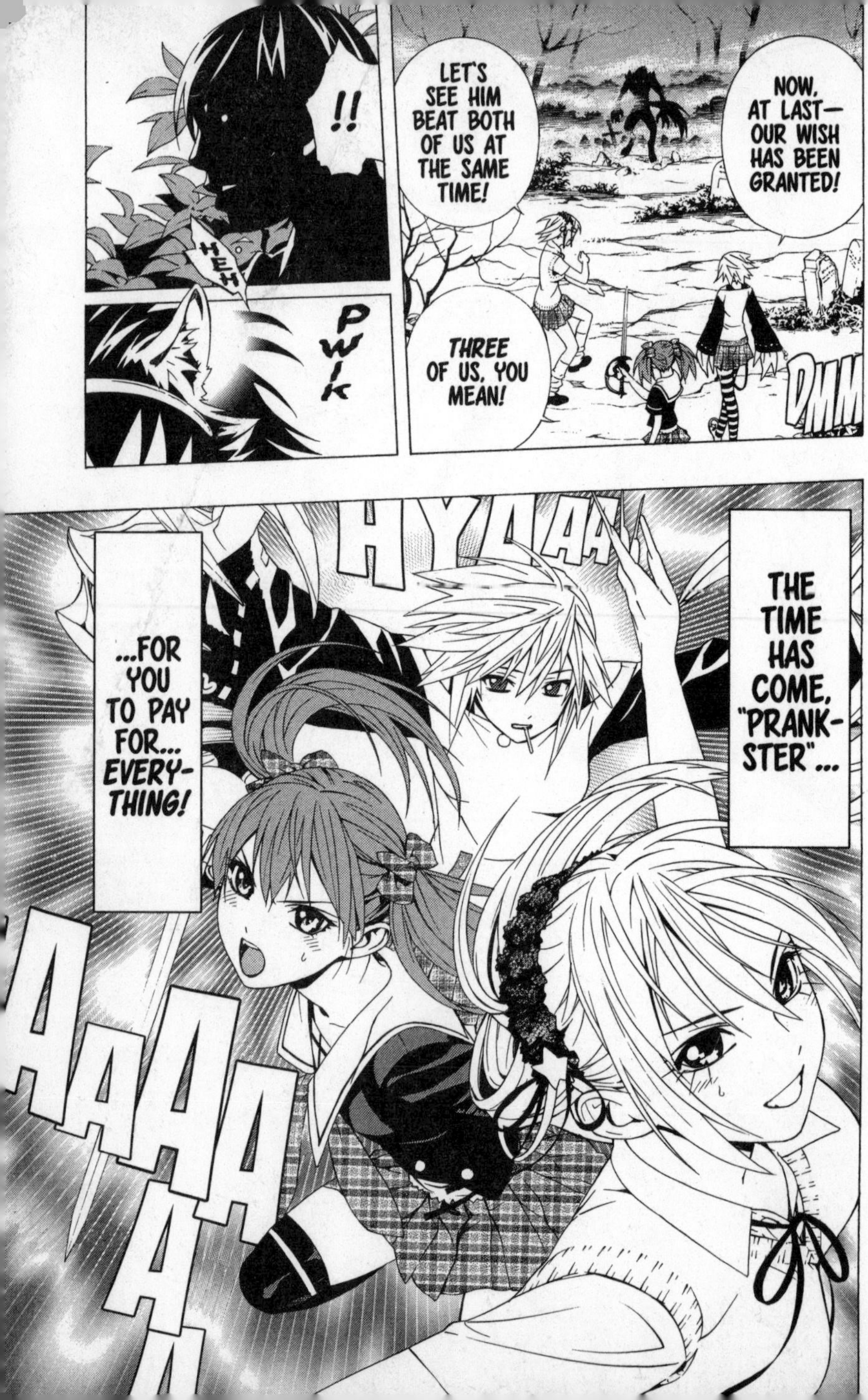
NOW, AT LAST— OUR WISH HAS BEEN GRANTED!
LET'S SEE HIM BEAT BOTH OF US AT THE SAME TIME!
THREE OF US, YOU MEAN!
DMM
!!
HEH
PWIK
THE TIME HAS COME, "PRANK-STER"...
...FOR YOU TO PAY FOR... EVERY-THING!
HYAAA
AAAAAAA

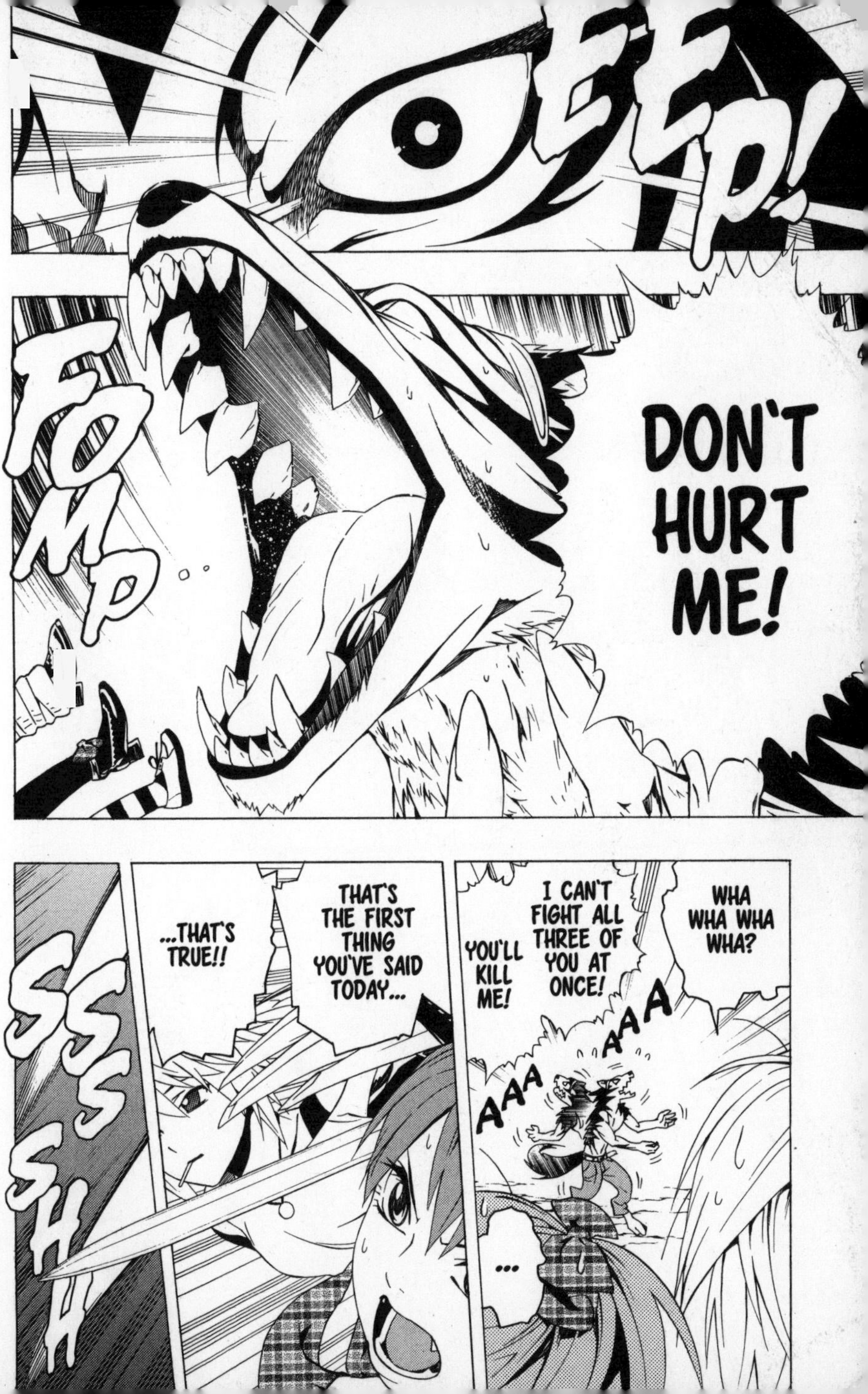
DON'T HURT ME!
FOMP
WHA WHA WHA WHA?
I CAN'T FIGHT ALL THREE OF YOU AT ONCE!
YOU'LL KILL ME!
AAAAAA
...
THAT'S THE FIRST THING YOU'VE SAID TODAY...
...THAT'S TRUE!!
SSSSHH

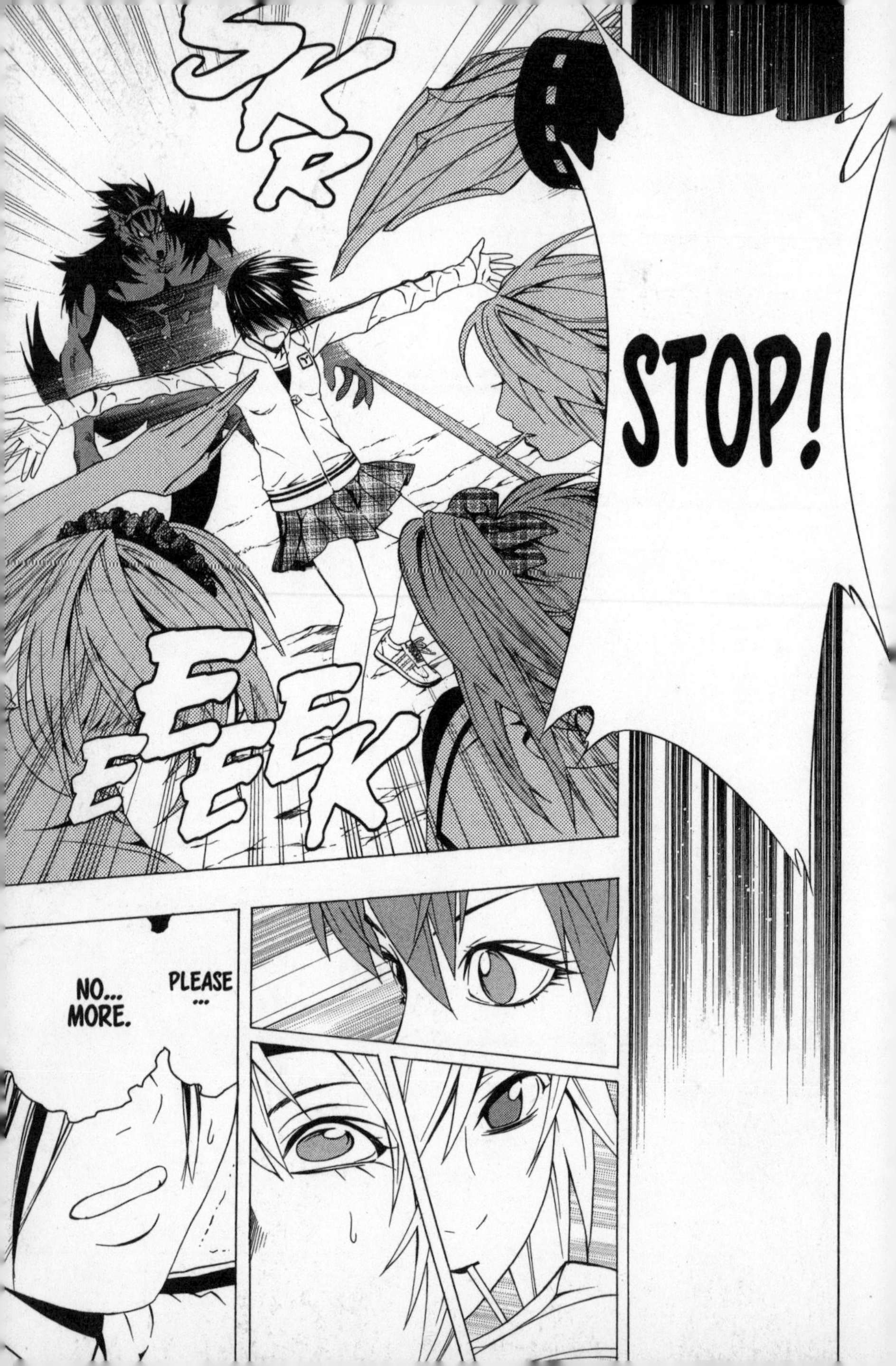
STOP!
SKR
EEEK
PLEASE ...
NO... MORE.

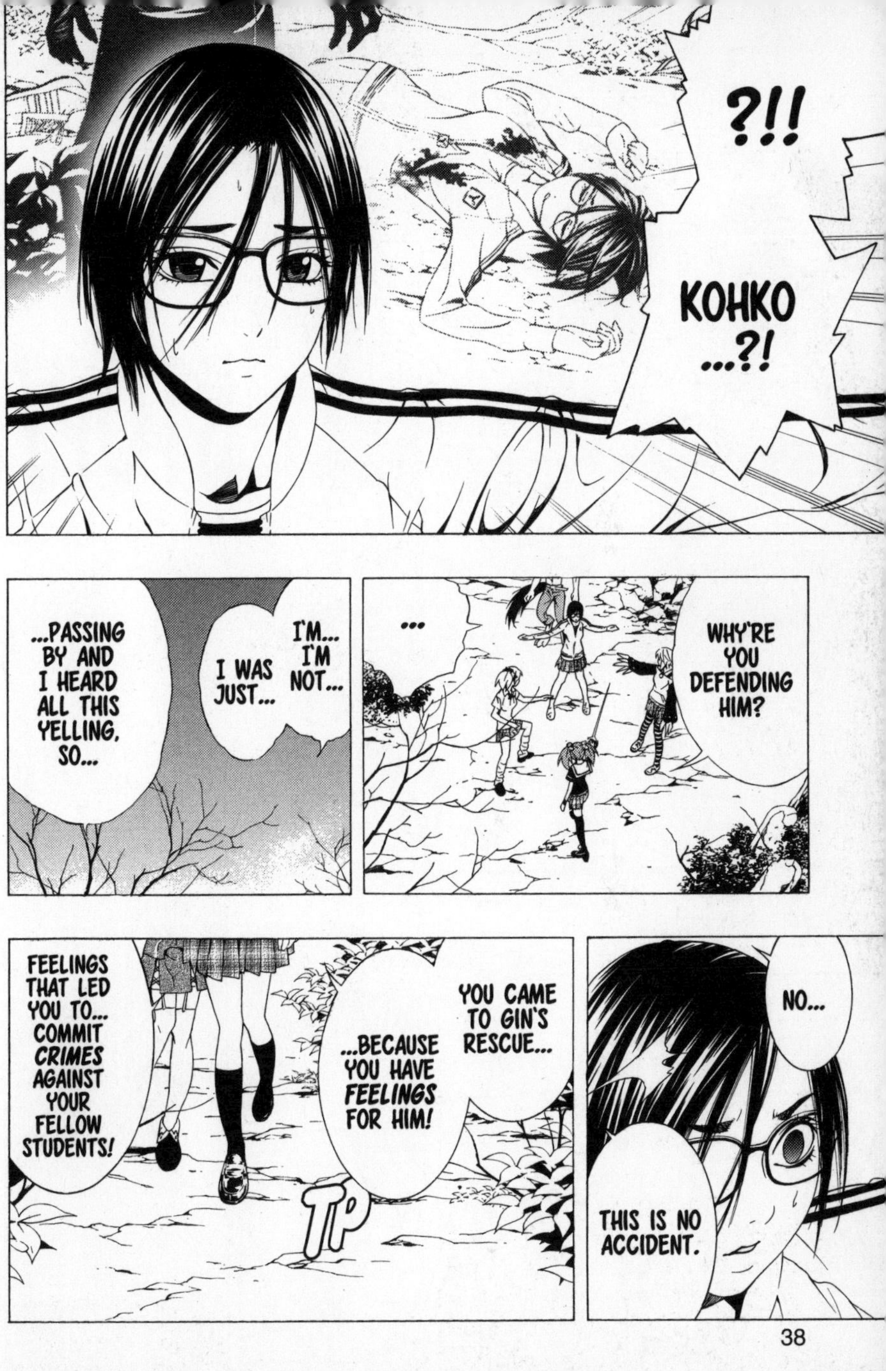
?!!
KOHKO ...?!
WHY'RE YOU DEFENDING HIM?
...
I'M... I'M NOT...
I WAS JUST...
...PASSING BY AND I HEARD ALL THIS YELLING, SO...
NO...
THIS IS NO ACCIDENT.
YOU CAME TO GIN'S RESCUE...
...BECAUSE YOU HAVE *FEELINGS* FOR HIM!
FEELINGS THAT LED YOU TO... COMMIT *CRIMES* AGAINST YOUR FELLOW STUDENTS!
TP

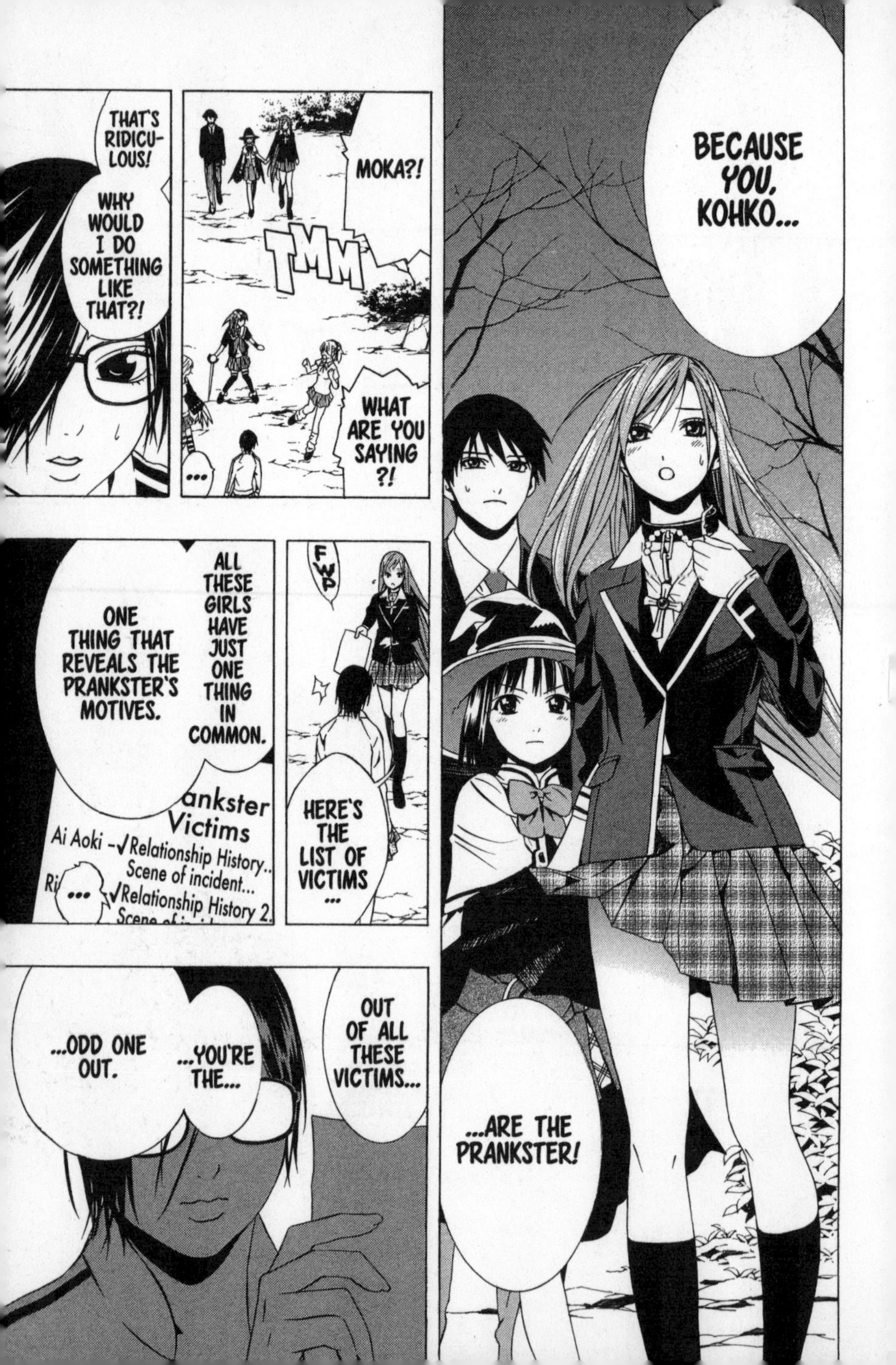
BECAUSE YOU, KOHKO...
...ARE THE PRANKSTER!
MOKA?!
TMM
WHAT ARE YOU SAYING ?!
...
THAT'S RIDICULOUS!
WHY WOULD I DO SOMETHING LIKE THAT?!
FWP
HERE'S THE LIST OF VICTIMS ...
ALL THESE GIRLS HAVE JUST ONE THING IN COMMON.
ONE THING THAT REVEALS THE PRANKSTER'S MOTIVES.
ankster Victims
Ai Aoki –√Relationship History..
Scene of incident...
√Relationship History 2.
...
OUT OF ALL THESE VICTIMS...
...YOU'RE THE...
...ODD ONE OUT.

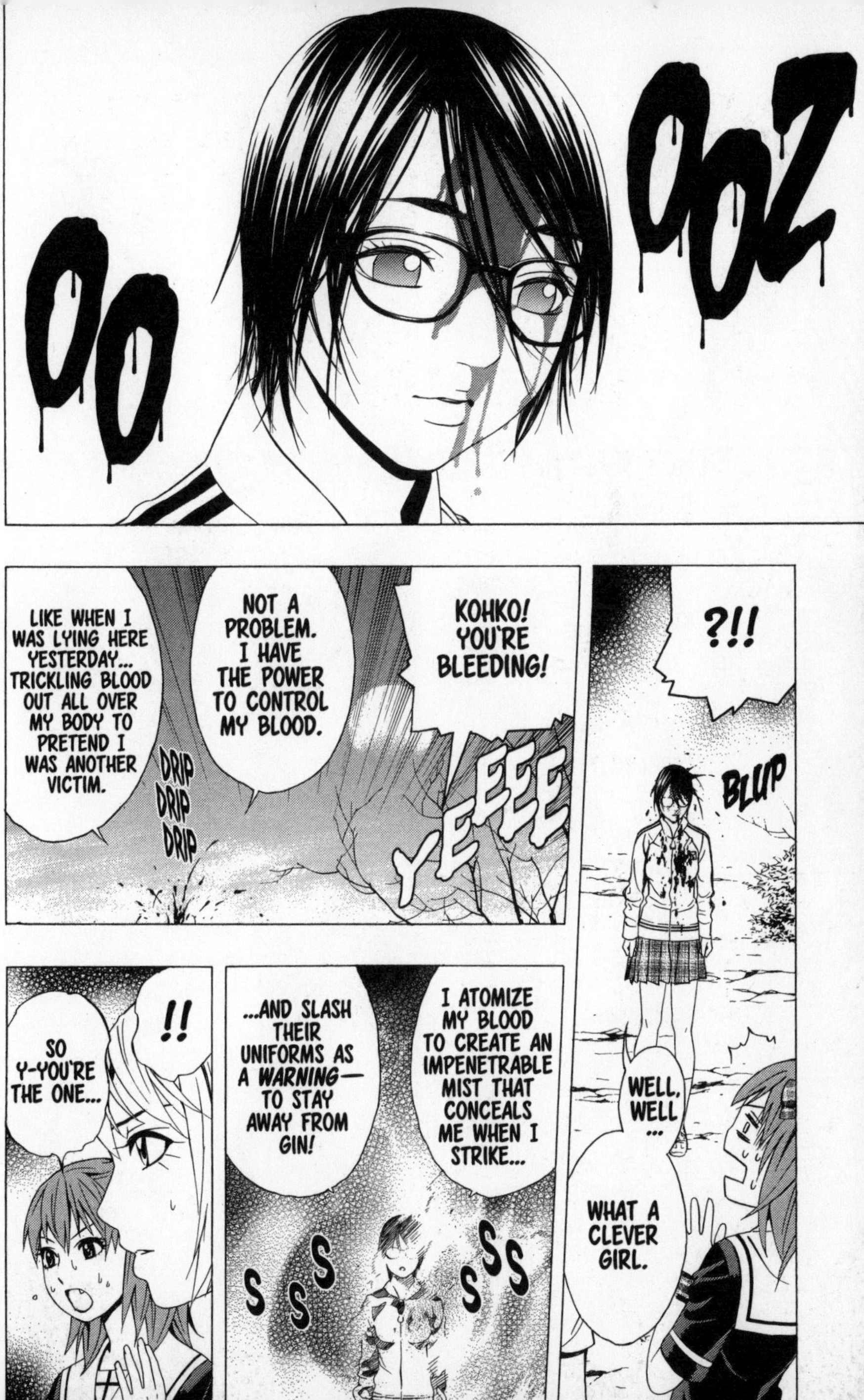
OOZ
OO
?!!
BLUP
KOHKO! YOU'RE BLEEDING!
YEEEE
NOT A PROBLEM. I HAVE THE POWER TO CONTROL MY BLOOD.
DRIP DRIP DRIP
LIKE WHEN I WAS LYING HERE YESTERDAY... TRICKLING BLOOD OUT ALL OVER MY BODY TO PRETEND I WAS ANOTHER VICTIM.
WELL, WELL ...
WHAT A CLEVER GIRL.
I ATOMIZE MY BLOOD TO CREATE AN IMPENETRABLE MIST THAT CONCEALS ME WHEN I STRIKE...
...AND SLASH THEIR UNIFORMS AS A *WARNING*— TO STAY AWAY FROM GIN!
S S S
S S S
!!
SO Y-YOU'RE THE ONE...

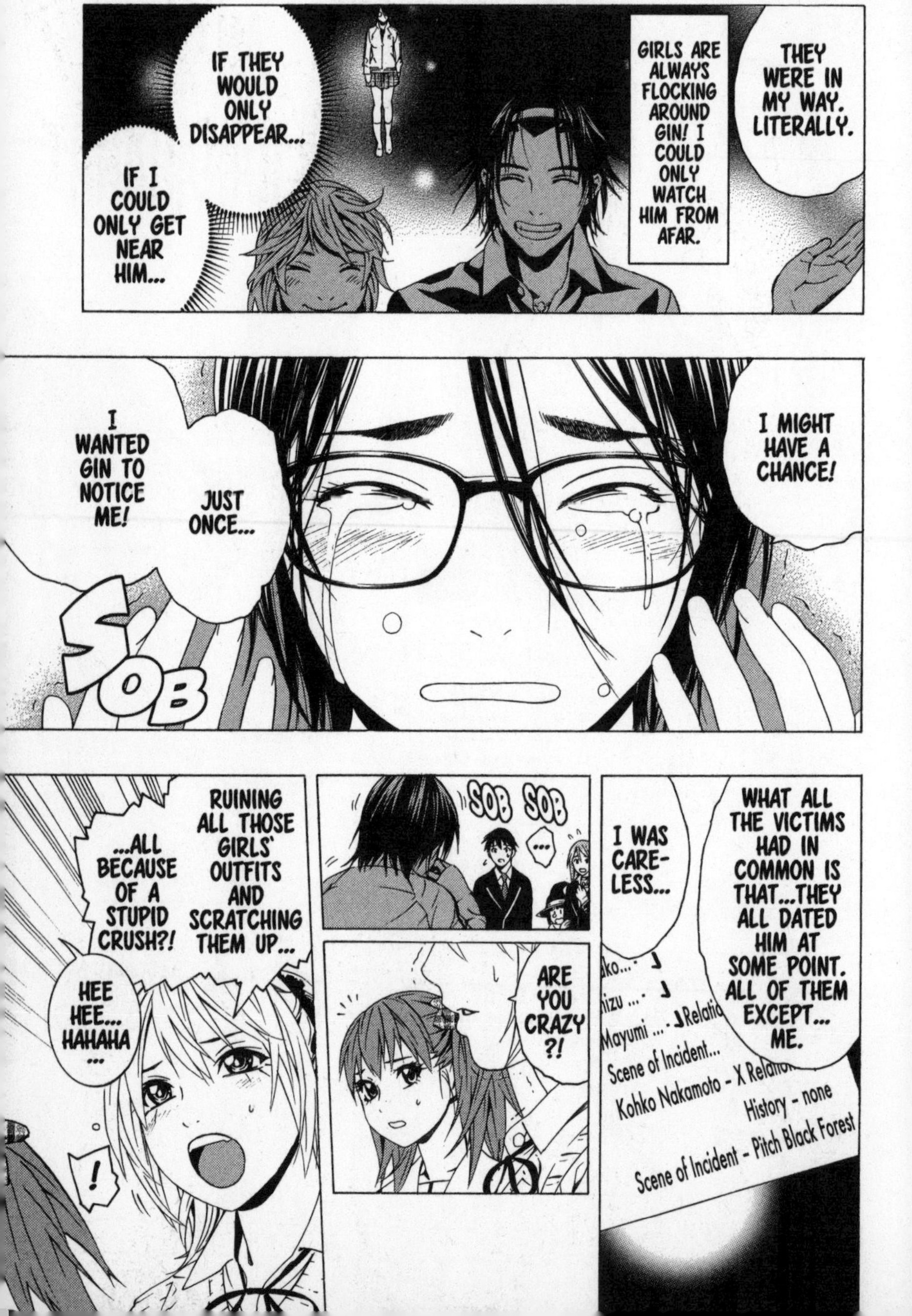
THEY WERE IN MY WAY. LITERALLY.
GIRLS ARE ALWAYS FLOCKING AROUND GIN! I COULD ONLY WATCH HIM FROM AFAR.
IF THEY WOULD ONLY DISAPPEAR...
IF I COULD ONLY GET NEAR HIM...
I MIGHT HAVE A CHANCE!
JUST ONCE...
I WANTED GIN TO NOTICE ME!
SOB
WHAT ALL THE VICTIMS HAD IN COMMON IS THAT...THEY ALL DATED HIM AT SOME POINT. ALL OF THEM EXCEPT... ME.
I WAS CARE-LESS...
Mayumi ...
Scene of Incident...
Kohko Nakamoto - X
History - none
Scene of Incident - Pitch Black Forest
SOB SOB
...
ARE YOU CRAZY?!
RUINING ALL THOSE GIRLS' OUTFITS AND SCRATCHING THEM UP...
...ALL BECAUSE OF A STUPID CRUSH?!
HEE HEE... HAHAHA ...
!

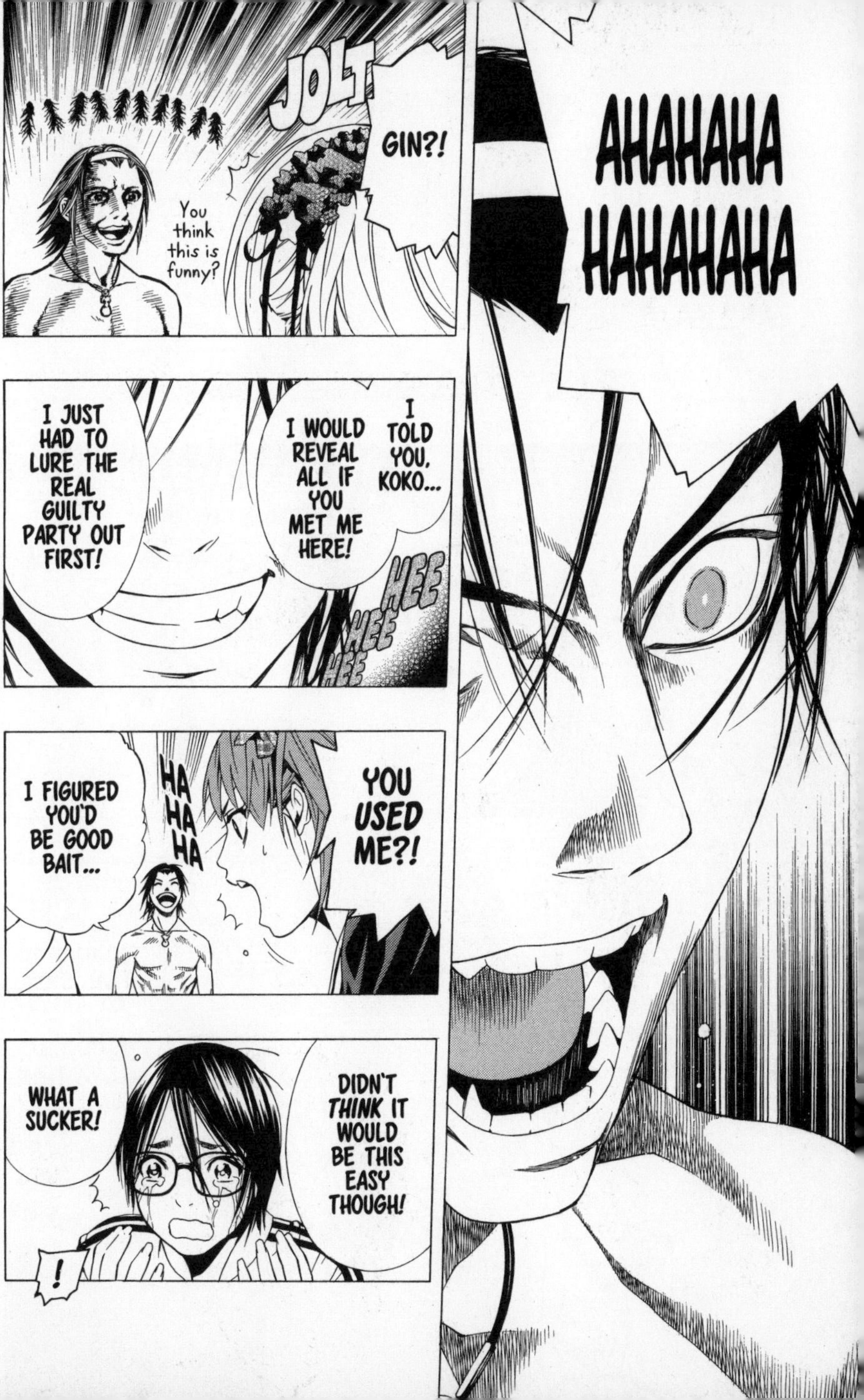
AHAHAHA HAHAHAHA
JOLT
GIN?!
You think this is funny?
I TOLD YOU, KOKO...
I WOULD REVEAL ALL IF YOU MET ME HERE!
HEE HEE HEE
I JUST HAD TO LURE THE REAL GUILTY PARTY OUT FIRST!
YOU *USED* ME?!
HA HA HA
I FIGURED YOU'D BE GOOD BAIT...
DIDN'T *THINK* IT WOULD BE THIS EASY THOUGH!
WHAT A SUCKER!
!

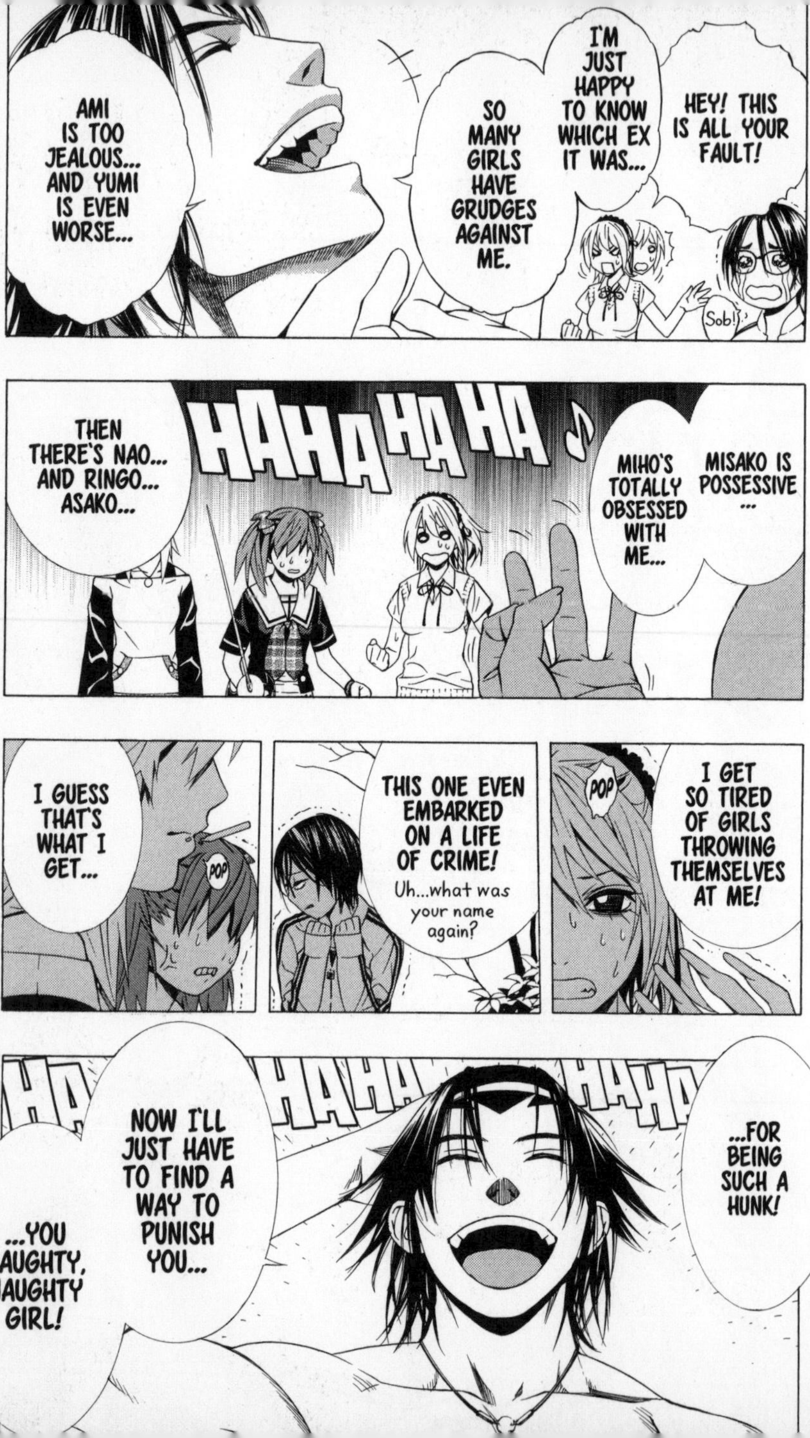
HEY! THIS IS ALL YOUR FAULT!
Sob!
I'M JUST HAPPY TO KNOW WHICH EX IT WAS...
SO MANY GIRLS HAVE GRUDGES AGAINST ME.
AMI IS TOO JEALOUS... AND YUMI IS EVEN WORSE...
MISAKO IS POSSESSIVE...
MIHO'S TOTALLY OBSESSED WITH ME...
HAHAHAHAHA
THEN THERE'S NAO... AND RINGO... ASAKO...
POP
I GET SO TIRED OF GIRLS THROWING THEMSELVES AT ME!
THIS ONE EVEN EMBARKED ON A LIFE OF CRIME!
Uh...what was your name again?
I GUESS THAT'S WHAT I GET...
POP
...FOR BEING SUCH A HUNK!
HAHA
HAHAHA
NOW I'LL JUST HAVE TO FIND A WAY TO PUNISH YOU...
...YOU NAUGHTY, NAUGHTY GIRL!

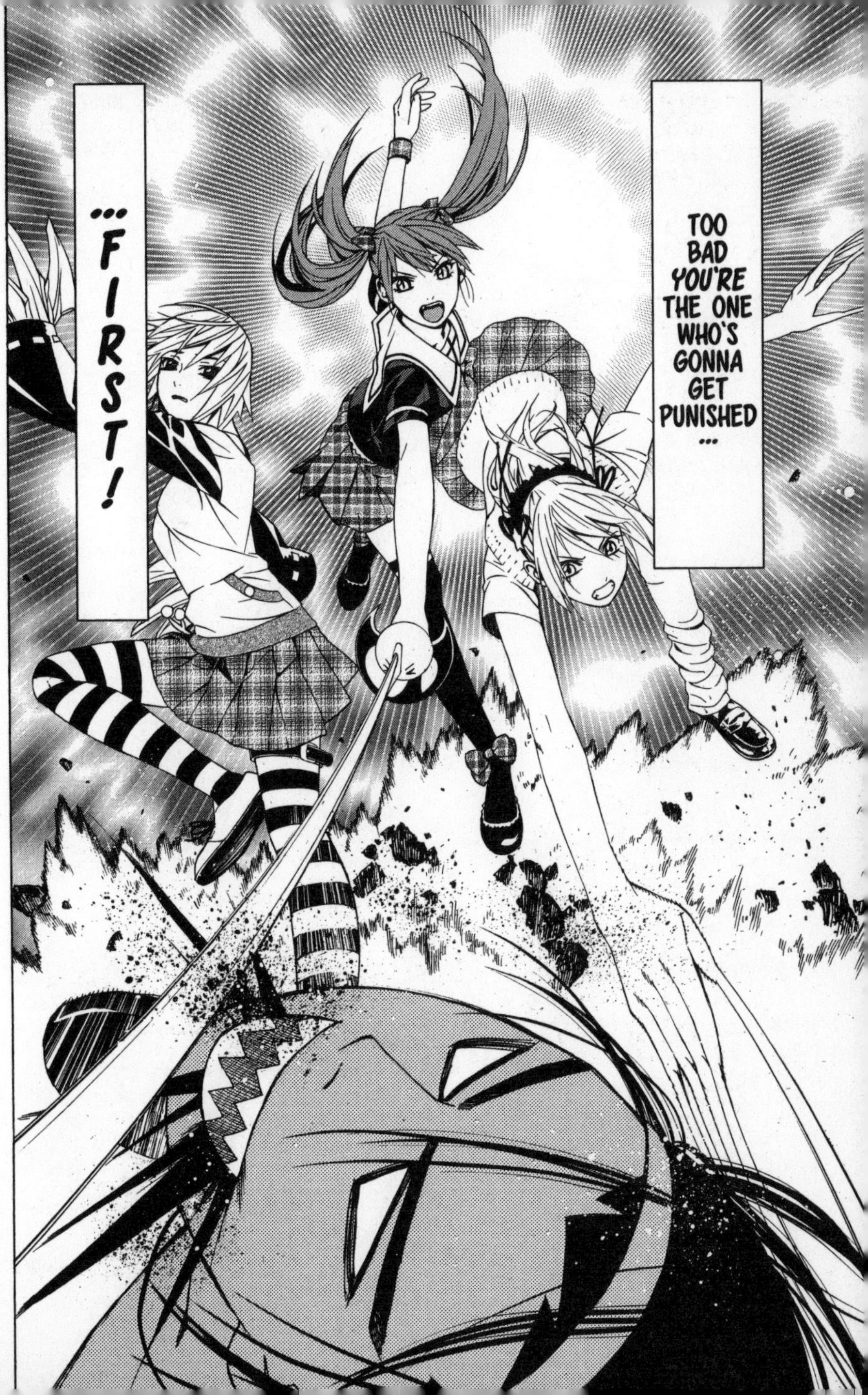
TOO BAD YOU'RE THE ONE WHO'S GONNA GET PUNISHED...
...FIRST!

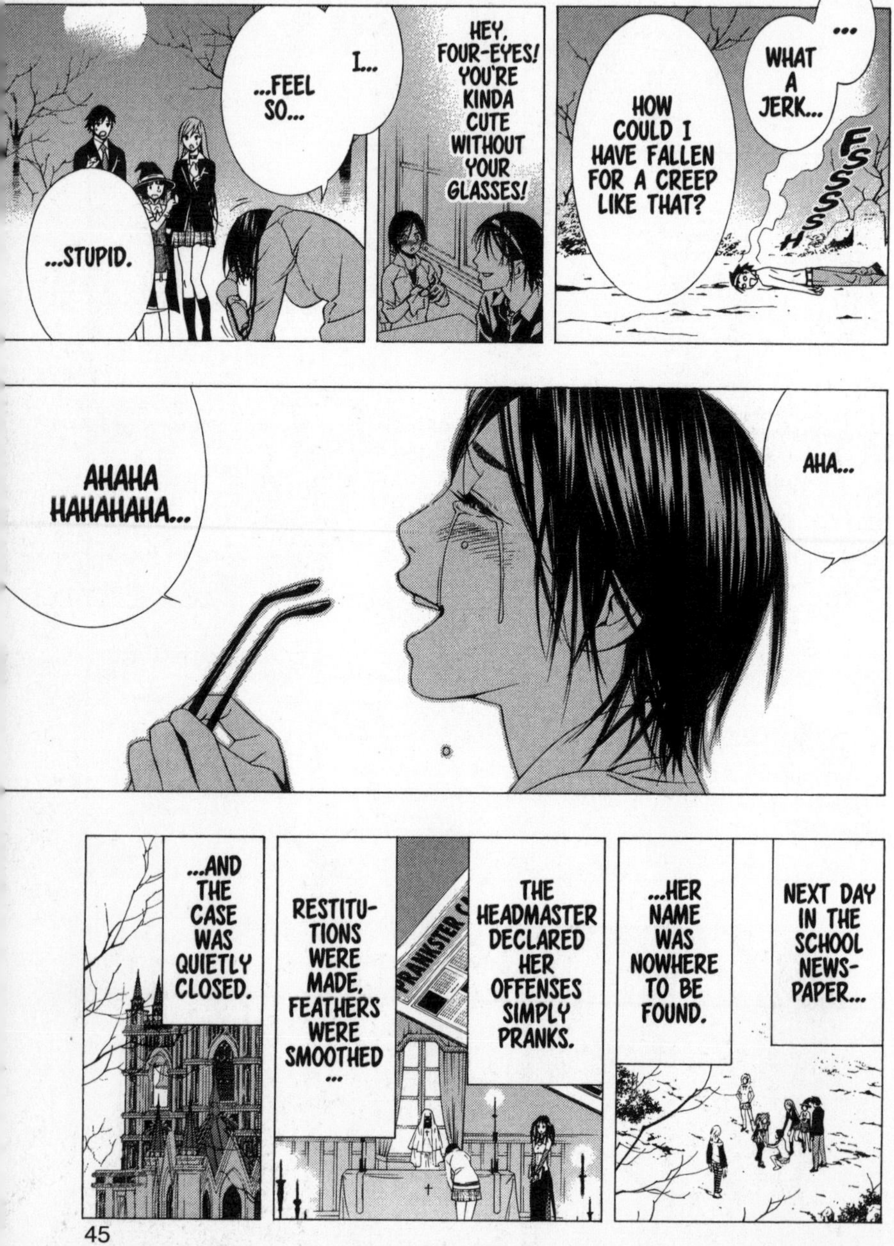
... WHAT A JERK...
FSSSSH
HOW COULD I HAVE FALLEN FOR A CREEP LIKE THAT?
HEY, FOUR-EYES! YOU'RE KINDA CUTE WITHOUT YOUR GLASSES!
I...
...FEEL SO...
...STUPID.
AHA...
AHAHA HAHAHAHA...
NEXT DAY IN THE SCHOOL NEWS-PAPER...
...HER NAME WAS NOWHERE TO BE FOUND.
THE HEADMASTER DECLARED HER OFFENSES SIMPLY PRANKS.
RESTITU-TIONS WERE MADE, FEATHERS WERE SMOOTHED...
...AND THE CASE WAS QUIETLY CLOSED.

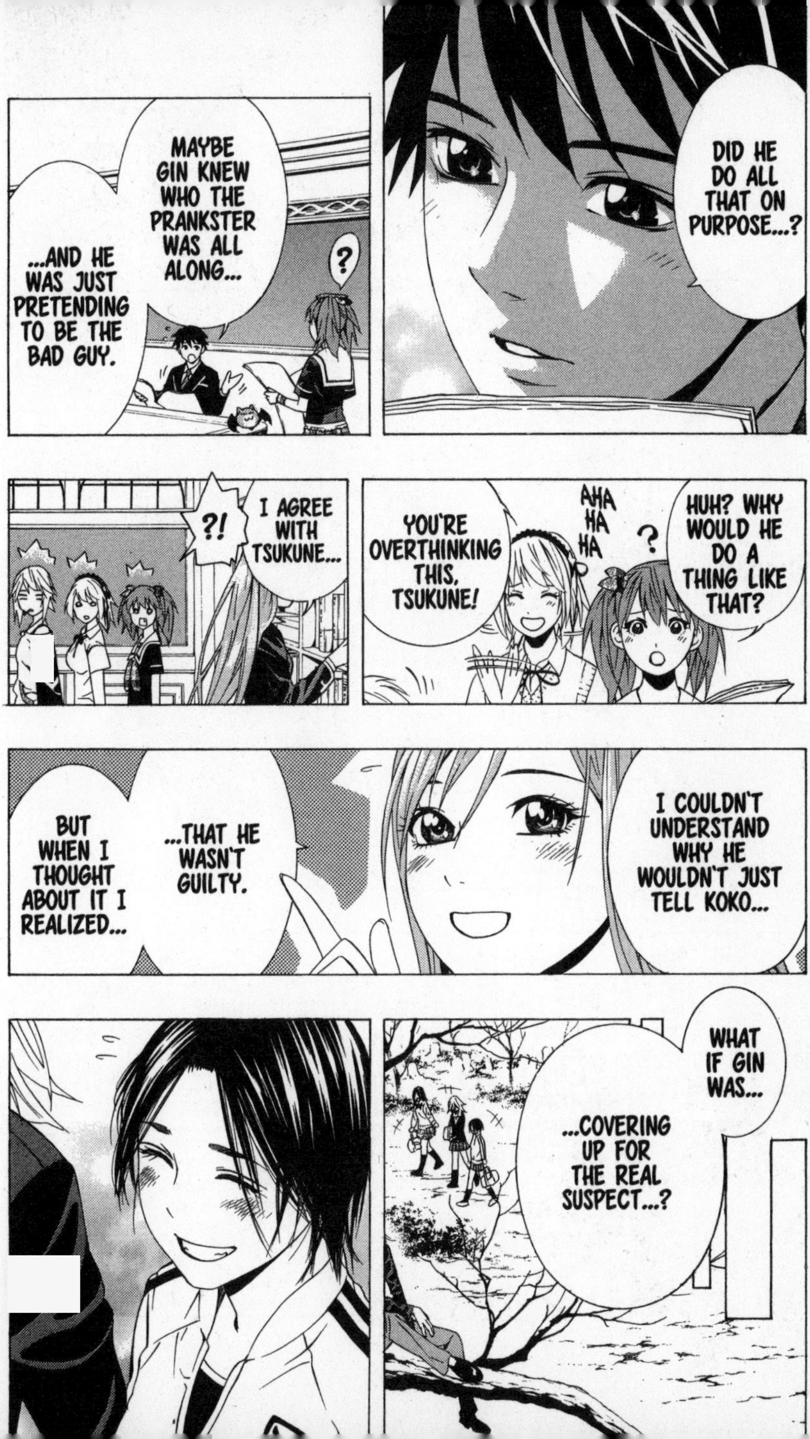
DID HE DO ALL THAT ON PURPOSE...?
MAYBE GIN KNEW WHO THE PRANKSTER WAS ALL ALONG...
?
...AND HE WAS JUST PRETENDING TO BE THE BAD GUY.
HUH? WHY WOULD HE DO A THING LIKE THAT?
?
AHA HA HA
YOU'RE OVERTHINKING THIS, TSUKUNE!
I AGREE WITH TSUKUNE...
?!
I COULDN'T UNDERSTAND WHY HE WOULDN'T JUST TELL KOKO...
BUT WHEN I THOUGHT ABOUT IT I REALIZED...
...THAT HE WASN'T GUILTY.
WHAT IF GIN WAS...
...COVERING UP FOR THE REAL SUSPECT...?

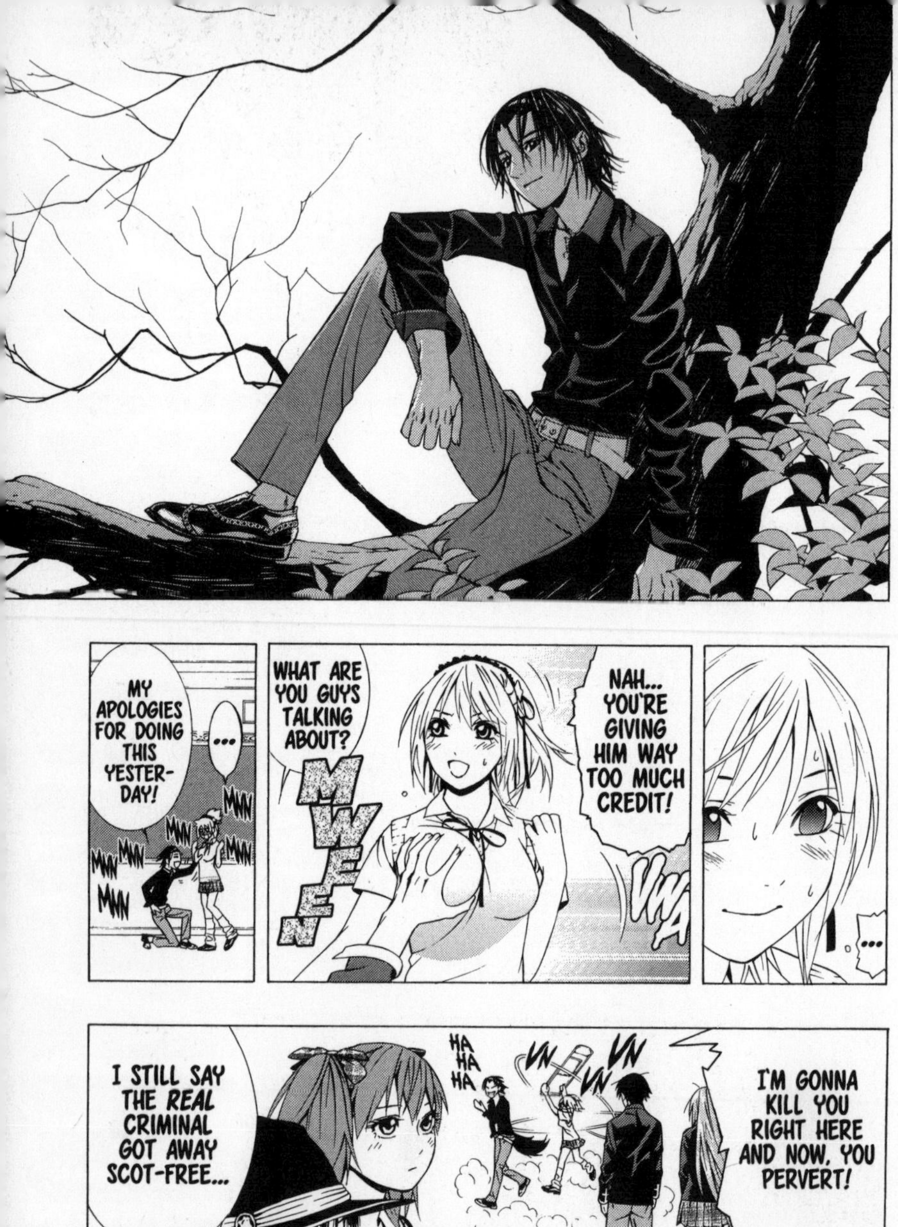
...
NAH... YOU'RE GIVING HIM WAY TOO MUCH CREDIT!
VWA
WHAT ARE YOU GUYS TALKING ABOUT?
MWEEN
MY APOLOGIES FOR DOING THIS YESTER-DAY!
...
MWN MWN MWN MWN MWN MWN
I'M GONNA KILL YOU RIGHT HERE AND NOW, YOU PERVERT!
VN VN VN VN
HA HA HA
I STILL SAY THE *REAL* CRIMINAL GOT AWAY SCOT-FREE...

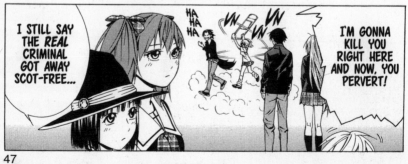

ROSARIO+VAMPIRE

Season II

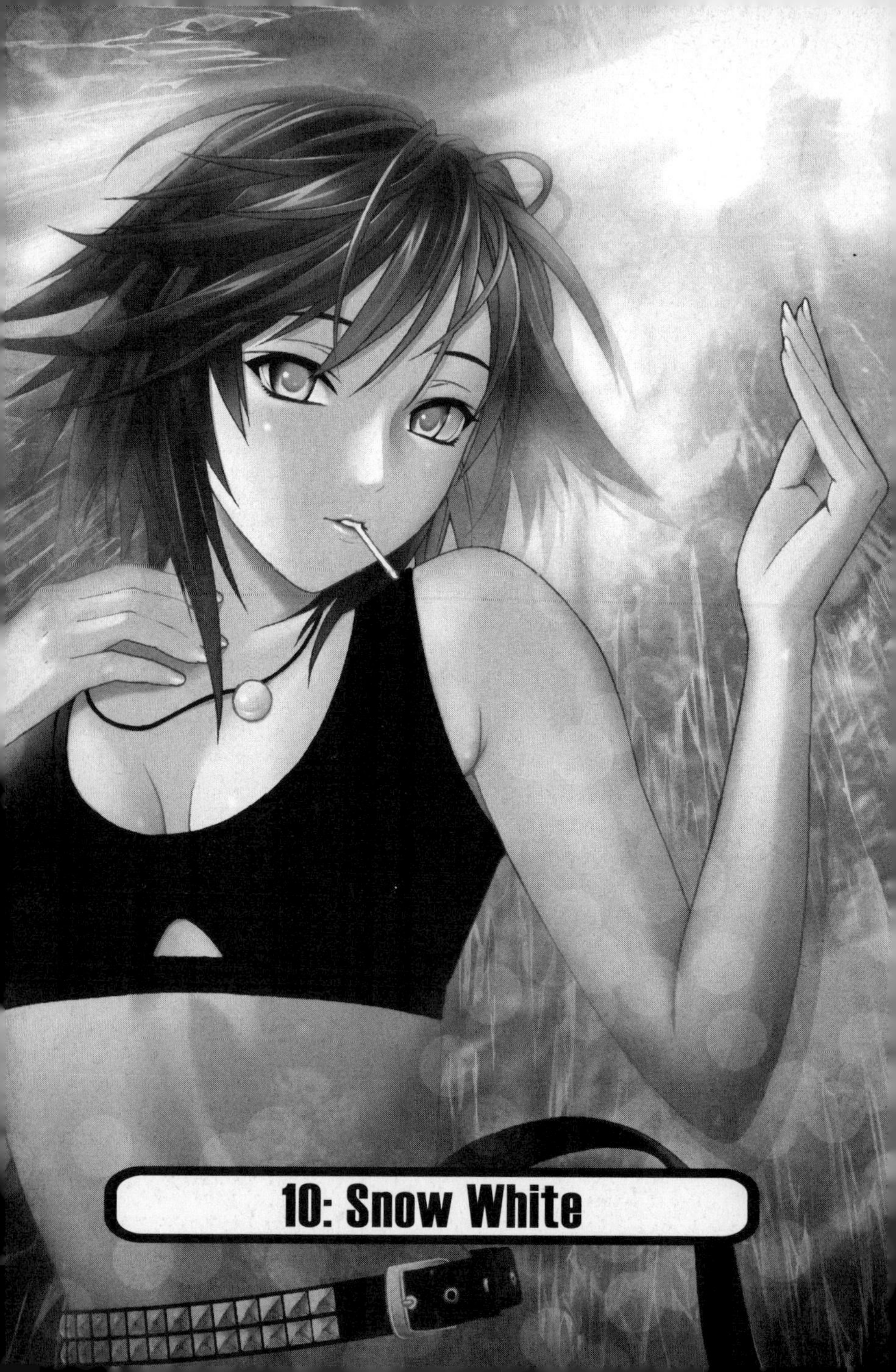
10: Snow White

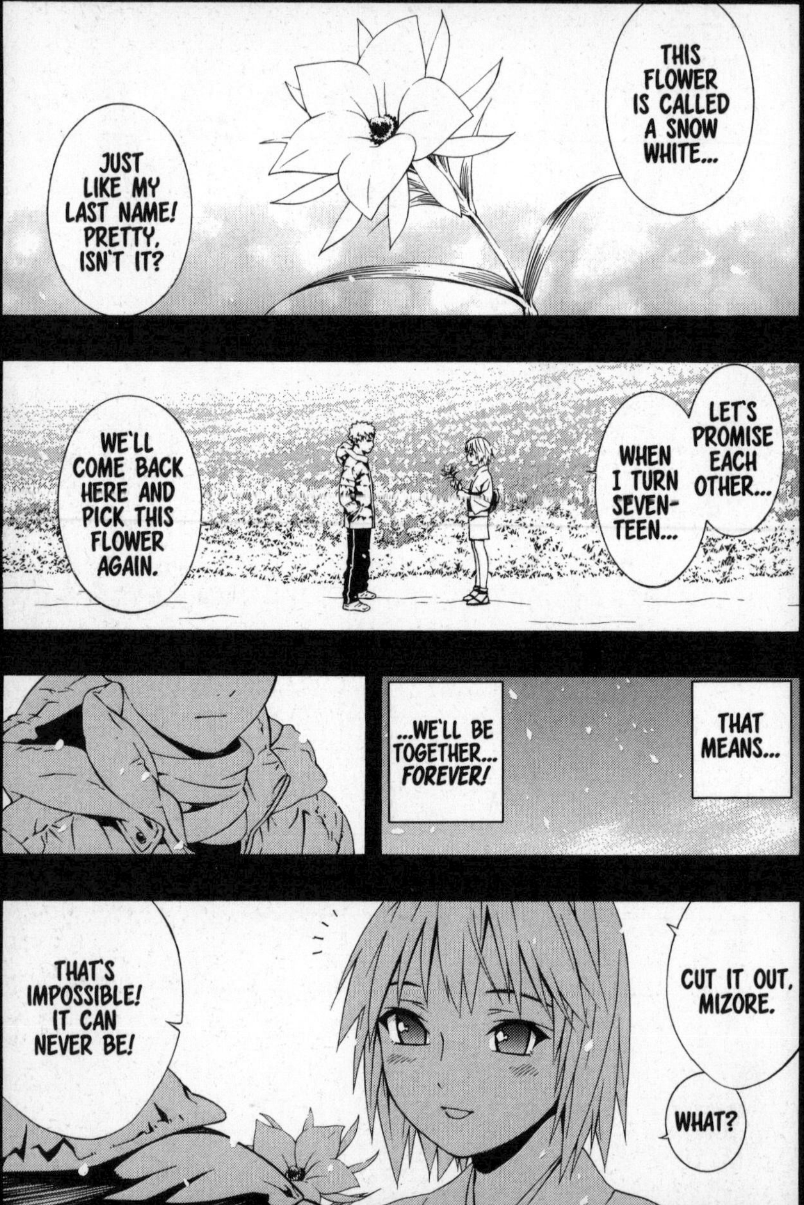
THIS FLOWER IS CALLED A SNOW WHITE...
JUST LIKE MY LAST NAME! PRETTY, ISN'T IT?
LET'S PROMISE EACH OTHER...
WHEN I TURN SEVENTEEN...
WE'LL COME BACK HERE AND PICK THIS FLOWER AGAIN.
THAT MEANS...
...WE'LL BE TOGETHER... FOREVER!
CUT IT OUT, MIZORE.
WHAT?
THAT'S IMPOSSIBLE! IT CAN NEVER BE!

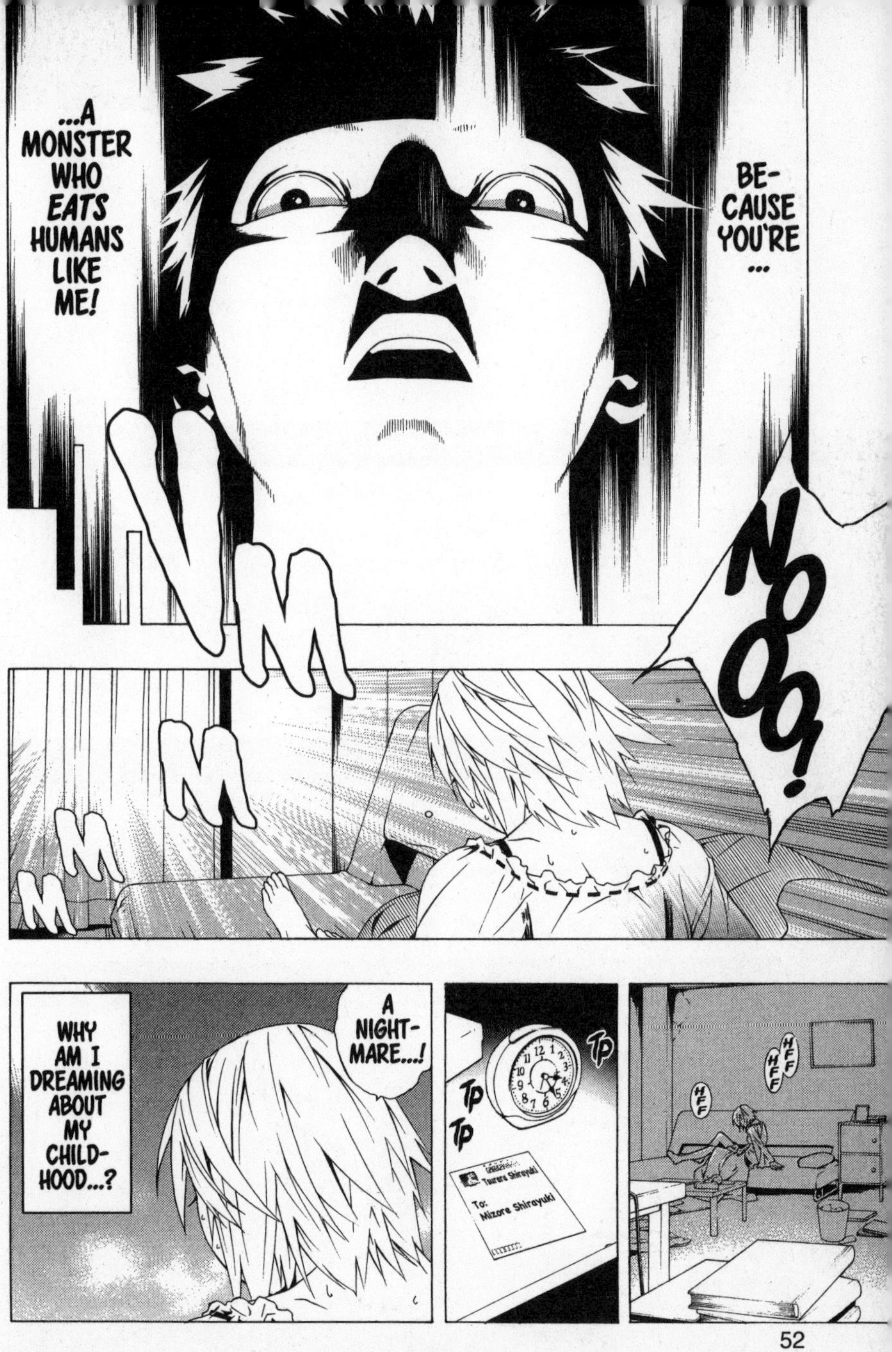
BE-CAUSE YOU'RE...
...A MONSTER WHO EATS HUMANS LIKE ME!
NOOO!
MMMM
HFF
HFF
HFF
Tp
Tp
Tp
Tsurara Shirayuki
To: Mizore Shirayuki
A NIGHT-MARE...!
WHY AM I DREAMING ABOUT MY CHILD-HOOD...?

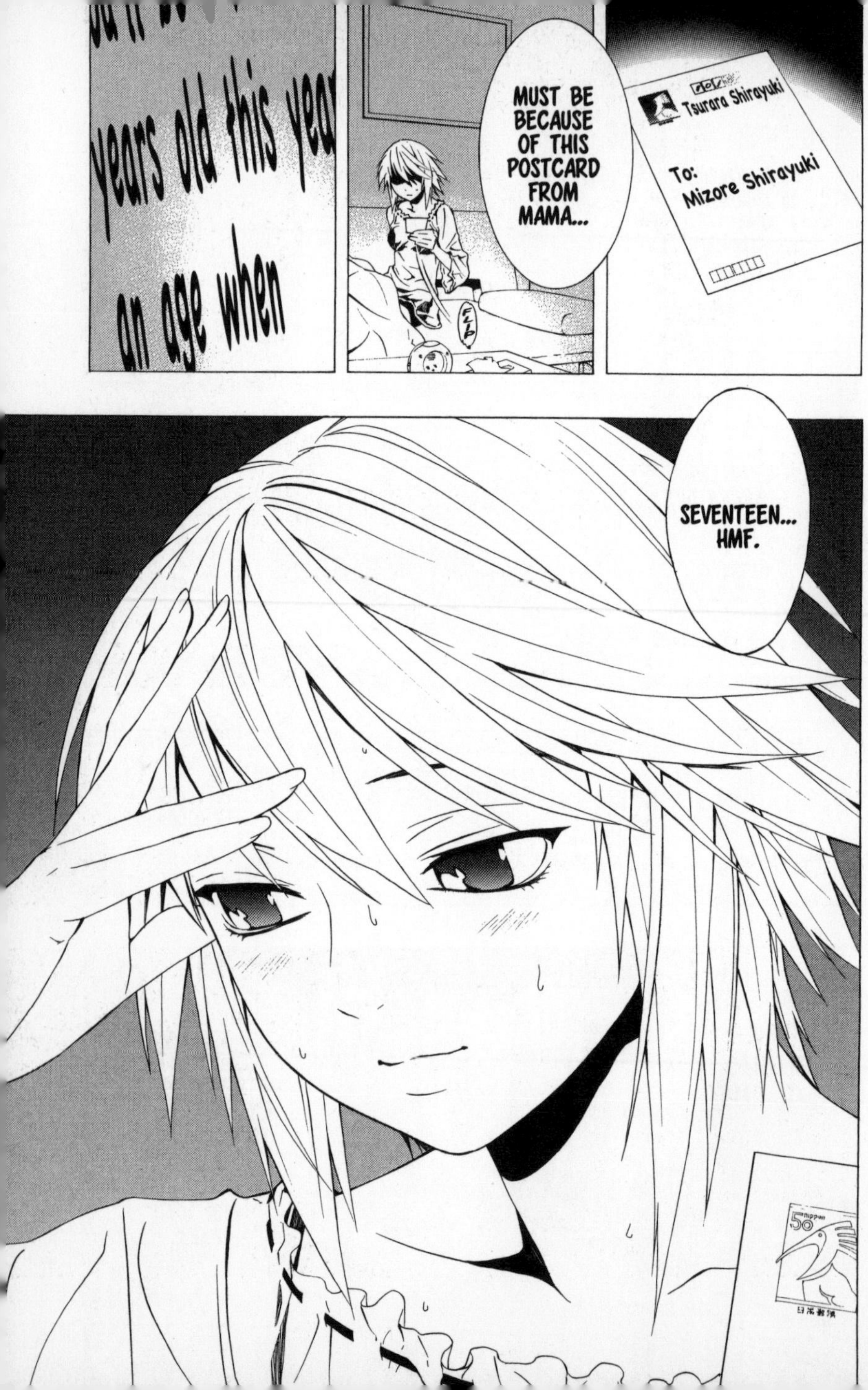
Tsurara Shirayuki
To:
Mizore Shirayuki
MUST BE BECAUSE OF THIS POSTCARD FROM MAMA...
years old this yea
an age when
SEVENTEEN... HMF.

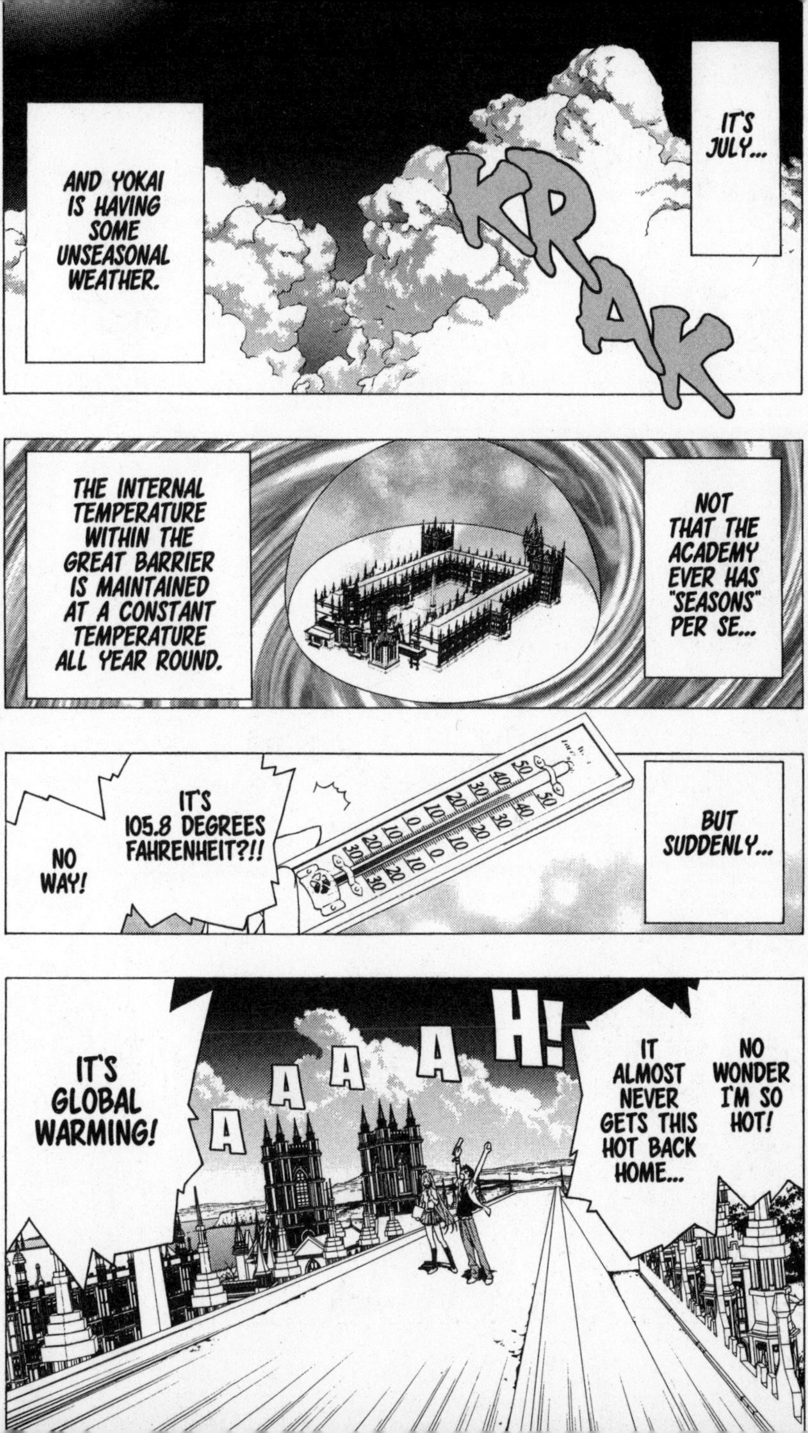
IT'S JULY...
KRAK
AND YOKAI IS HAVING SOME UNSEASONAL WEATHER.
NOT THAT THE ACADEMY EVER HAS "SEASONS" PER SE...
THE INTERNAL TEMPERATURE WITHIN THE GREAT BARRIER IS MAINTAINED AT A CONSTANT TEMPERATURE ALL YEAR ROUND.
BUT SUDDENLY...
IT'S 105.8 DEGREES FAHRENHEIT?!!
NO WAY!
NO WONDER I'M SO HOT!
IT ALMOST NEVER GETS THIS HOT BACK HOME...
AAAAH!
IT'S GLOBAL WARMING!

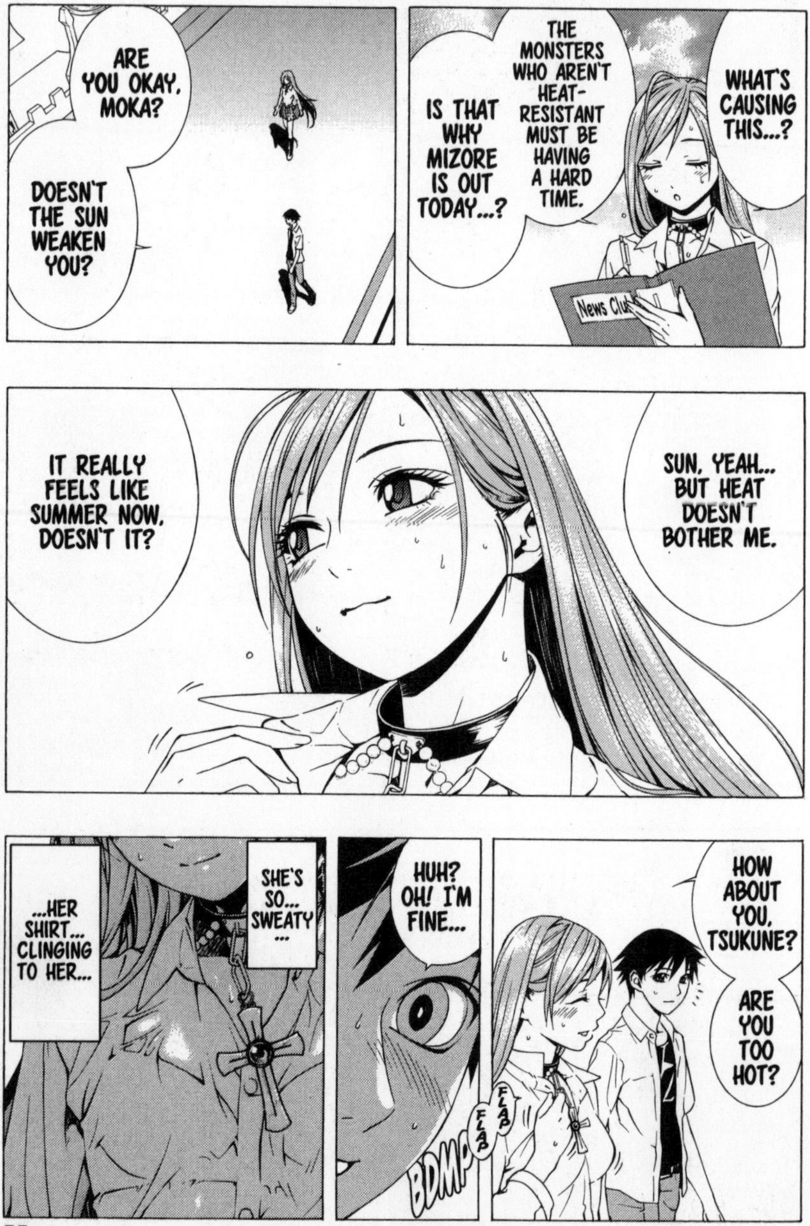
WHAT'S CAUSING THIS...?
THE MONSTERS WHO AREN'T HEAT-RESISTANT MUST BE HAVING A HARD TIME.
IS THAT WHY MIZORE IS OUT TODAY...?
News Club
ARE YOU OKAY, MOKA?
DOESN'T THE SUN WEAKEN YOU?
SUN, YEAH... BUT HEAT DOESN'T BOTHER ME.
IT REALLY FEELS LIKE SUMMER NOW, DOESN'T IT?
HOW ABOUT YOU, TSUKUNE?
ARE YOU TOO HOT?
FLAP FLAP FLAP
BDMP
HUH? OH! I'M FINE...
SHE'S SO... SWEATY ...
...HER SHIRT... CLINGING TO HER...

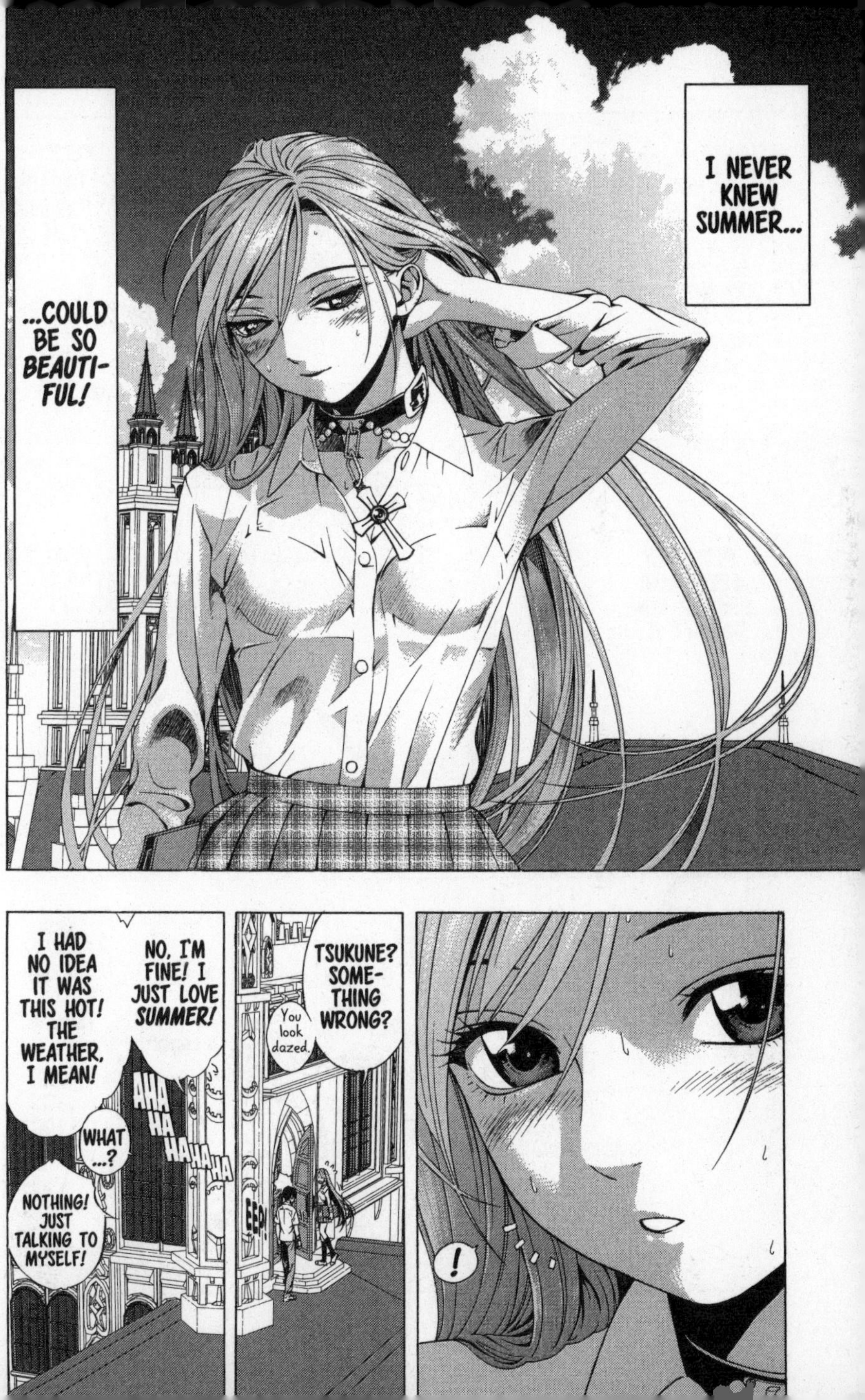
I NEVER KNEW SUMMER...
...COULD BE SO BEAUTIFUL!
!
TSUKUNE? SOMETHING WRONG?
You look dazed.
EEP!
NO, I'M FINE! I JUST LOVE SUMMER!
I HAD NO IDEA IT WAS THIS HOT! THE WEATHER, I MEAN!
AHA HA HAHAHA
WHAT...?
NOTHING! JUST TALKING TO MYSELF!

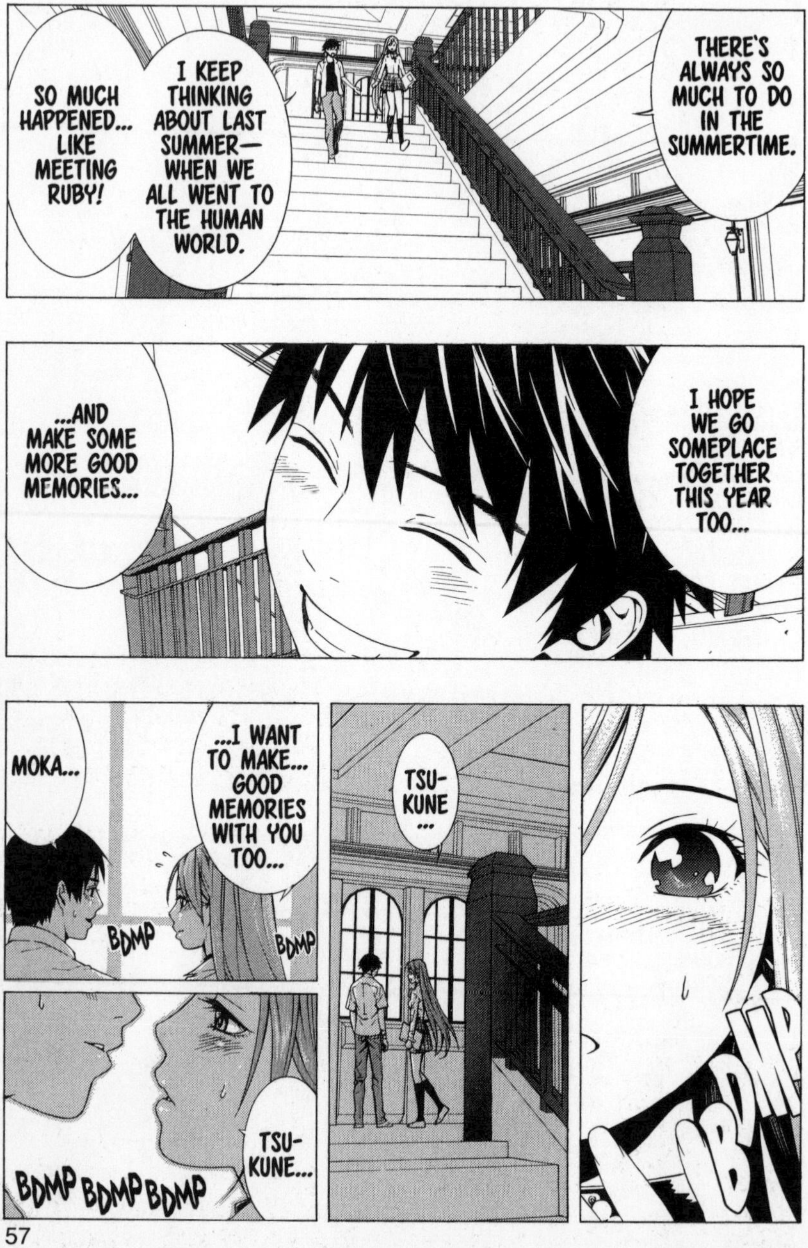
THERE'S ALWAYS SO MUCH TO DO IN THE SUMMERTIME.
I KEEP THINKING ABOUT LAST SUMMER— WHEN WE ALL WENT TO THE HUMAN WORLD.
SO MUCH HAPPENED... LIKE MEETING RUBY!
I HOPE WE GO SOMEPLACE TOGETHER THIS YEAR TOO...
...AND MAKE SOME MORE GOOD MEMORIES...
BDMP
BDMP
TSU-KUNE ...
...I WANT TO MAKE... GOOD MEMORIES WITH YOU TOO...
MOKA...
BDMP
BDMP
TSU-KUNE...
BDMP BDMP BDMP

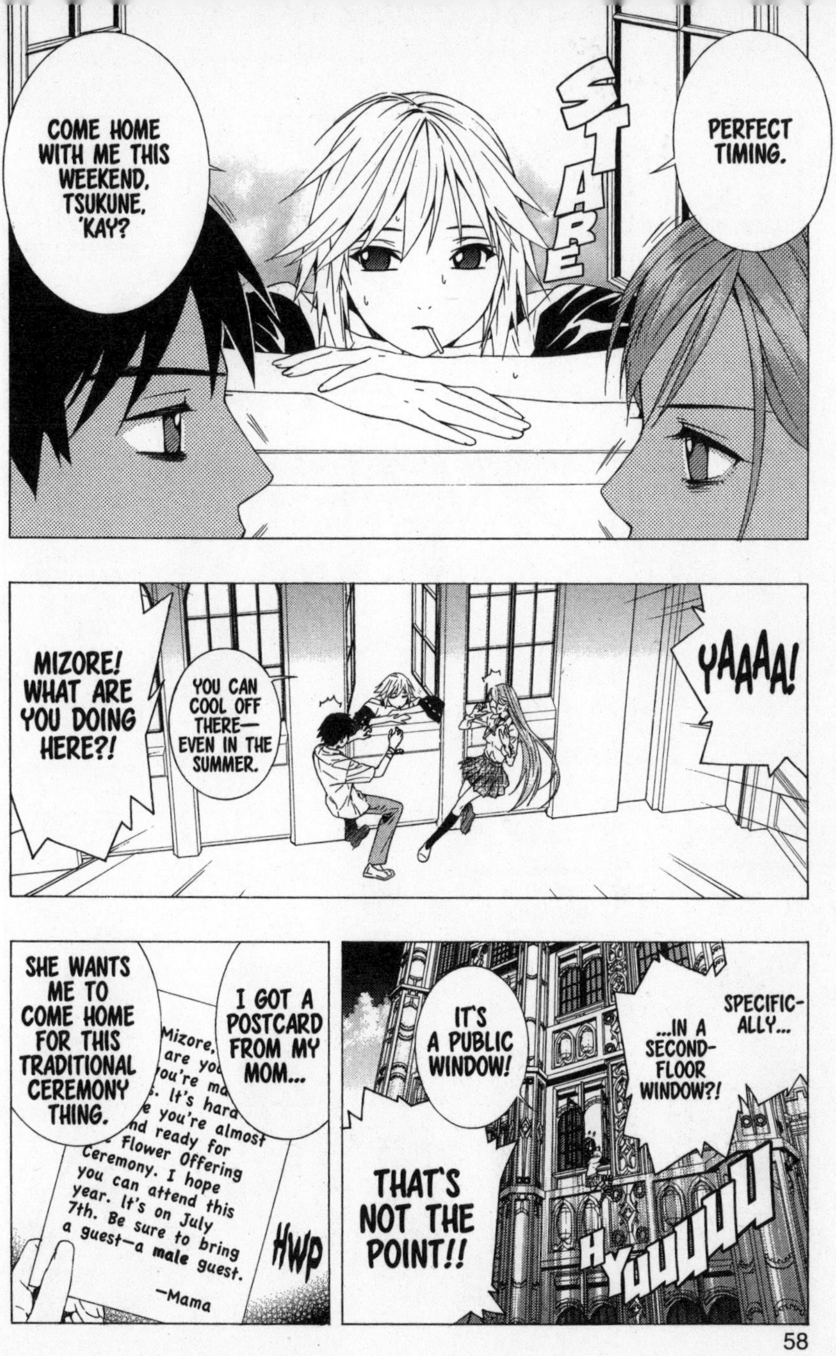
PERFECT TIMING.
STARE
COME HOME WITH ME THIS WEEKEND, TSUKUNE, 'KAY?
YAAAA!
MIZORE! WHAT ARE YOU DOING HERE?!
YOU CAN COOL OFF THERE—EVEN IN THE SUMMER.
SPECIFIC-ALLY...
...IN A SECOND-FLOOR WINDOW?!
IT'S A PUBLIC WINDOW!
THAT'S NOT THE POINT!!
HYUUUUU
I GOT A POSTCARD FROM MY MOM...
SHE WANTS ME TO COME HOME FOR THIS TRADITIONAL CEREMONY THING.
Mizore,
Ceremony. I hope you can attend this year. It's on July 7th. Be sure to bring a guest—a male guest.
—Mama
HWP

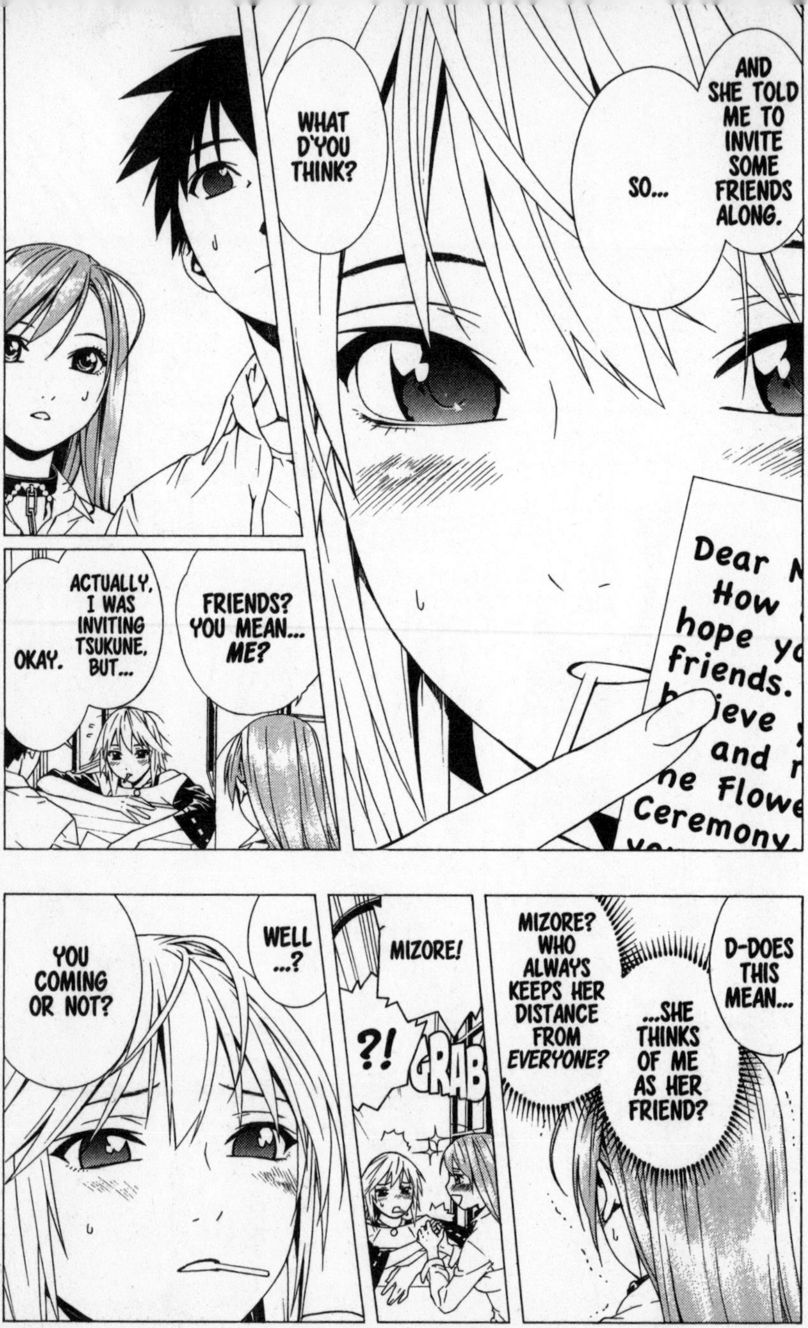
AND SHE TOLD ME TO INVITE SOME FRIENDS ALONG.
SO...
WHAT D'YOU THINK?
Dear
How
friends.
and
Ceremony.
FRIENDS? YOU MEAN... ME?
ACTUALLY, I WAS INVITING TSUKUNE, BUT...
OKAY.
D-DOES THIS MEAN...
...SHE THINKS OF ME AS HER FRIEND?
MIZORE? WHO ALWAYS KEEPS HER DISTANCE FROM EVERYONE?
MIZORE!
GRAB
?!
WELL ...?
YOU COMING OR NOT?

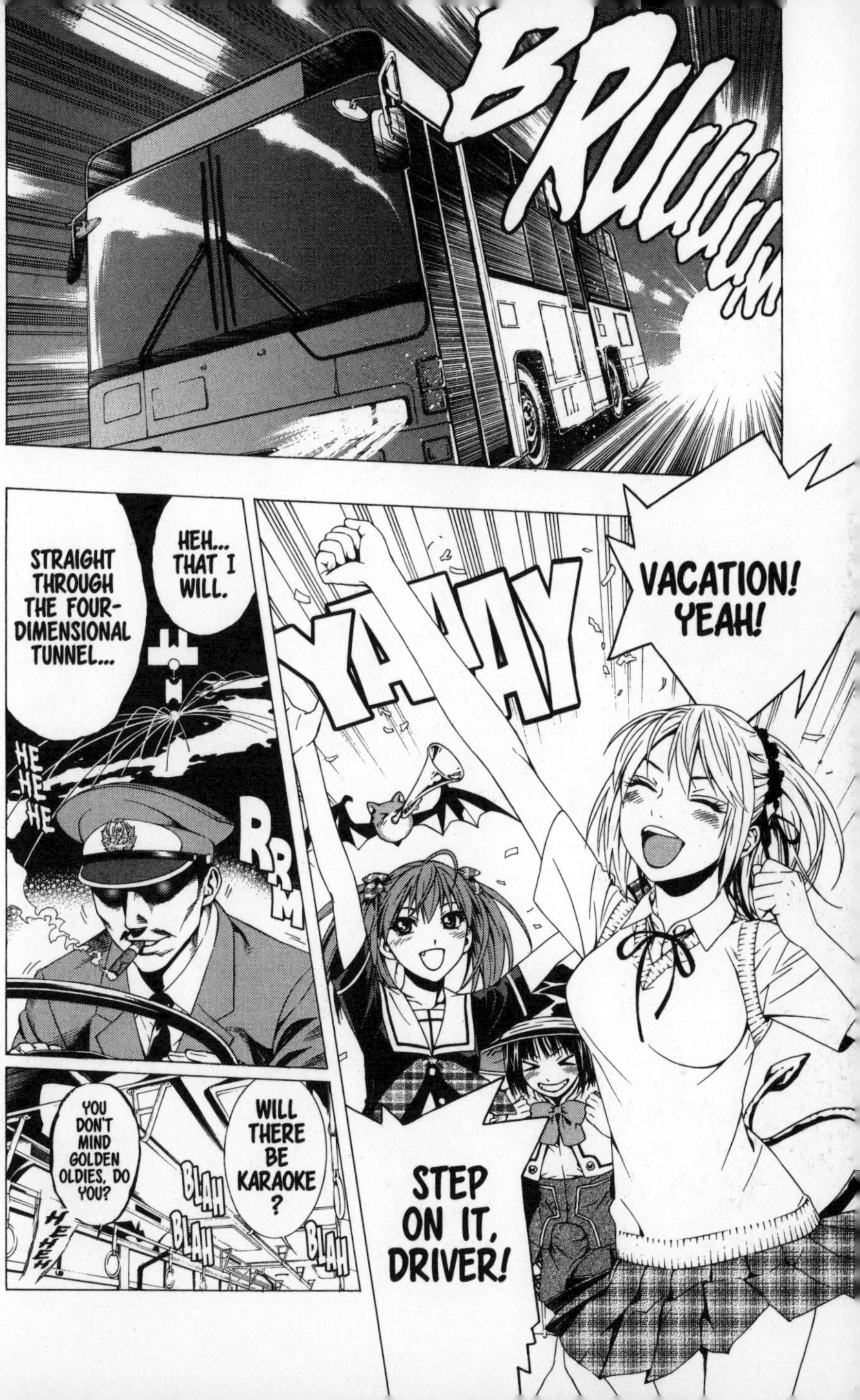

VACATION! YEAH!
STEP ON IT, DRIVER!
HEH... THAT I WILL.
STRAIGHT THROUGH THE FOUR-DIMENSIONAL TUNNEL...
HE HE HE
RRM
WILL THERE BE KARAOKE?
YOU DON'T MIND GOLDEN OLDIES, DO YOU?
BLAH
BLAH
BLAH
HEHEH

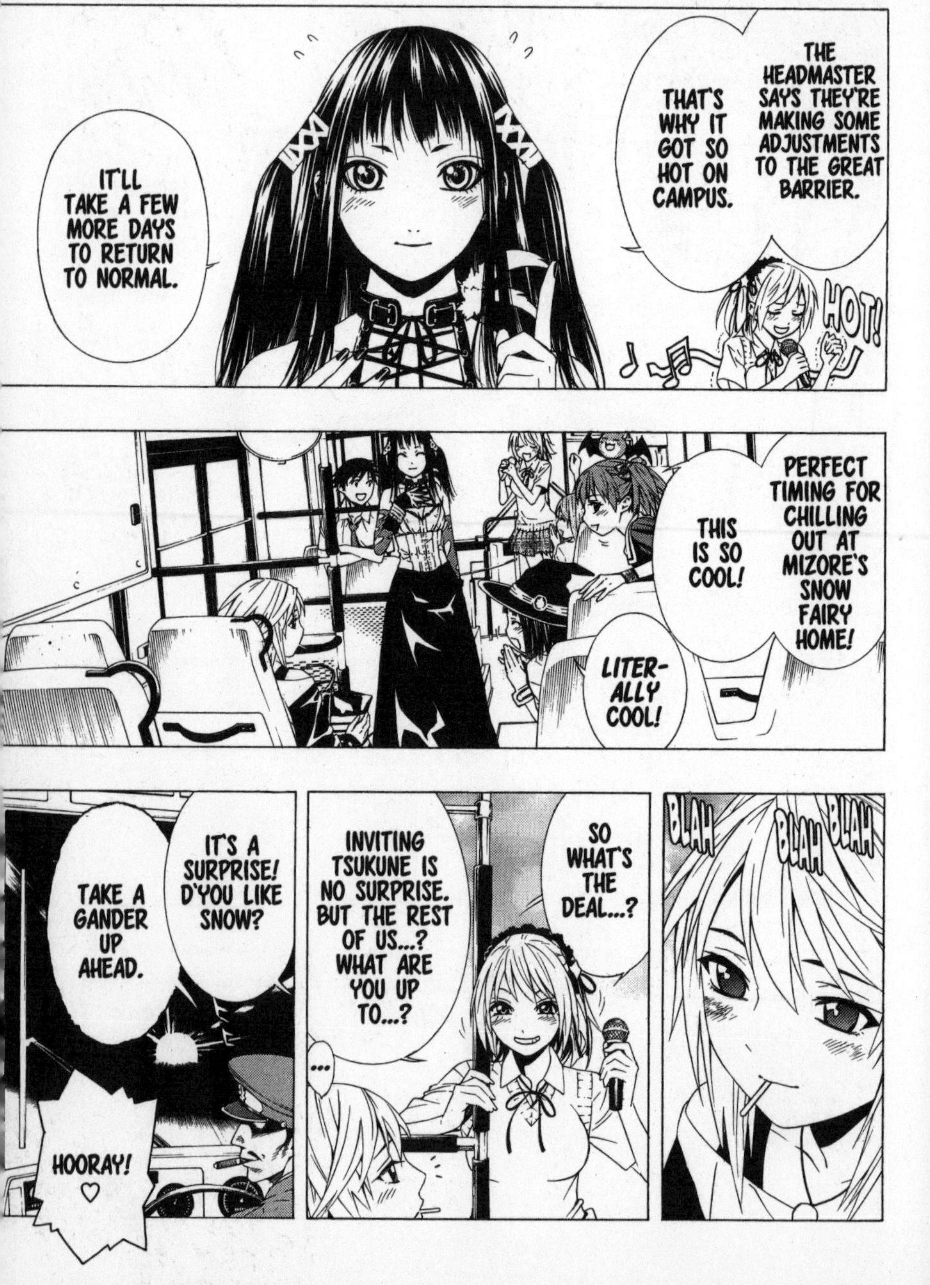
THE HEADMASTER SAYS THEY'RE MAKING SOME ADJUSTMENTS TO THE GREAT BARRIER.
THAT'S WHY IT GOT SO HOT ON CAMPUS.
HOT!
IT'LL TAKE A FEW MORE DAYS TO RETURN TO NORMAL.
PERFECT TIMING FOR CHILLING OUT AT MIZORE'S SNOW FAIRY HOME!
THIS IS SO COOL!
LITER-ALLY COOL!
BLAH BLAH BLAH
SO WHAT'S THE DEAL...?
INVITING TSUKUNE IS NO SURPRISE. BUT THE REST OF US...? WHAT ARE YOU UP TO...?
...
IT'S A SURPRISE! D'YOU LIKE SNOW?
TAKE A GANDER UP AHEAD.
HOORAY! ♡

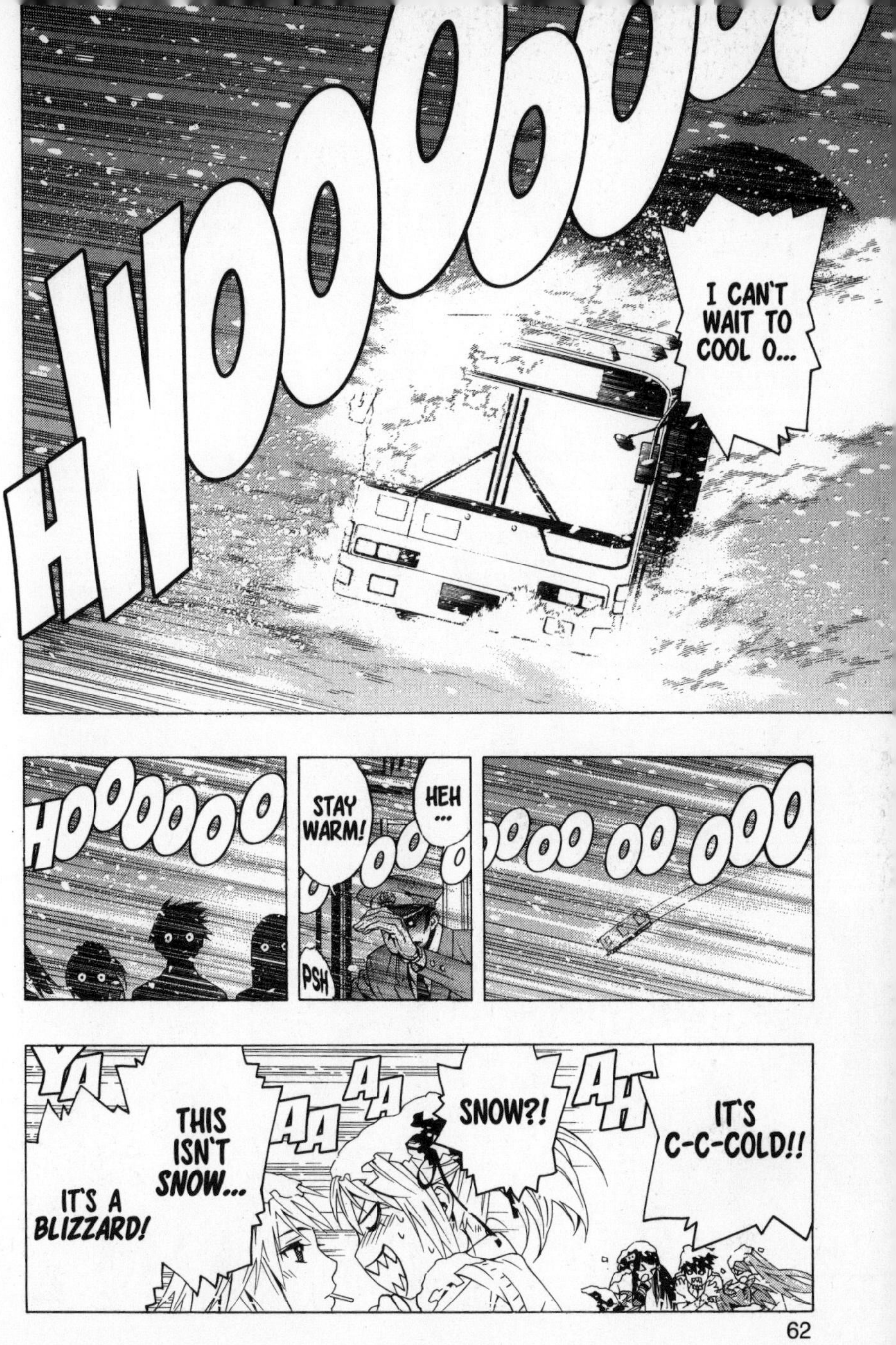
HWOOOOOO
I CAN'T WAIT TO COOL O...
OOOOO OO OOO
HEH ...
STAY WARM!
PSH
HOOOOOO
IT'S C-C-COLD!!
AH
SNOW?!
AAA
AA
THIS ISN'T SNOW...
IT'S A BLIZZARD!
YA

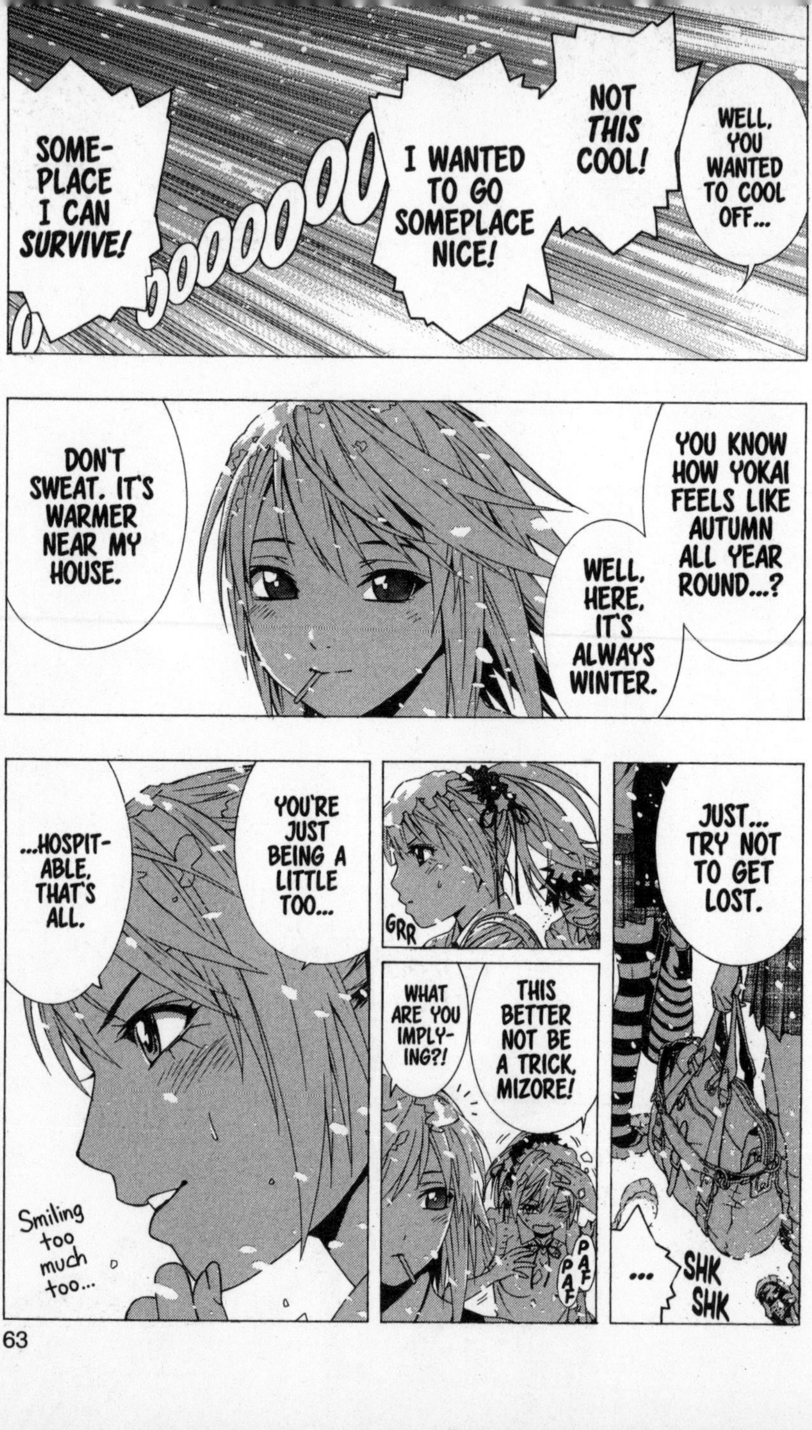
WELL, YOU WANTED TO COOL OFF...
NOT THIS COOL!
I WANTED TO GO SOMEPLACE NICE!
OOOOOOOOO
SOME-PLACE I CAN SURVIVE!
YOU KNOW HOW YOKAI FEELS LIKE AUTUMN ALL YEAR ROUND...?
WELL, HERE, IT'S ALWAYS WINTER.
DON'T SWEAT. IT'S WARMER NEAR MY HOUSE.
JUST... TRY NOT TO GET LOST.
...
SHK SHK
GRR
THIS BETTER NOT BE A TRICK, MIZORE!
WHAT ARE YOU IMPLY-ING?!
PAF PAF
YOU'RE JUST BEING A LITTLE TOO...
...HOSPIT-ABLE, THAT'S ALL.
Smiling too much too...

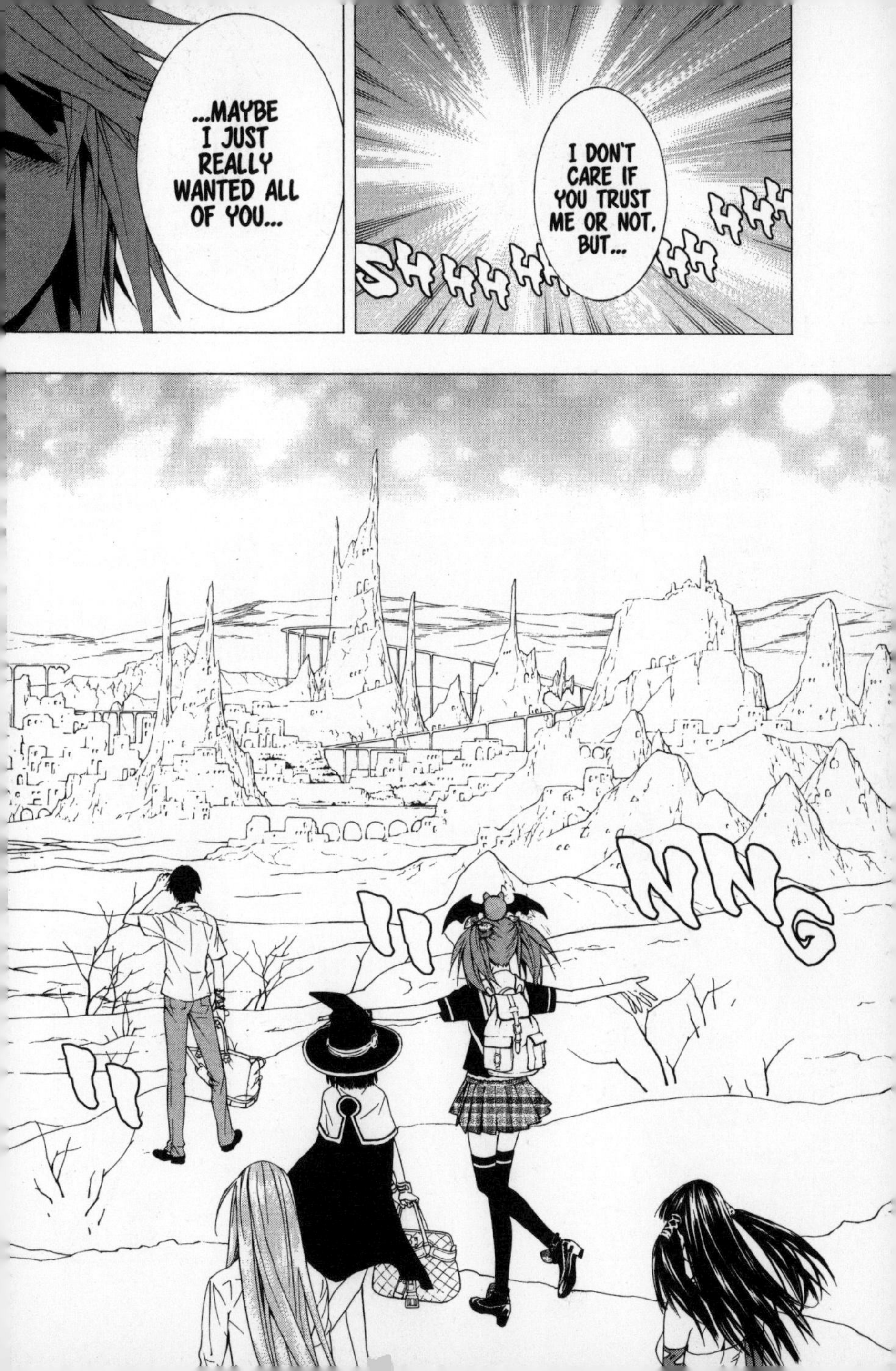
I DON'T CARE IF YOU TRUST ME OR NOT, BUT...
SHHHHHHHHHHH
...MAYBE I JUST REALLY WANTED ALL OF YOU...
NNG

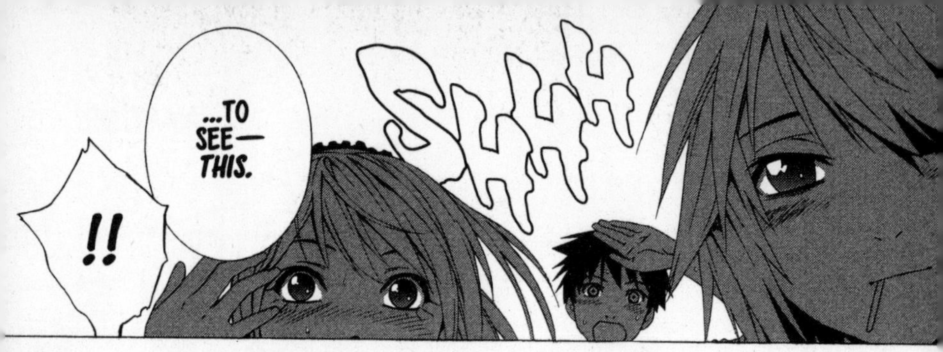
SHHH
...TO SEE— THIS.
!!

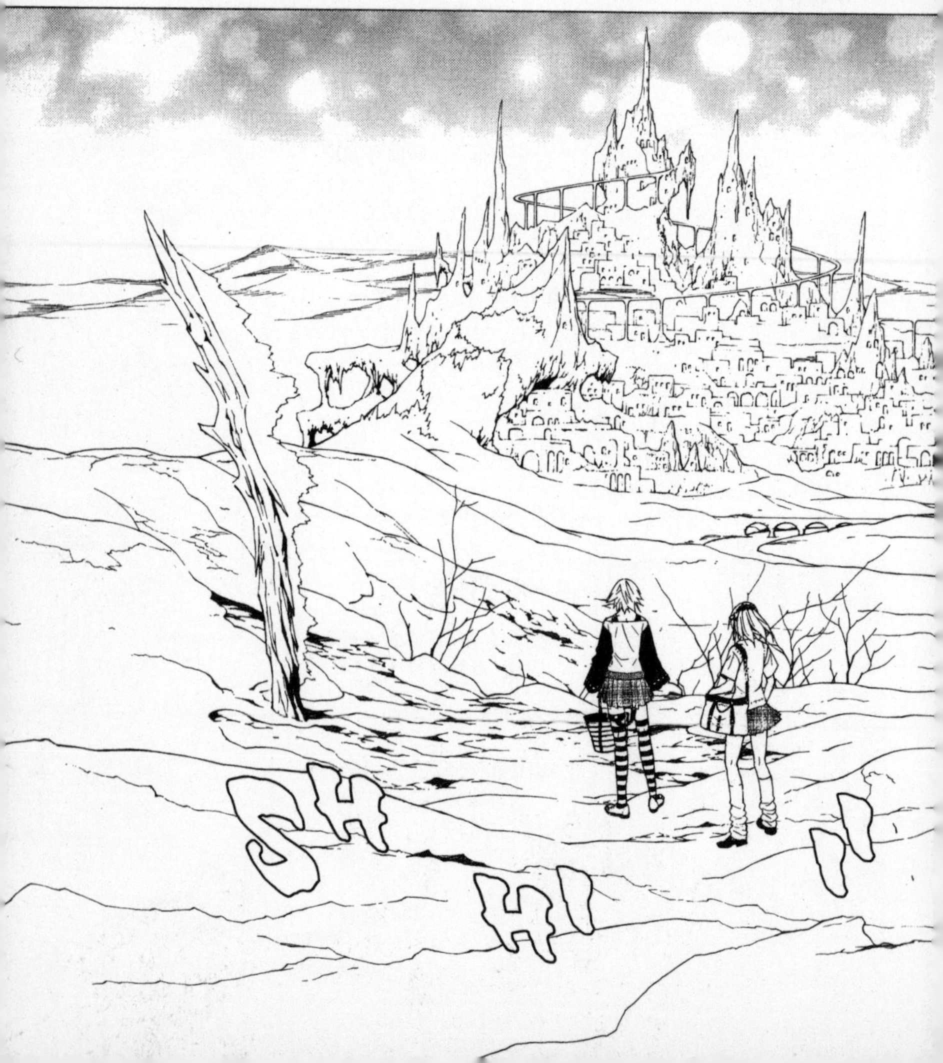
SHH!!

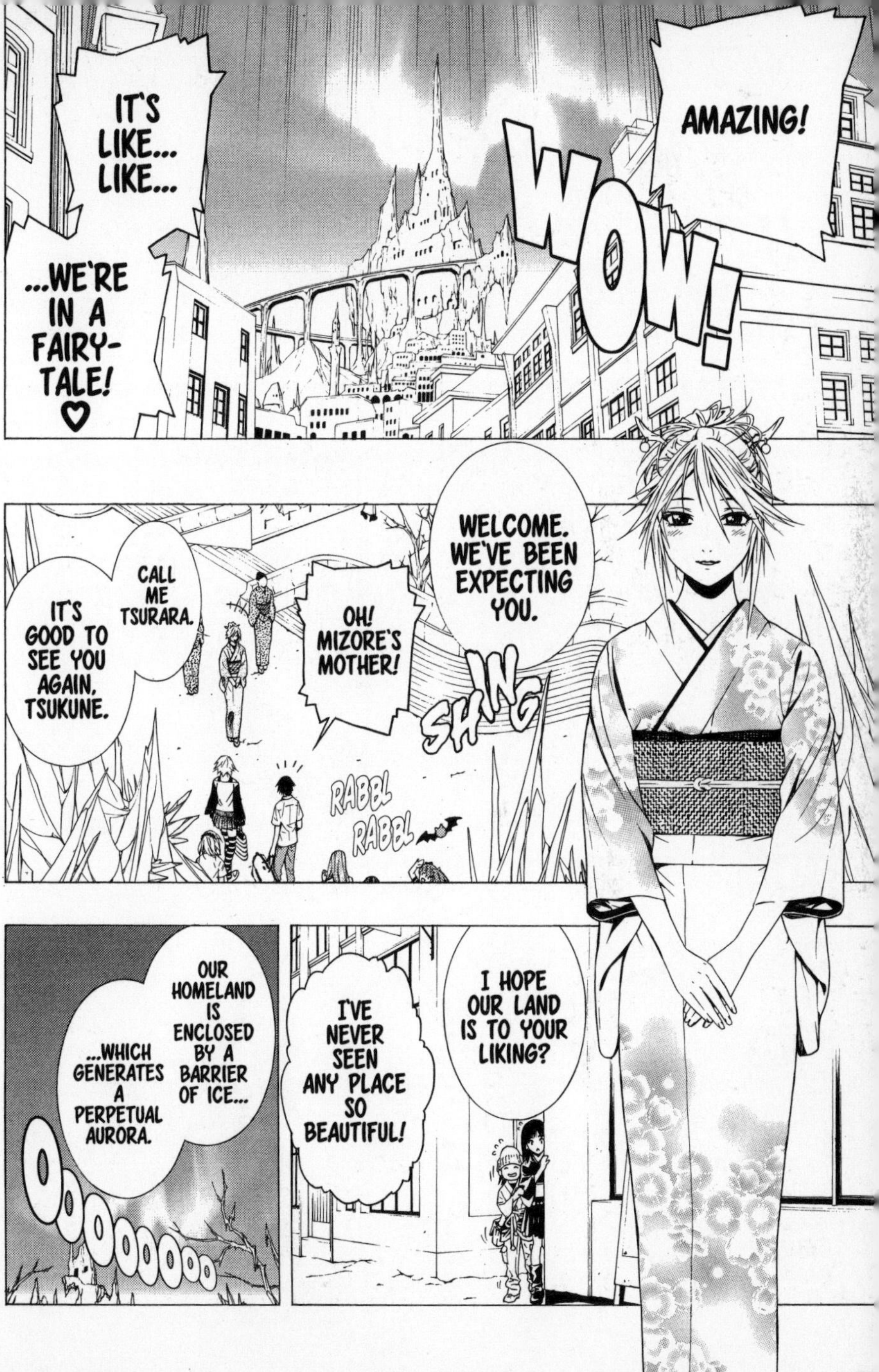
AMAZING!
WOW!
IT'S LIKE... LIKE...
...WE'RE IN A FAIRY-TALE! ♥
WELCOME. WE'VE BEEN EXPECTING YOU.
SHING
OH! MIZORE'S MOTHER!
RABBL RABBL
CALL ME TSURARA.
IT'S GOOD TO SEE YOU AGAIN, TSUKUNE.
I HOPE OUR LAND IS TO YOUR LIKING?
I'VE NEVER SEEN ANY PLACE SO BEAUTIFUL!
OUR HOMELAND IS ENCLOSED BY A BARRIER OF ICE...
...WHICH GENERATES A PERPETUAL AURORA.
OOOOOOOOOO

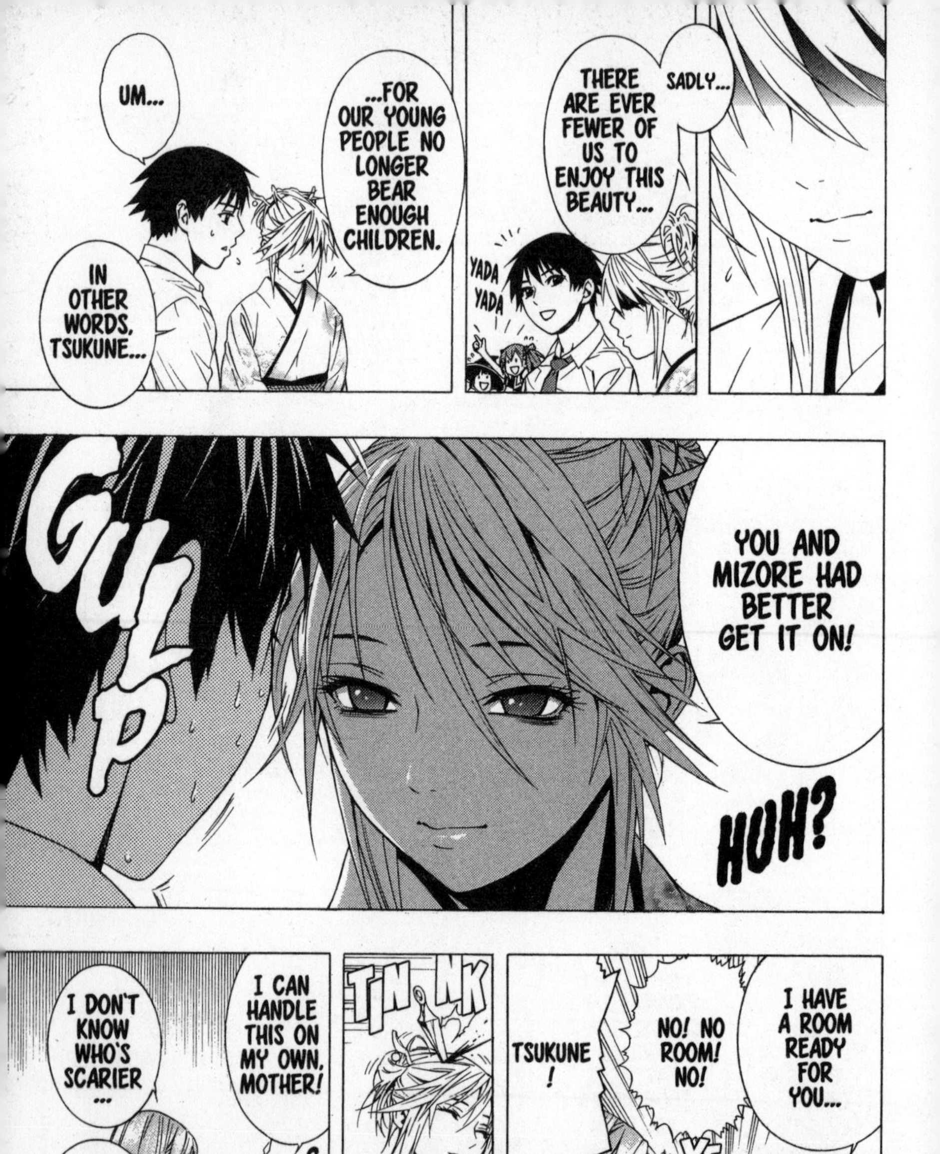
SADLY...
THERE ARE EVER FEWER OF US TO ENJOY THIS BEAUTY...
YADA YADA
...FOR OUR YOUNG PEOPLE NO LONGER BEAR ENOUGH CHILDREN.
UM...
IN OTHER WORDS, TSUKUNE...
YOU AND MIZORE HAD BETTER GET IT ON!
HUH?
GULP
I HAVE A ROOM READY FOR YOU...
NO! NO ROOM! NO!
TSUKUNE!
YEEEE
DRAGG
TINNK
I CAN HANDLE THIS ON MY OWN, MOTHER!
I DON'T KNOW WHO'S SCARIER...
SPRT
BRRR
LIKE MOTHER, LIKE DAUGHTER...

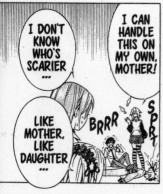

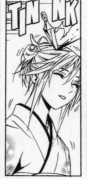

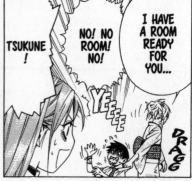

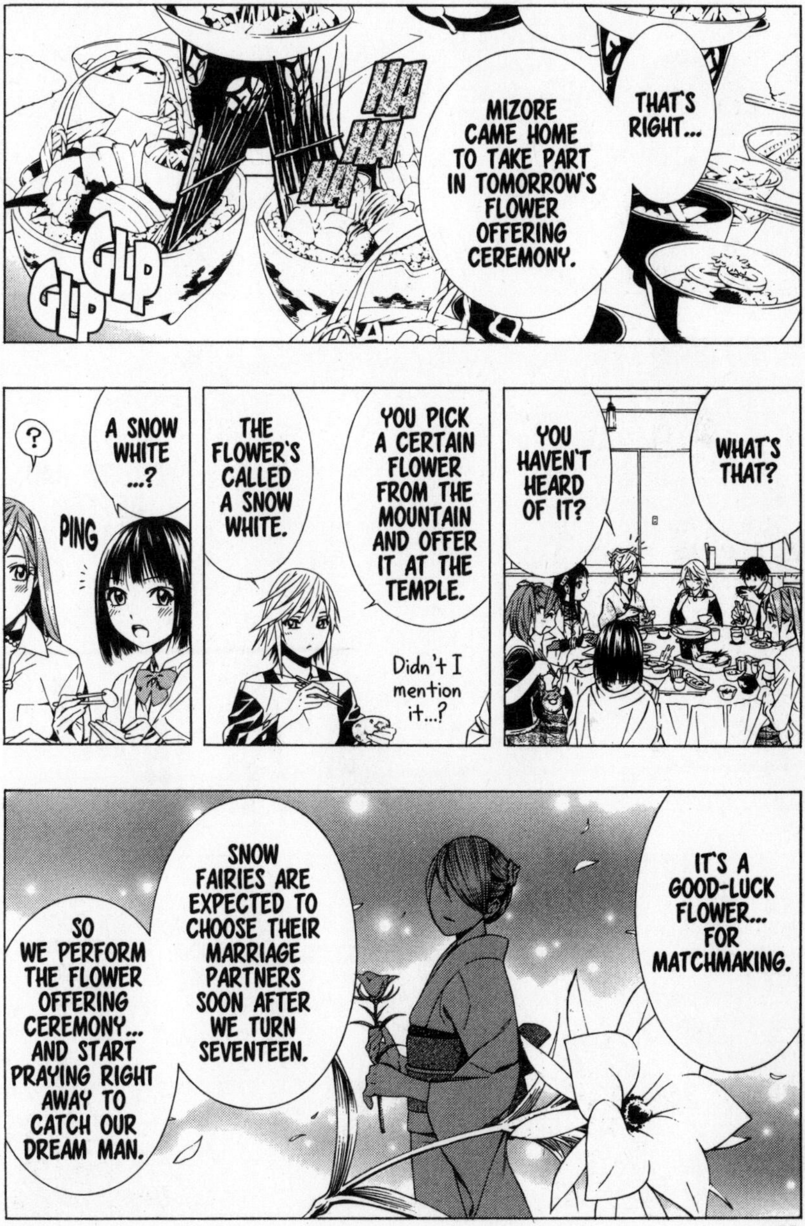
THAT'S RIGHT...
MIZORE CAME HOME TO TAKE PART IN TOMORROW'S FLOWER OFFERING CEREMONY.
HA HA HA
GLP GLP
WHAT'S THAT?
YOU HAVEN'T HEARD OF IT?
YOU PICK A CERTAIN FLOWER FROM THE MOUNTAIN AND OFFER IT AT THE TEMPLE.
THE FLOWER'S CALLED A SNOW WHITE.
Didn't I mention it...?
A SNOW WHITE ...?
?
PING
IT'S A GOOD-LUCK FLOWER... FOR MATCHMAKING.
SNOW FAIRIES ARE EXPECTED TO CHOOSE THEIR MARRIAGE PARTNERS SOON AFTER WE TURN SEVENTEEN.
SO WE PERFORM THE FLOWER OFFERING CEREMONY... AND START PRAYING RIGHT AWAY TO CATCH OUR DREAM MAN.

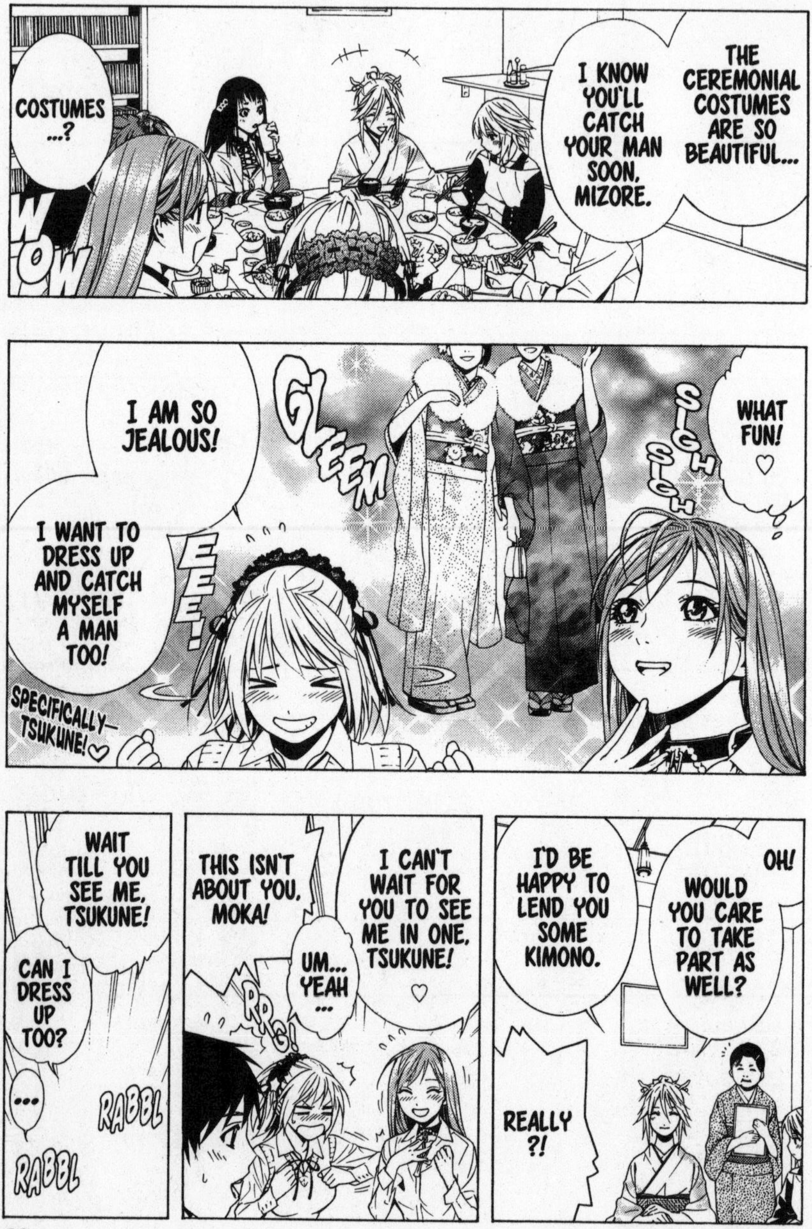
THE CEREMONIAL COSTUMES ARE SO BEAUTIFUL...
I KNOW YOU'LL CATCH YOUR MAN SOON, MIZORE.
COSTUMES ...?
WOW
WHAT FUN! ♡
SIGH SIGH
GLEEM
I AM SO JEALOUS!
I WANT TO DRESS UP AND CATCH MYSELF A MAN TOO!
EEE!
SPECIFICALLY— TSUKUNE! ♡
OH!
WOULD YOU CARE TO TAKE PART AS WELL?
I'D BE HAPPY TO LEND YOU SOME KIMONO.
REALLY ?!
I CAN'T WAIT FOR YOU TO SEE ME IN ONE, TSUKUNE! ♡
THIS ISN'T ABOUT YOU, MOKA!
UM... YEAH...
RPG!
WAIT TILL YOU SEE ME, TSUKUNE!
CAN I DRESS UP TOO?
...
RABBL
RABBL

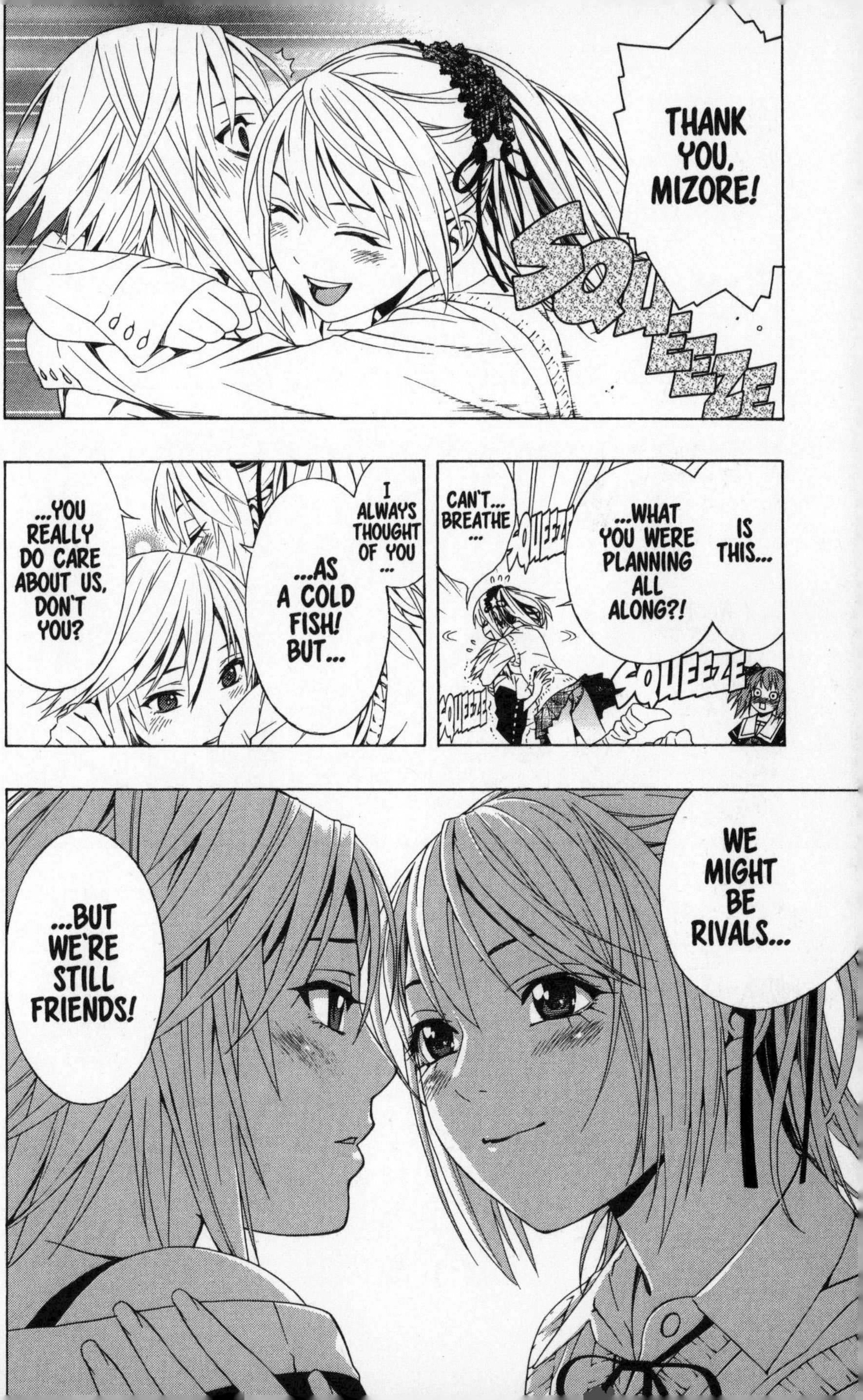
THANK YOU, MIZORE!
SQUEEEZE
IS THIS...
...WHAT YOU WERE PLANNING ALL ALONG?!
CAN'T... BREATHE...
SQUEEZE
SQUEEZE
SQUEEZE
I ALWAYS THOUGHT OF YOU...
...AS A COLD FISH! BUT...
...YOU REALLY DO CARE ABOUT US, DON'T YOU?
WE MIGHT BE RIVALS...
...BUT WE'RE STILL FRIENDS!

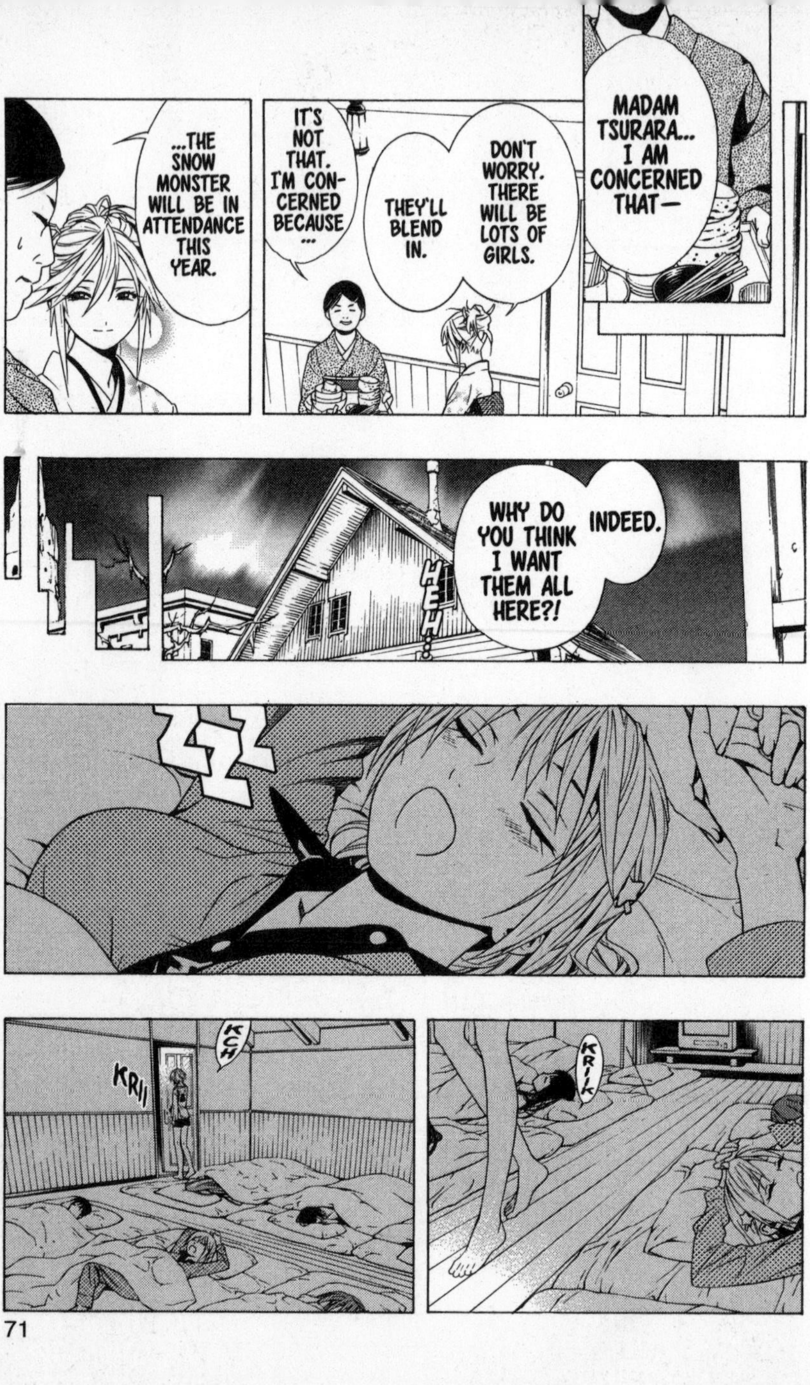
MADAM TSURARA... I AM CONCERNED THAT—
DON'T WORRY. THERE WILL BE LOTS OF GIRLS.
THEY'LL BLEND IN.
IT'S NOT THAT. I'M CONCERNED BECAUSE ...
...THE SNOW MONSTER WILL BE IN ATTENDANCE THIS YEAR.
INDEED.
WHY DO YOU THINK I WANT THEM ALL HERE?!
HEH...
ZZZ
KRIK
KCH
KRII

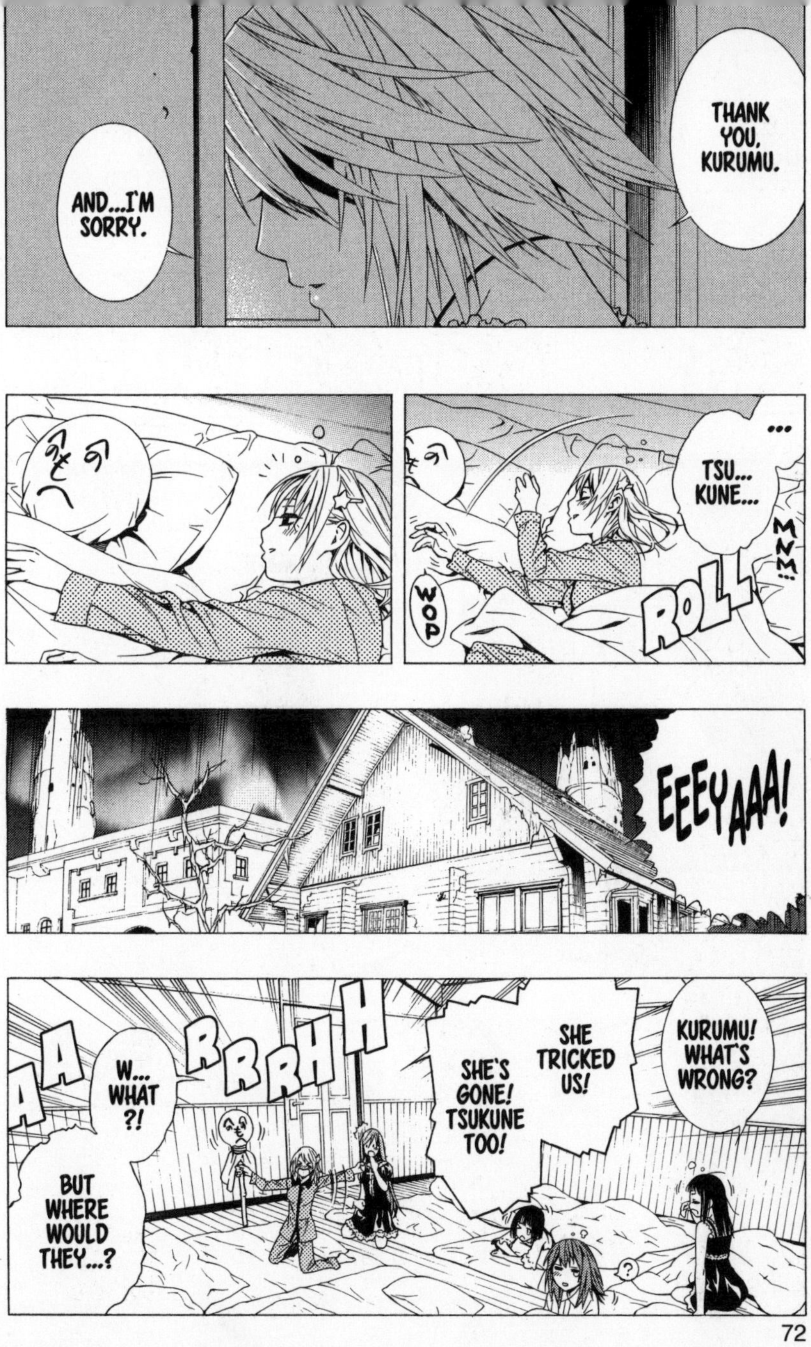
THANK YOU, KURUMU.
AND...I'M SORRY.
...
TSU... KUNE...
MNM..
ROLL
WOP
EEEYAAA!
KURUMU! WHAT'S WRONG?
SHE TRICKED US!
SHE'S GONE! TSUKUNE TOO!
AARRRHH
W... WHAT ?!
BUT WHERE WOULD THEY...?

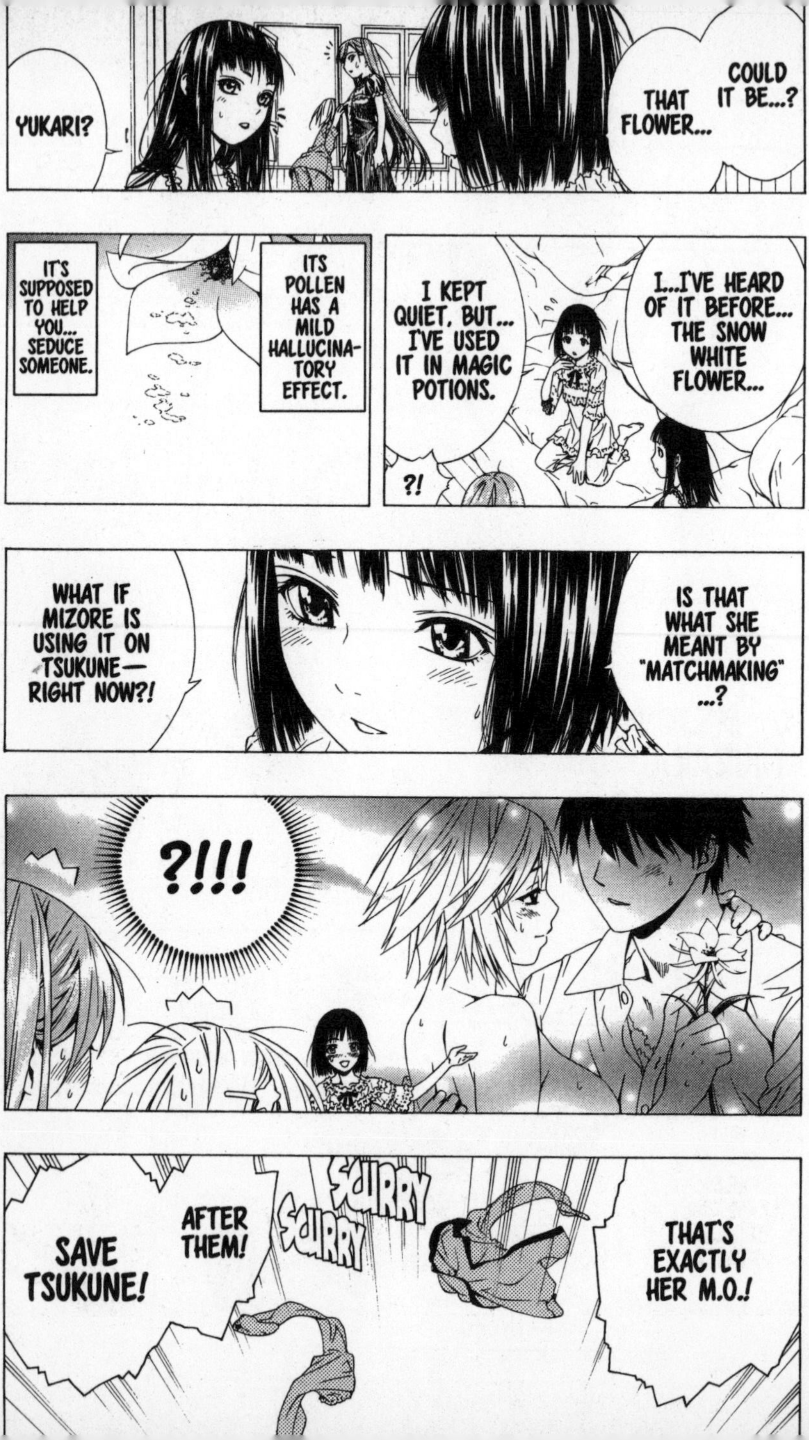
THAT FLOWER... COULD IT BE...?
YUKARI?
I...I'VE HEARD OF IT BEFORE... THE SNOW WHITE FLOWER...
I KEPT QUIET, BUT... I'VE USED IT IN MAGIC POTIONS.
?!
ITS POLLEN HAS A MILD HALLUCINATORY EFFECT.
IT'S SUPPOSED TO HELP YOU... SEDUCE SOMEONE.
IS THAT WHAT SHE MEANT BY "MATCHMAKING" ...?
WHAT IF MIZORE IS USING IT ON TSUKUNE— RIGHT NOW?!
?!!!
THAT'S EXACTLY HER M.O.!
SCURRY
SCURRY
AFTER THEM!
SAVE TSUKUNE!

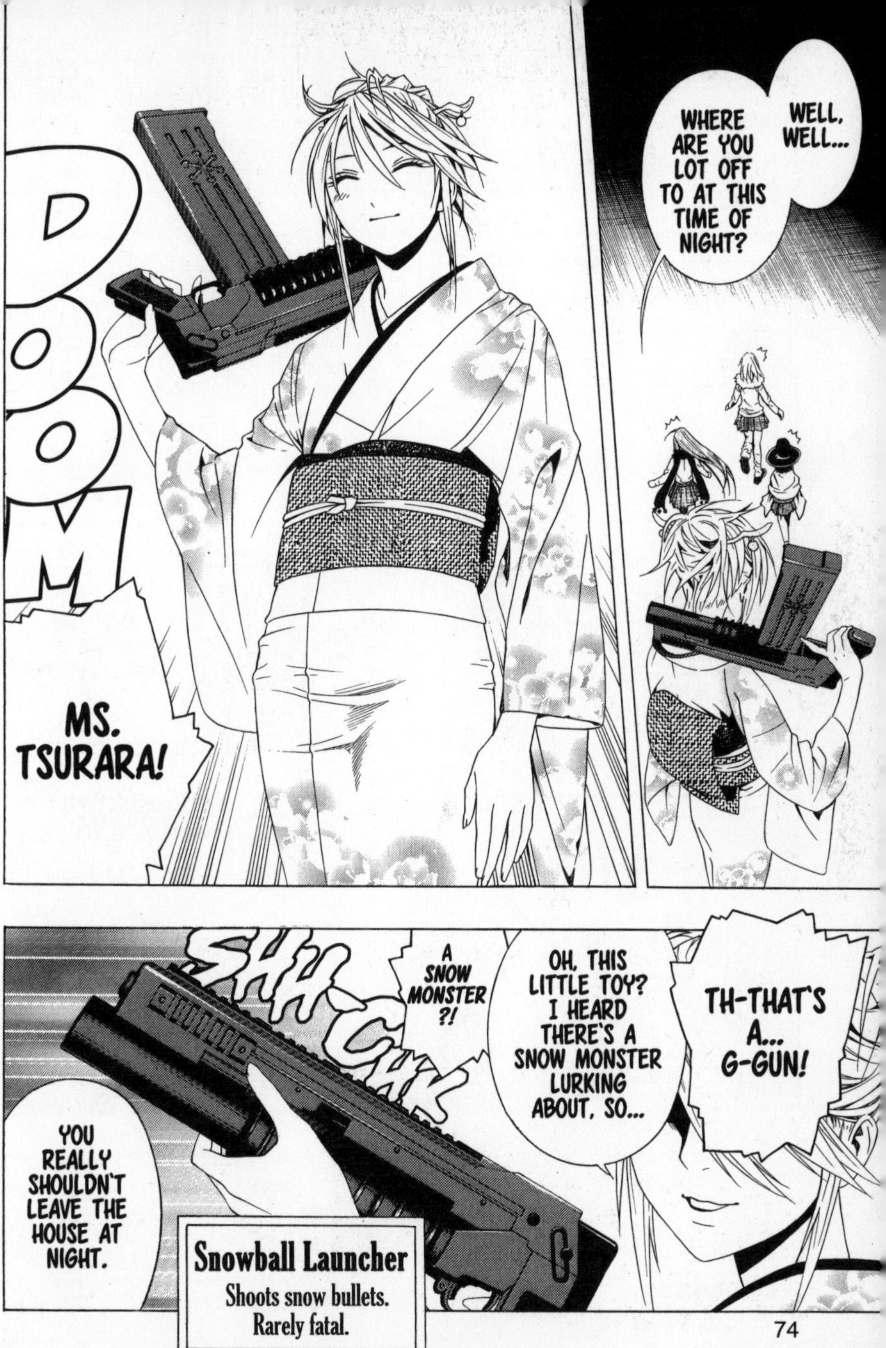
WELL, WELL...
WHERE ARE YOU LOT OFF TO AT THIS TIME OF NIGHT?
DOOOM
MS. TSURARA!
TH-THAT'S A... G-GUN!
OH, THIS LITTLE TOY? I HEARD THERE'S A SNOW MONSTER LURKING ABOUT, SO...
A SNOW MONSTER?!
SHK CHK
YOU REALLY SHOULDN'T LEAVE THE HOUSE AT NIGHT.
Snowball Launcher
Shoots snow bullets. Rarely fatal.

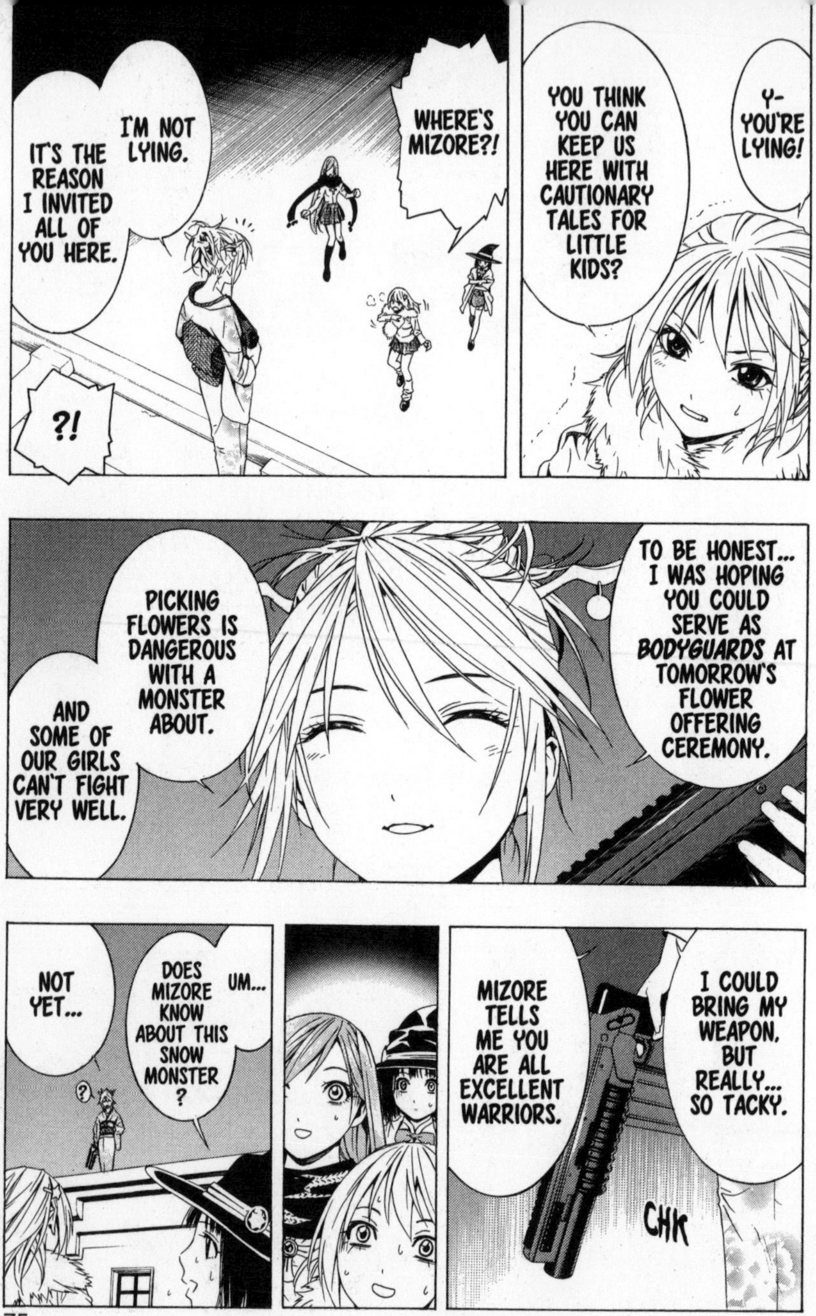
Y-
YOU'RE LYING!
YOU THINK YOU CAN KEEP US HERE WITH CAUTIONARY TALES FOR LITTLE KIDS?
WHERE'S MIZORE?!
I'M NOT LYING.
IT'S THE REASON I INVITED ALL OF YOU HERE.
?!
TO BE HONEST... I WAS HOPING YOU COULD SERVE AS BODYGUARDS AT TOMORROW'S FLOWER OFFERING CEREMONY.
PICKING FLOWERS IS DANGEROUS WITH A MONSTER ABOUT.
AND SOME OF OUR GIRLS CAN'T FIGHT VERY WELL.
I COULD BRING MY WEAPON, BUT REALLY... SO TACKY.
CHK
MIZORE TELLS ME YOU ARE ALL EXCELLENT WARRIORS.
UM...
DOES MIZORE KNOW ABOUT THIS SNOW MONSTER?
NOT YET...
?

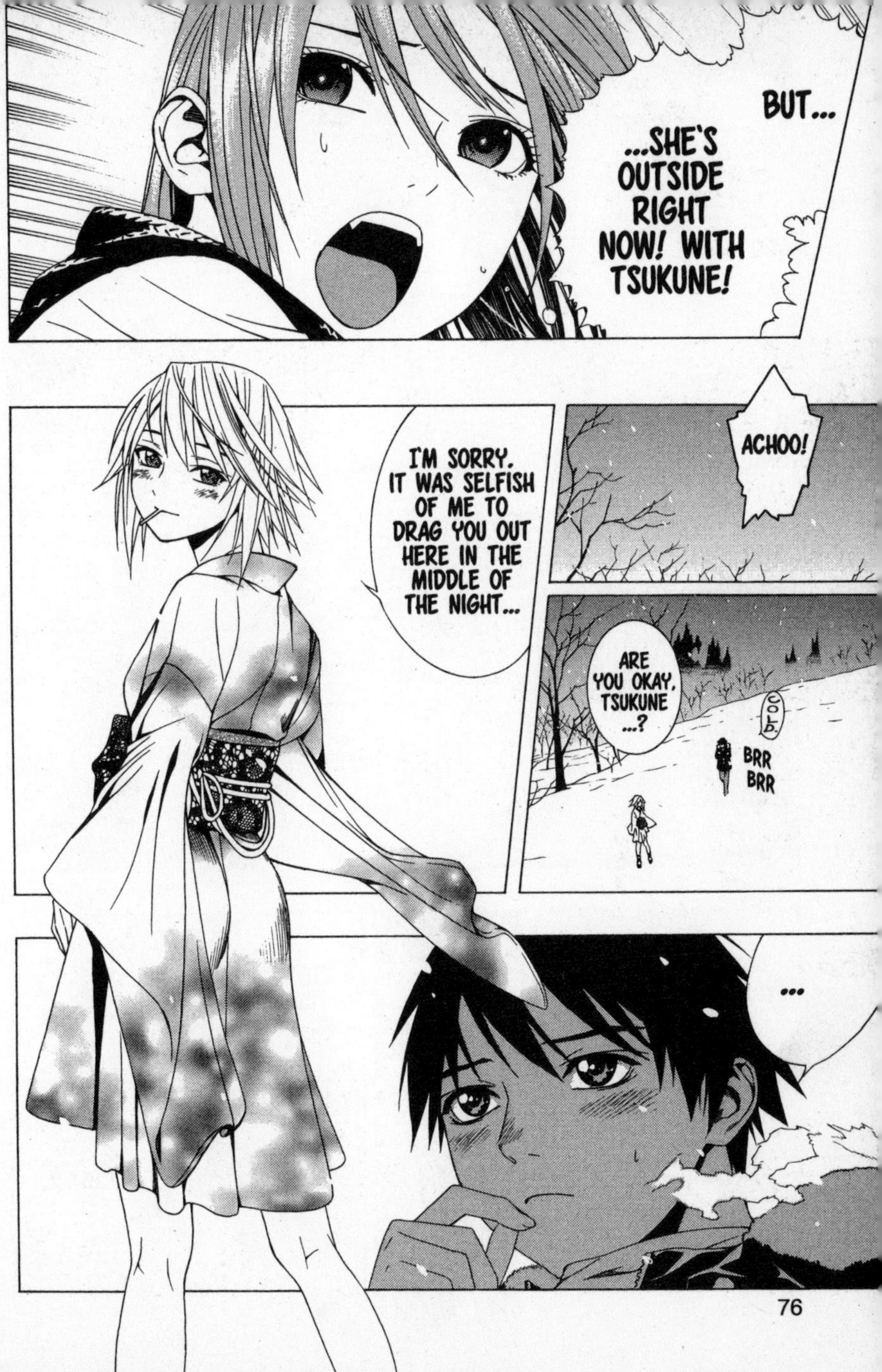
BUT...
...SHE'S OUTSIDE RIGHT NOW! WITH TSUKUNE!
ACHOO!
ARE YOU OKAY, TSUKUNE ...?
COLD
BRR BRR
I'M SORRY. IT WAS SELFISH OF ME TO DRAG YOU OUT HERE IN THE MIDDLE OF THE NIGHT...
...

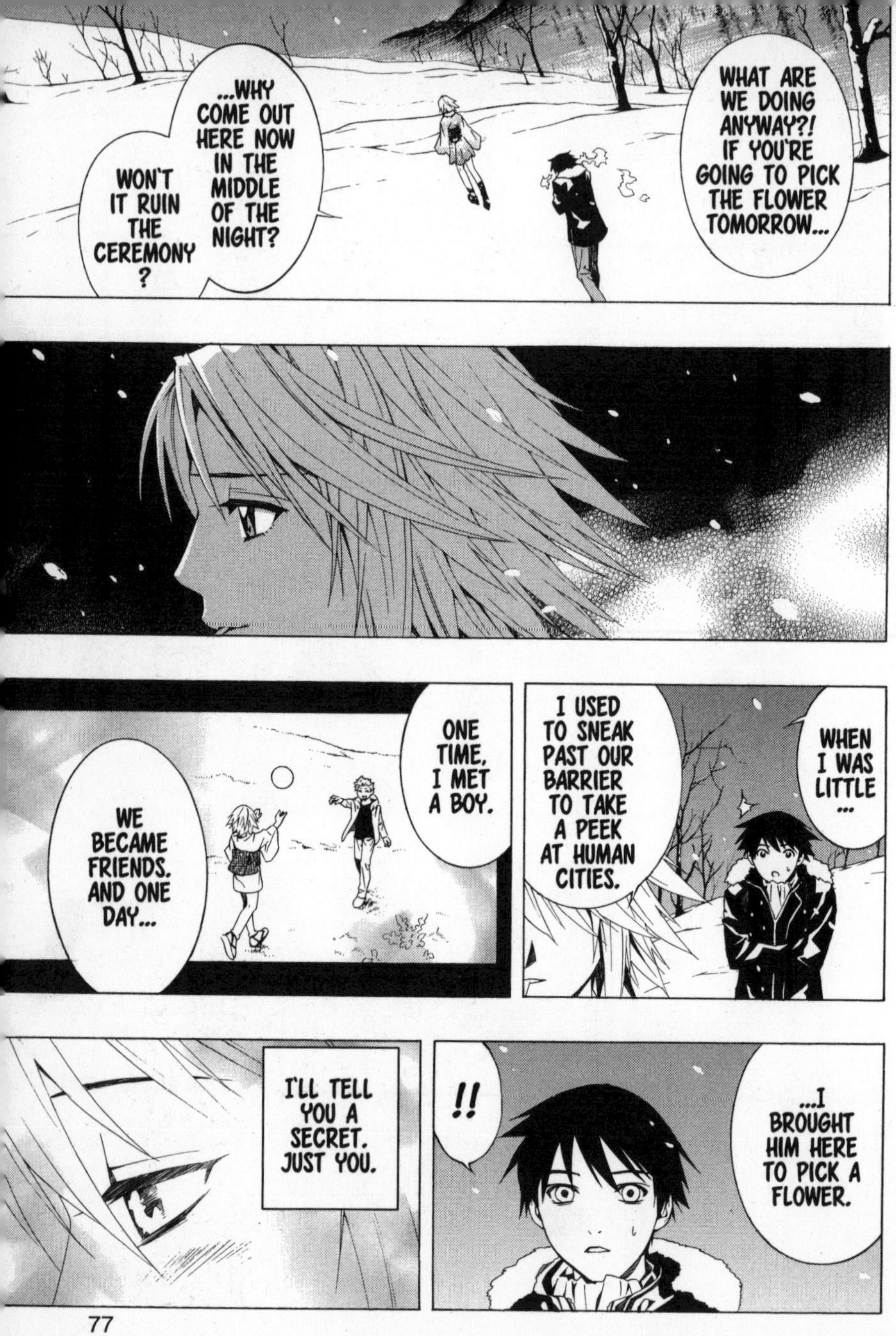
WHAT ARE WE DOING ANYWAY?! IF YOU'RE GOING TO PICK THE FLOWER TOMORROW...
...WHY COME OUT HERE NOW IN THE MIDDLE OF THE NIGHT?
WON'T IT RUIN THE CEREMONY?
WHEN I WAS LITTLE...
I USED TO SNEAK PAST OUR BARRIER TO TAKE A PEEK AT HUMAN CITIES.
ONE TIME, I MET A BOY.
WE BECAME FRIENDS. AND ONE DAY...
...I BROUGHT HIM HERE TO PICK A FLOWER.
!!
I'LL TELL YOU A SECRET. JUST YOU.

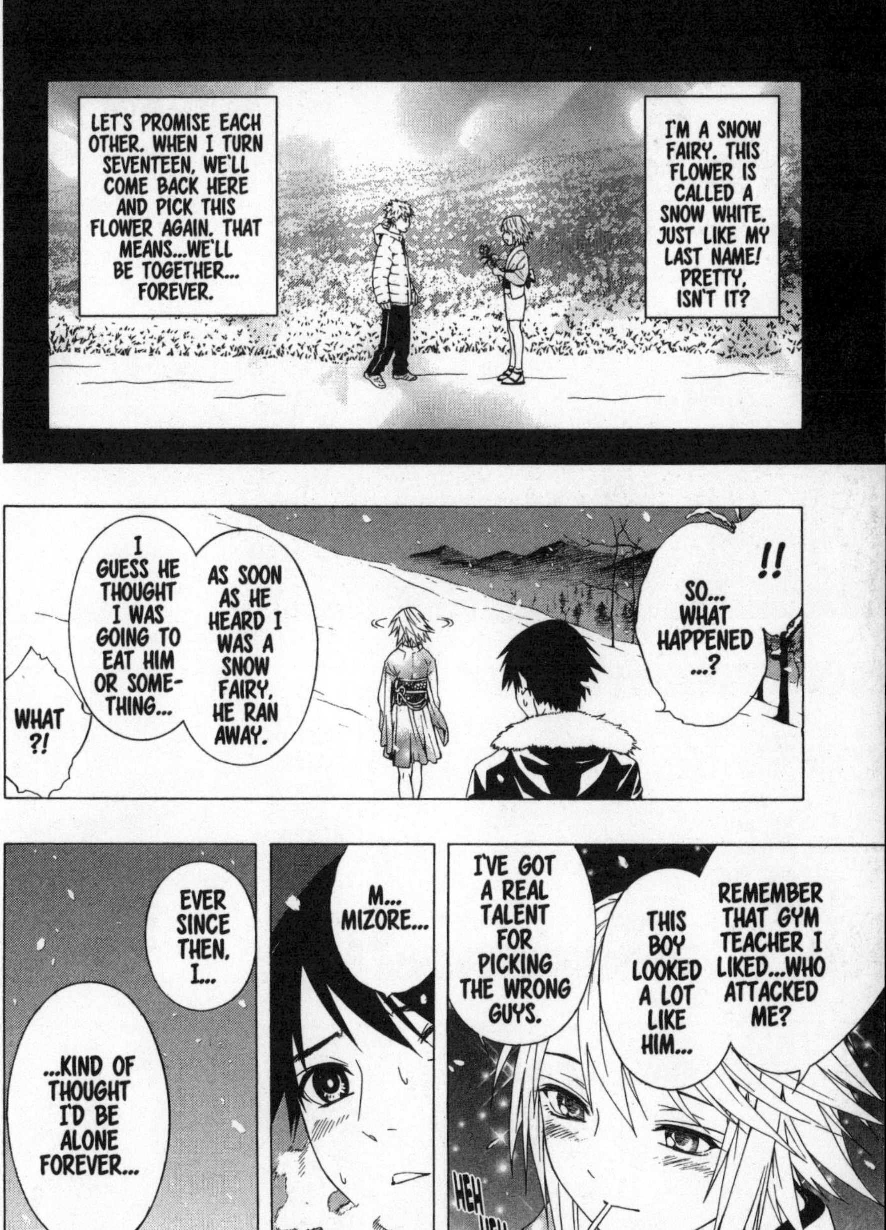
I'M A SNOW FAIRY. THIS FLOWER IS CALLED A SNOW WHITE. JUST LIKE MY LAST NAME! PRETTY, ISN'T IT?
LET'S PROMISE EACH OTHER. WHEN I TURN SEVENTEEN, WE'LL COME BACK HERE AND PICK THIS FLOWER AGAIN. THAT MEANS...WE'LL BE TOGETHER... FOREVER.
!!
SO... WHAT HAPPENED ...?
AS SOON AS HE HEARD I WAS A SNOW FAIRY, HE RAN AWAY.
I GUESS HE THOUGHT I WAS GOING TO EAT HIM OR SOME-THING...
WHAT ?!
REMEMBER THAT GYM TEACHER I LIKED...WHO ATTACKED ME?
THIS BOY LOOKED A LOT LIKE HIM...
I'VE GOT A REAL TALENT FOR PICKING THE WRONG GUYS.
HEH HEH
M... MIZORE...
EVER SINCE THEN, I...
...KIND OF THOUGHT I'D BE ALONE FOREVER...

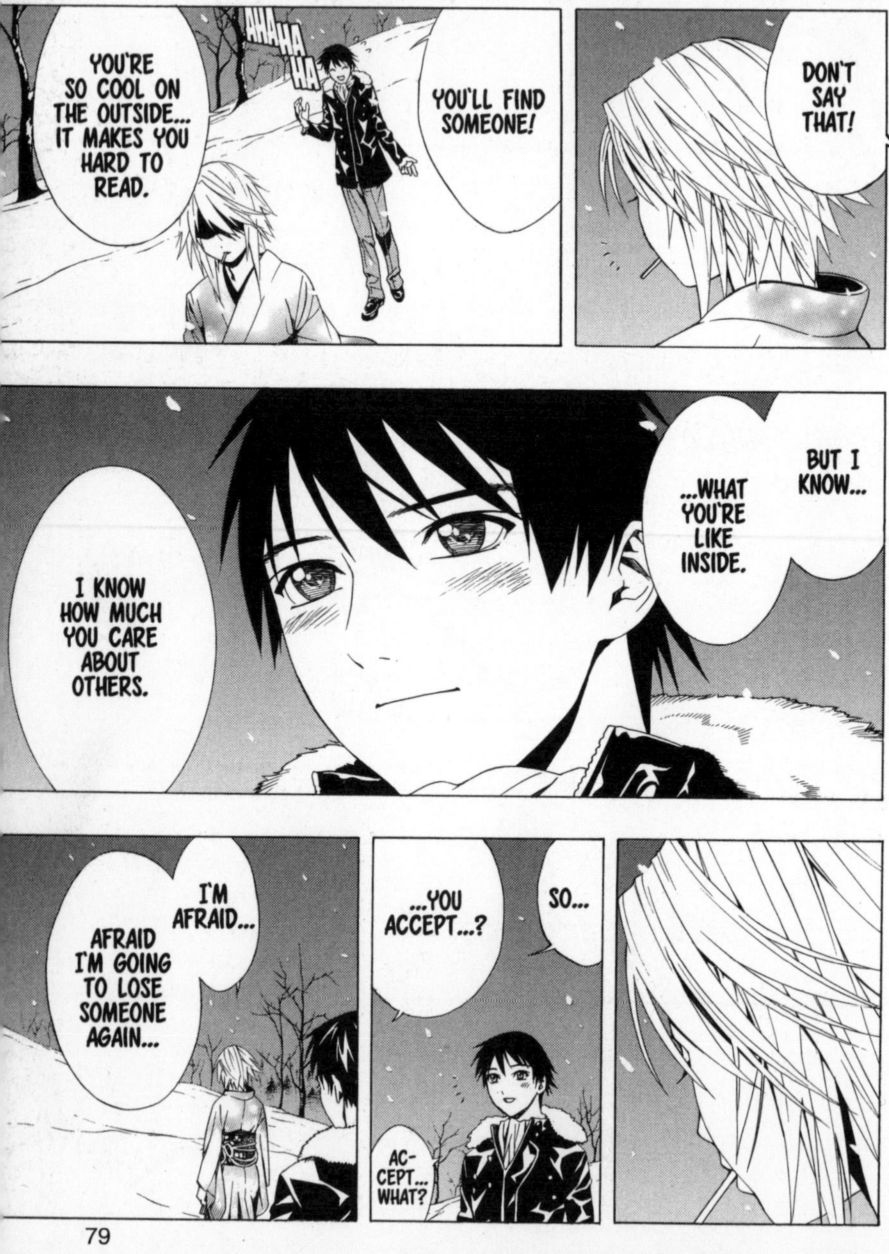
DON'T SAY THAT!
YOU'LL FIND SOMEONE!
AHAHAHA
YOU'RE SO COOL ON THE OUTSIDE... IT MAKES YOU HARD TO READ.
BUT I KNOW...
...WHAT YOU'RE LIKE INSIDE.
I KNOW HOW MUCH YOU CARE ABOUT OTHERS.
SO...
...YOU ACCEPT...?
AC-CEPT... WHAT?
I'M AFRAID...
AFRAID I'M GOING TO LOSE SOMEONE AGAIN...

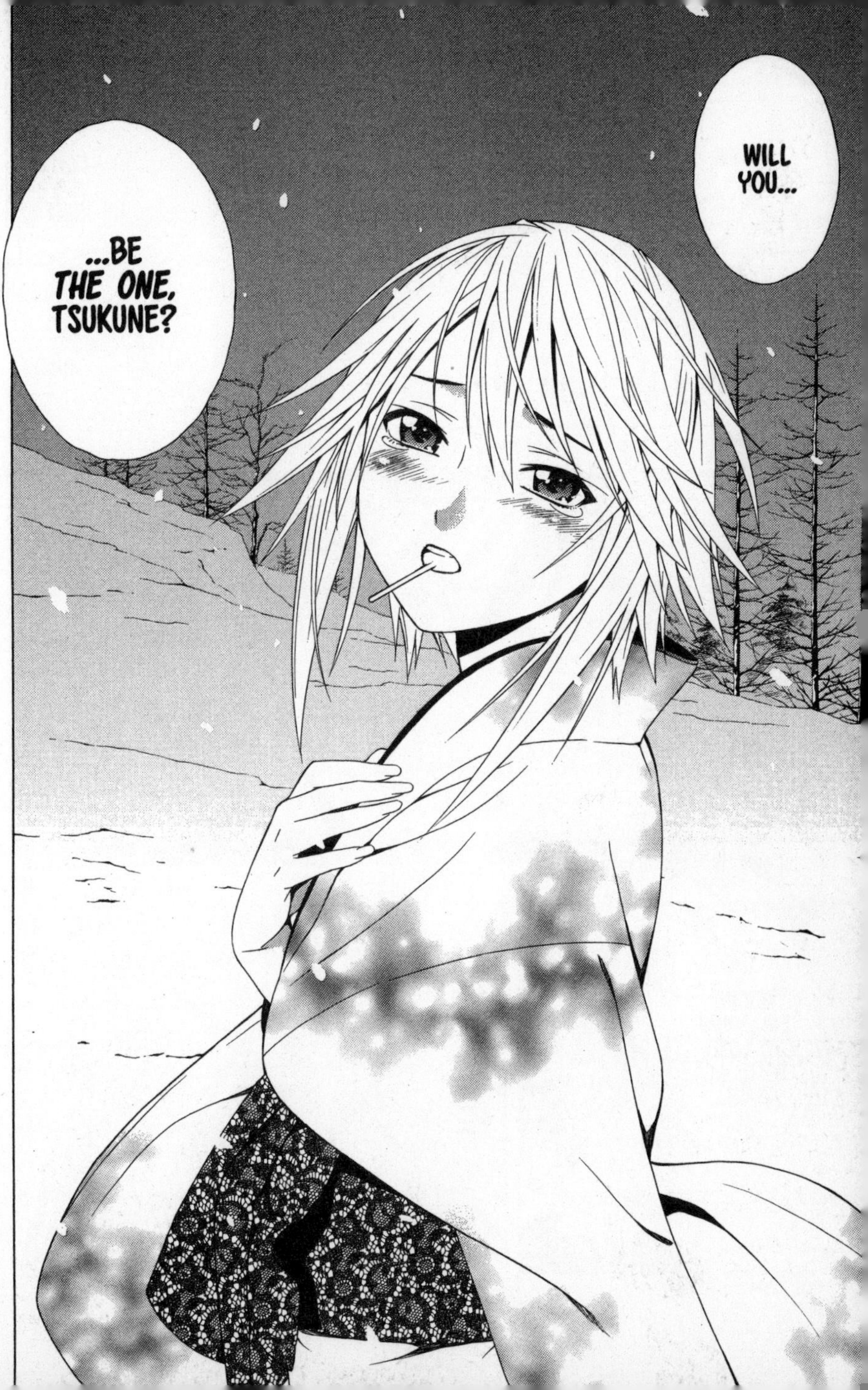
WILL YOU...
...BE THE ONE, TSUKUNE?

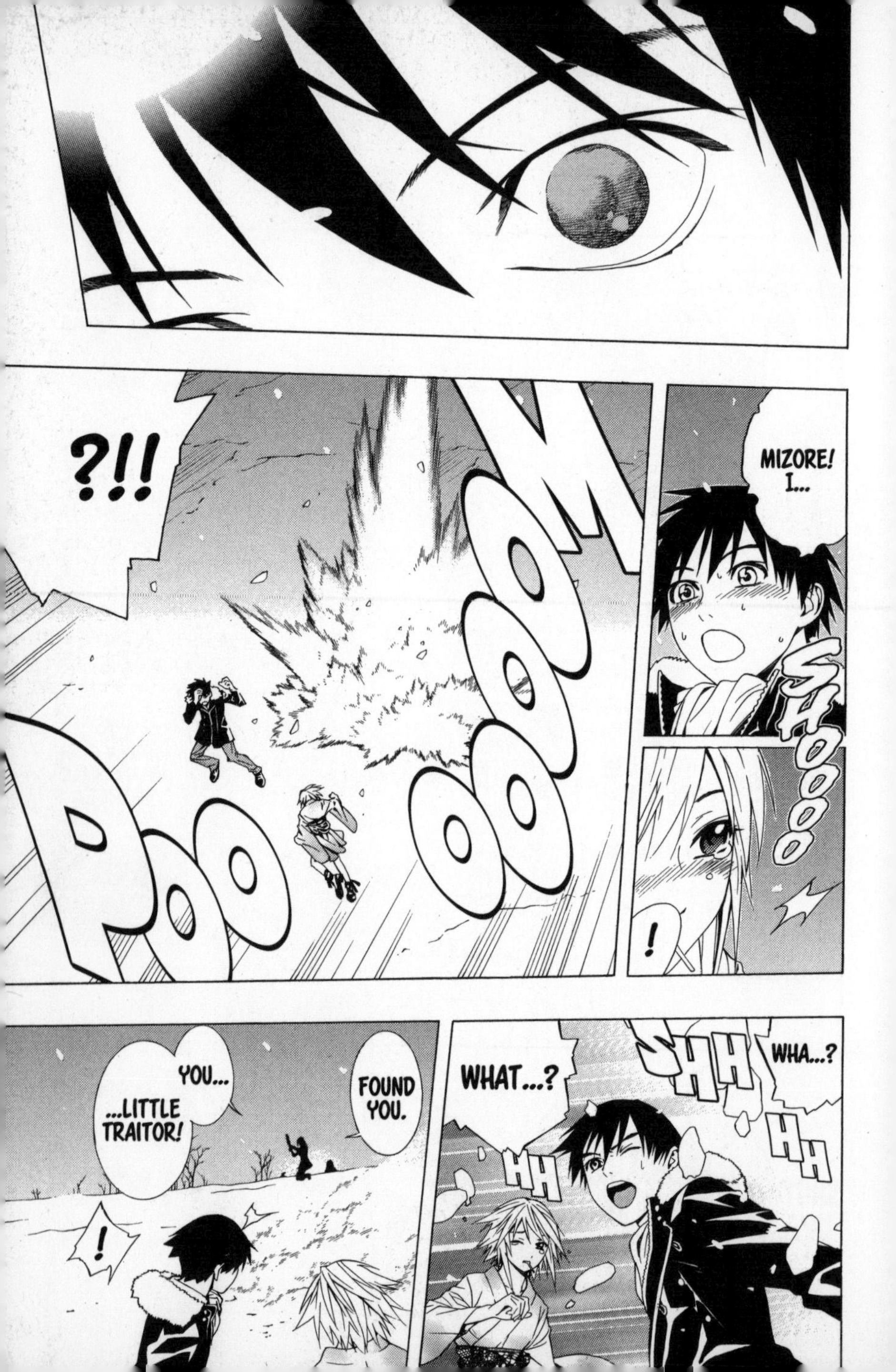
MIZORE! I...
SHOOOOO
!
?!!
POOOOOOOOM
WHA...?
SHHHHH
WHAT...?
FOUND YOU.
YOU...
...LITTLE TRAITOR!
!

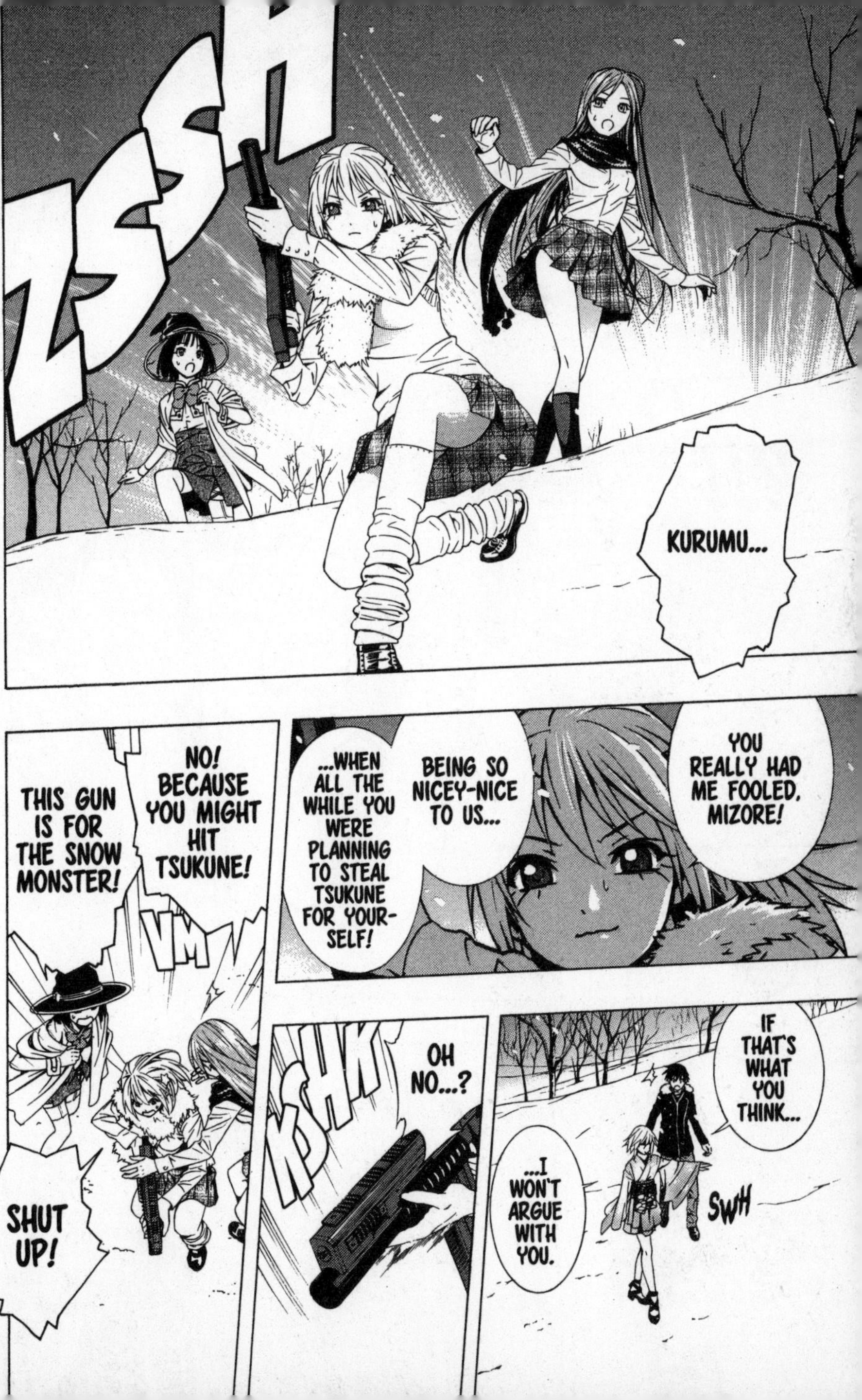
KURUMU...
ZSSH
YOU REALLY HAD ME FOOLED, MIZORE!
BEING SO NICEY-NICE TO US...
...WHEN ALL THE WHILE YOU WERE PLANNING TO STEAL TSUKUNE FOR YOUR-SELF!
IF THAT'S WHAT YOU THINK...
...I WON'T ARGUE WITH YOU.
SWH
OH NO...?
KSHK
NO! BECAUSE YOU MIGHT HIT TSUKUNE!
THIS GUN IS FOR THE SNOW MONSTER!
VM
SHUT UP!

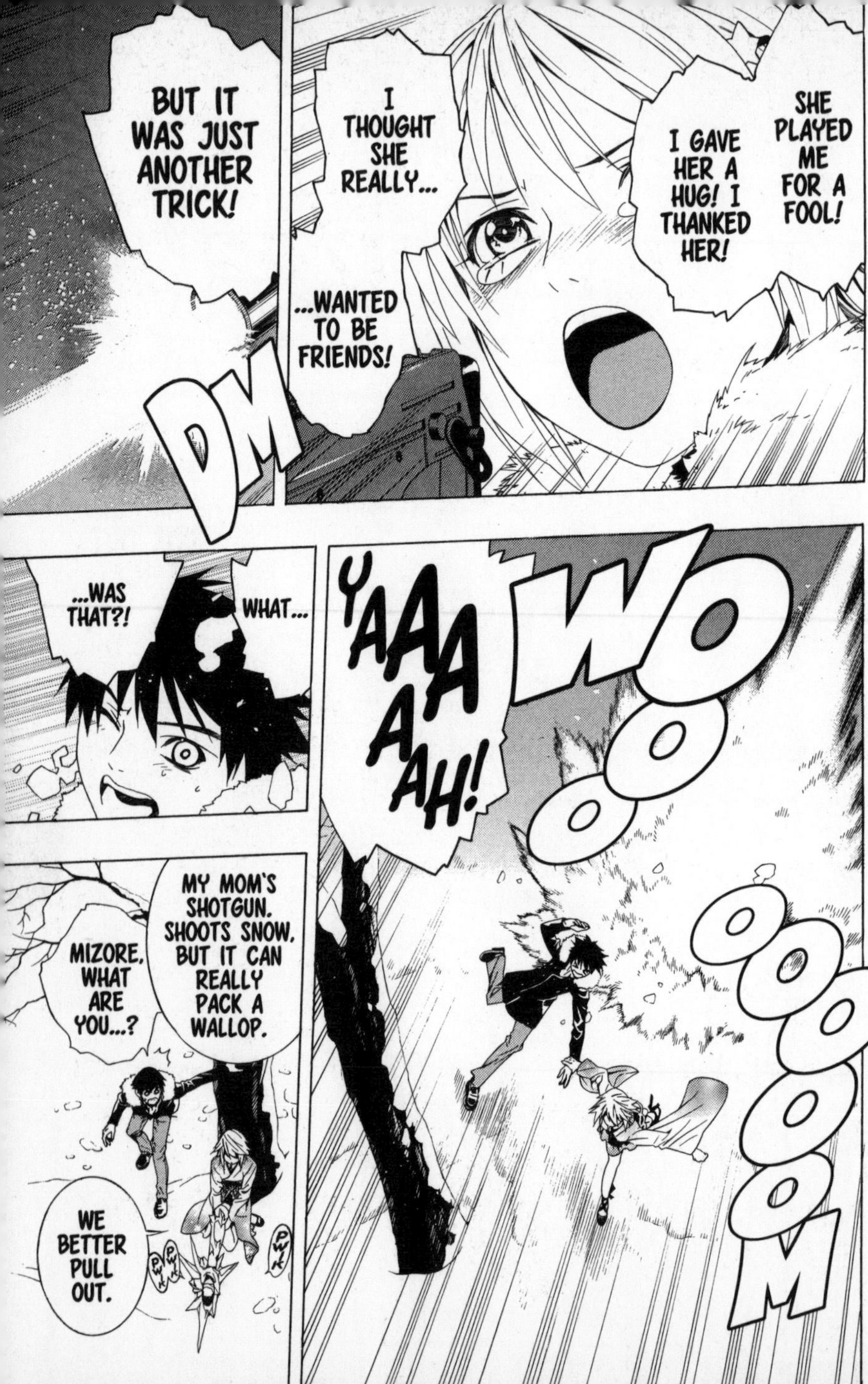
SHE PLAYED ME FOR A FOOL!
I GAVE HER A HUG! I THANKED HER!
I THOUGHT SHE REALLY...
...WANTED TO BE FRIENDS!
BUT IT WAS JUST ANOTHER TRICK!
DM
YAAAAAH!
WOOOOOOOOOM
WHAT...
...WAS THAT?!
MY MOM'S SHOTGUN. SHOOTS SNOW, BUT IT CAN REALLY PACK A WALLOP.
MIZORE, WHAT ARE YOU...?
WE BETTER PULL OUT.
PWIK
PWIK
PWIK

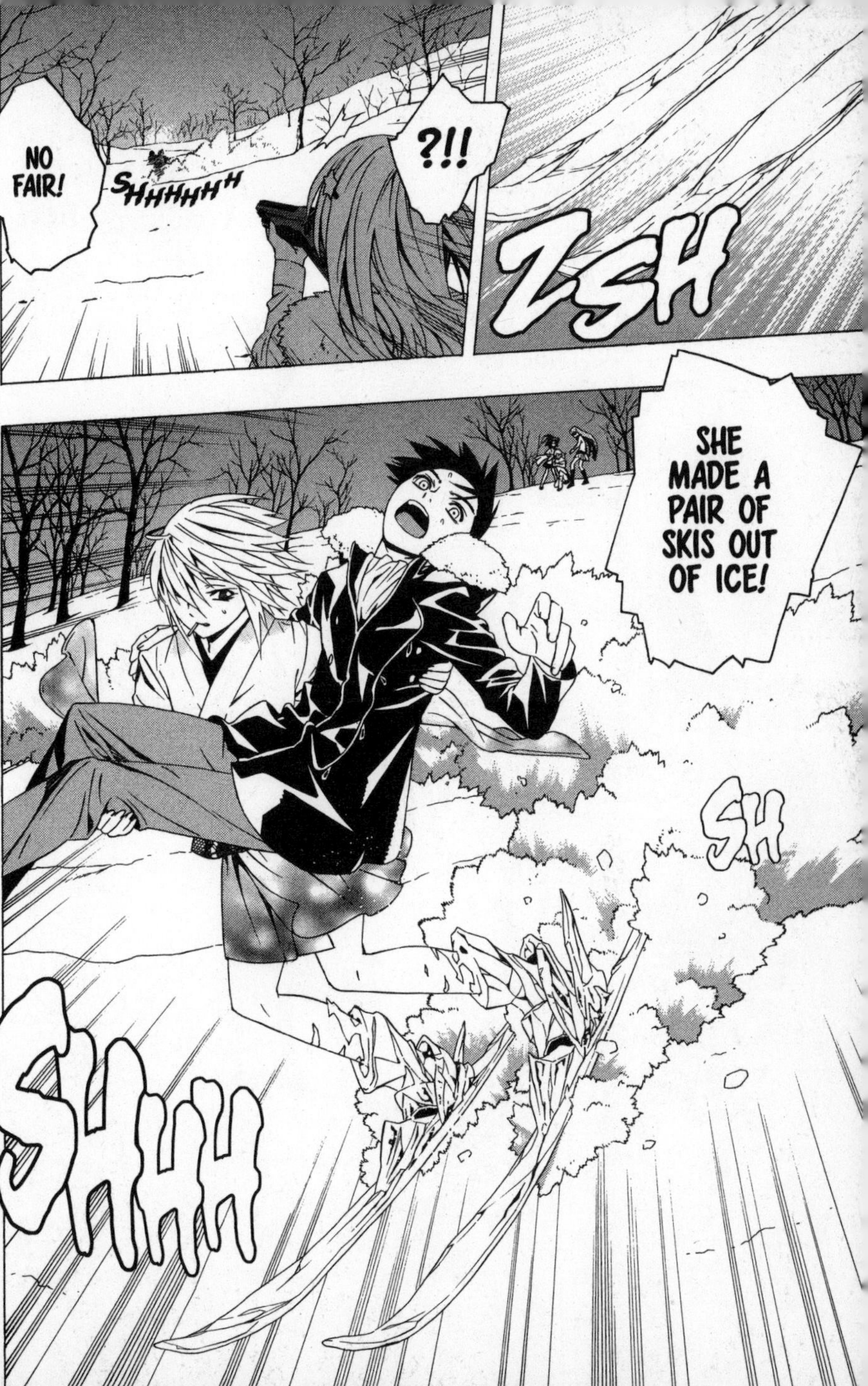
ZSH
?!!
NO FAIR!
SHHHHHH
SHE MADE A PAIR OF SKIS OUT OF ICE!
SH
SHHH

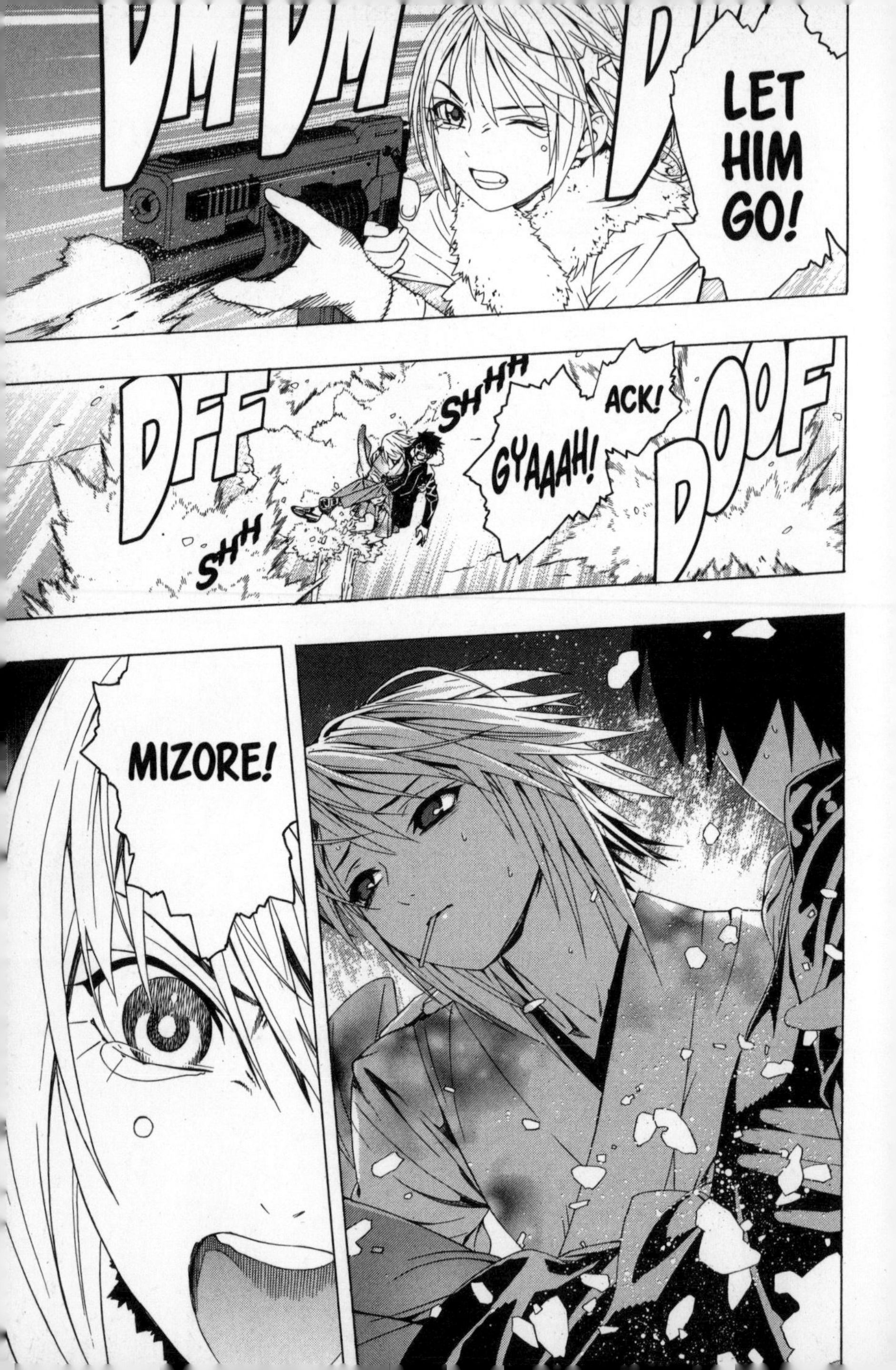

LET HIM GO!
DMDM
DOOF
ACK!
GYAAAH!
SHHH
DFF
SHH
MIZORE!

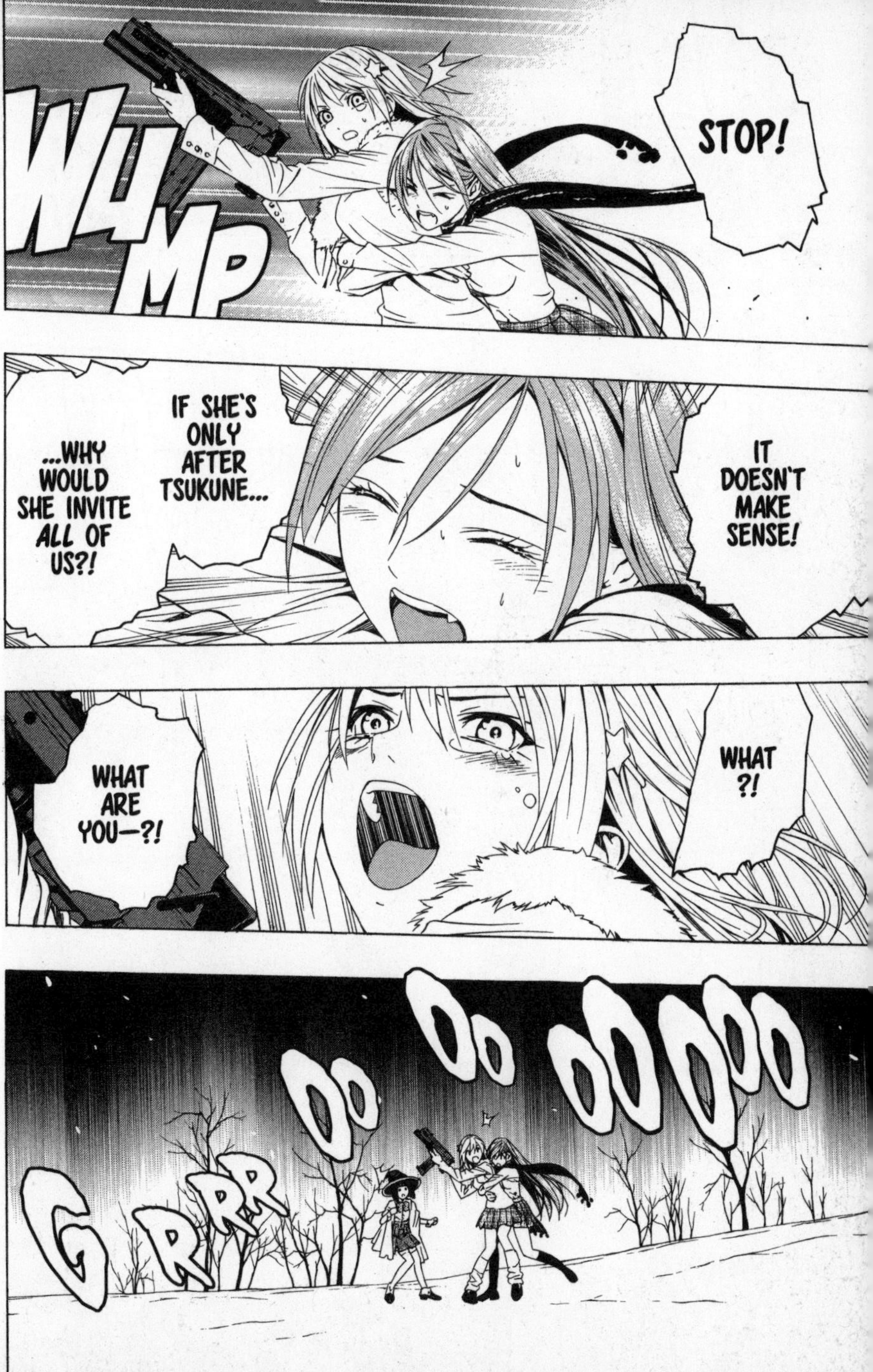
STOP!
WUMP
IT DOESN'T MAKE SENSE!
IF SHE'S ONLY AFTER TSUKUNE...
...WHY WOULD SHE INVITE ALL OF US?!
WHAT?!
WHAT ARE YOU—?!
OOOOOOOOOO
GRRR

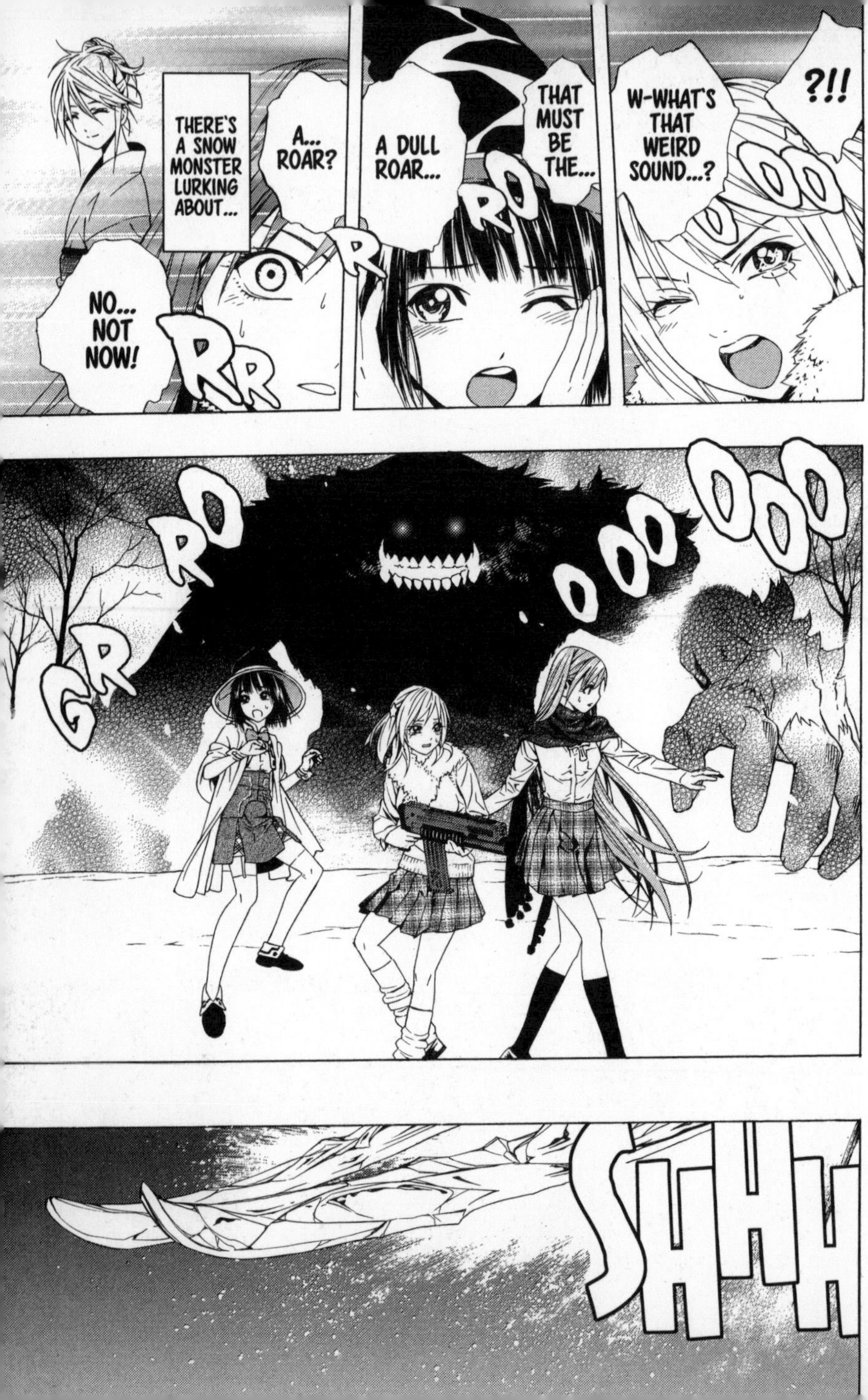
?!!
W-WHAT'S THAT WEIRD SOUND...?
OOOO
THAT MUST BE THE...
A DULL ROAR...
RO
A... ROAR?
THERE'S A SNOW MONSTER LURKING ABOUT...
R
NO... NOT NOW!
RR
GR
RO
OOOOOOO
SHHH

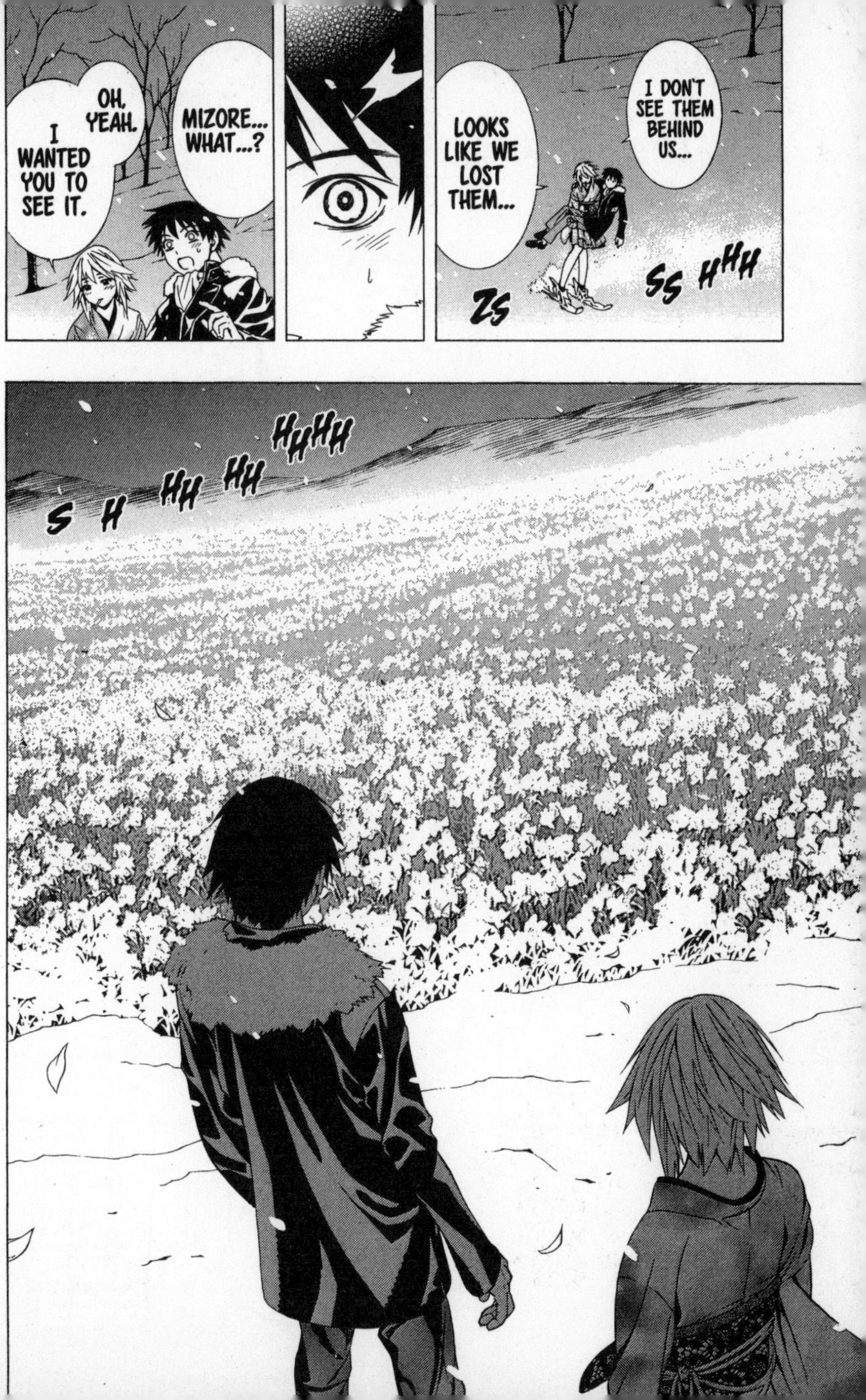
I DON'T SEE THEM BEHIND US...
LOOKS LIKE WE LOST THEM...
SSHHH
ZS
MIZORE... WHAT...?
OH, YEAH. I WANTED YOU TO SEE IT.
S H HH HH HHHH

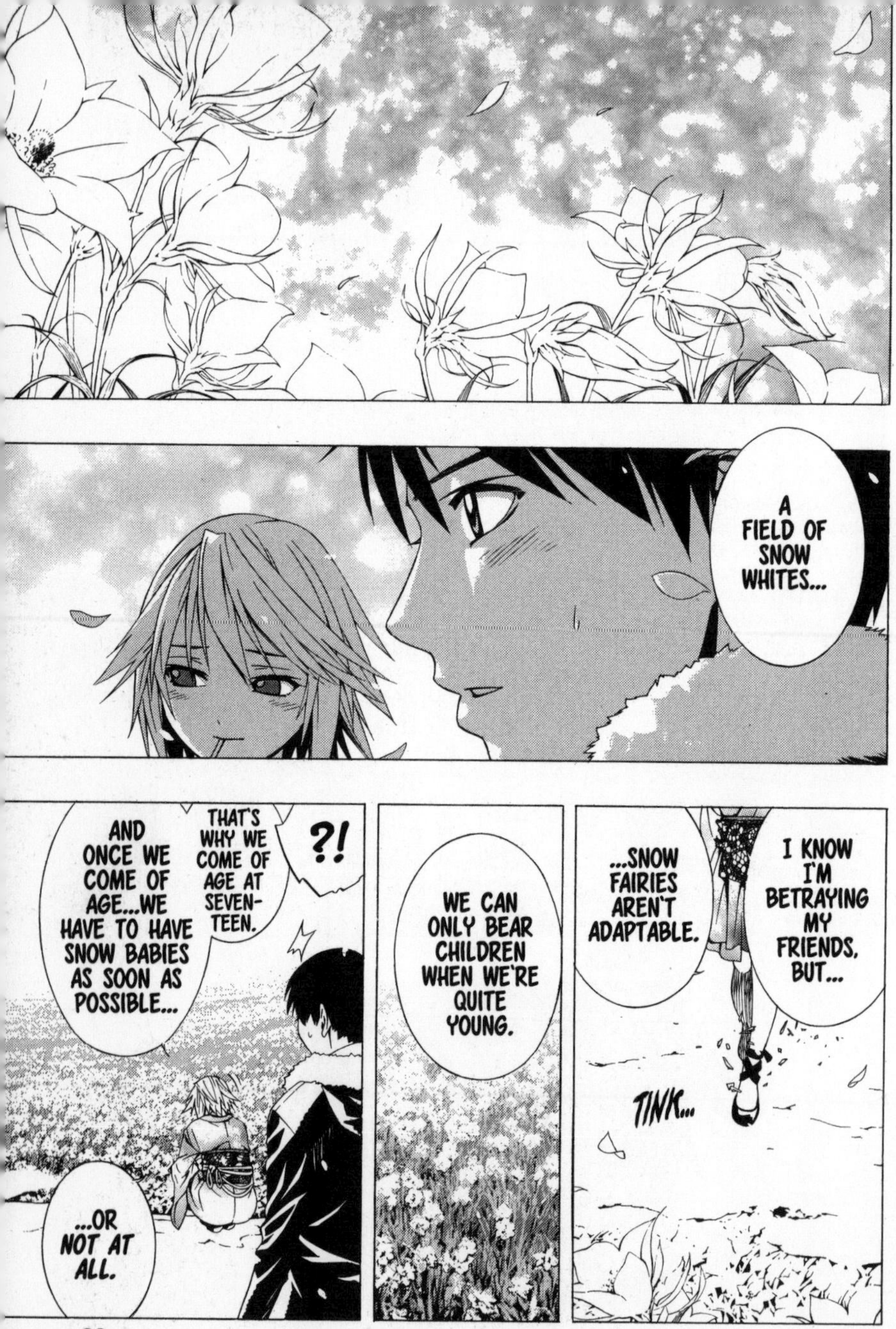
A FIELD OF SNOW WHITES...
I KNOW I'M BETRAYING MY FRIENDS, BUT...
...SNOW FAIRIES AREN'T ADAPTABLE.
TINK...
WE CAN ONLY BEAR CHILDREN WHEN WE'RE QUITE YOUNG.
THAT'S WHY WE COME OF AGE AT SEVENTEEN.
?!
AND ONCE WE COME OF AGE...WE HAVE TO HAVE SNOW BABIES AS SOON AS POSSIBLE...
...OR NOT AT ALL.

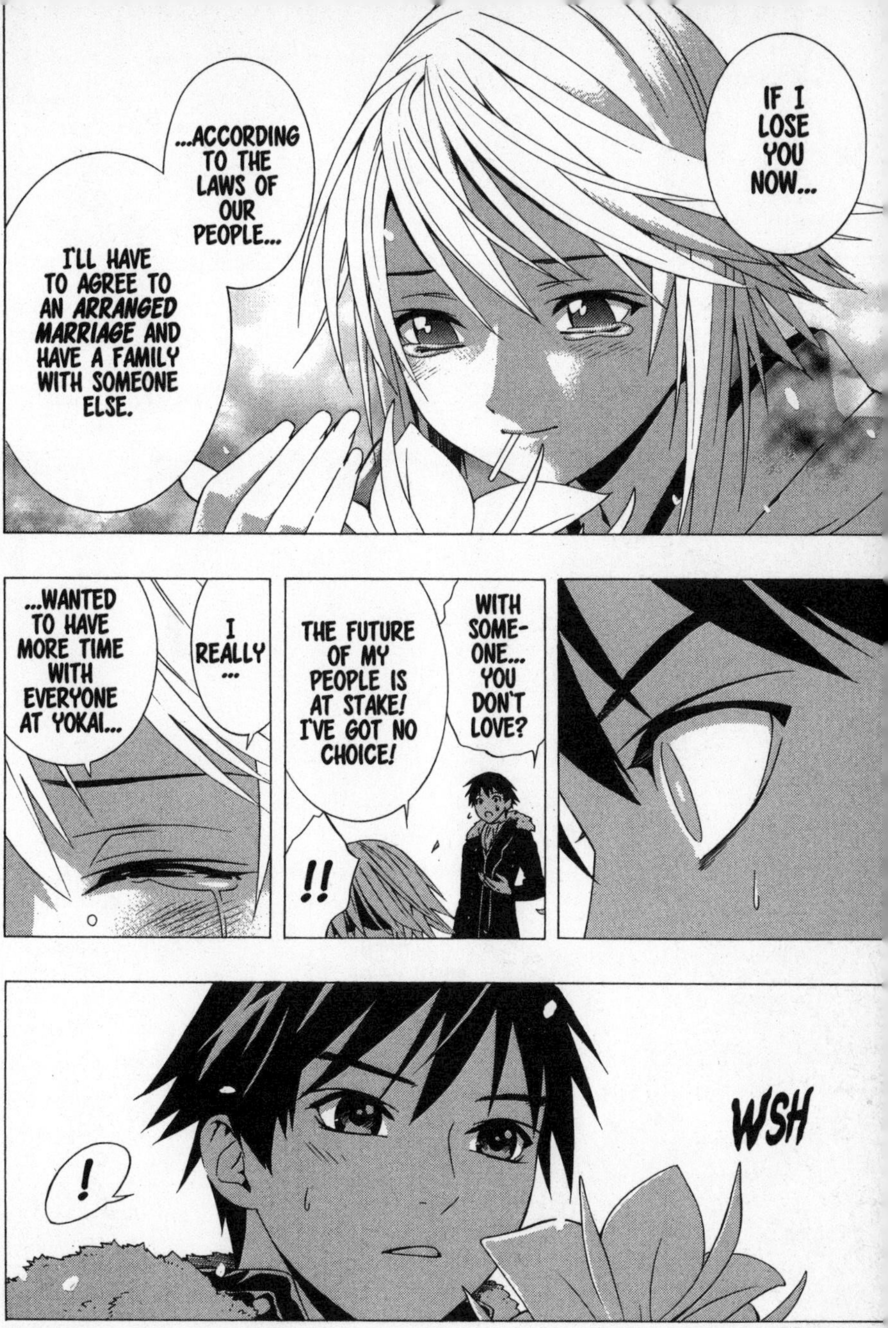

IF I LOSE YOU NOW...
...ACCORDING TO THE LAWS OF OUR PEOPLE...
I'LL HAVE TO AGREE TO AN *ARRANGED MARRIAGE* AND HAVE A FAMILY WITH SOMEONE ELSE.
WITH SOME-ONE... YOU DON'T LOVE?
THE FUTURE OF MY PEOPLE IS AT STAKE! I'VE GOT NO CHOICE!
!!
I REALLY ...
...WANTED TO HAVE MORE TIME WITH EVERYONE AT YOKAI...
WSH
!

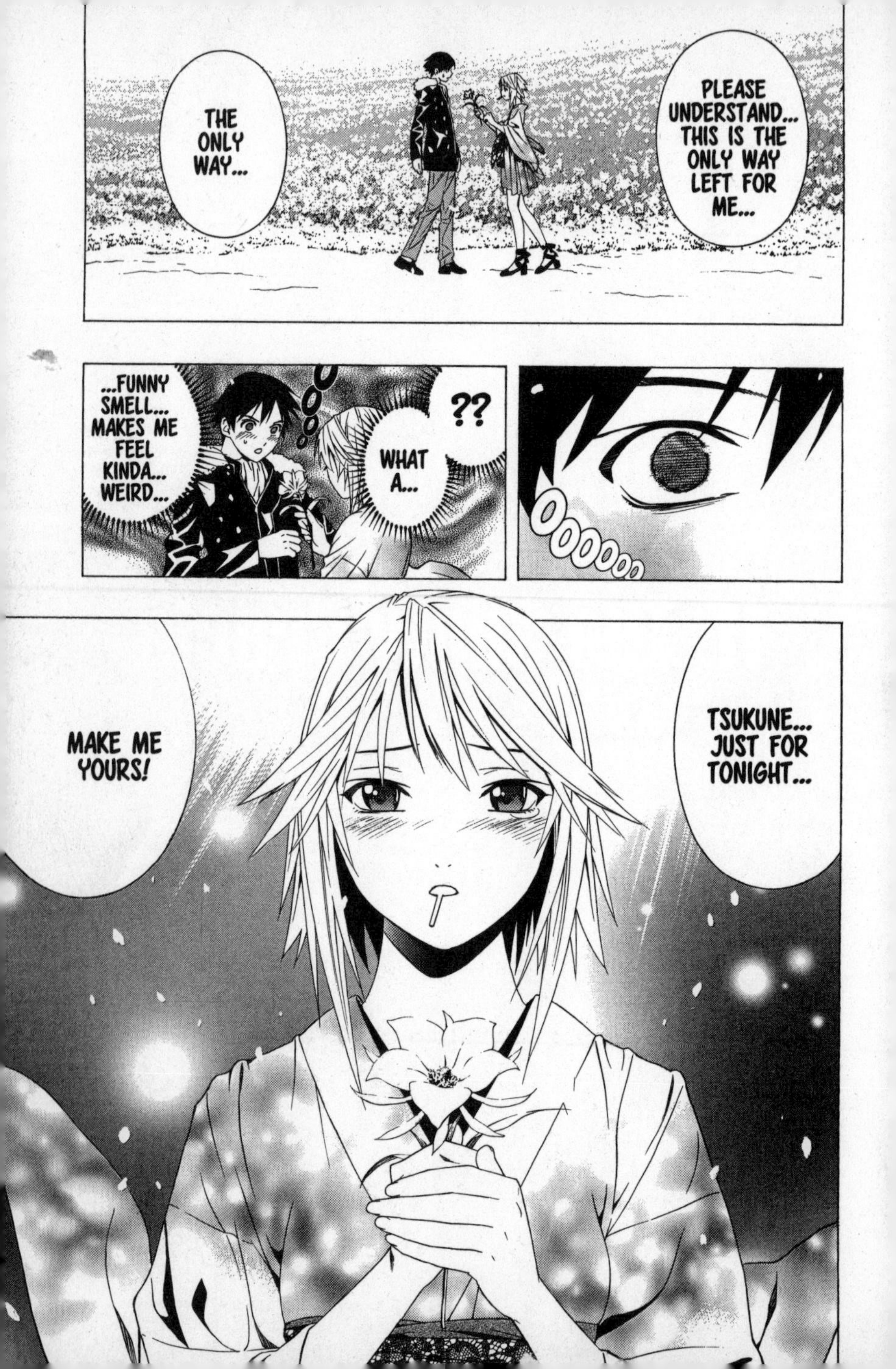
PLEASE UNDERSTAND... THIS IS THE ONLY WAY LEFT FOR ME...
THE ONLY WAY...
OOOOOOO
??
WHAT A...
...FUNNY SMELL... MAKES ME FEEL KINDA... WEIRD...
TSUKUNE... JUST FOR TONIGHT...
MAKE ME YOURS!

11: The Snow Oracle

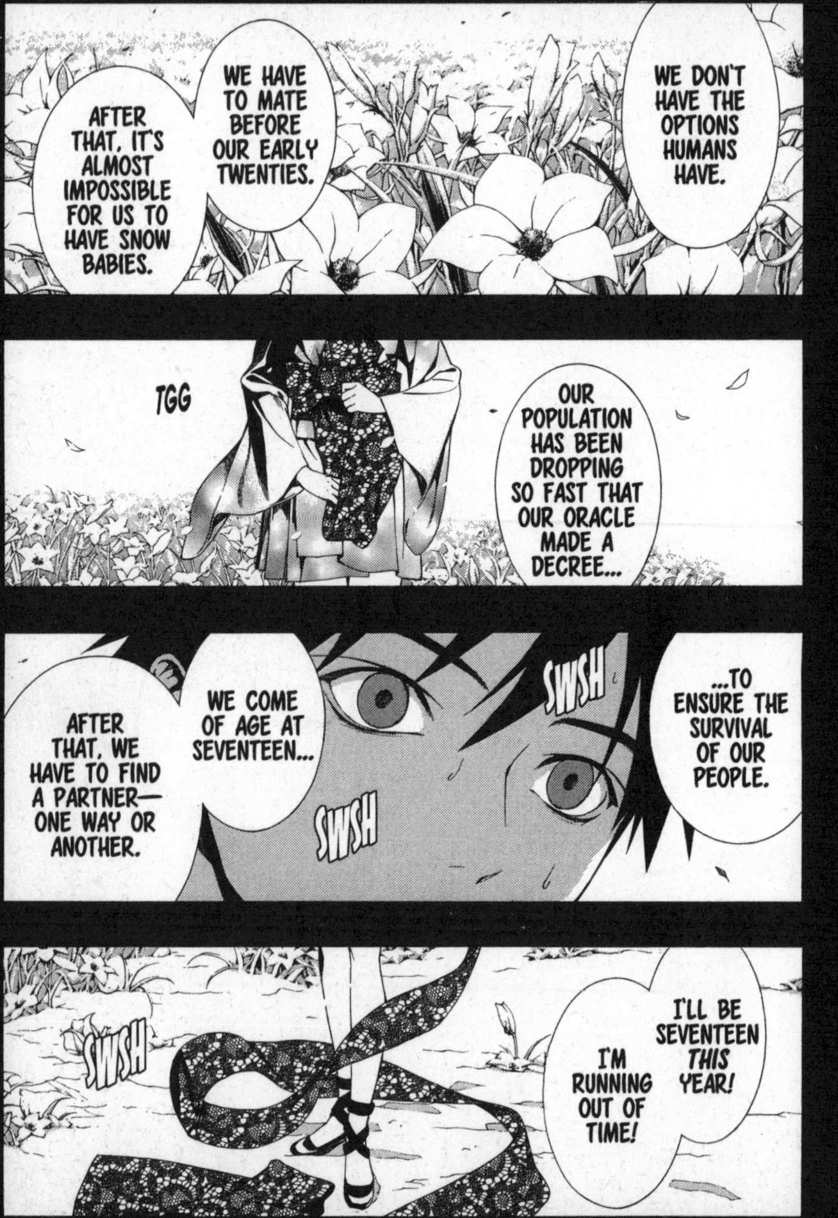
WE DON'T HAVE THE OPTIONS HUMANS HAVE.
WE HAVE TO MATE BEFORE OUR EARLY TWENTIES.
AFTER THAT, IT'S ALMOST IMPOSSIBLE FOR US TO HAVE SNOW BABIES.
OUR POPULATION HAS BEEN DROPPING SO FAST THAT OUR ORACLE MADE A DECREE...
TGG
...TO ENSURE THE SURVIVAL OF OUR PEOPLE.
SWSH
WE COME OF AGE AT SEVENTEEN...
SWSH
AFTER THAT, WE HAVE TO FIND A PARTNER—ONE WAY OR ANOTHER.
I'LL BE SEVENTEEN *THIS* YEAR!
I'M RUNNING OUT OF TIME!
SWSH

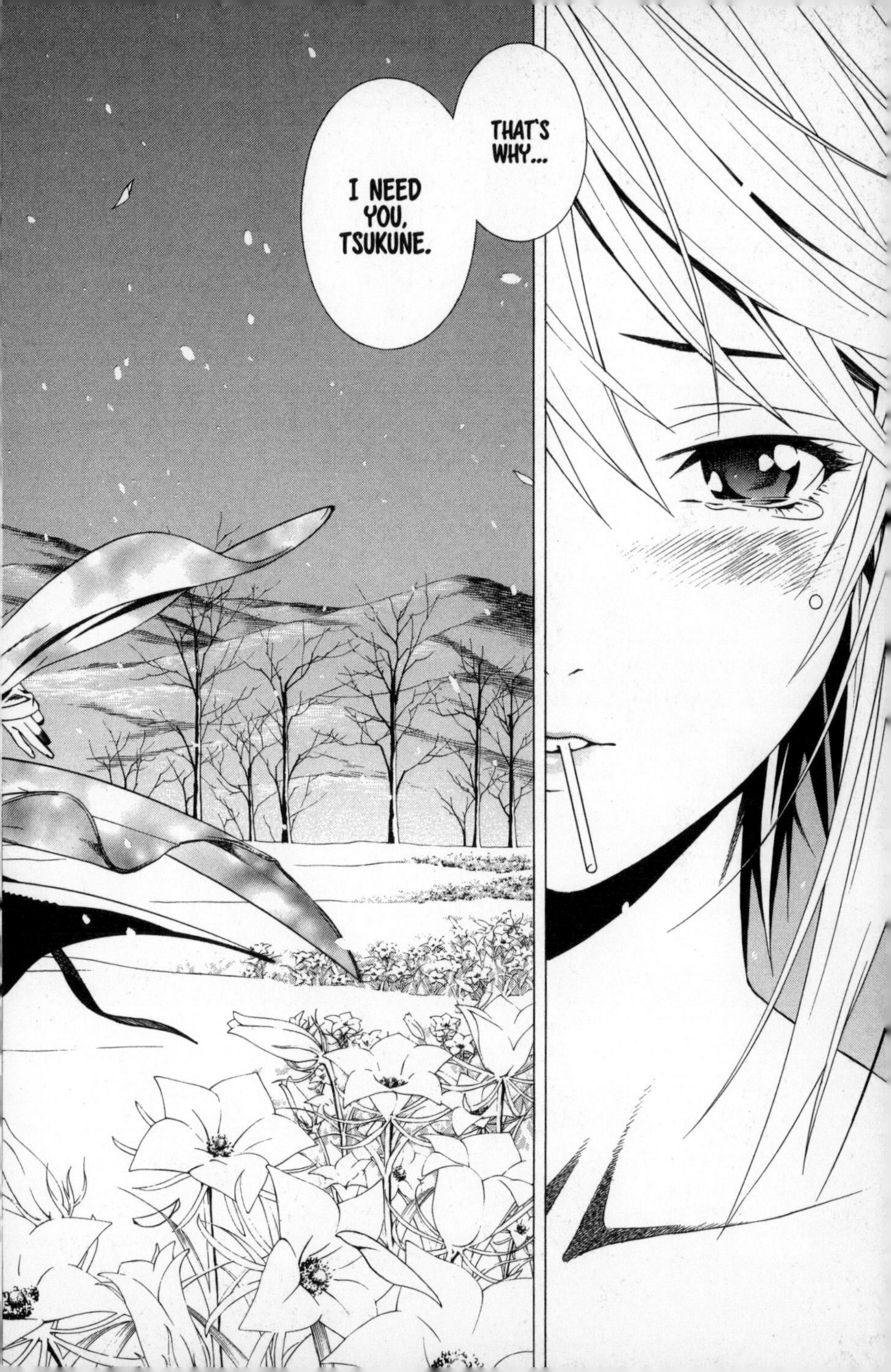
THAT'S WHY...
I NEED YOU, TSUKUNE.

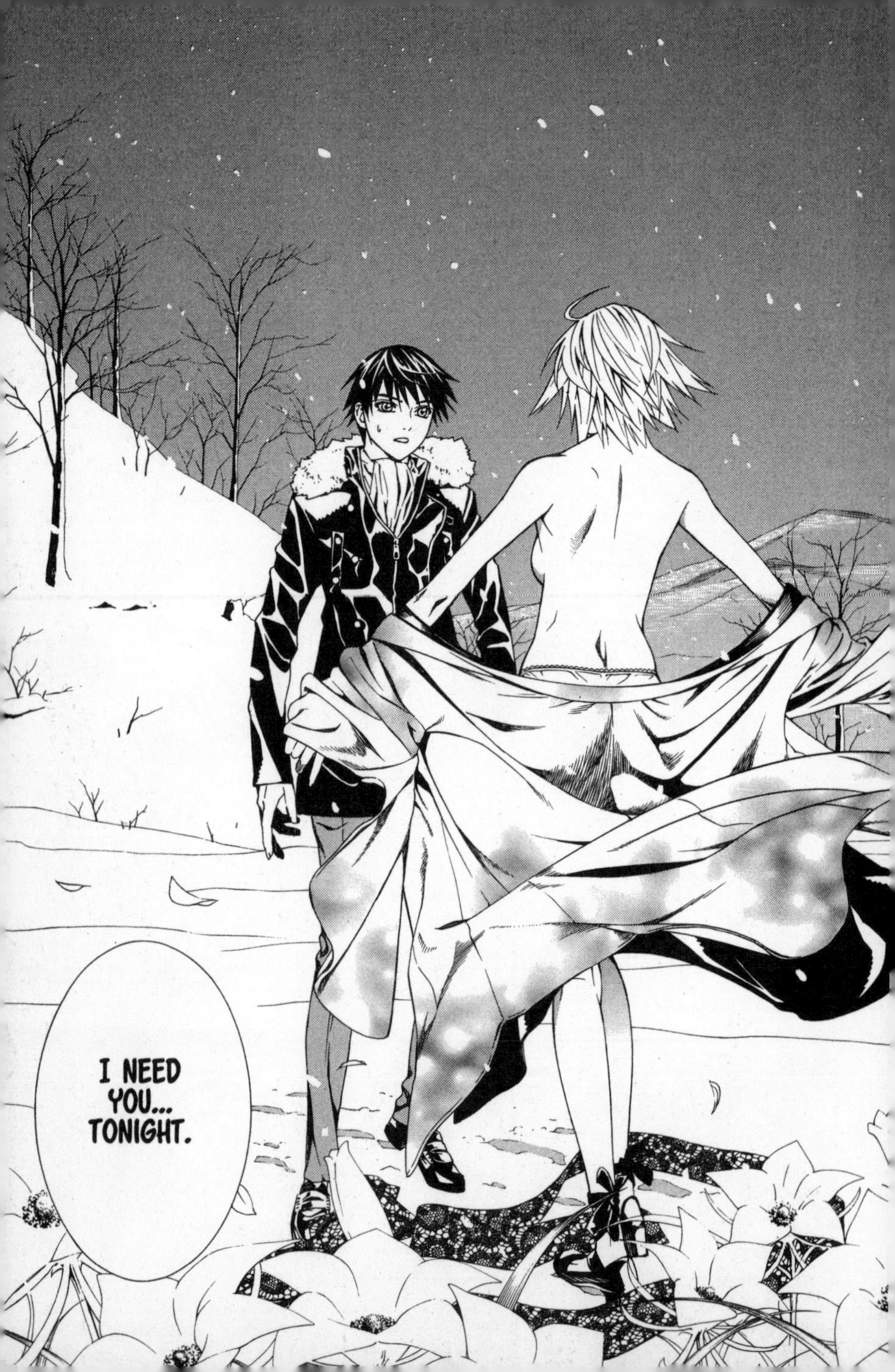
I NEED YOU... TONIGHT.

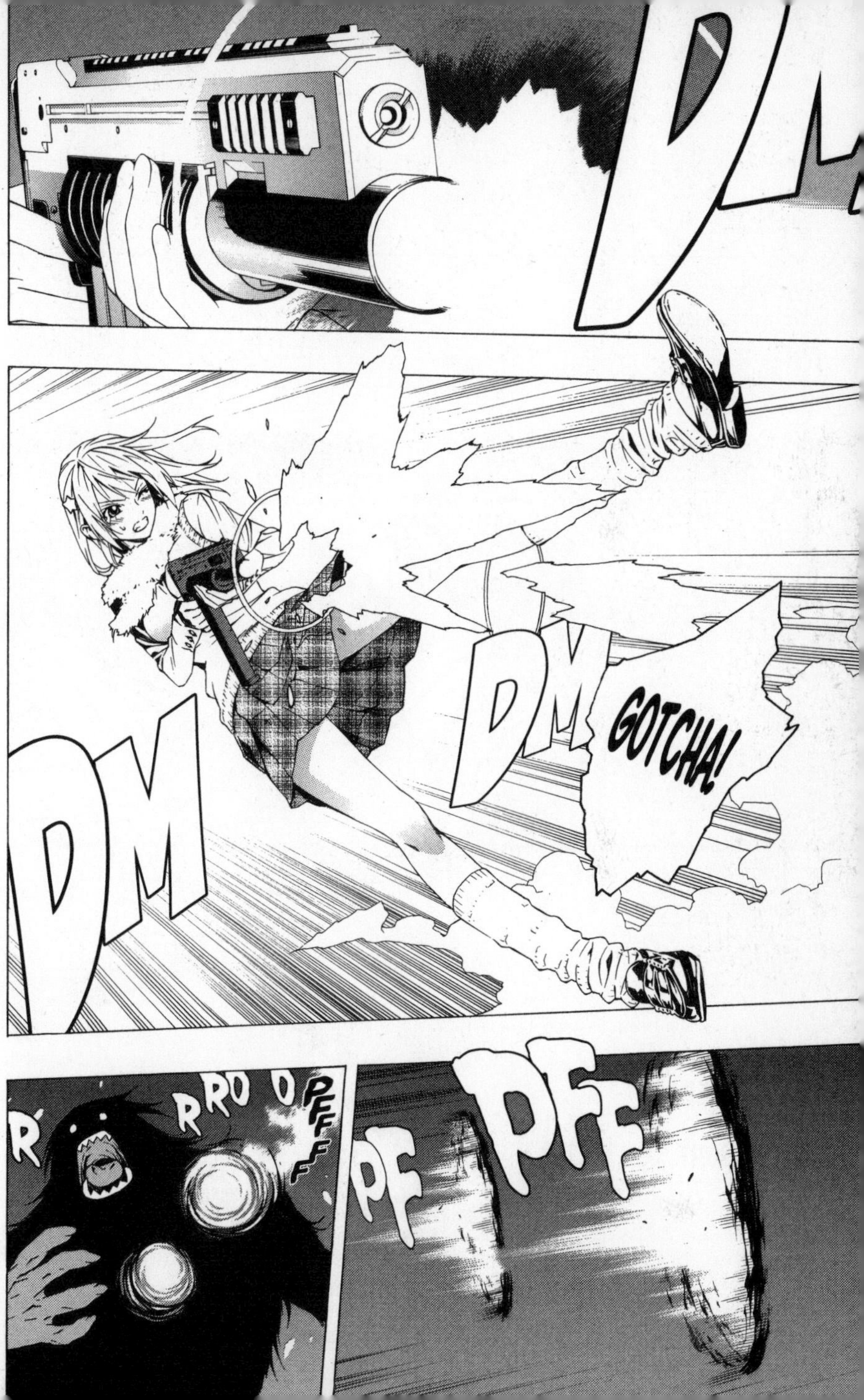
D
GOTCHA!
DM
DM
PFF
PF
RRO O
PFFFF
R

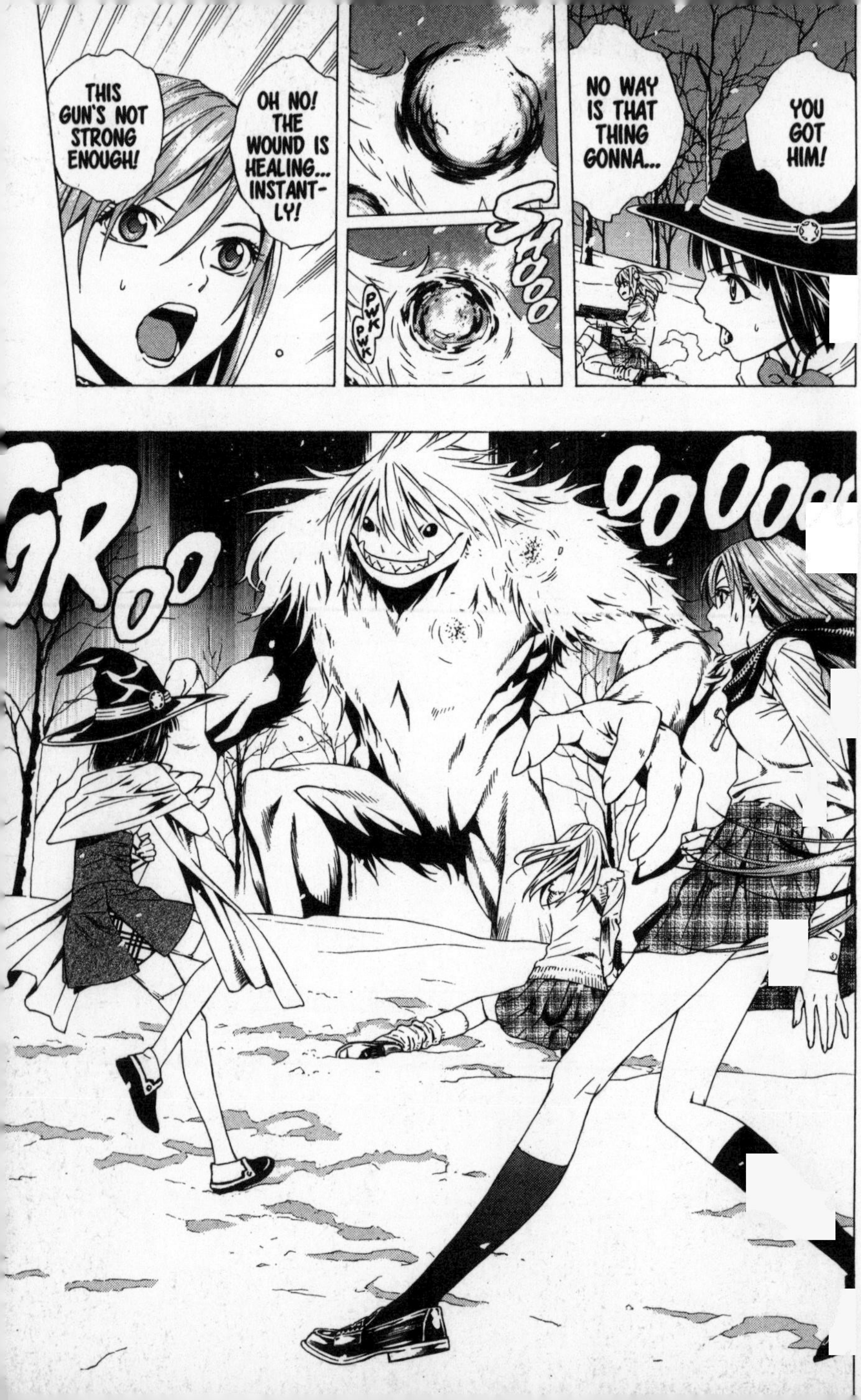
YOU GOT HIM!
NO WAY IS THAT THING GONNA...
SHOOO
PWK PWK PWK
OH NO! THE WOUND IS HEALING... INSTANT-LY!
THIS GUN'S NOT STRONG ENOUGH!
GROOOOOOO

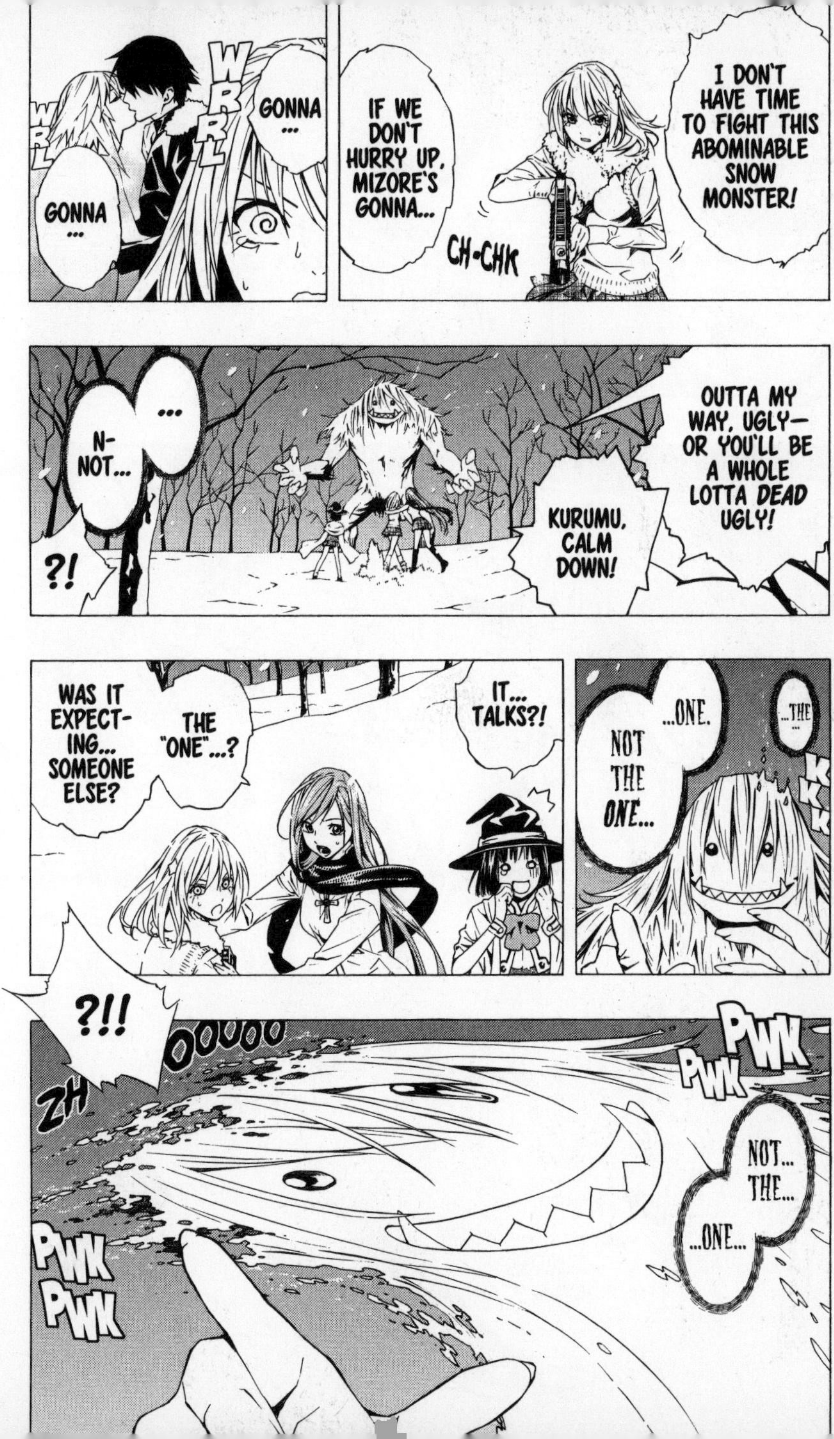
I DON'T HAVE TIME TO FIGHT THIS ABOMINABLE SNOW MONSTER!
IF WE DON'T HURRY UP, MIZORE'S GONNA...
CH-CHK
WRRL
GONNA ...
WRRL
GONNA ...
OUTTA MY WAY, UGLY— OR YOU'LL BE A WHOLE LOTTA DEAD UGLY!
KURUMU, CALM DOWN!
...
N-NOT...
?!
...THE ...
KKK
...ONE.
NOT THE ONE...
IT... TALKS?!
THE "ONE"...?
WAS IT EXPECTING... SOMEONE ELSE?
PWK PWK
NOT... THE... ...ONE...
?!!
ZHOOOOOO
PWK PWK

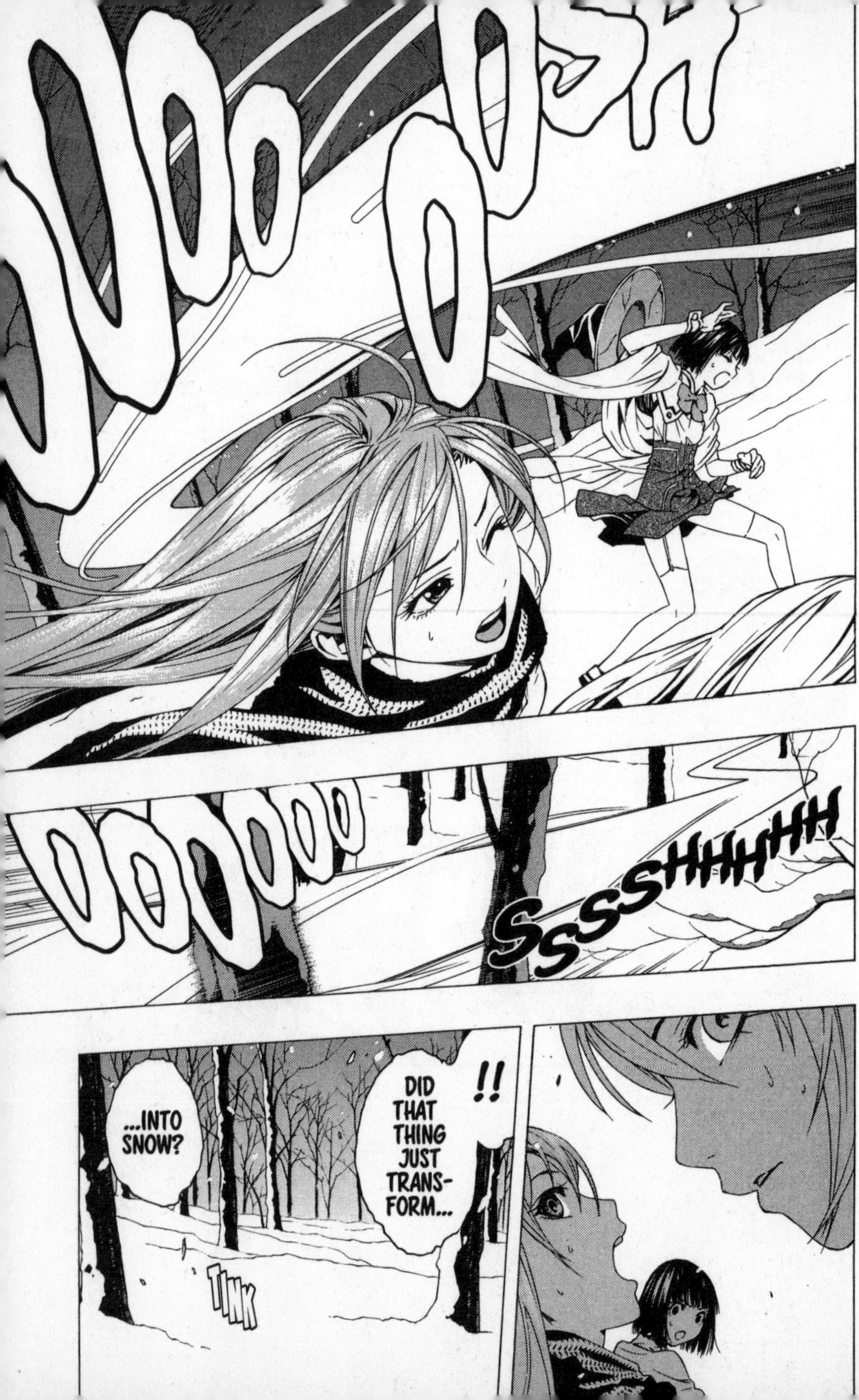
WOOOOOOSH
OOOOOOO
SSSSHHHHHH
!!
DID THAT THING JUST TRANS-FORM...
...INTO SNOW?
TINK

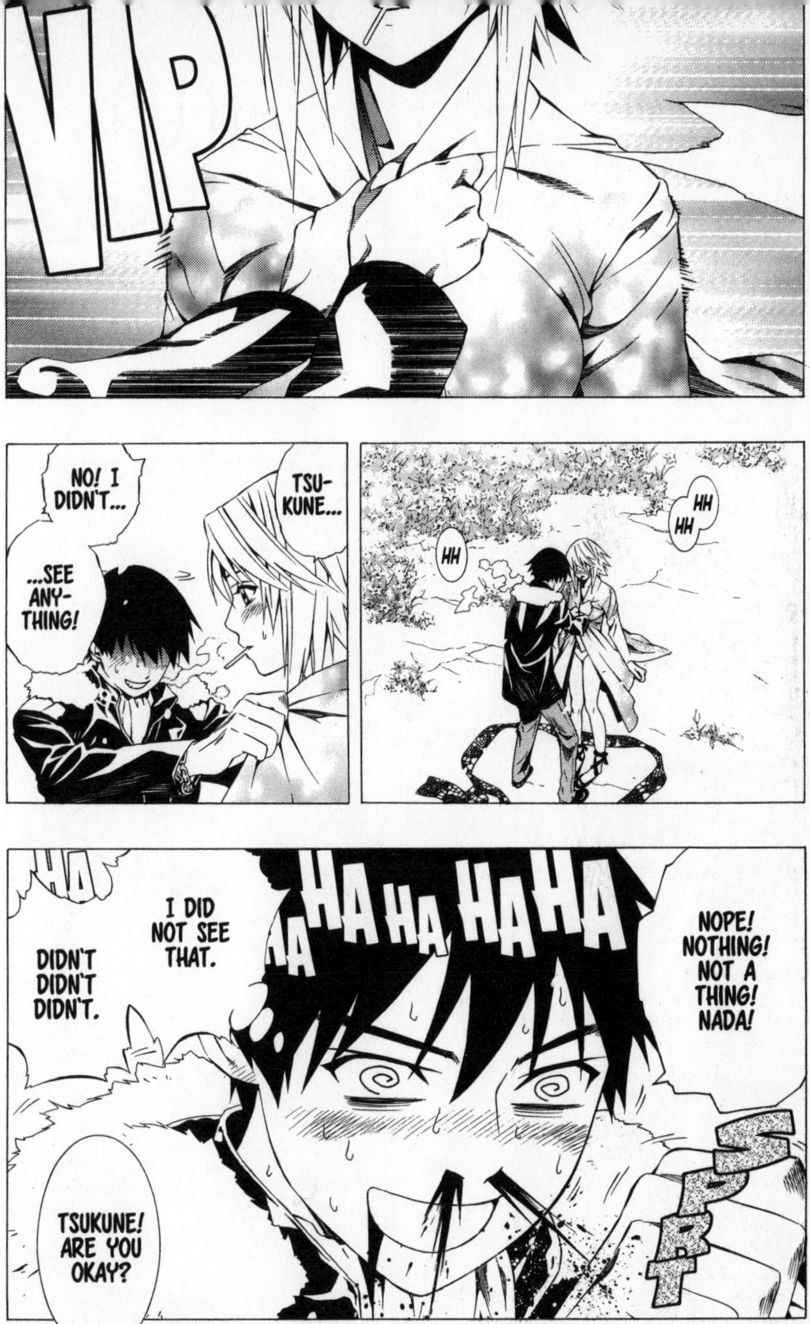
VIP
HH HH
HH
TSU-KUNE...
NO! I DIDN'T...
...SEE ANY-THING!
NOPE! NOTHING! NOT A THING! NADA!
HA HA HA HA HA HA HA
I DID NOT SEE THAT.
HA
DIDN'T DIDN'T DIDN'T.
SPRT
TSUKUNE! ARE YOU OKAY?

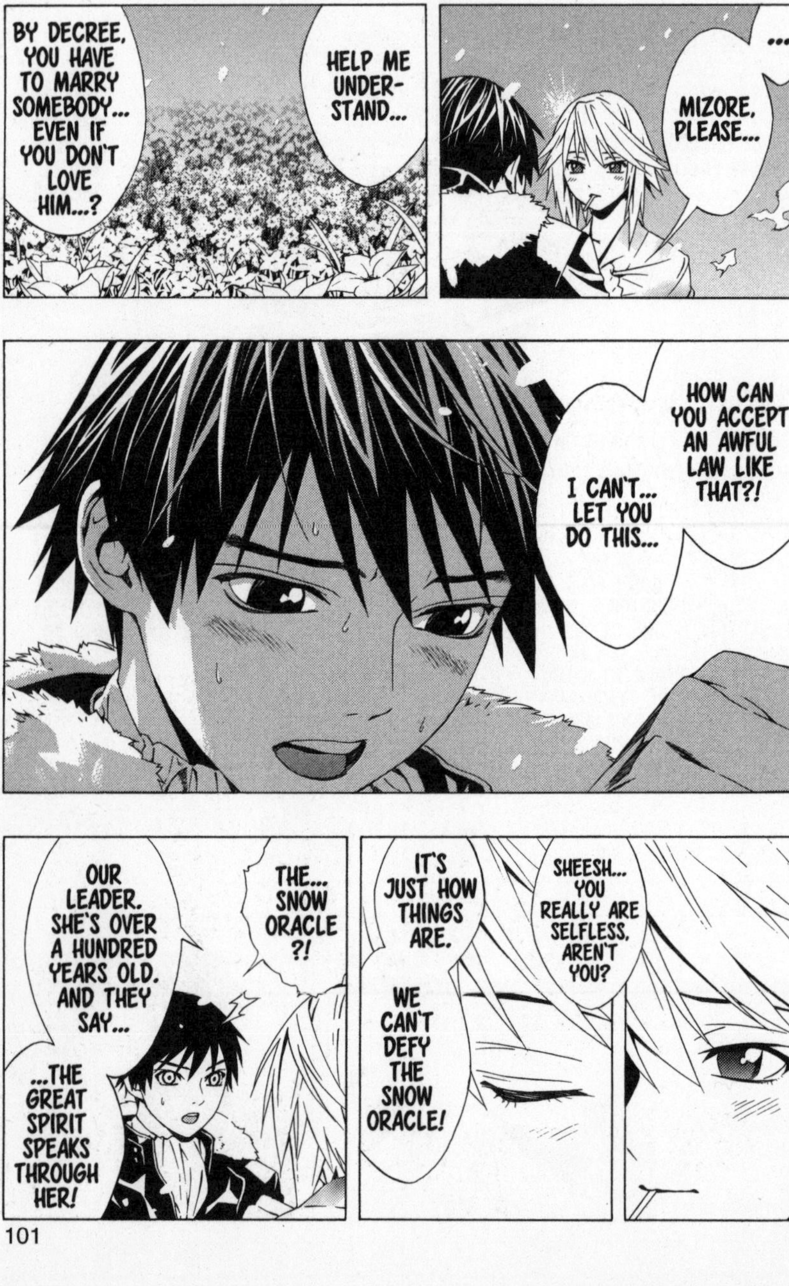
...
MIZORE, PLEASE...
HELP ME UNDERSTAND...
BY DECREE, YOU HAVE TO MARRY SOMEBODY... EVEN IF YOU DON'T LOVE HIM...?
HOW CAN YOU ACCEPT AN AWFUL LAW LIKE THAT?!
I CAN'T... LET YOU DO THIS...
SHEESH... YOU REALLY ARE SELFLESS, AREN'T YOU?
IT'S JUST HOW THINGS ARE.
WE CAN'T DEFY THE SNOW ORACLE!
THE... SNOW ORACLE?!
OUR LEADER. SHE'S OVER A HUNDRED YEARS OLD. AND THEY SAY...
...THE GREAT SPIRIT SPEAKS THROUGH HER!

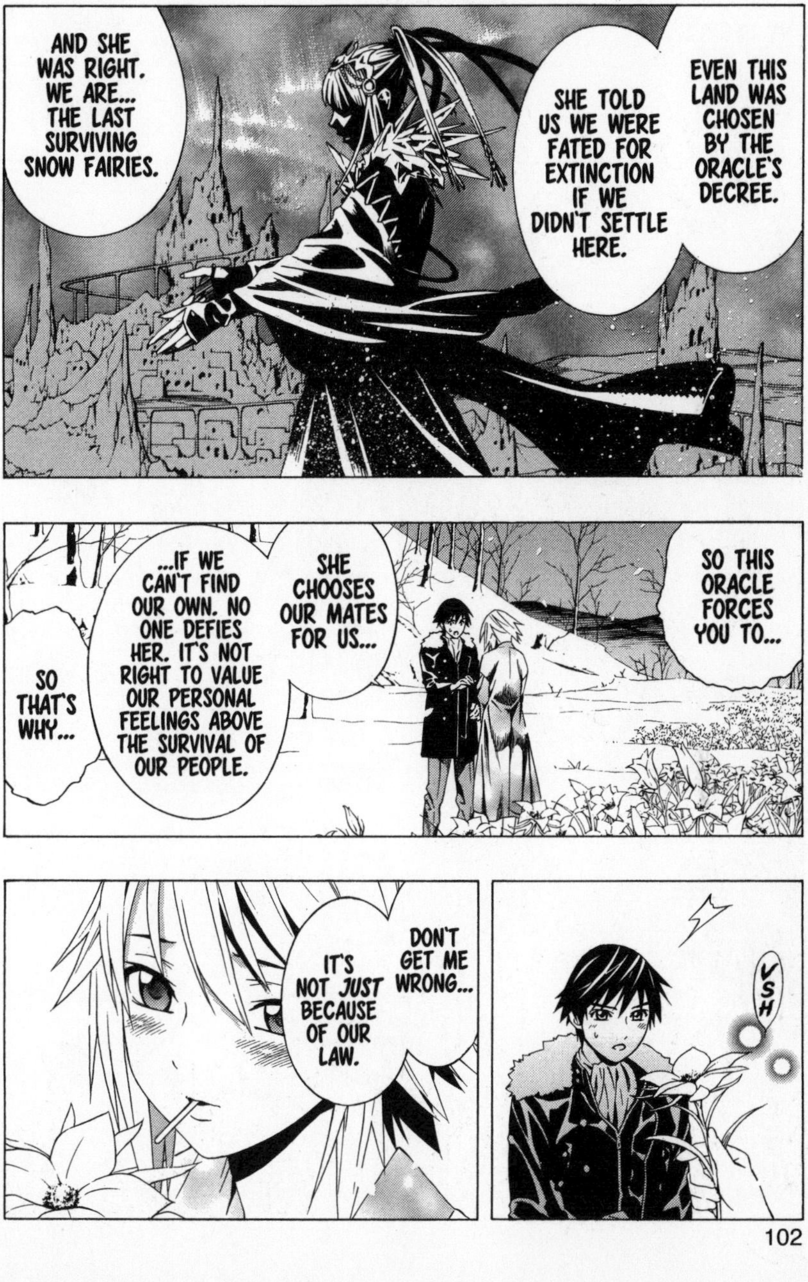
EVEN THIS LAND WAS CHOSEN BY THE ORACLE'S DECREE.
SHE TOLD US WE WERE FATED FOR EXTINCTION IF WE DIDN'T SETTLE HERE.
AND SHE WAS RIGHT. WE ARE... THE LAST SURVIVING SNOW FAIRIES.
SO THIS ORACLE FORCES YOU TO...
SHE CHOOSES OUR MATES FOR US...
...IF WE CAN'T FIND OUR OWN. NO ONE DEFIES HER. IT'S NOT RIGHT TO VALUE OUR PERSONAL FEELINGS ABOVE THE SURVIVAL OF OUR PEOPLE.
SO THAT'S WHY...
VSH
DON'T GET ME WRONG...
IT'S NOT *JUST* BECAUSE OF OUR LAW.

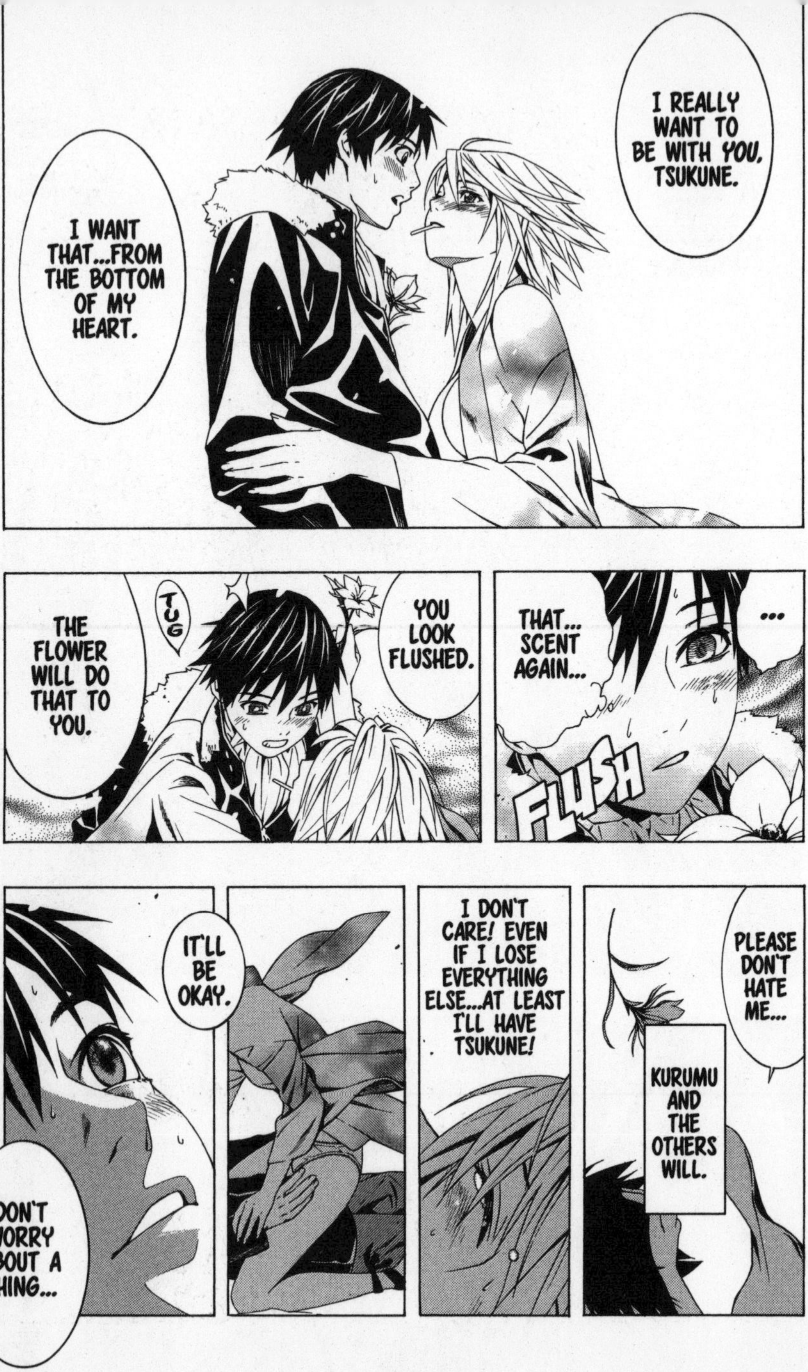
I REALLY WANT TO BE WITH YOU, TSUKUNE.
I WANT THAT...FROM THE BOTTOM OF MY HEART.
...
THAT... SCENT AGAIN...
FLUSH
YOU LOOK FLUSHED.
TUG
THE FLOWER WILL DO THAT TO YOU.
PLEASE DON'T HATE ME...
KURUMU AND THE OTHERS WILL.
I DON'T CARE! EVEN IF I LOSE EVERYTHING ELSE...AT LEAST I'LL HAVE TSUKUNE!
IT'LL BE OKAY.
DON'T WORRY ABOUT A THING...

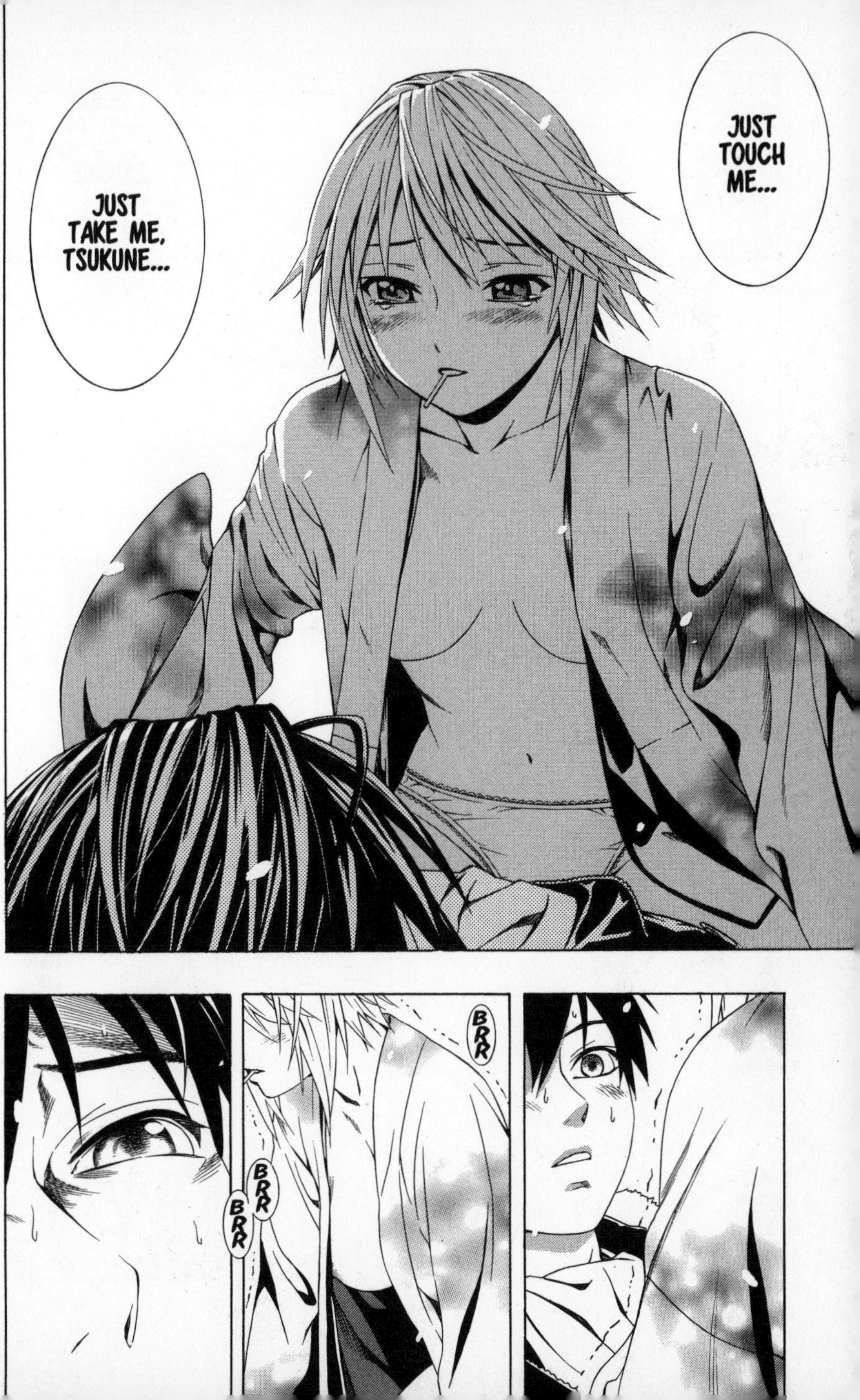
JUST TOUCH ME...
JUST TAKE ME, TSUKUNE...
BRR
BRR
BRR

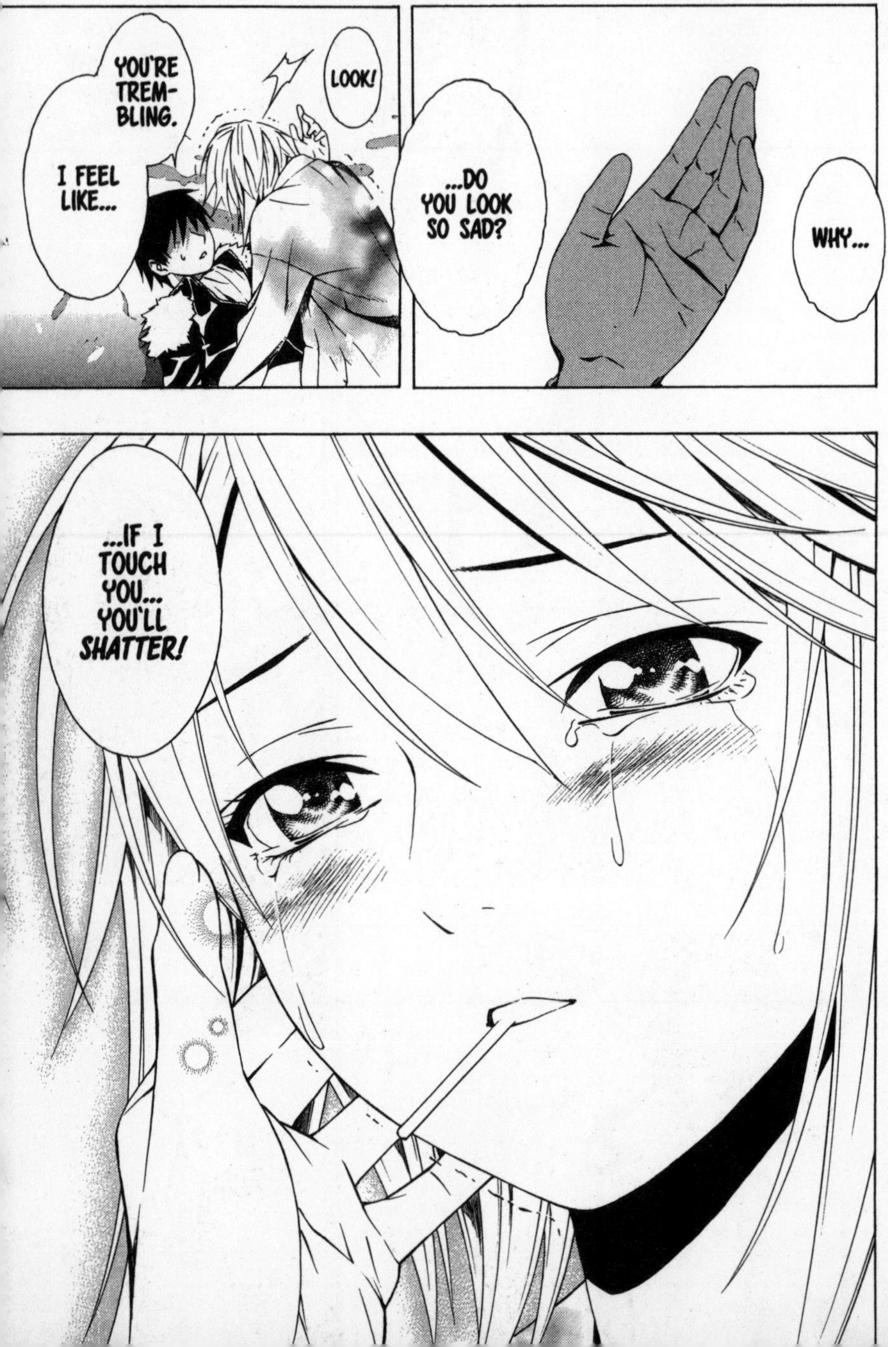
WHY...
...DO YOU LOOK SO SAD?
LOOK!
YOU'RE TREMBLING.
I FEEL LIKE...
...IF I TOUCH YOU... YOU'LL SHATTER!

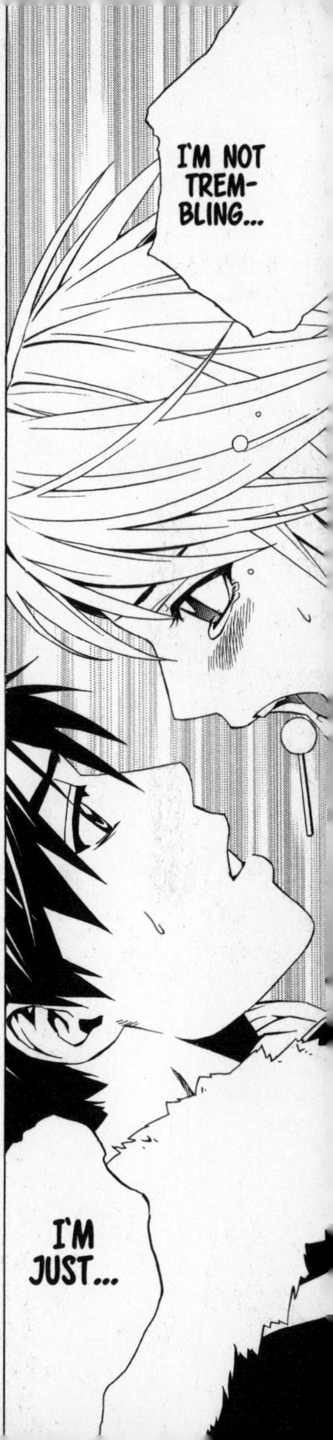
I'M NOT TREM-BLING...
I'M JUST...
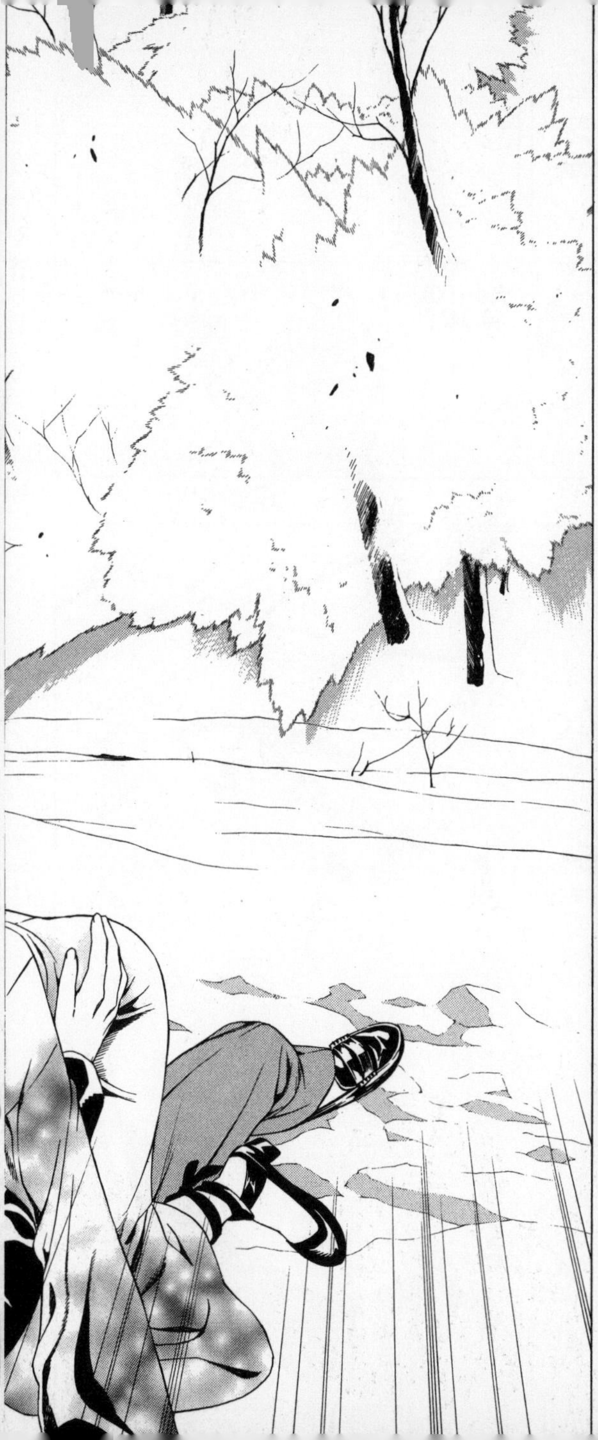

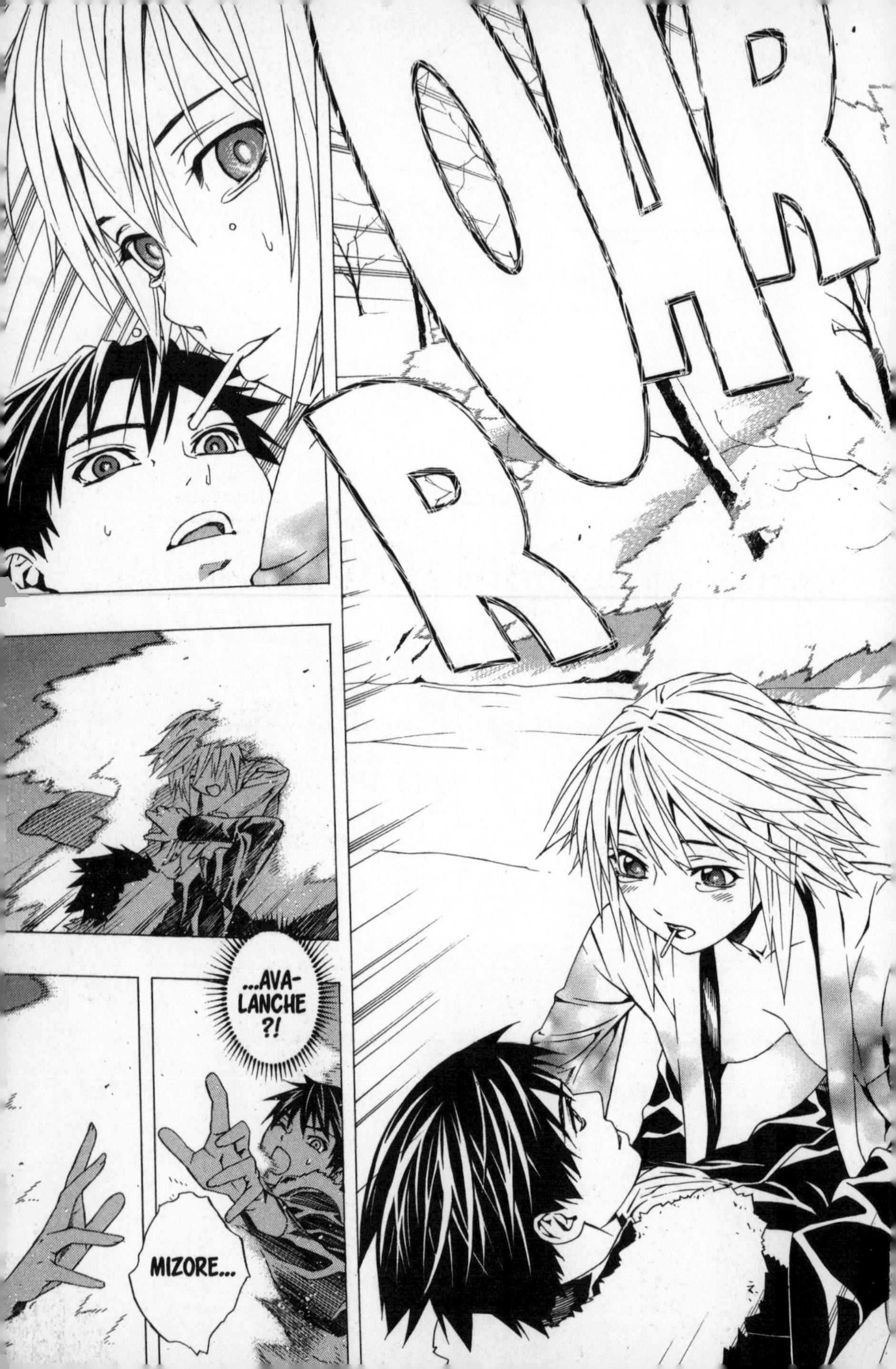
...AVA-
LANCHE
?!
MIZORE...

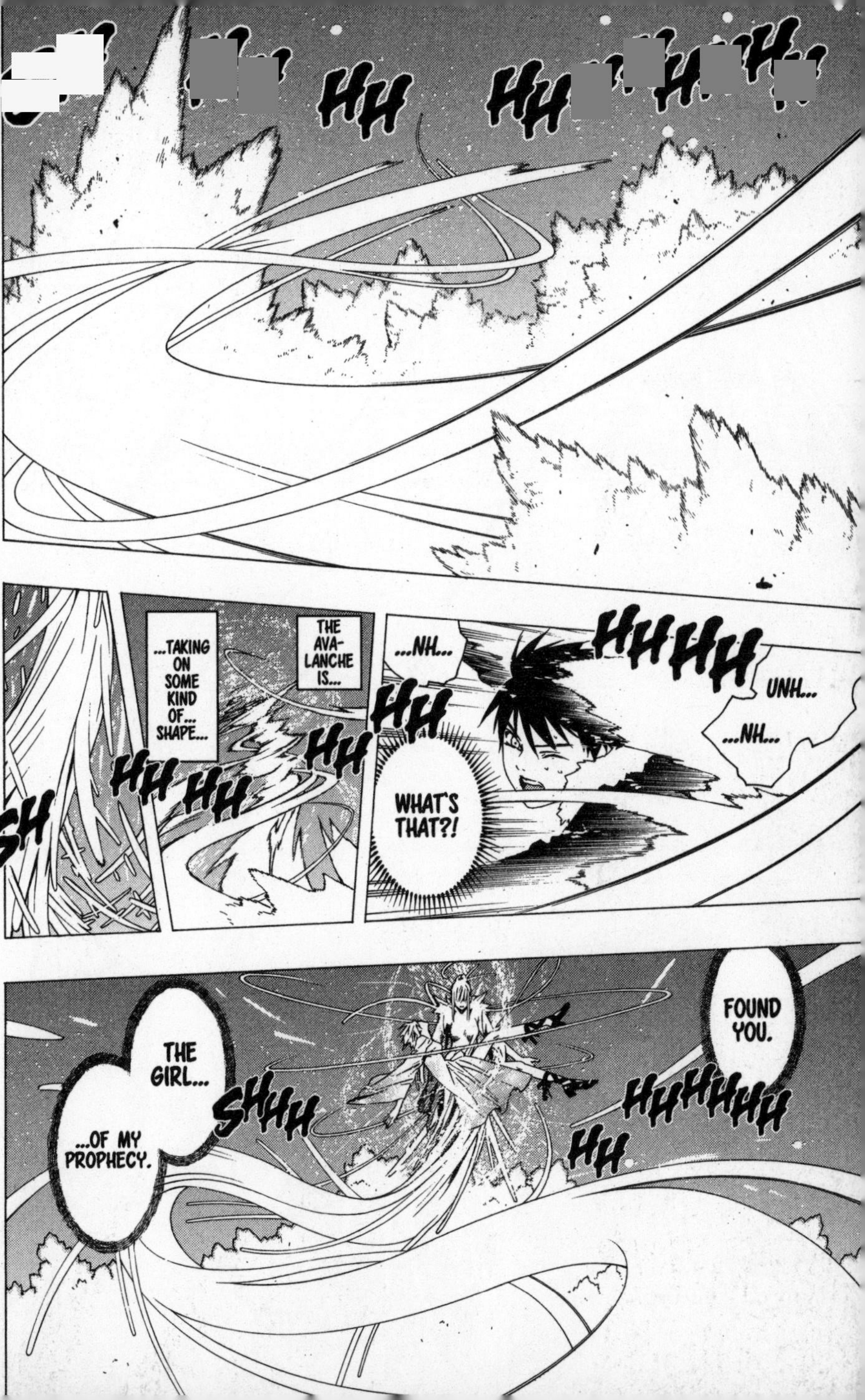
HH
HH
UNH...
...NH...
HHHHH
...NH...
WHAT'S THAT?!
HH
THE AVA-LANCHE IS...
HH
...TAKING ON SOME KIND OF... SHAPE...
HH
HH
SH
FOUND YOU.
HHHHHHH
HH
SHHH
THE GIRL...
...OF MY PROPHECY.

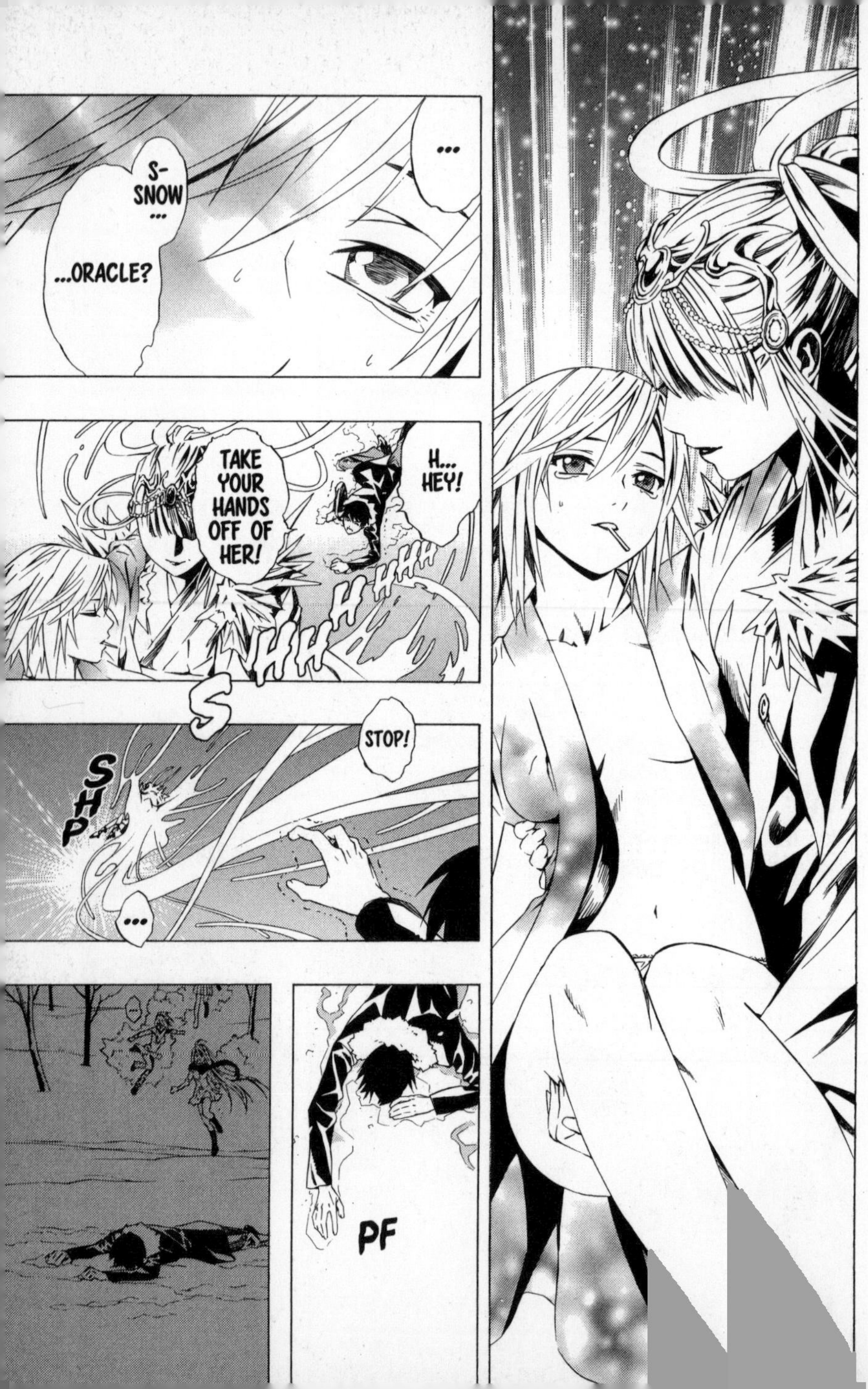
...
S- SNOW ...
...ORACLE?
H... HEY!
TAKE YOUR HANDS OFF OF HER!
SHHHHHHHHH
STOP!
SHP
...
PF

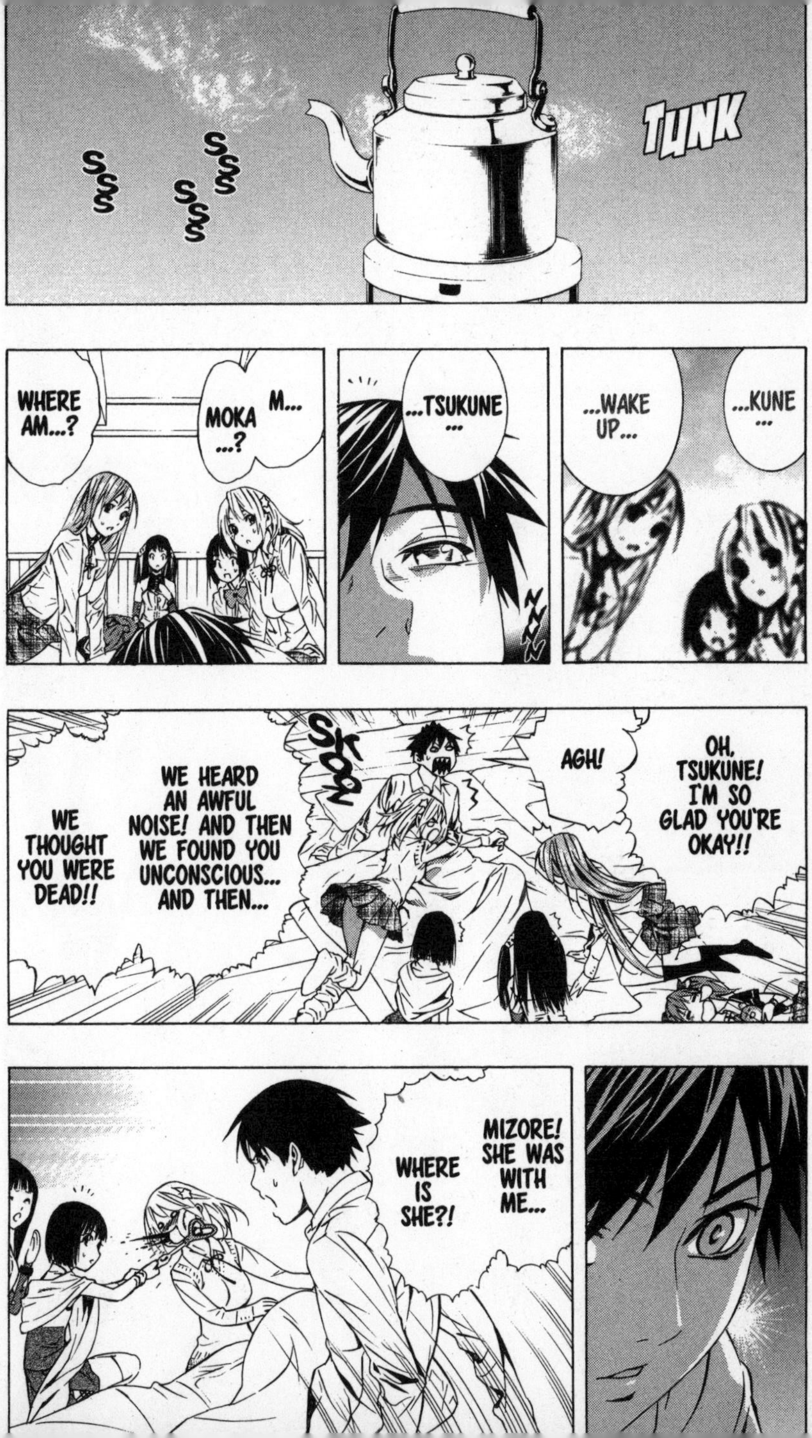
TUNK
SSS
SSS
SSS
...KUNE ...
...WAKE UP...
...TSUKUNE ...
NNN
M...
MOKA ...?
WHERE AM...?
OH, TSUKUNE! I'M SO GLAD YOU'RE OKAY!!
AGH!
SKOON
WE HEARD AN AWFUL NOISE! AND THEN WE FOUND YOU UNCONSCIOUS... AND THEN...
WE THOUGHT YOU WERE DEAD!!
MIZORE! SHE WAS WITH ME...
WHERE IS SHE?!

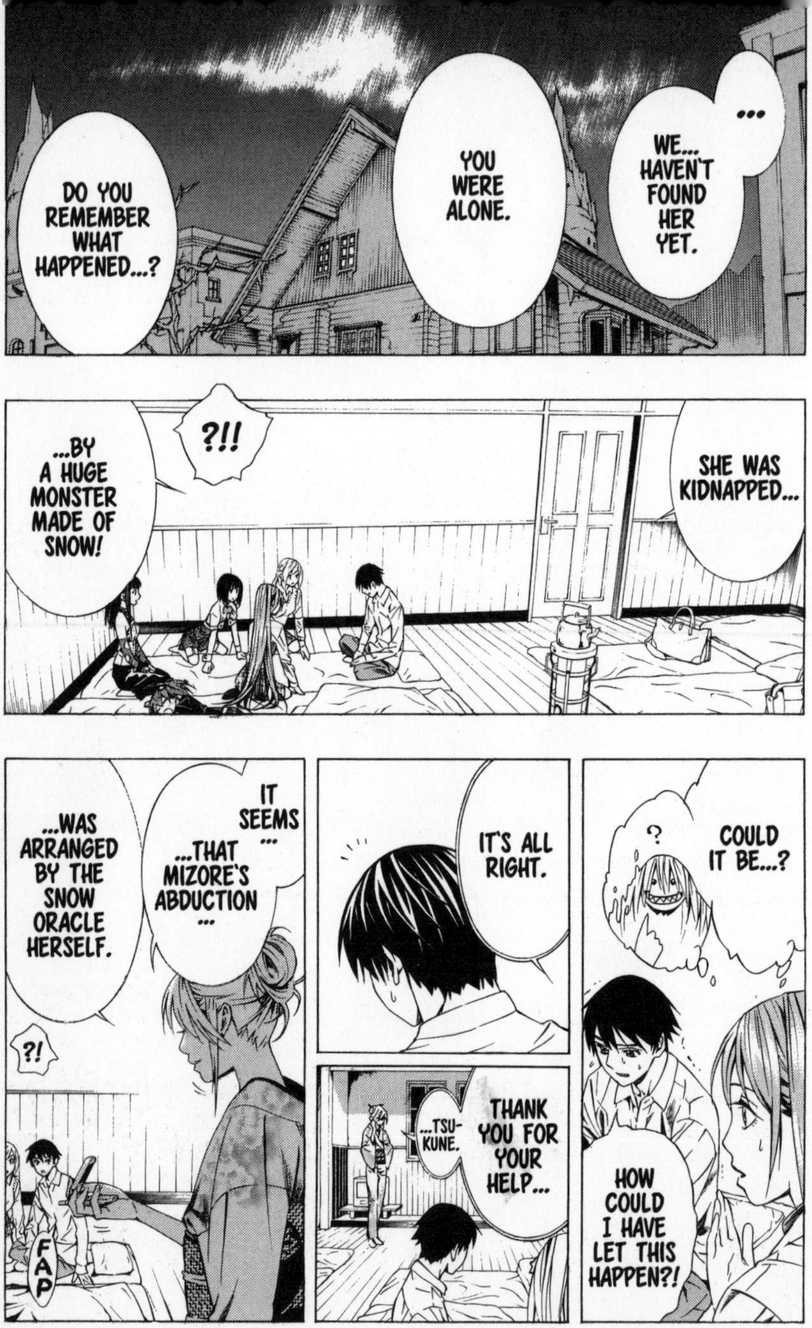
...
WE... HAVEN'T FOUND HER YET.
YOU WERE ALONE.
DO YOU REMEMBER WHAT HAPPENED...?
SHE WAS KIDNAPPED...
?!!
...BY A HUGE MONSTER MADE OF SNOW!
COULD IT BE...?
?
HOW COULD I HAVE LET THIS HAPPEN?!
IT'S ALL RIGHT.
THANK YOU FOR YOUR HELP...
...TSU-KUNE.
IT SEEMS...
...THAT MIZORE'S ABDUCTION...
...WAS ARRANGED BY THE SNOW ORACLE HERSELF.
?!
FAP

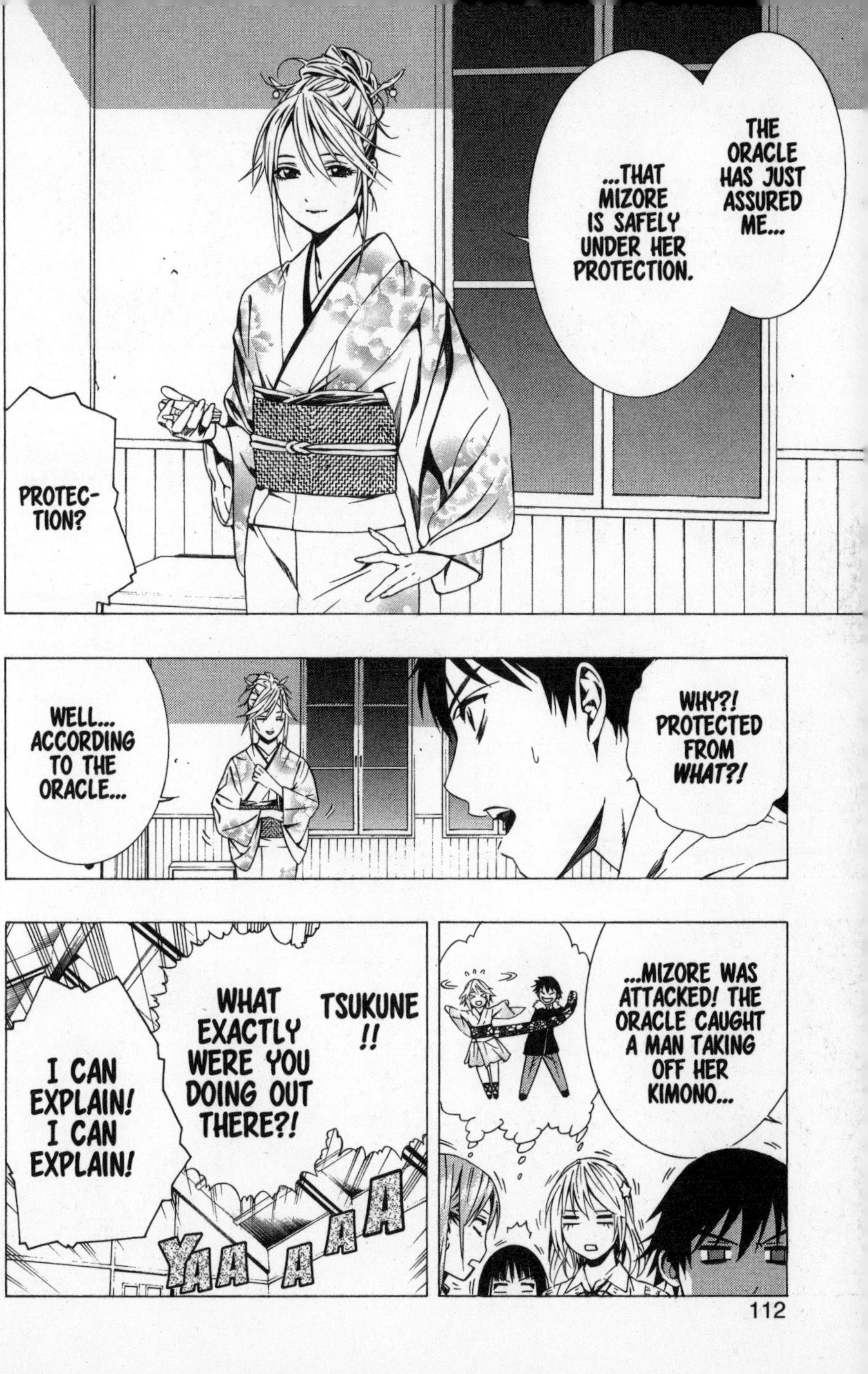
THE ORACLE HAS JUST ASSURED ME...
...THAT MIZORE IS SAFELY UNDER HER PROTECTION.
PROTECTION?
WHY?! PROTECTED FROM WHAT?!
WELL... ACCORDING TO THE ORACLE...
...MIZORE WAS ATTACKED! THE ORACLE CAUGHT A MAN TAKING OFF HER KIMONO...
TSUKUNE!!
WHAT EXACTLY WERE YOU DOING OUT THERE?!
I CAN EXPLAIN! I CAN EXPLAIN!
YAAAAAA

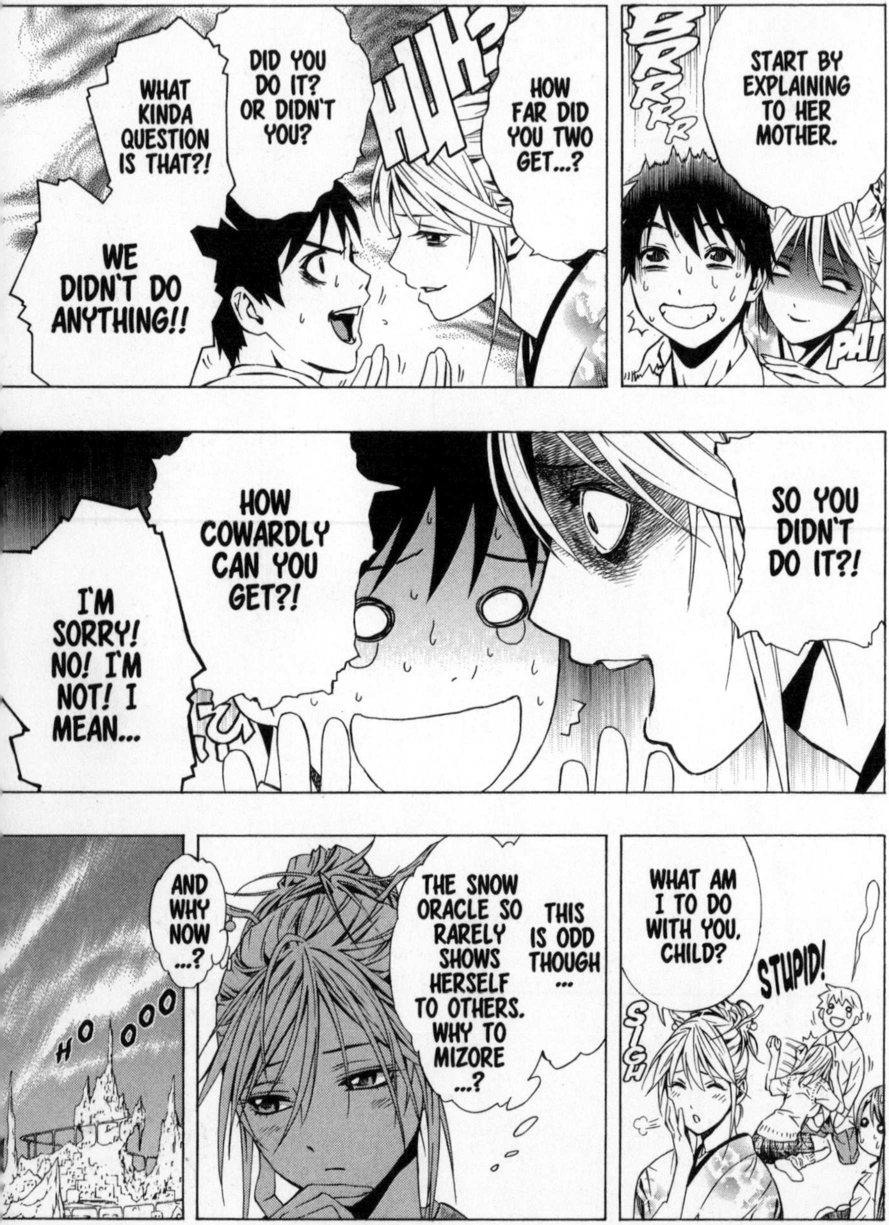
BRRRR
START BY EXPLAINING TO HER MOTHER.
PAT
HOW FAR DID YOU TWO GET...?
HUH?
DID YOU DO IT? OR DIDN'T YOU?
WHAT KINDA QUESTION IS THAT?!
WE DIDN'T DO ANYTHING!!
SO YOU DIDN'T DO IT?!
HOW COWARDLY CAN YOU GET?!
I'M SORRY! NO! I'M NOT! I MEAN...
WHAT AM I TO DO WITH YOU, CHILD?
STUPID!
SIGH
THIS IS ODD THOUGH...
THE SNOW ORACLE SO RARELY SHOWS HERSELF TO OTHERS. WHY TO MIZORE...?
AND WHY NOW...?
HO OOO

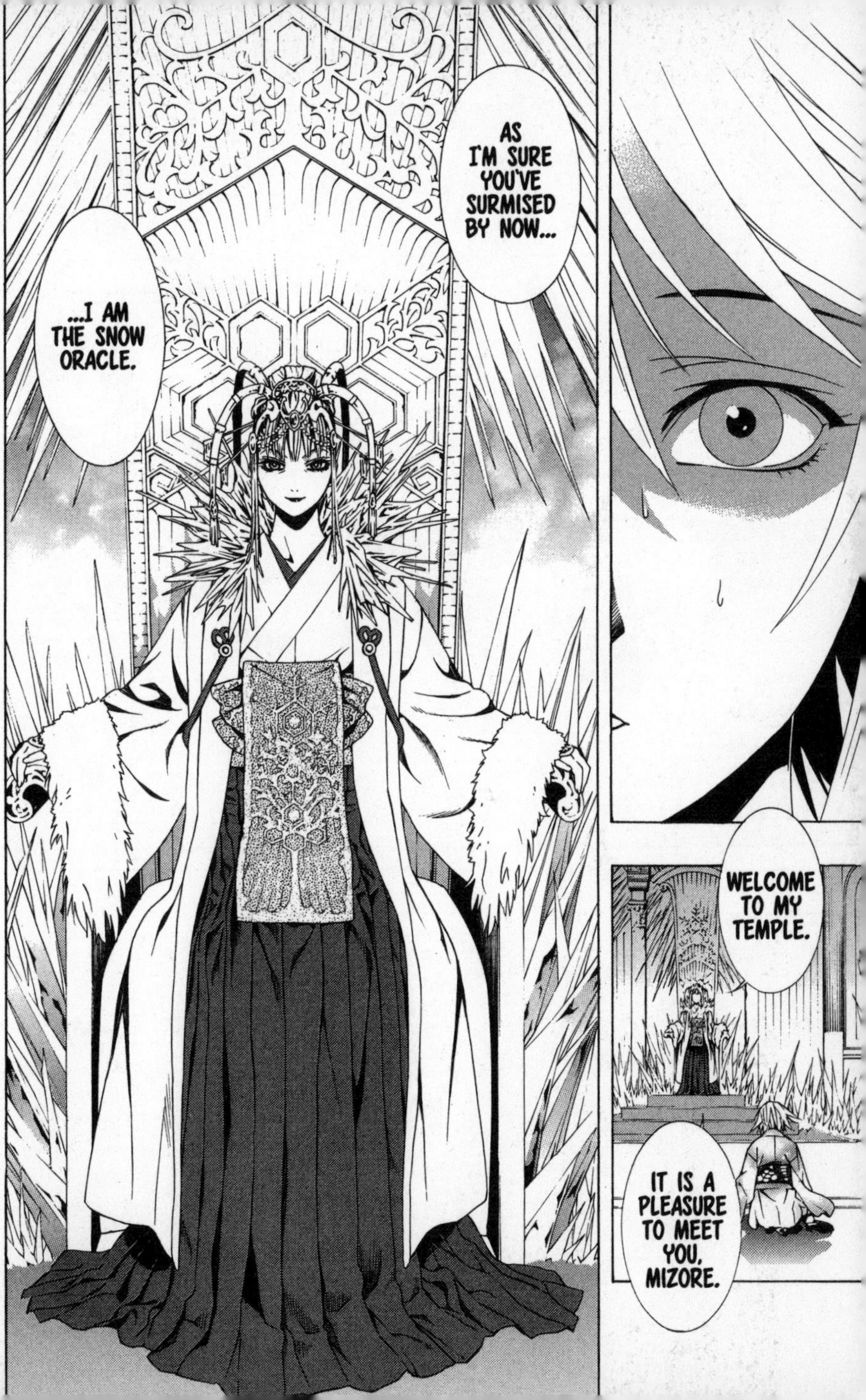
WELCOME TO MY TEMPLE.
IT IS A PLEASURE TO MEET YOU, MIZORE.
AS I'M SURE YOU'VE SURMISED BY NOW...
...I AM THE SNOW ORACLE.

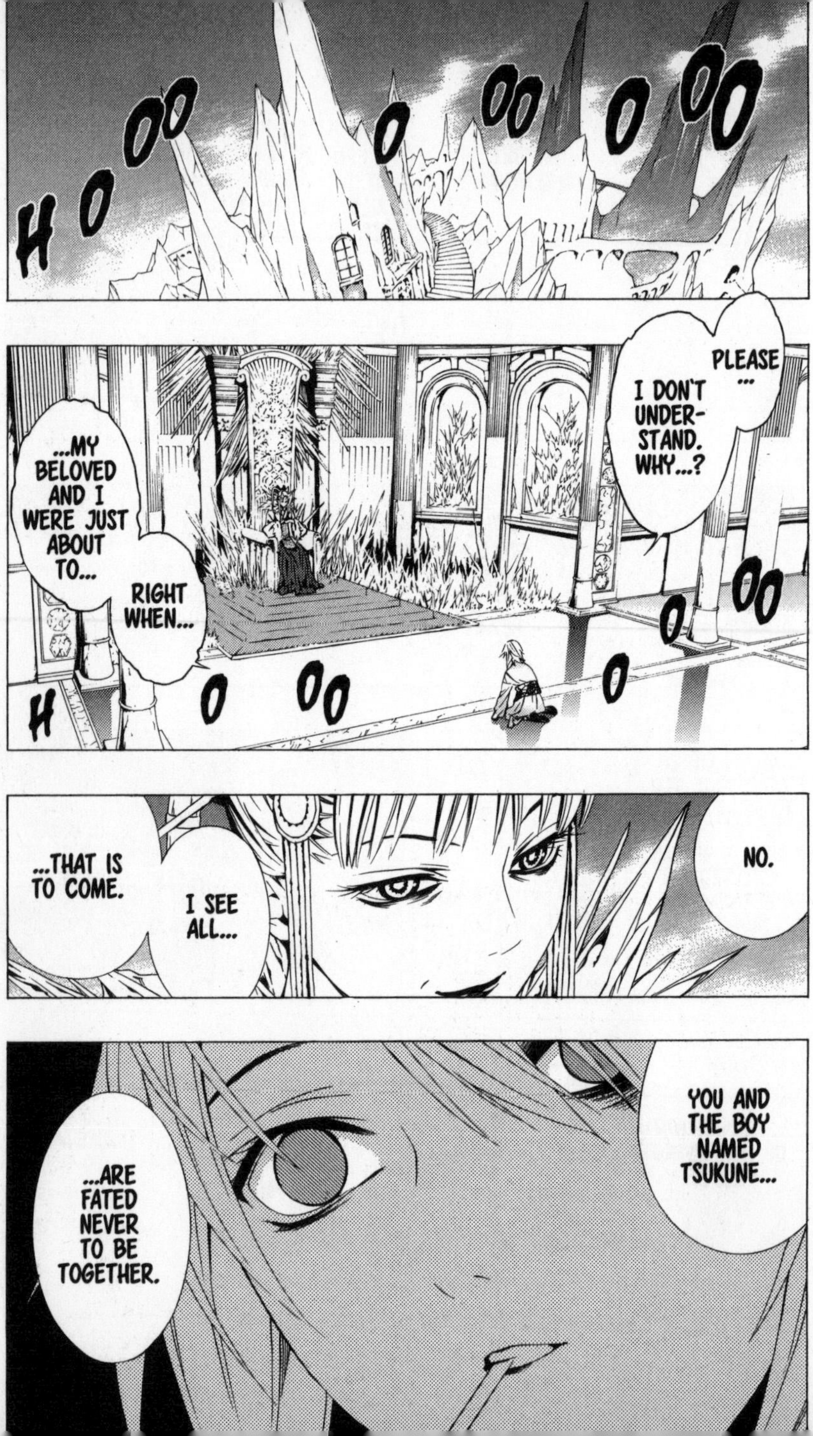
HOOOOOOOOOO
PLEASE...
I DON'T UNDERSTAND. WHY...?
...MY BELOVED AND I WERE JUST ABOUT TO...
RIGHT WHEN...
HOOOOOOO
NO.
I SEE ALL...
...THAT IS TO COME.
YOU AND THE BOY NAMED TSUKUNE...
...ARE FATED NEVER TO BE TOGETHER.

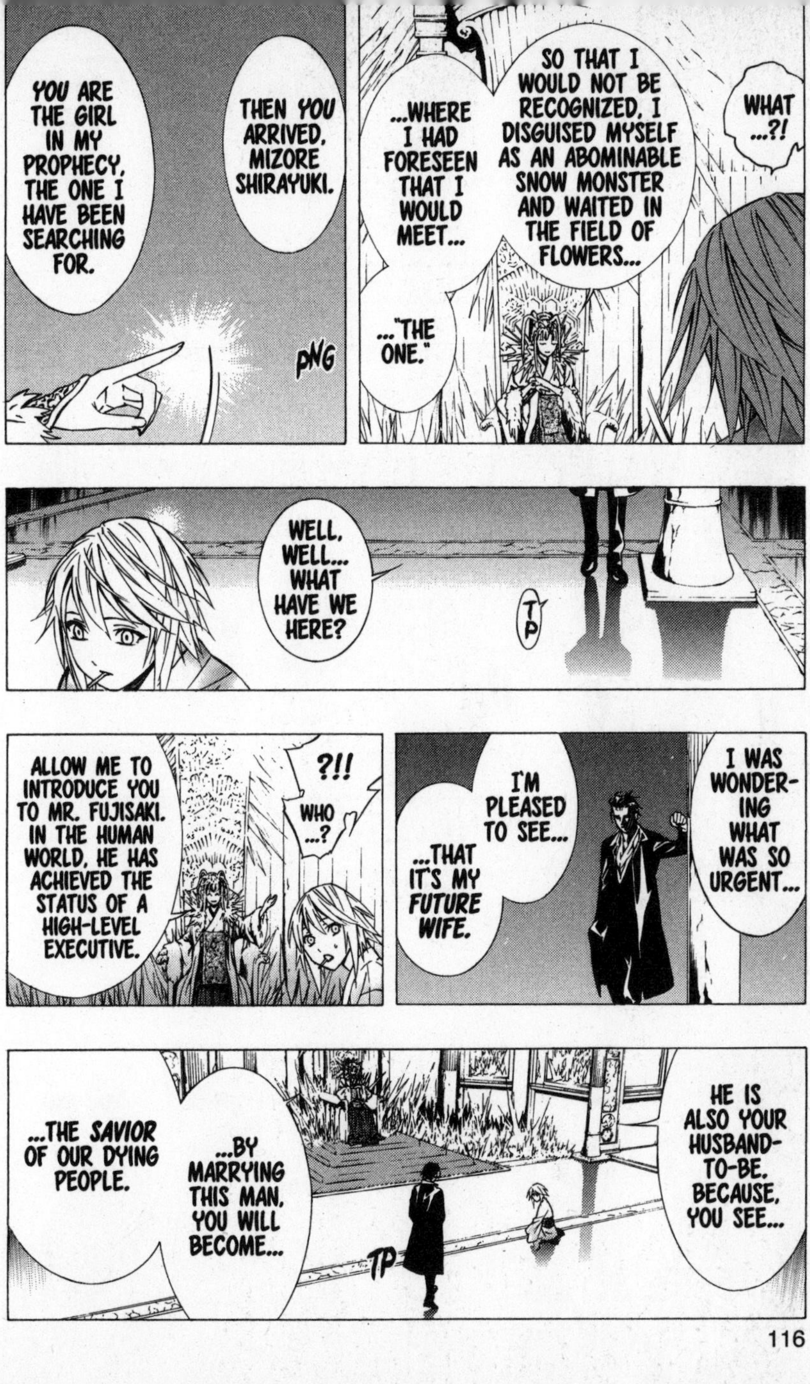
WHAT ...?!
SO THAT I WOULD NOT BE RECOGNIZED, I DISGUISED MYSELF AS AN ABOMINABLE SNOW MONSTER AND WAITED IN THE FIELD OF FLOWERS...
...WHERE I HAD FORESEEN THAT I WOULD MEET...
..."THE ONE."
THEN YOU ARRIVED, MIZORE SHIRAYUKI.
PNG
YOU ARE THE GIRL IN MY PROPHECY, THE ONE I HAVE BEEN SEARCHING FOR.
TP
WELL, WELL... WHAT HAVE WE HERE?
I WAS WONDER-ING WHAT WAS SO URGENT...
I'M PLEASED TO SEE...
...THAT IT'S MY FUTURE WIFE.
?!!
WHO ...?
ALLOW ME TO INTRODUCE YOU TO MR. FUJISAKI. IN THE HUMAN WORLD, HE HAS ACHIEVED THE STATUS OF A HIGH-LEVEL EXECUTIVE.
HE IS ALSO YOUR HUSBAND-TO-BE. BECAUSE, YOU SEE...
...BY MARRYING THIS MAN, YOU WILL BECOME...
...THE SAVIOR OF OUR DYING PEOPLE.
TP

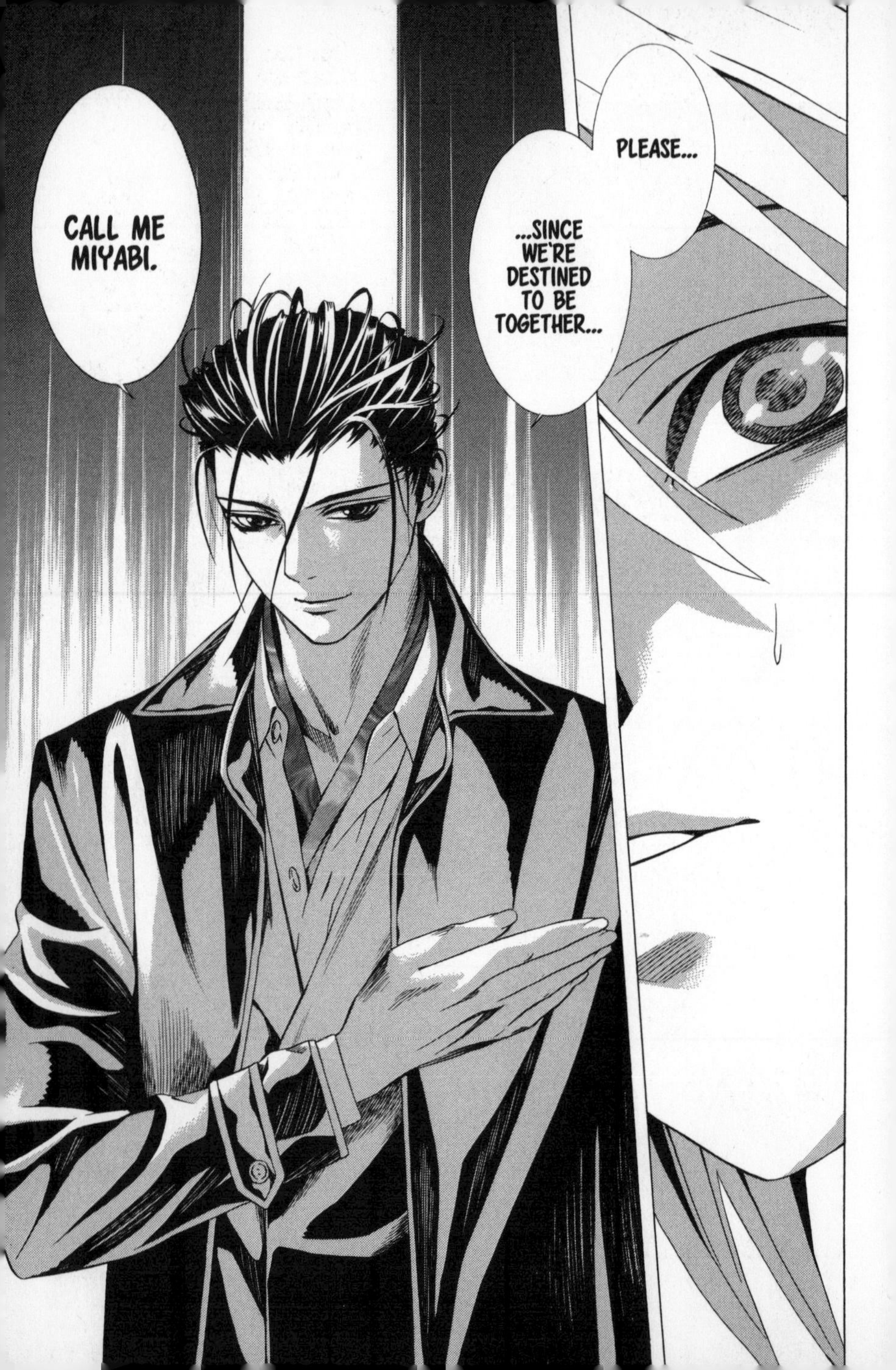
PLEASE...
...SINCE WE'RE DESTINED TO BE TOGETHER...
CALL ME MIYABI.

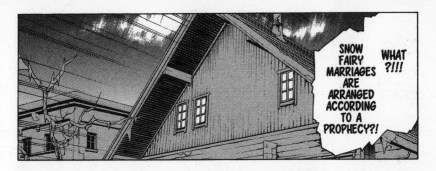

SNOW FAIRY MARRIAGES ARE ARRANGED ACCORDING TO A PROPHECY?!
WHAT ?!!!
TH-THAT'S TERRIBLE!
•••
WE'VE ALL BEEN THROUGH IT.
BUT THERE IS ONE SECRET ONLY WE ADULTS ARE PRIVY TO.
AT TOMOR-ROW'S FLOWER OFFERING...
...MIZORE WILL RECEIVE HER PROPHECY.

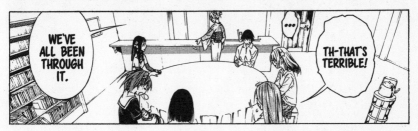

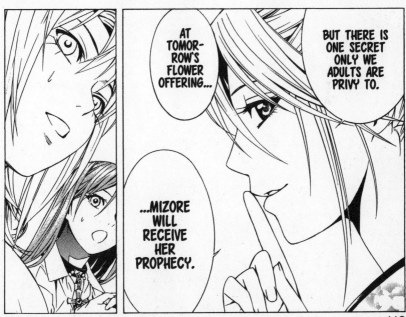

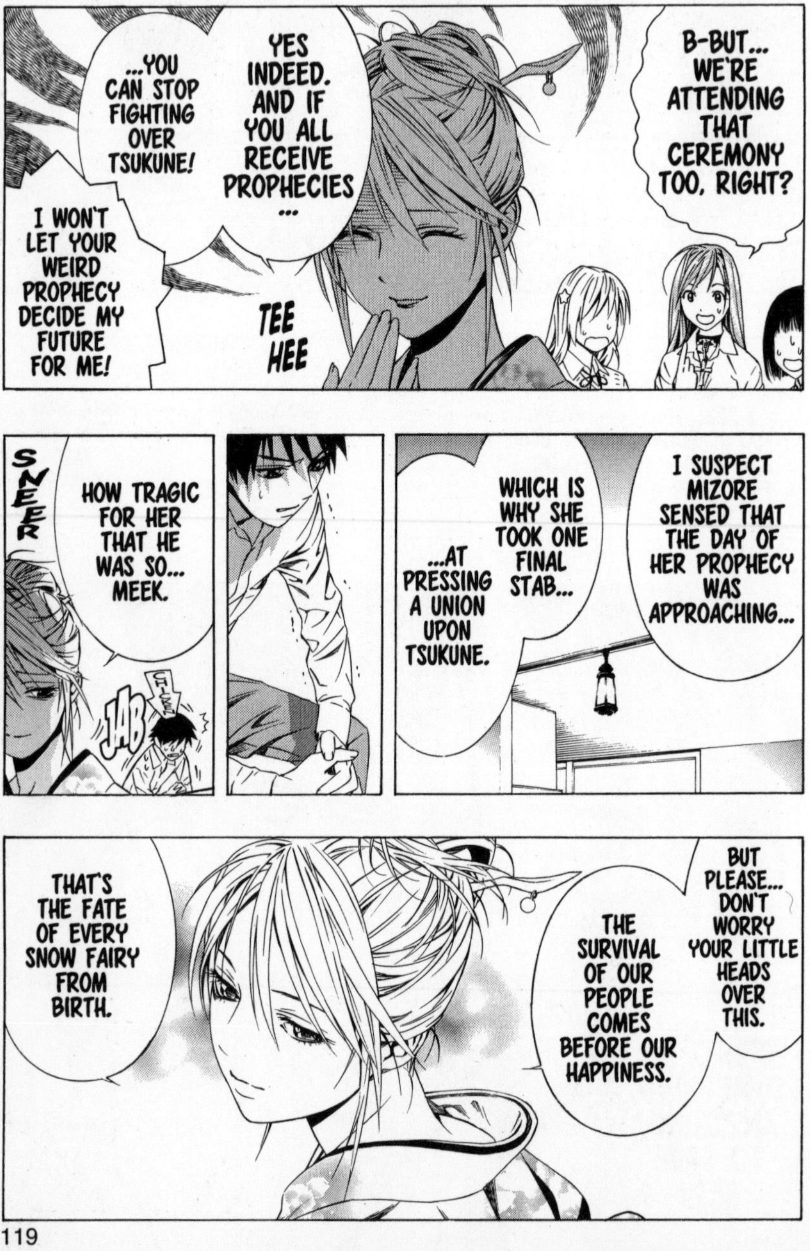
B-BUT... WE'RE ATTENDING THAT CEREMONY TOO, RIGHT?
YES INDEED. AND IF YOU ALL RECEIVE PROPHECIES ...
...YOU CAN STOP FIGHTING OVER TSUKUNE!
TEE HEE
I WON'T LET YOUR WEIRD PROPHECY DECIDE MY FUTURE FOR ME!
I SUSPECT MIZORE SENSED THAT THE DAY OF HER PROPHECY WAS APPROACHING...
WHICH IS WHY SHE TOOK ONE FINAL STAB...
...AT PRESSING A UNION UPON TSUKUNE.
SNEER
HOW TRAGIC FOR HER THAT HE WAS SO... MEEK.
JAB
BUT PLEASE... DON'T WORRY YOUR LITTLE HEADS OVER THIS.
THE SURVIVAL OF OUR PEOPLE COMES BEFORE OUR HAPPINESS.
THAT'S THE FATE OF EVERY SNOW FAIRY FROM BIRTH.

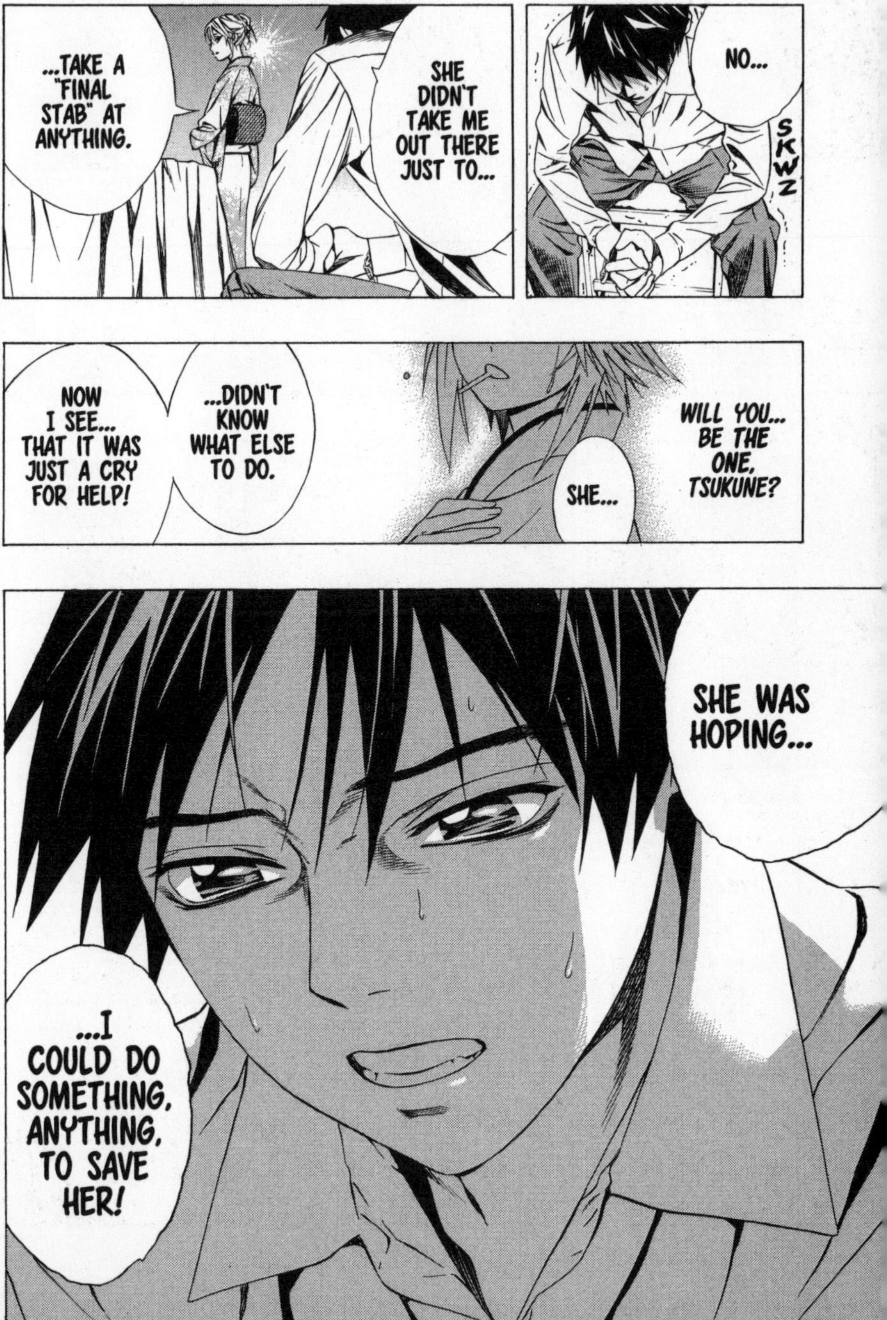
NO...
SKWZ
SHE DIDN'T TAKE ME OUT THERE JUST TO...
...TAKE A "FINAL STAB" AT ANYTHING.
WILL YOU... BE THE ONE, TSUKUNE?
SHE...
...DIDN'T KNOW WHAT ELSE TO DO.
NOW I SEE... THAT IT WAS JUST A CRY FOR HELP!
SHE WAS HOPING...
...I COULD DO SOMETHING, ANYTHING, TO SAVE HER!

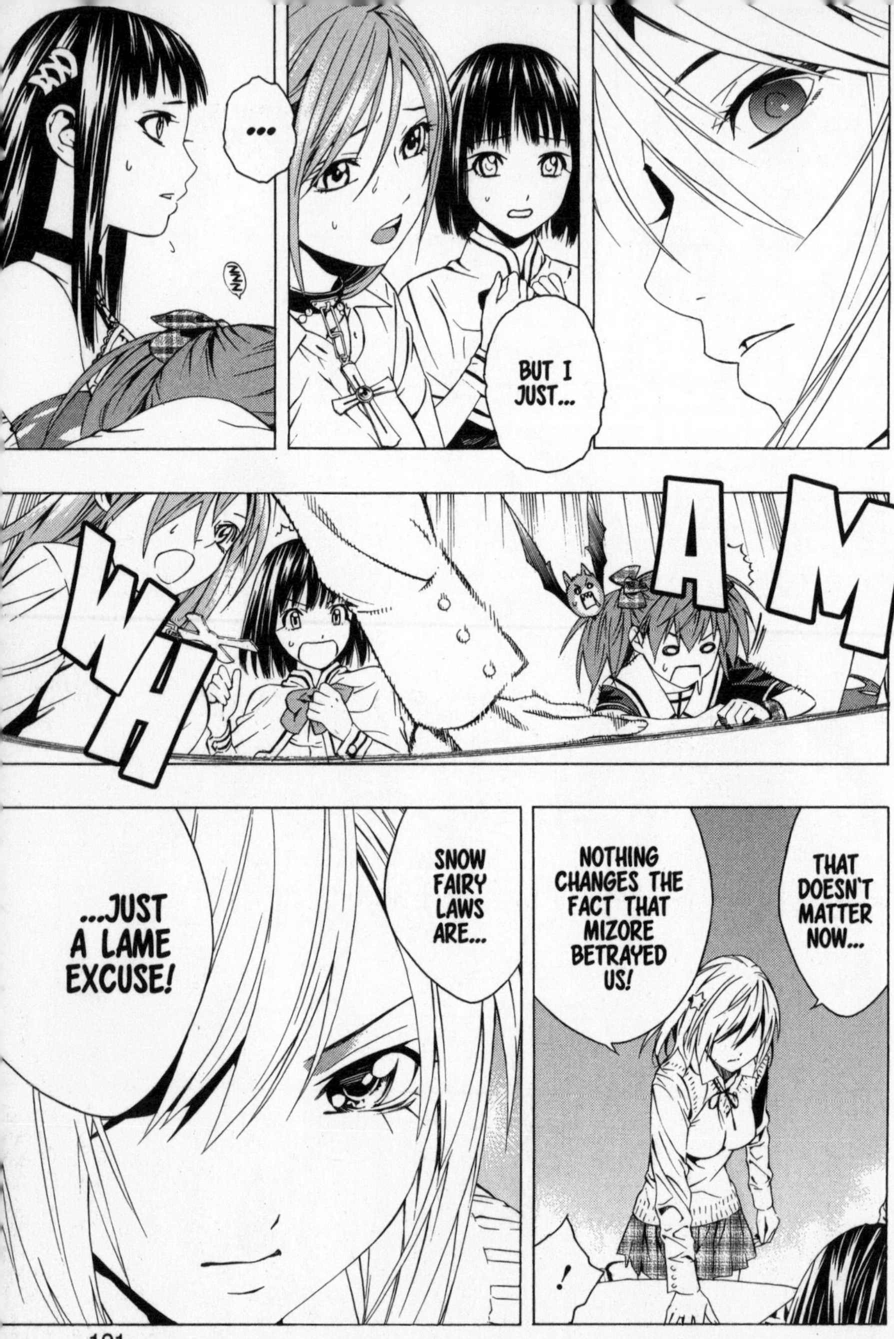
BUT I JUST...
...
NNN
WHAM
THAT DOESN'T MATTER NOW...
NOTHING CHANGES THE FACT THAT MIZORE BETRAYED US!
!
SNOW FAIRY LAWS ARE...
...JUST A LAME EXCUSE!

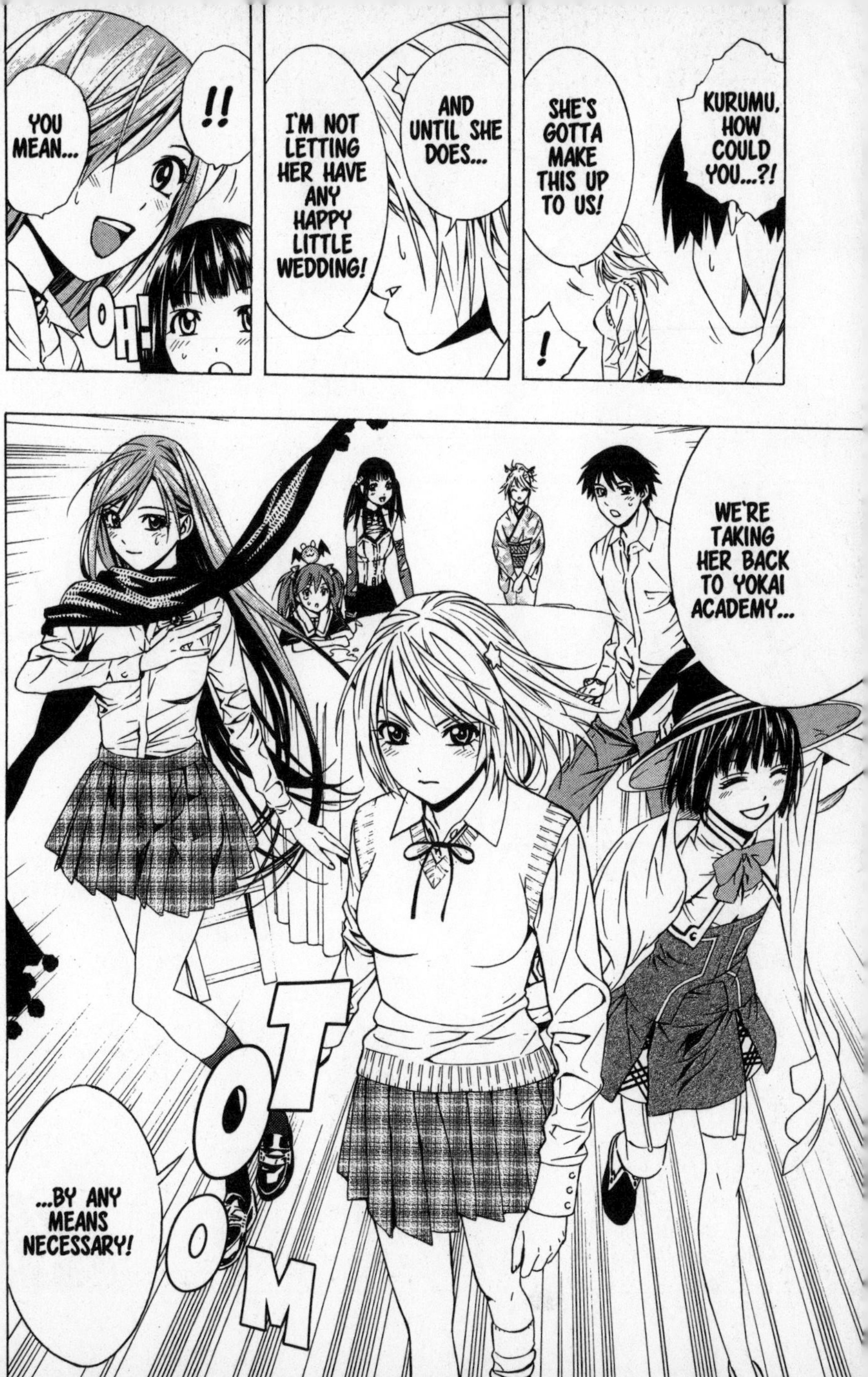
KURUMU, HOW COULD YOU...?!
SHE'S GOTTA MAKE THIS UP TO US!
!
AND UNTIL SHE DOES...
I'M NOT LETTING HER HAVE ANY HAPPY LITTLE WEDDING!
!!
YOU MEAN...
OH!
WE'RE TAKING HER BACK TO YOKAI ACADEMY...
TOOOM
...BY ANY MEANS NECESSARY!

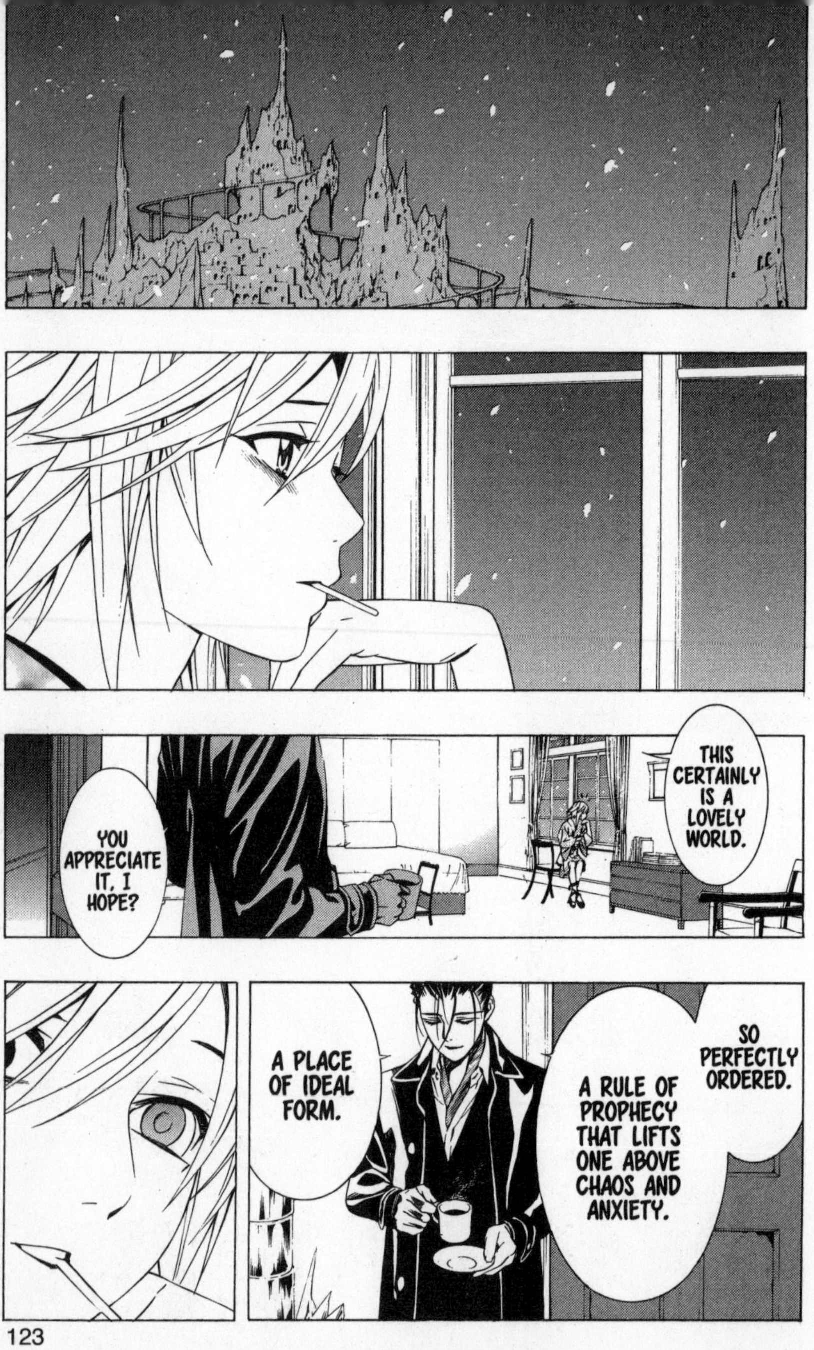
THIS CERTAINLY IS A LOVELY WORLD.
YOU APPRECIATE IT, I HOPE?
SO PERFECTLY ORDERED.
A RULE OF PROPHECY THAT LIFTS ONE ABOVE CHAOS AND ANXIETY.
A PLACE OF IDEAL FORM.

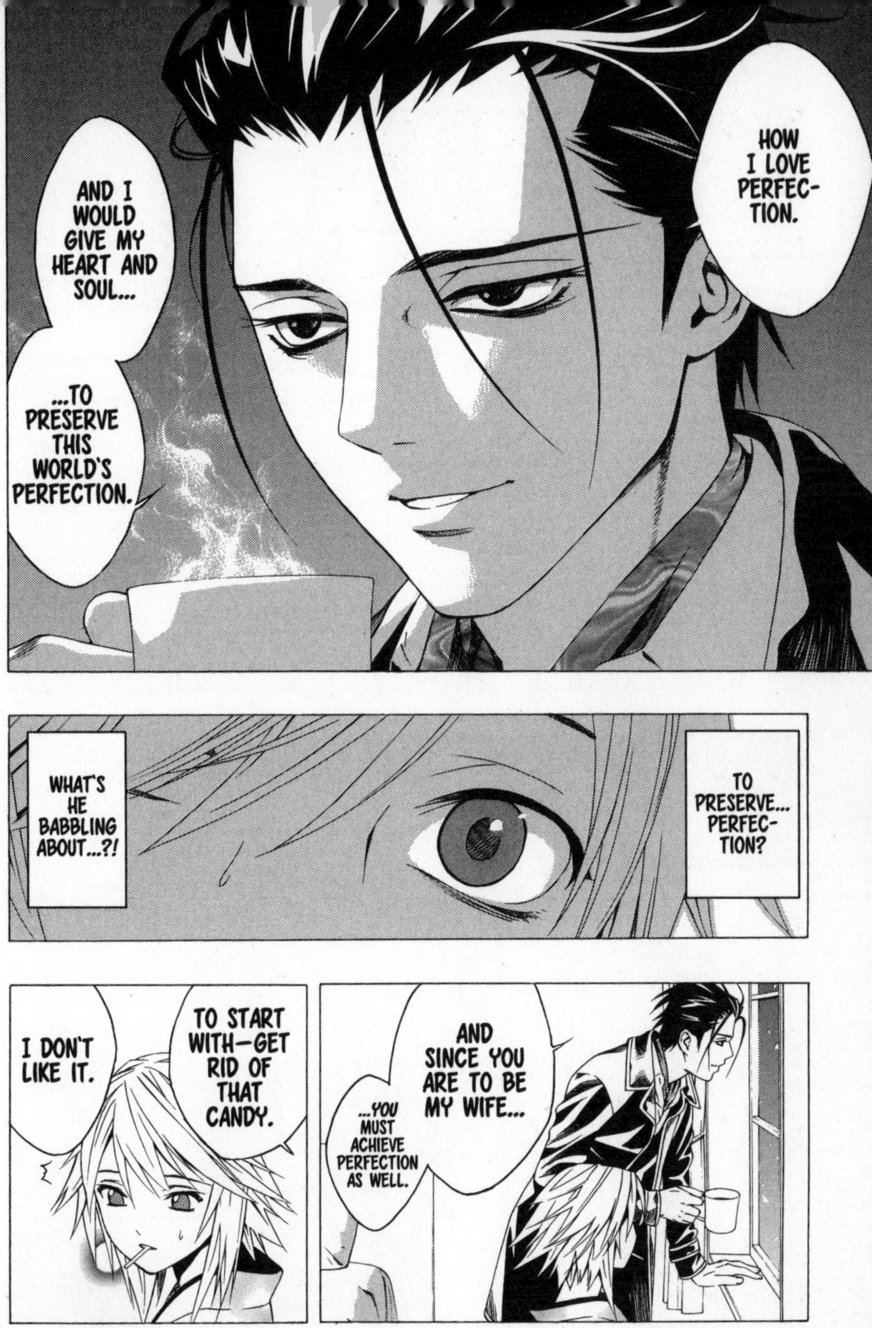
HOW I LOVE PERFECTION.
AND I WOULD GIVE MY HEART AND SOUL...
...TO PRESERVE THIS WORLD'S PERFECTION.
TO PRESERVE... PERFECTION?
WHAT'S HE BABBLING ABOUT...?!
AND SINCE YOU ARE TO BE MY WIFE...
...YOU MUST ACHIEVE PERFECTION AS WELL.
TO START WITH—GET RID OF THAT CANDY.
I DON'T LIKE IT.

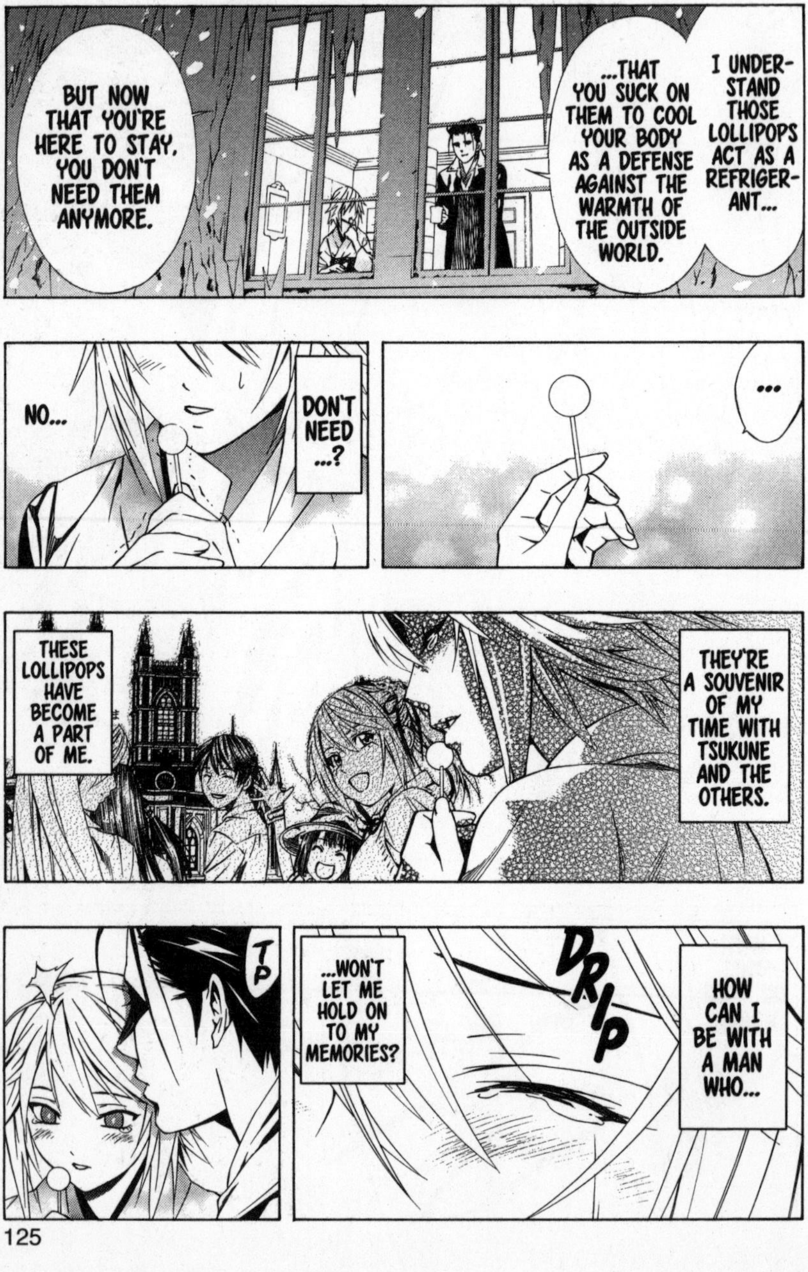
I UNDER-STAND THOSE LOLLIPOPS ACT AS A REFRIGER-ANT...
...THAT YOU SUCK ON THEM TO COOL YOUR BODY AS A DEFENSE AGAINST THE WARMTH OF THE OUTSIDE WORLD.
BUT NOW THAT YOU'RE HERE TO STAY, YOU DON'T NEED THEM ANYMORE.
...
DON'T NEED ...?
NO...
THEY'RE A SOUVENIR OF MY TIME WITH TSUKUNE AND THE OTHERS.
THESE LOLLIPOPS HAVE BECOME A PART OF ME.
HOW CAN I BE WITH A MAN WHO...
...WON'T LET ME HOLD ON TO MY MEMORIES?
DRIP
TP

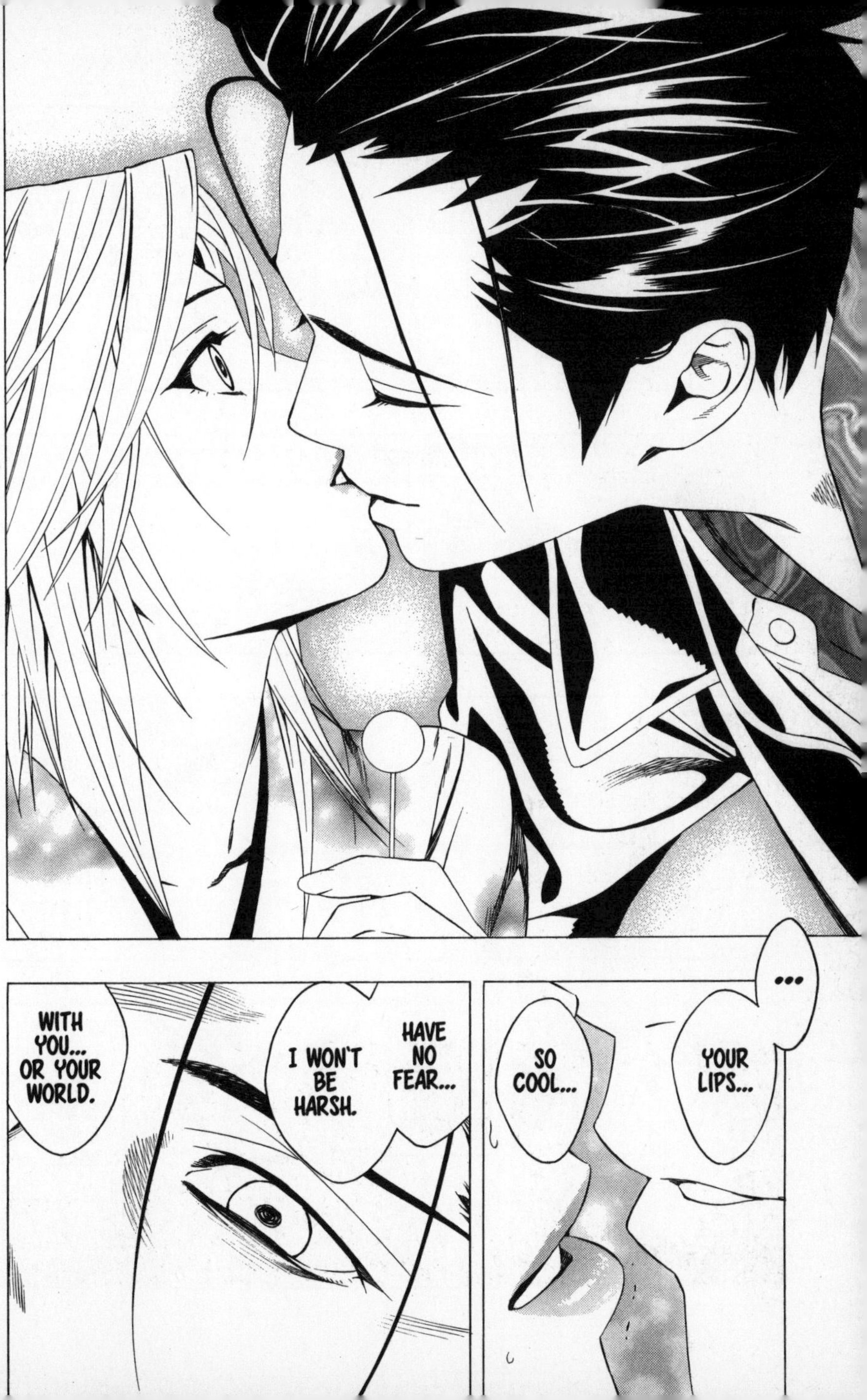
...
YOUR LIPS...
SO COOL...
HAVE NO FEAR...
I WON'T BE HARSH.
WITH YOU... OR YOUR WORLD.

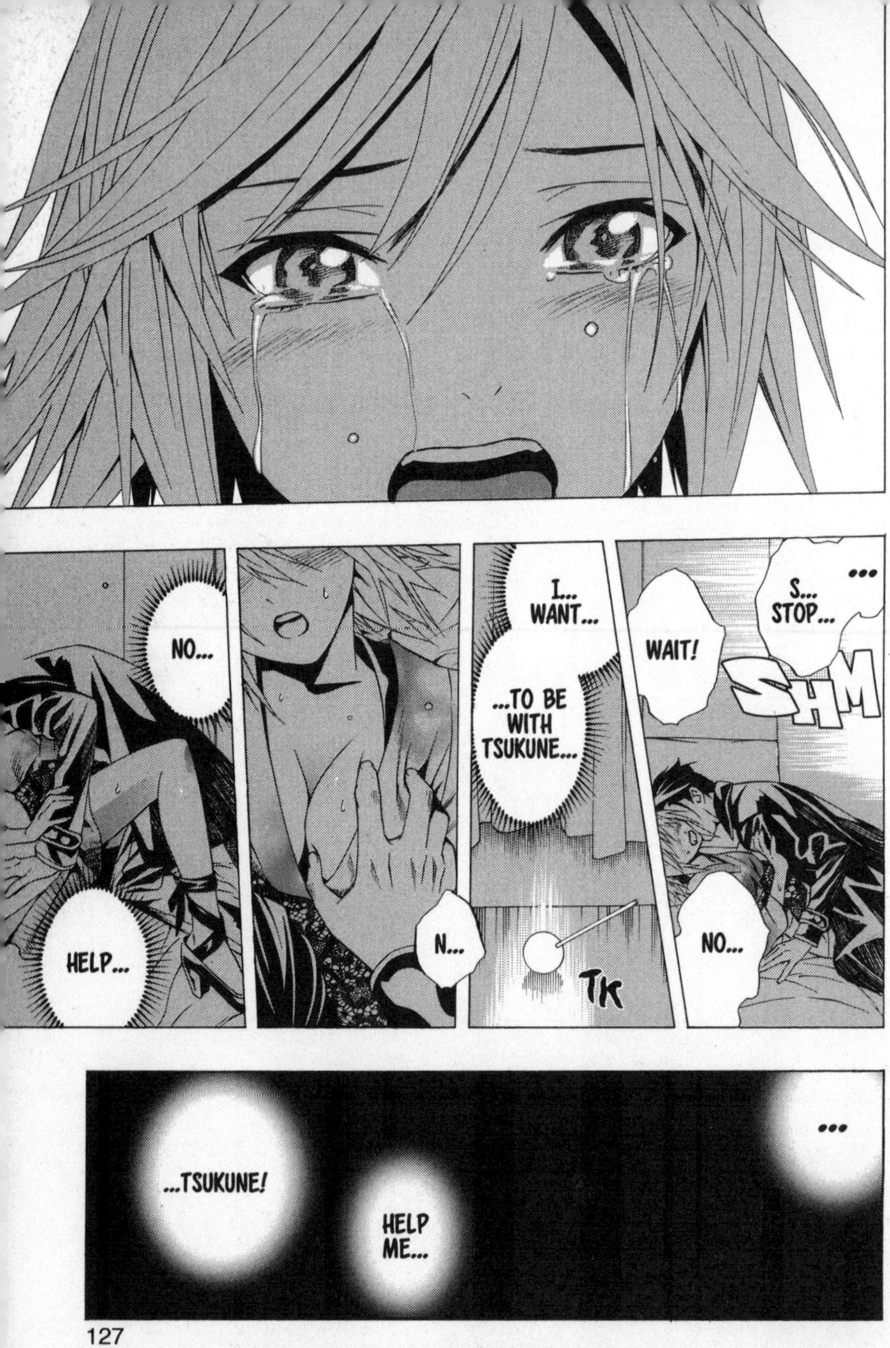
...
S... STOP...
WAIT!
SHM
NO...
I... WANT...
...TO BE WITH TSUKUNE...
TK
N...
NO...
HELP...
...
HELP ME...
...TSUKUNE!

12: The Offering
of the Flower

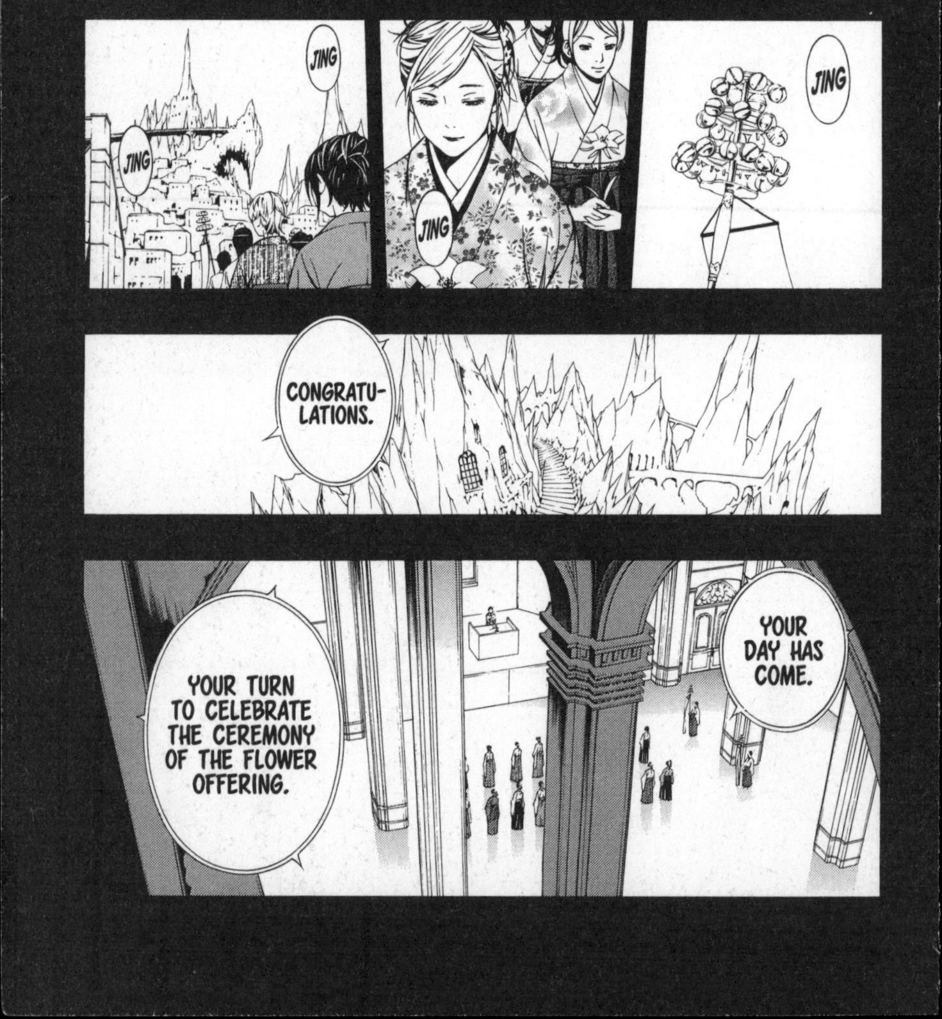
JING
JING
JING
JING
CONGRATU-LATIONS.
YOUR DAY HAS COME.
YOUR TURN TO CELEBRATE THE CEREMONY OF THE FLOWER OFFERING.

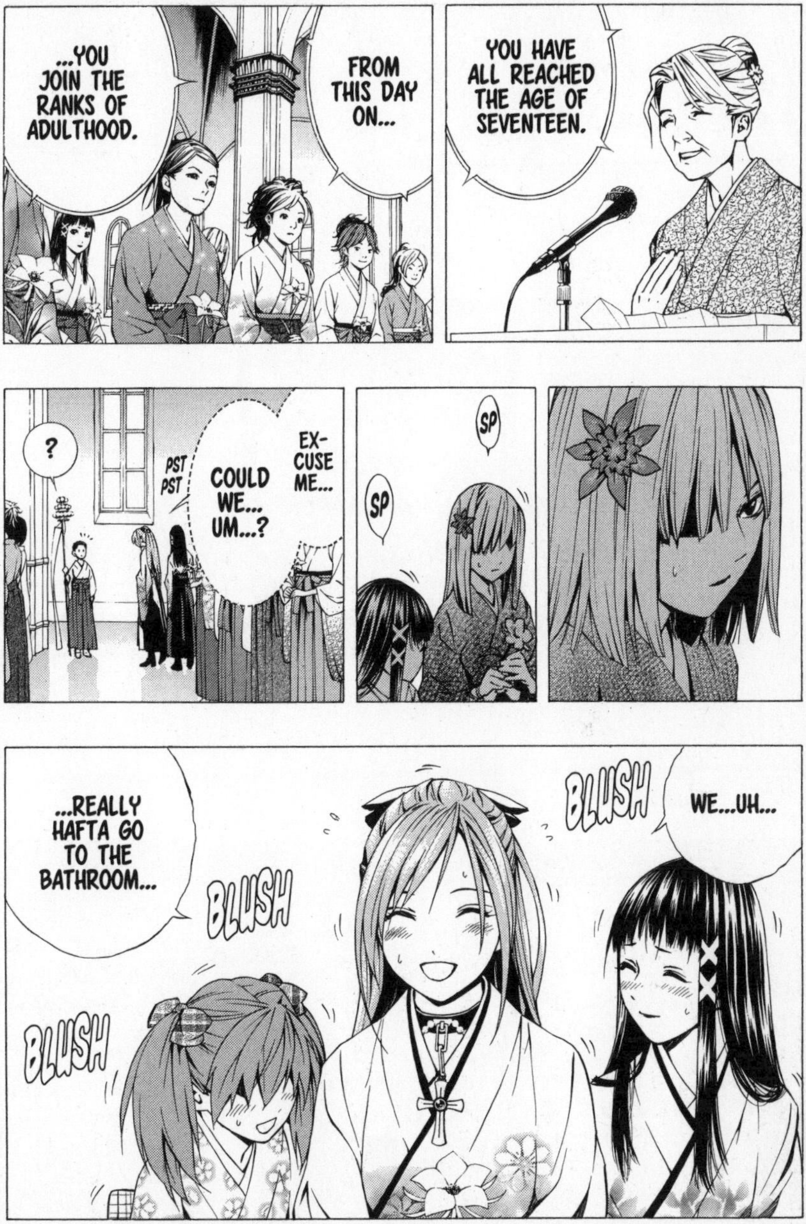
YOU HAVE ALL REACHED THE AGE OF SEVENTEEN.
FROM THIS DAY ON...
...YOU JOIN THE RANKS OF ADULTHOOD.
SP
SP
EX-CUSE ME...
COULD WE... UM...?
PST PST
?
WE...UH...
BLUSH
...REALLY HAFTA GO TO THE BATHROOM...
BLUSH
BLUSH

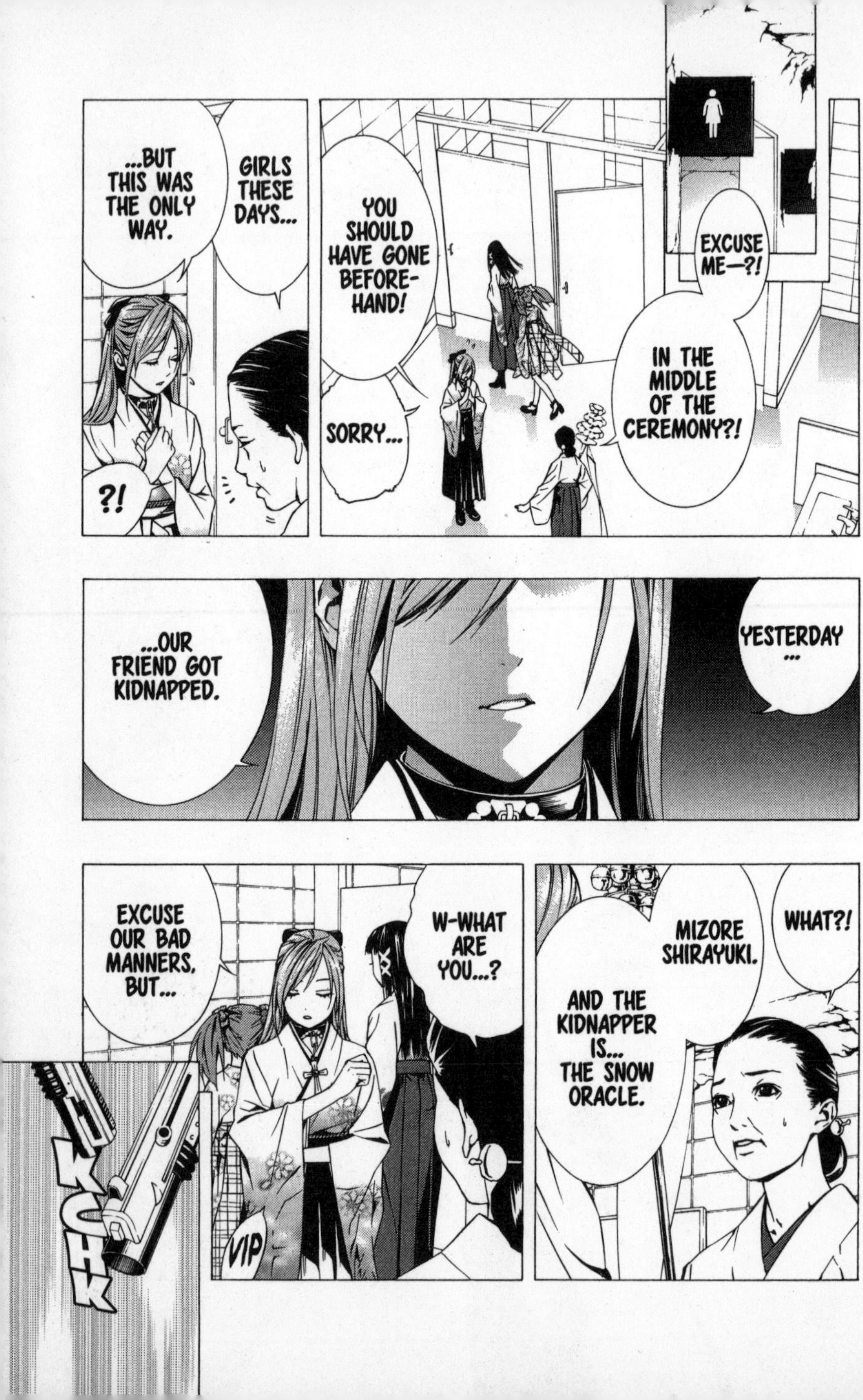
EXCUSE ME—?!
IN THE MIDDLE OF THE CEREMONY?!
YOU SHOULD HAVE GONE BEFORE-HAND!
SORRY...
GIRLS THESE DAYS...
...BUT THIS WAS THE ONLY WAY.
?!
YESTERDAY ...
...OUR FRIEND GOT KIDNAPPED.
WHAT?!
MIZORE SHIRAYUKI.
AND THE KIDNAPPER IS... THE SNOW ORACLE.
W-WHAT ARE YOU...?
EXCUSE OUR BAD MANNERS, BUT...
VIP
KCHK

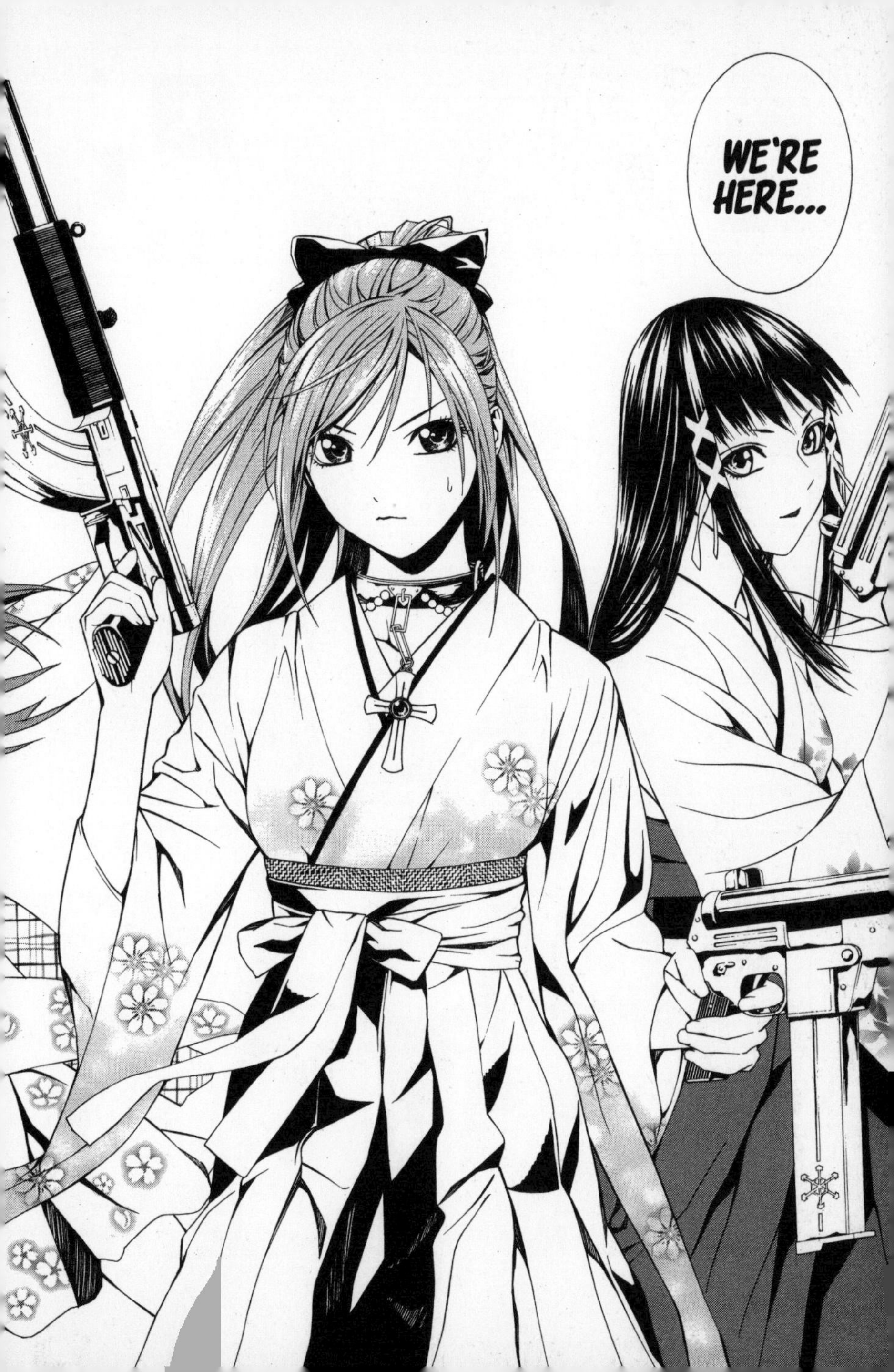
WE'RE HERE...

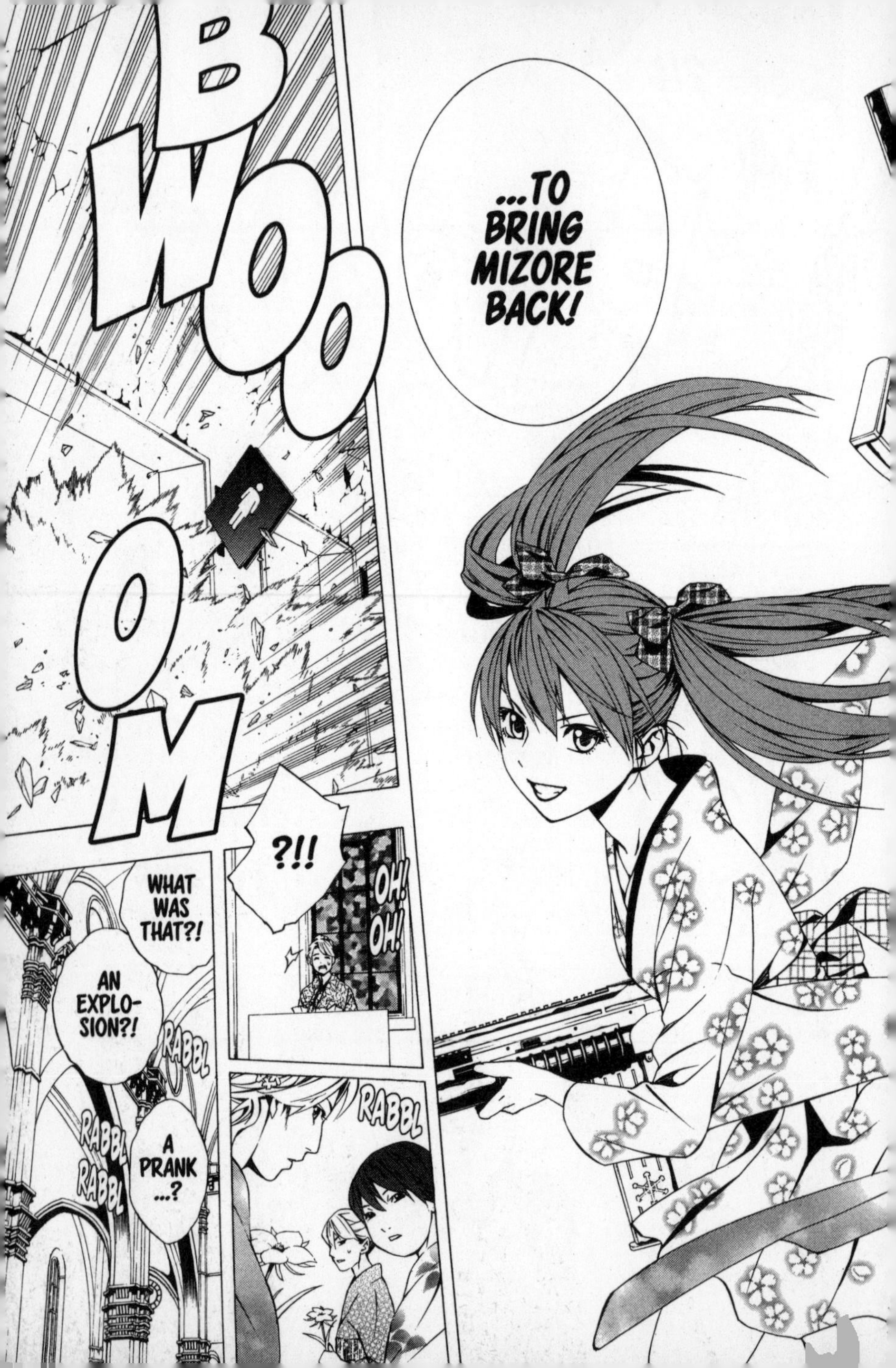
...TO BRING MIZORE BACK!
BWOOOOM
?!!
OH! OH!
RABBL
WHAT WAS THAT?!
AN EXPLOSION?!
RABBL
RABBL RABBL
A PRANK ...?

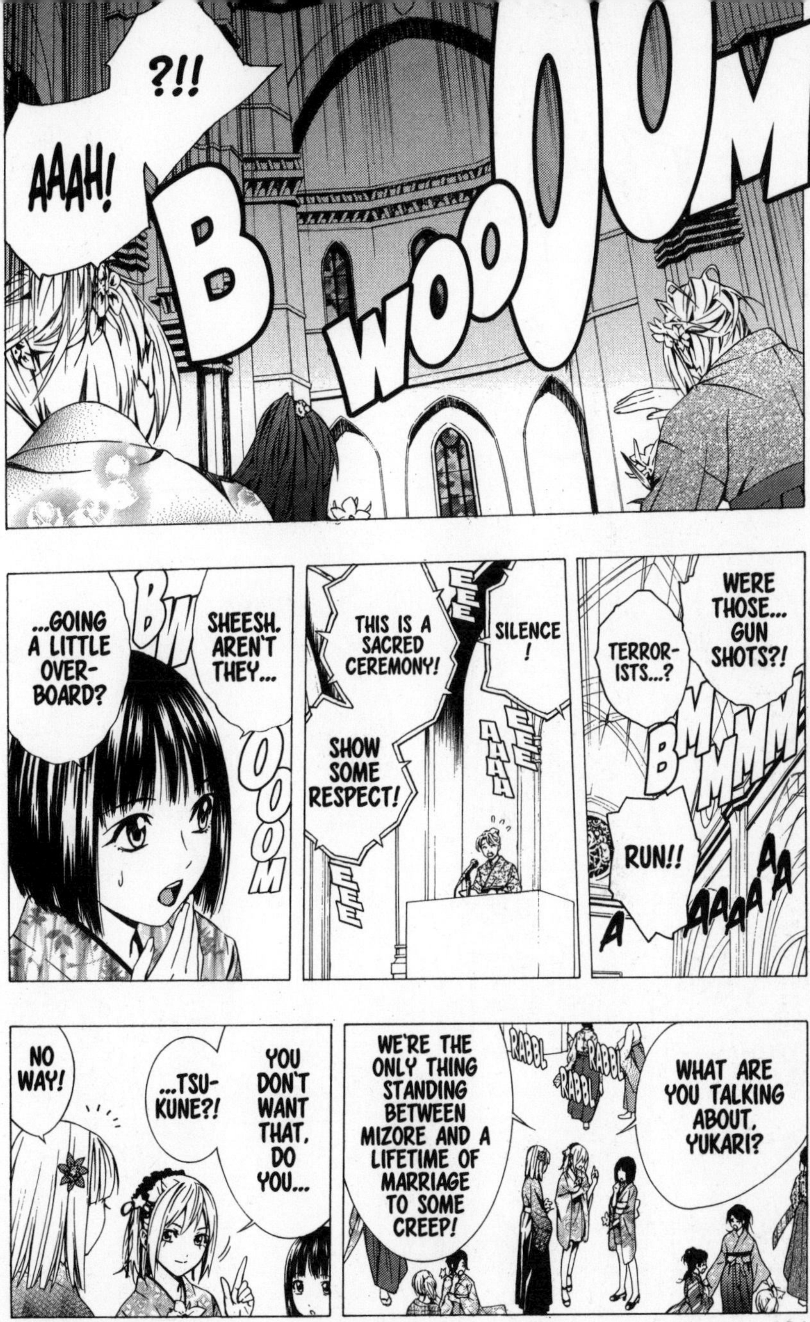
BWOOOOM
?!!
AAAH!
WERE THOSE... GUN SHOTS?!
TERRORISTS...?
BMMMMMMM
RUN!!
AAAAAAA
SILENCE!
THIS IS A SACRED CEREMONY!
SHOW SOME RESPECT!
EEEEEEAAAAEEE
SHEESH. AREN'T THEY...
...GOING A LITTLE OVERBOARD?
BWOOOOM
WHAT ARE YOU TALKING ABOUT, YUKARI?
RABBL RABBL RABBL
WE'RE THE ONLY THING STANDING BETWEEN MIZORE AND A LIFETIME OF MARRIAGE TO SOME CREEP!
YOU DON'T WANT THAT, DO YOU...
...TSUKUNE?!
NO WAY!

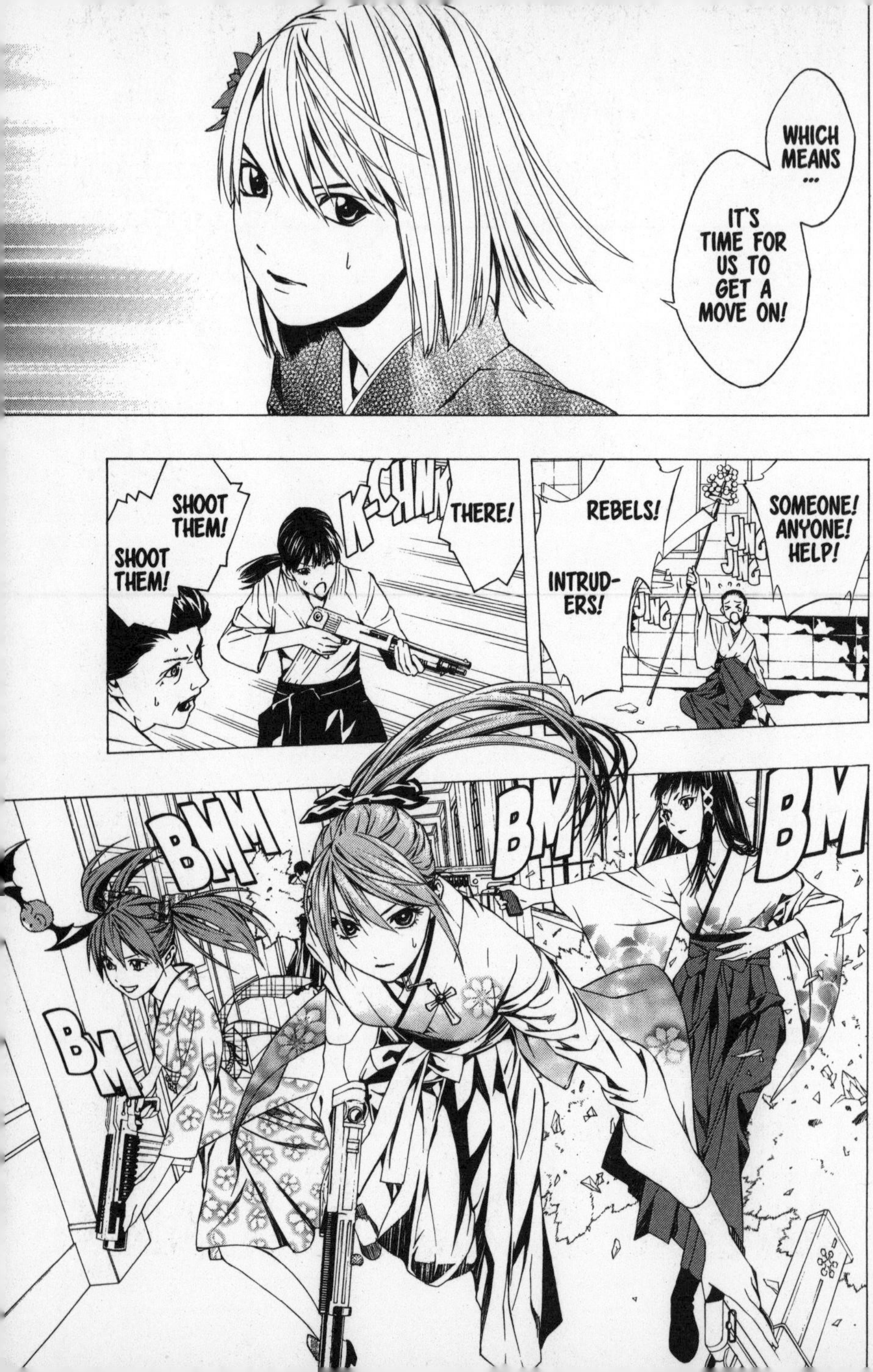
WHICH MEANS ...
IT'S TIME FOR US TO GET A MOVE ON!
SOMEONE! ANYONE! HELP!
JING JING
REBELS!
JING
INTRUD-ERS!
THERE!
K-CHUNK
SHOOT THEM!
SHOOT THEM!
BM
BM
BMM
BM

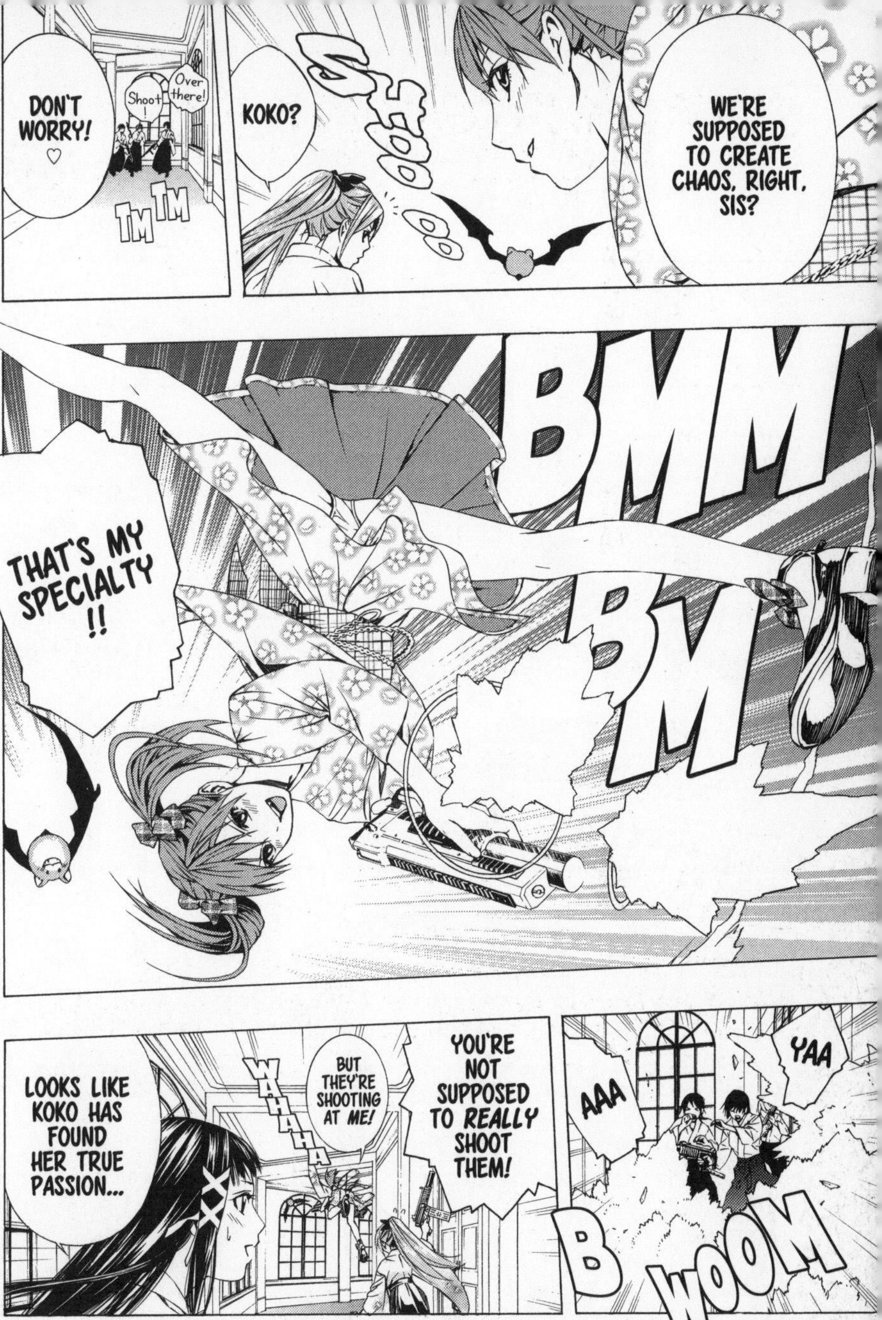
WE'RE SUPPOSED TO CREATE CHAOS, RIGHT, SIS?
SHOOOOO
KOKO?
Over there!
Shoot!
DON'T WORRY! ♡
TM TM
BMM
BM
THAT'S MY SPECIALTY !!
YAA
AAA
BWOOM
YOU'RE NOT SUPPOSED TO *REALLY* SHOOT THEM!
BUT THEY'RE SHOOTING AT *ME!*
WAHAHA
LOOKS LIKE KOKO HAS FOUND HER TRUE PASSION...

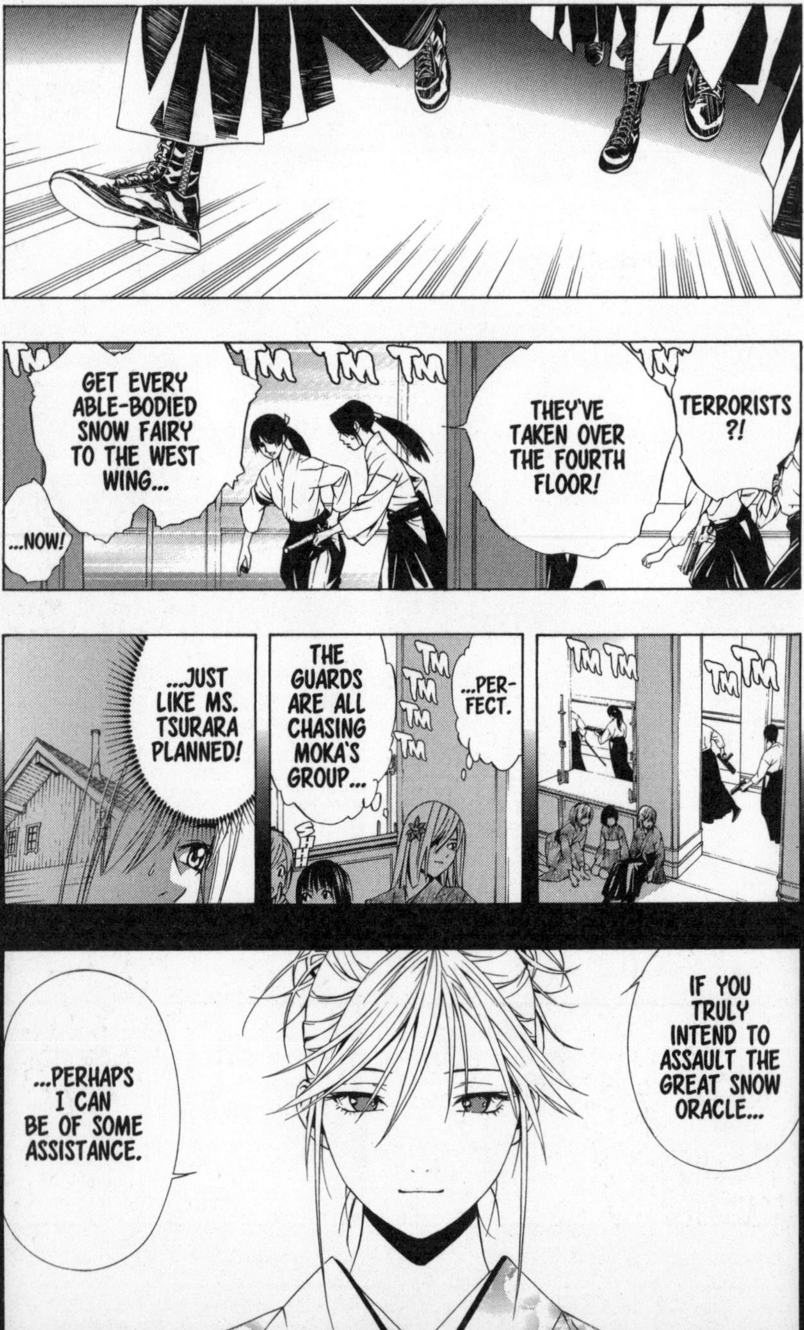
TM
TERRORISTS?!
THEY'VE TAKEN OVER THE FOURTH FLOOR!
TM TM TM
GET EVERY ABLE-BODIED SNOW FAIRY TO THE WEST WING...
TM
...NOW!
TM TM TM TM
THE GUARDS ARE ALL CHASING MOKA'S GROUP...
...PER-FECT.
TM TM TM TM
SHH
...JUST LIKE MS. TSURARA PLANNED!
IF YOU TRULY INTEND TO ASSAULT THE GREAT SNOW ORACLE...
...PERHAPS I CAN BE OF SOME ASSISTANCE.

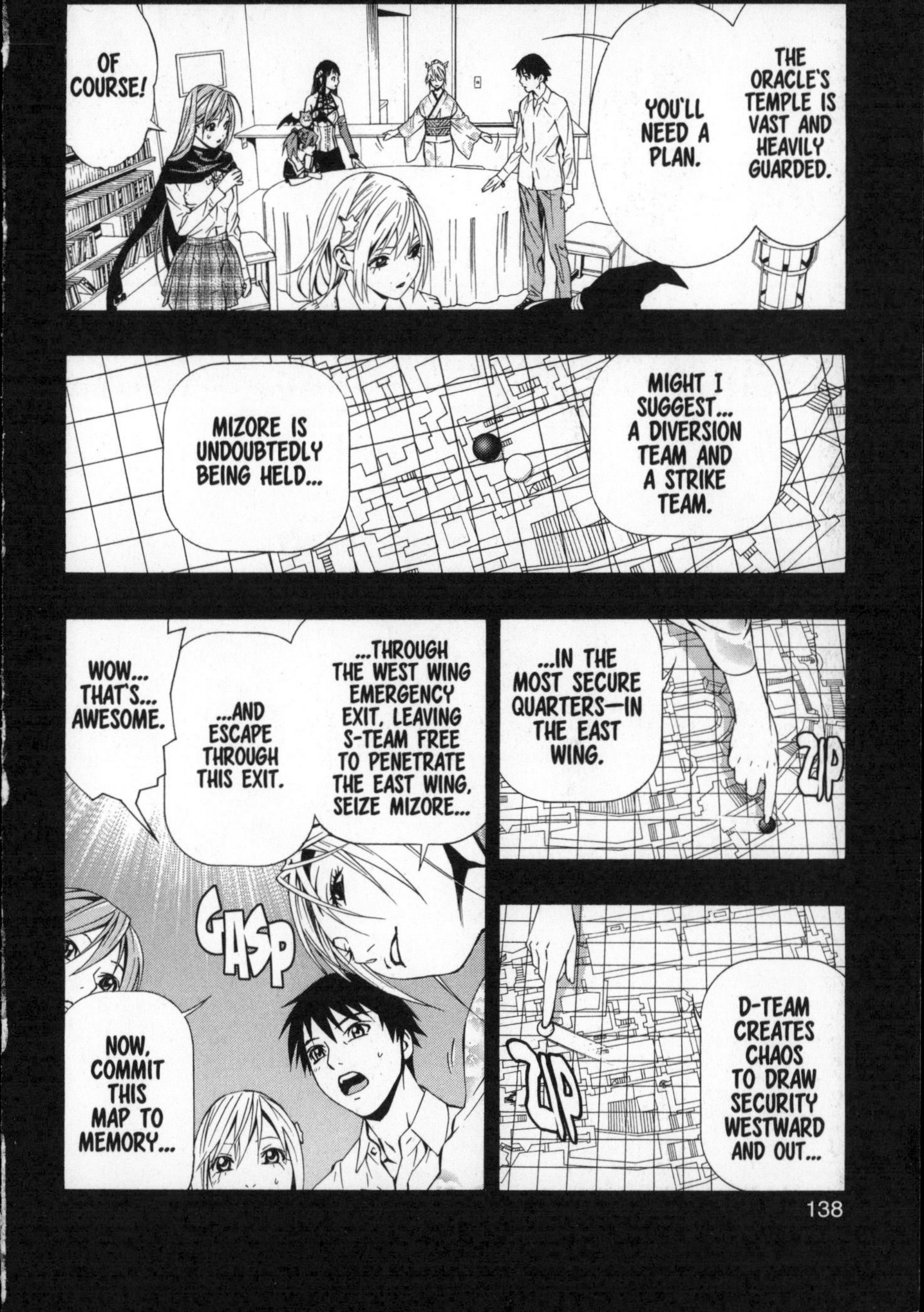
THE ORACLE'S TEMPLE IS VAST AND HEAVILY GUARDED.
YOU'LL NEED A PLAN.
OF COURSE!
MIGHT I SUGGEST... A DIVERSION TEAM AND A STRIKE TEAM.
MIZORE IS UNDOUBTEDLY BEING HELD...
...IN THE MOST SECURE QUARTERS—IN THE EAST WING.
ZIP
D-TEAM CREATES CHAOS TO DRAW SECURITY WESTWARD AND OUT...
ZIP
...THROUGH THE WEST WING EMERGENCY EXIT, LEAVING S-TEAM FREE TO PENETRATE THE EAST WING, SEIZE MIZORE...
...AND ESCAPE THROUGH THIS EXIT.
WOW... THAT'S... AWESOME.
GASP
NOW, COMMIT THIS MAP TO MEMORY...

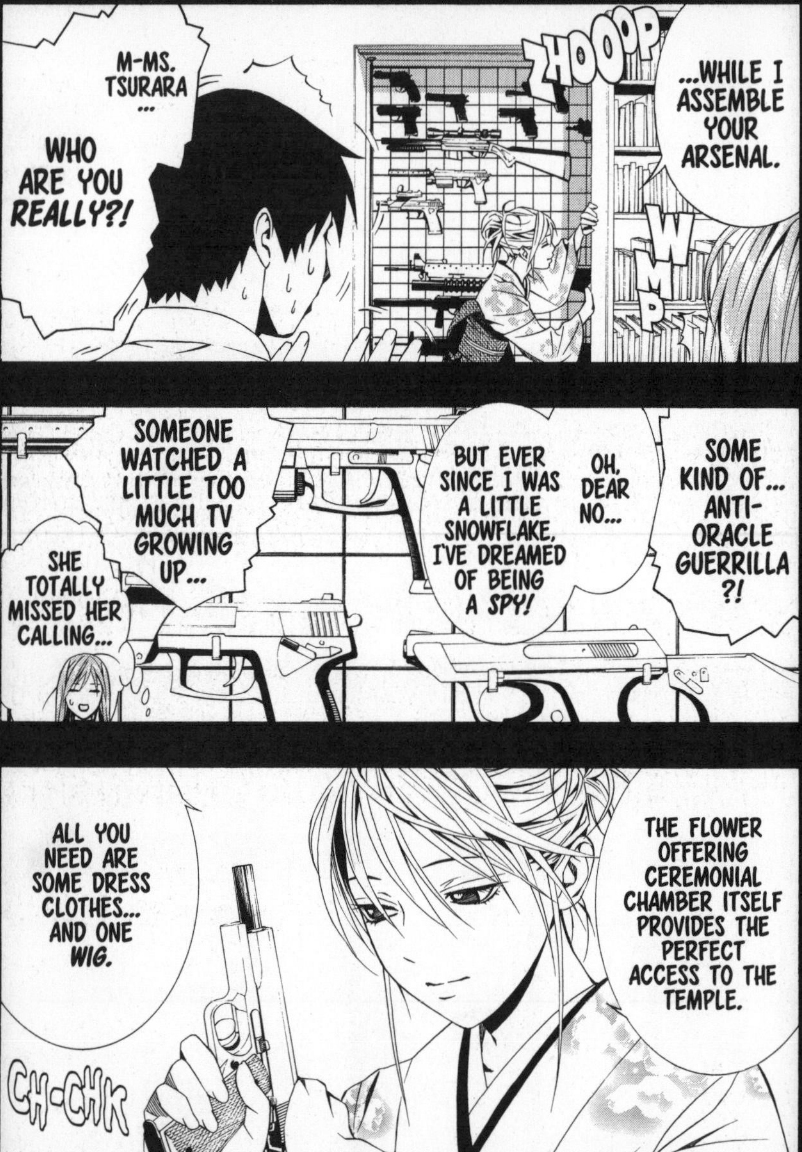
...WHILE I ASSEMBLE YOUR ARSENAL.
ZHOOOP
WMP
M-MS. TSURARA...
WHO ARE YOU REALLY?!
SOME KIND OF... ANTI-ORACLE GUERRILLA?!
OH, DEAR NO...
BUT EVER SINCE I WAS A LITTLE SNOWFLAKE, I'VE DREAMED OF BEING A SPY!
SOMEONE WATCHED A LITTLE TOO MUCH TV GROWING UP...
SHE TOTALLY MISSED HER CALLING...
THE FLOWER OFFERING CEREMONIAL CHAMBER ITSELF PROVIDES THE PERFECT ACCESS TO THE TEMPLE.
ALL YOU NEED ARE SOME DRESS CLOTHES... AND ONE WIG.
CH-CHK

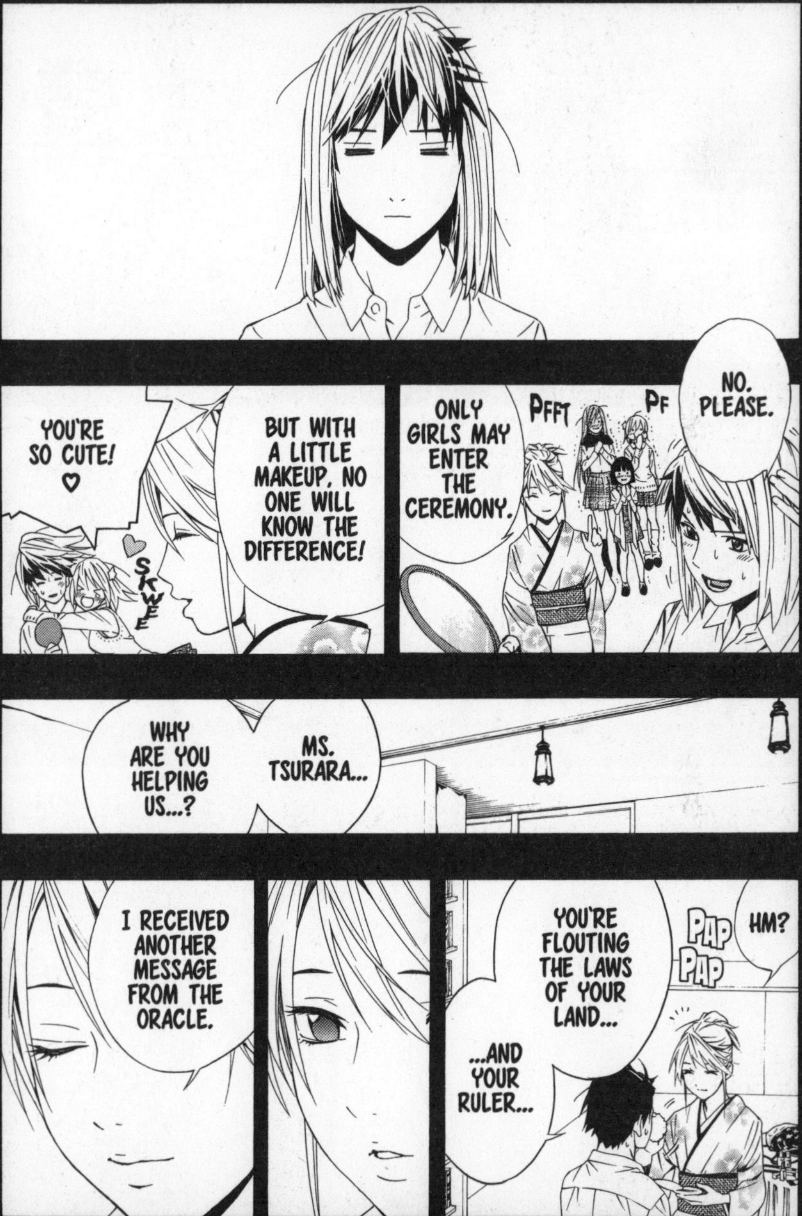
NO. PLEASE.
PF
PFFT
ONLY GIRLS MAY ENTER THE CEREMONY.
BUT WITH A LITTLE MAKEUP, NO ONE WILL KNOW THE DIFFERENCE!
SKWEE
YOU'RE SO CUTE! ♡
MS. TSURARA...
WHY ARE YOU HELPING US...?
HM?
PAP PAP
YOU'RE FLOUTING THE LAWS OF YOUR LAND...
...AND YOUR RULER...
I RECEIVED ANOTHER MESSAGE FROM THE ORACLE.

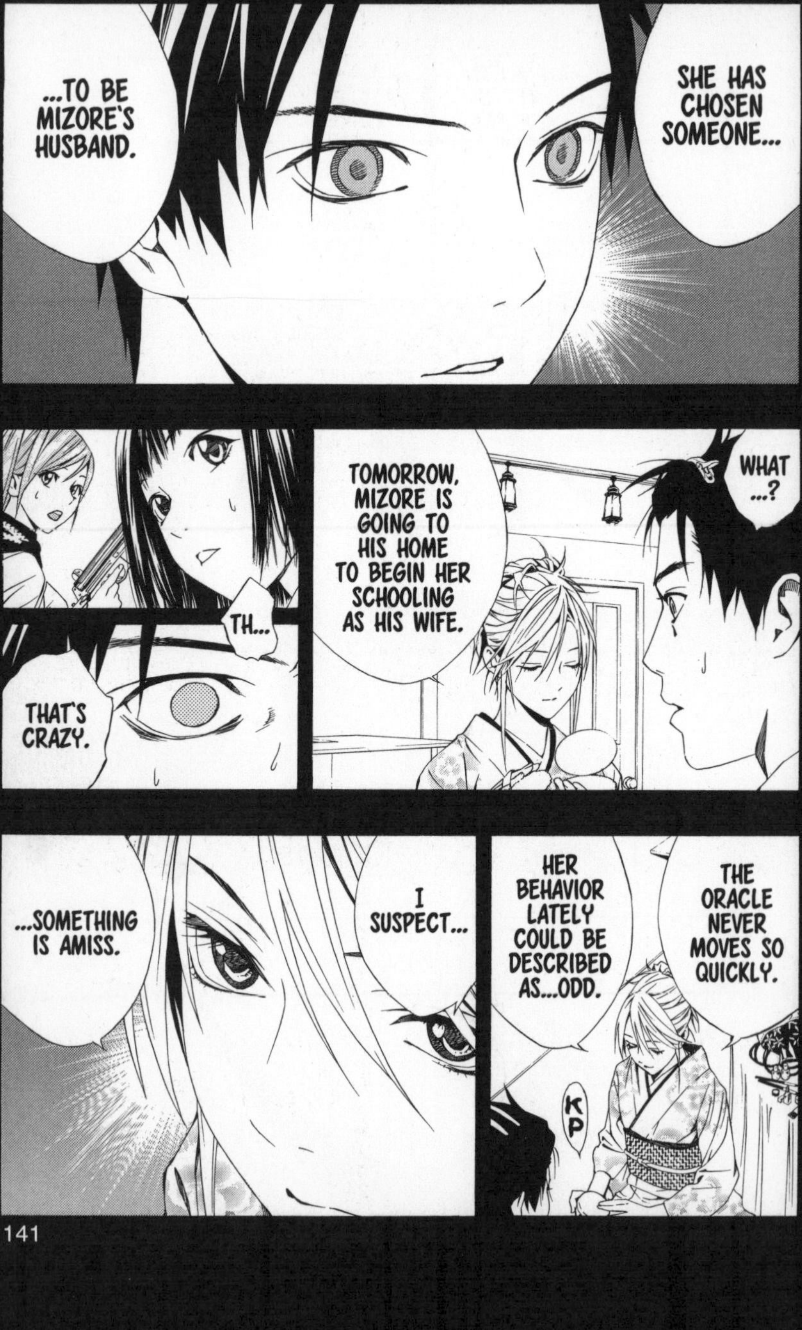
SHE HAS CHOSEN SOMEONE...
...TO BE MIZORE'S HUSBAND.
WHAT ...?
TOMORROW, MIZORE IS GOING TO HIS HOME TO BEGIN HER SCHOOLING AS HIS WIFE.
TH...
THAT'S CRAZY.
THE ORACLE NEVER MOVES SO QUICKLY.
HER BEHAVIOR LATELY COULD BE DESCRIBED AS...ODD.
KP
I SUSPECT...
...SOMETHING IS AMISS.

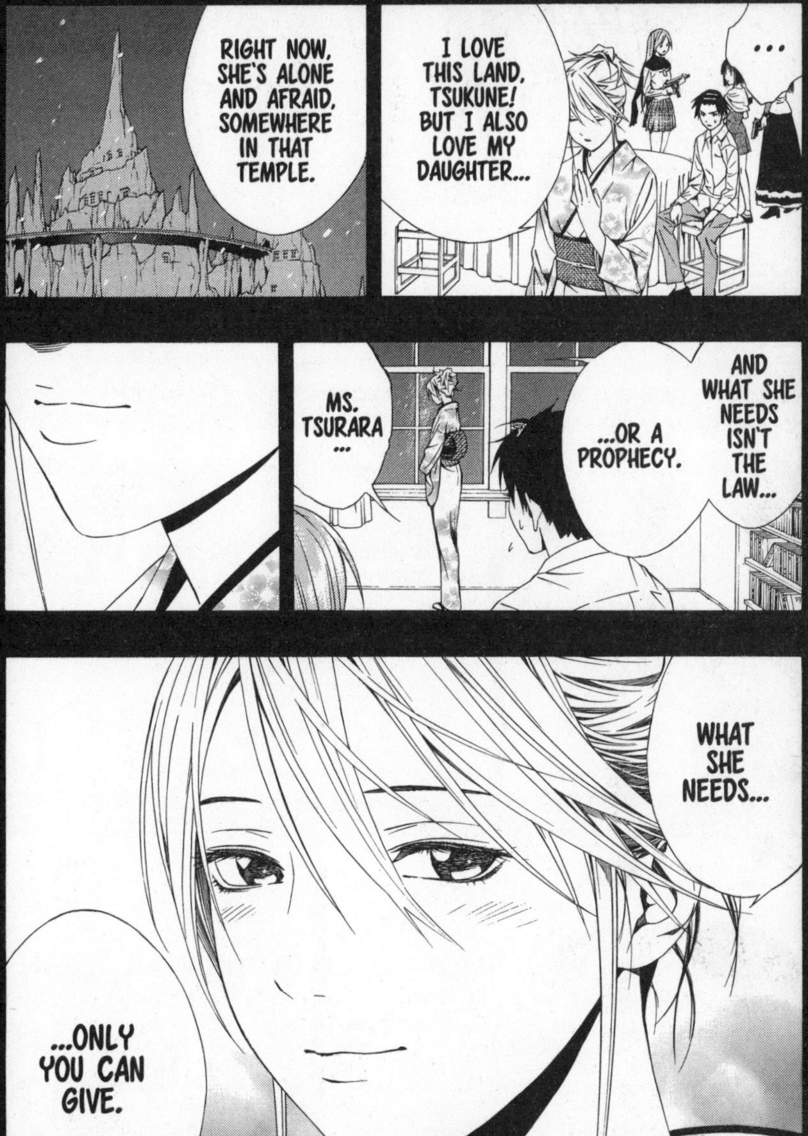
...
I LOVE THIS LAND, TSUKUNE! BUT I ALSO LOVE MY DAUGHTER...
RIGHT NOW, SHE'S ALONE AND AFRAID, SOMEWHERE IN THAT TEMPLE.
AND WHAT SHE NEEDS ISN'T THE LAW...
...OR A PROPHECY.
MS. TSURARA ...
WHAT SHE NEEDS...
...ONLY YOU CAN GIVE.

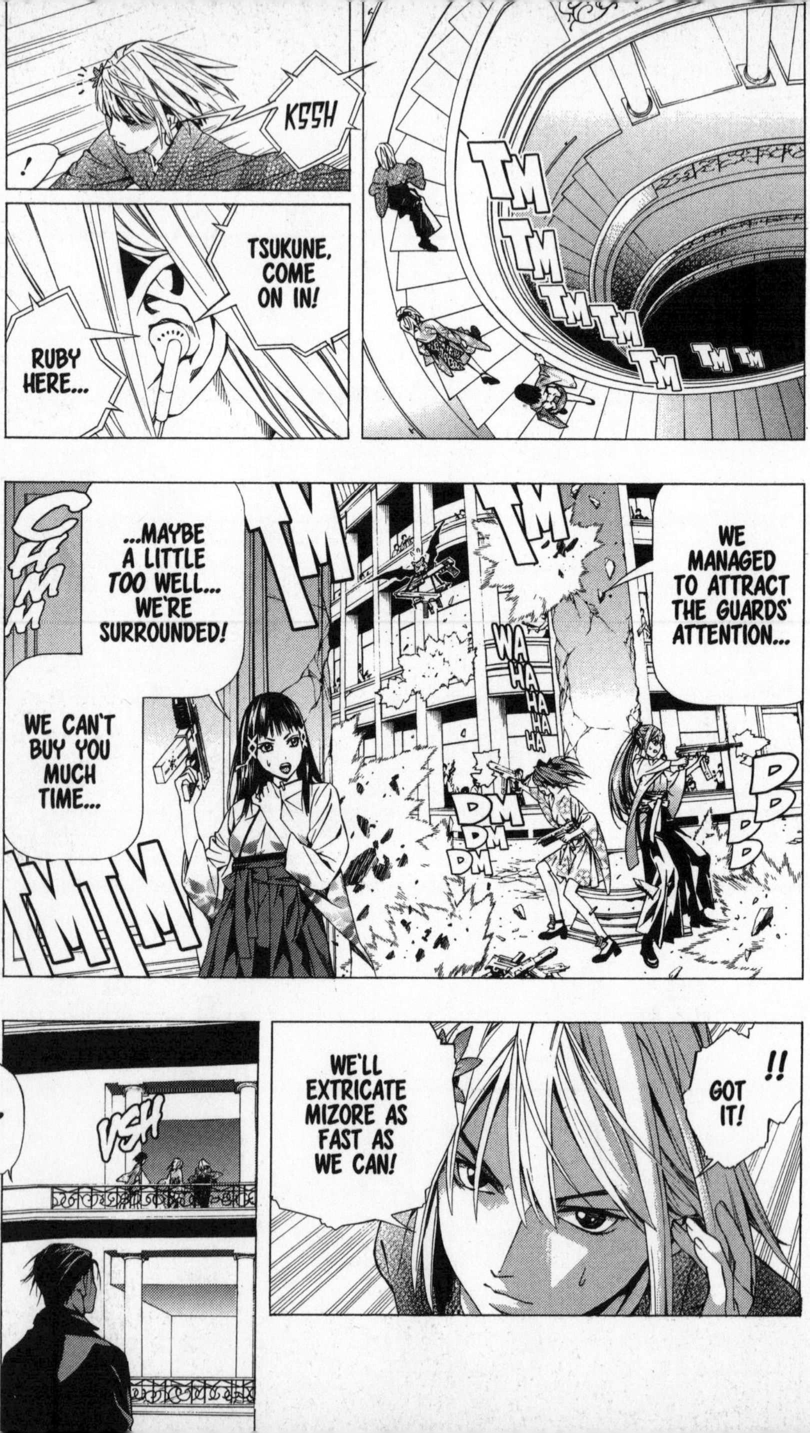
TM TM TM TM TM TM TM TM
KSSH
!
TSUKUNE, COME ON IN!
RUBY HERE...
WE MANAGED TO ATTRACT THE GUARDS' ATTENTION...
TM
TM
...MAYBE A LITTLE TOO WELL... WE'RE SURROUNDED!
CHMM
WA HA HA HA HA HA
D D D D
DM DM DM DM
WE CAN'T BUY YOU MUCH TIME...
TMTM
!!
GOT IT!
WE'LL EXTRICATE MIZORE AS FAST AS WE CAN!
VSH
...

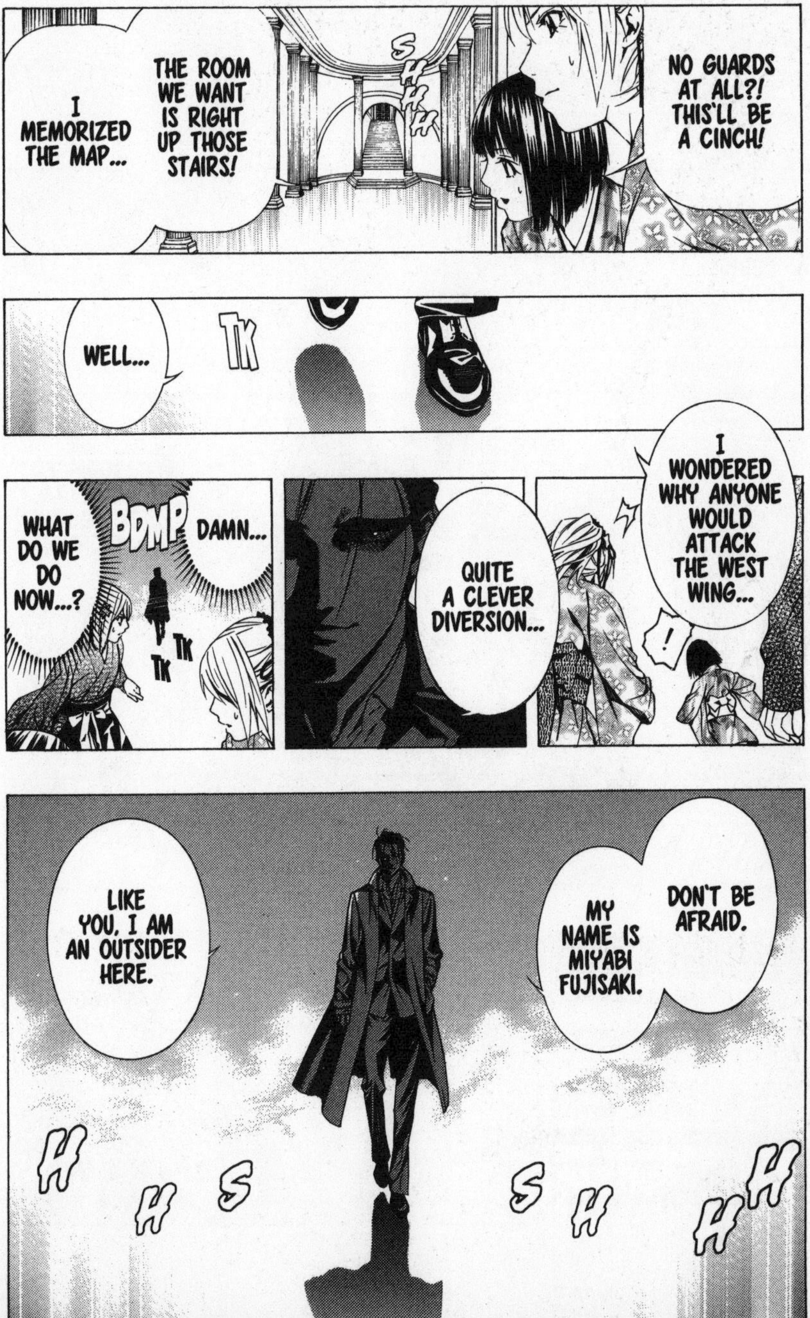
NO GUARDS AT ALL?! THIS'LL BE A CINCH!
SHHH
THE ROOM WE WANT IS RIGHT UP THOSE STAIRS!
I MEMORIZED THE MAP...
TK
WELL...
I WONDERED WHY ANYONE WOULD ATTACK THE WEST WING...
!
QUITE A CLEVER DIVERSION...
DAMN...
BDMP
WHAT DO WE DO NOW...?
TK
TK
DON'T BE AFRAID.
MY NAME IS MIYABI FUJISAKI.
LIKE YOU, I AM AN OUTSIDER HERE.

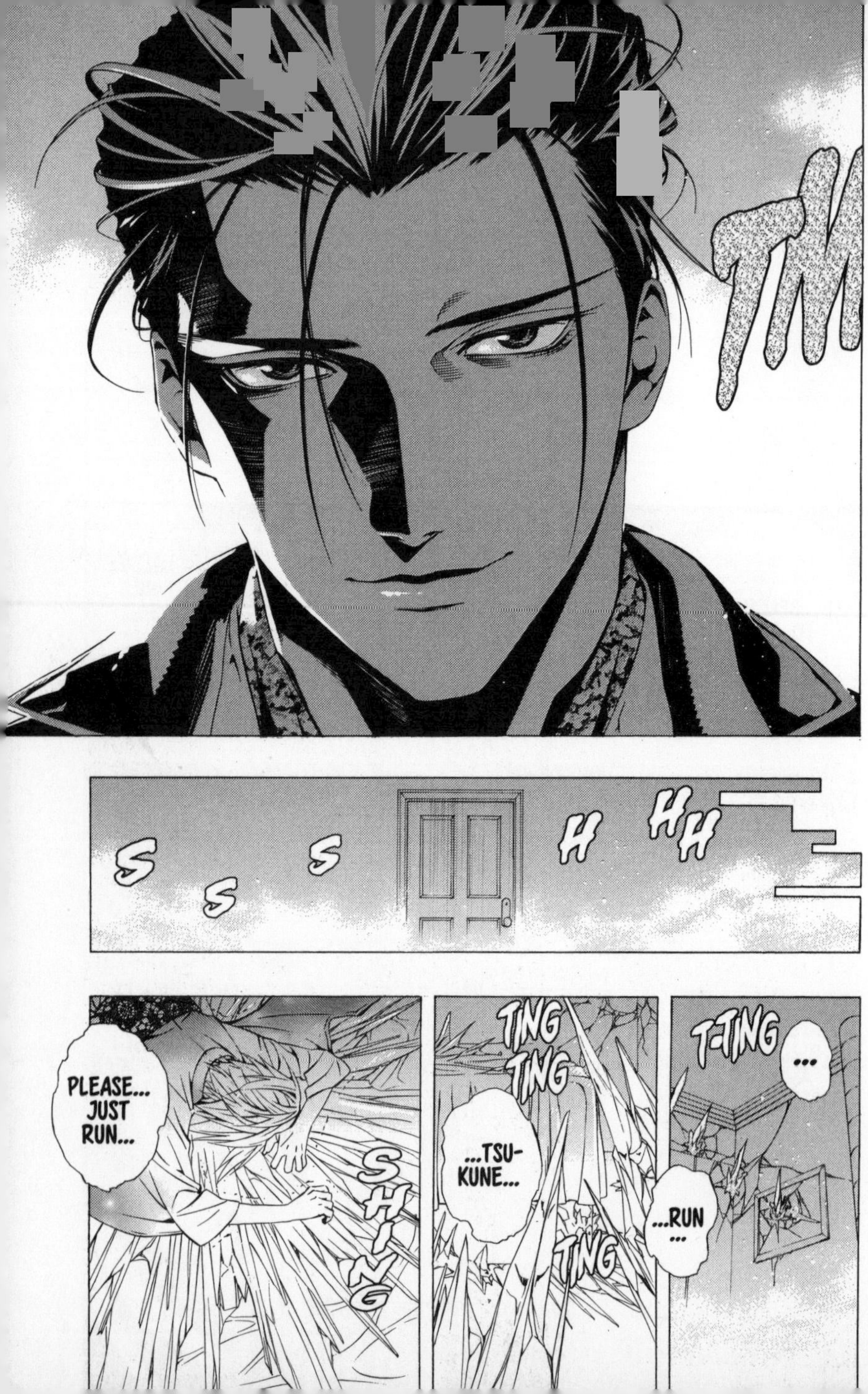
TM
HHH
SSS
T-TING
...
...RUN ...
TING
TING
...TSU-KUNE...
TING
PLEASE... JUST RUN...
SHING

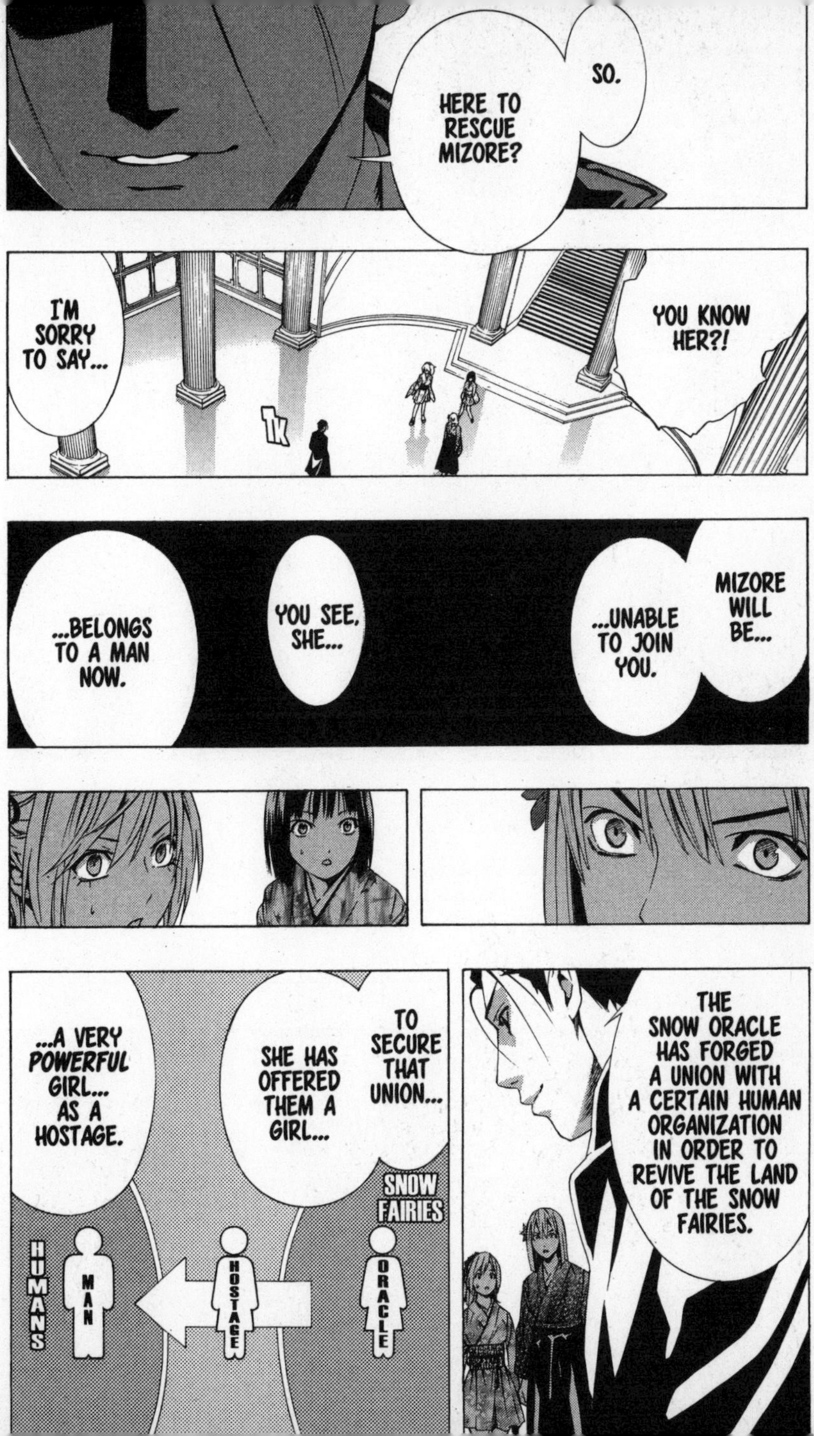
SO.
HERE TO RESCUE MIZORE?
YOU KNOW HER?!
I'M SORRY TO SAY...
TK
MIZORE WILL BE...
...UNABLE TO JOIN YOU.
YOU SEE, SHE...
...BELONGS TO A MAN NOW.
THE SNOW ORACLE HAS FORGED A UNION WITH A CERTAIN HUMAN ORGANIZATION IN ORDER TO REVIVE THE LAND OF THE SNOW FAIRIES.
TO SECURE THAT UNION...
SHE HAS OFFERED THEM A GIRL...
...A VERY POWERFUL GIRL... AS A HOSTAGE.
SNOW FAIRIES
ORACLE
HOSTAGE
MAN
HUMANS

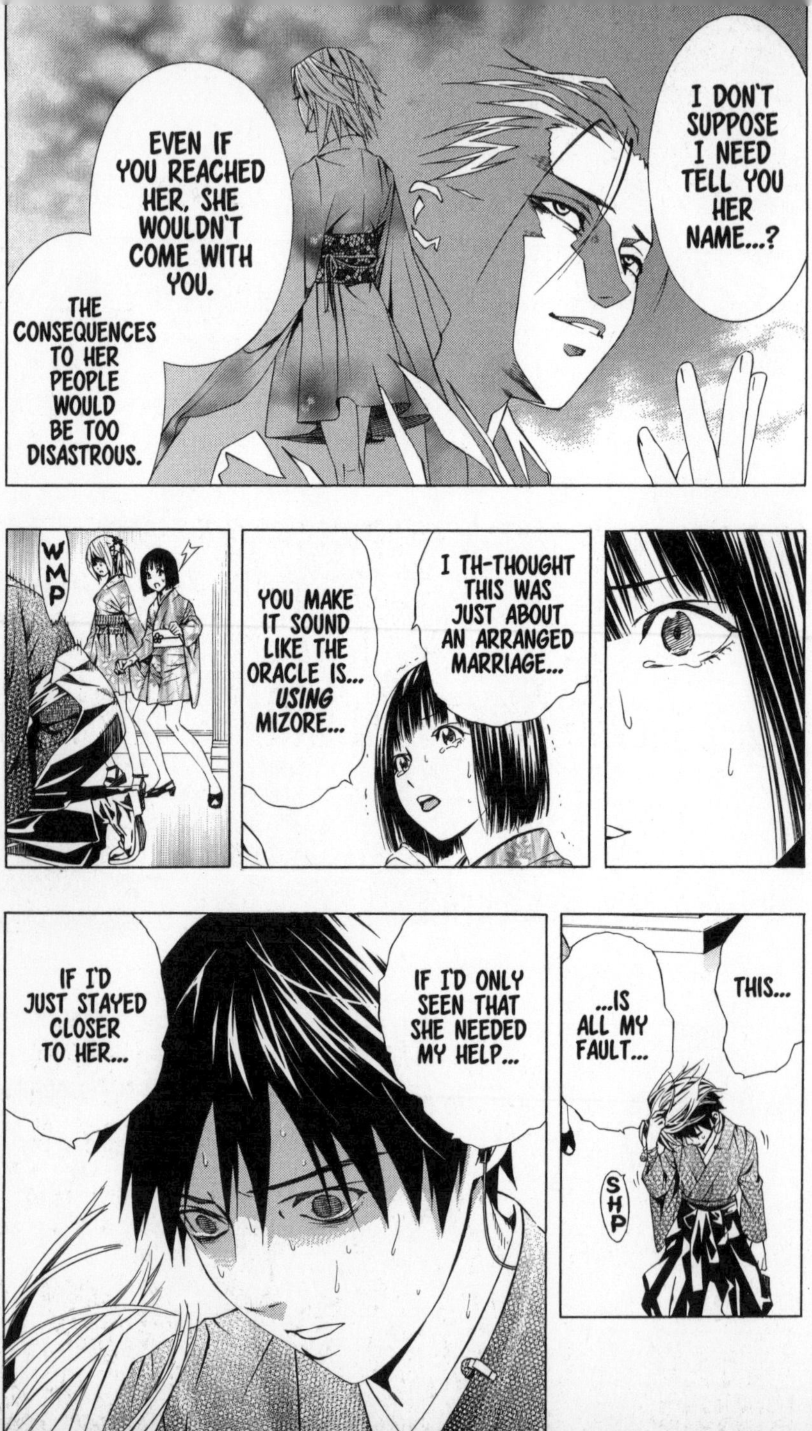
I DON'T SUPPOSE I NEED TELL YOU HER NAME...?
EVEN IF YOU REACHED HER, SHE WOULDN'T COME WITH YOU.
THE CONSEQUENCES TO HER PEOPLE WOULD BE TOO DISASTROUS.
I TH-THOUGHT THIS WAS JUST ABOUT AN ARRANGED MARRIAGE...
YOU MAKE IT SOUND LIKE THE ORACLE IS... USING MIZORE...
WMP
THIS...
...IS ALL MY FAULT...
SHP
IF I'D ONLY SEEN THAT SHE NEEDED MY HELP...
IF I'D JUST STAYED CLOSER TO HER...

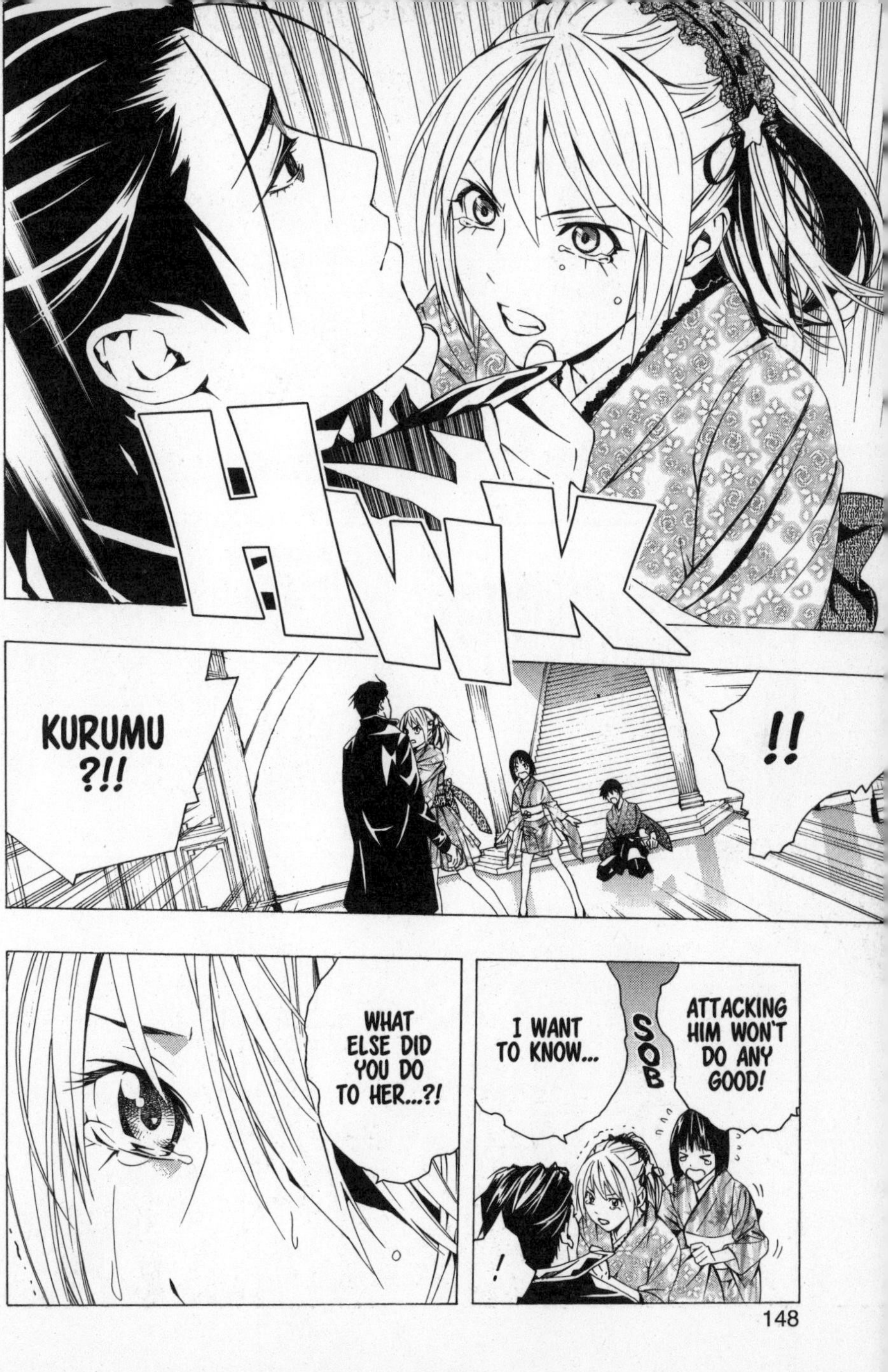
HAWK
!!
KURUMU ?!!
ATTACKING HIM WON'T DO ANY GOOD!
SOB
I WANT TO KNOW...
WHAT ELSE DID YOU DO TO HER...?!

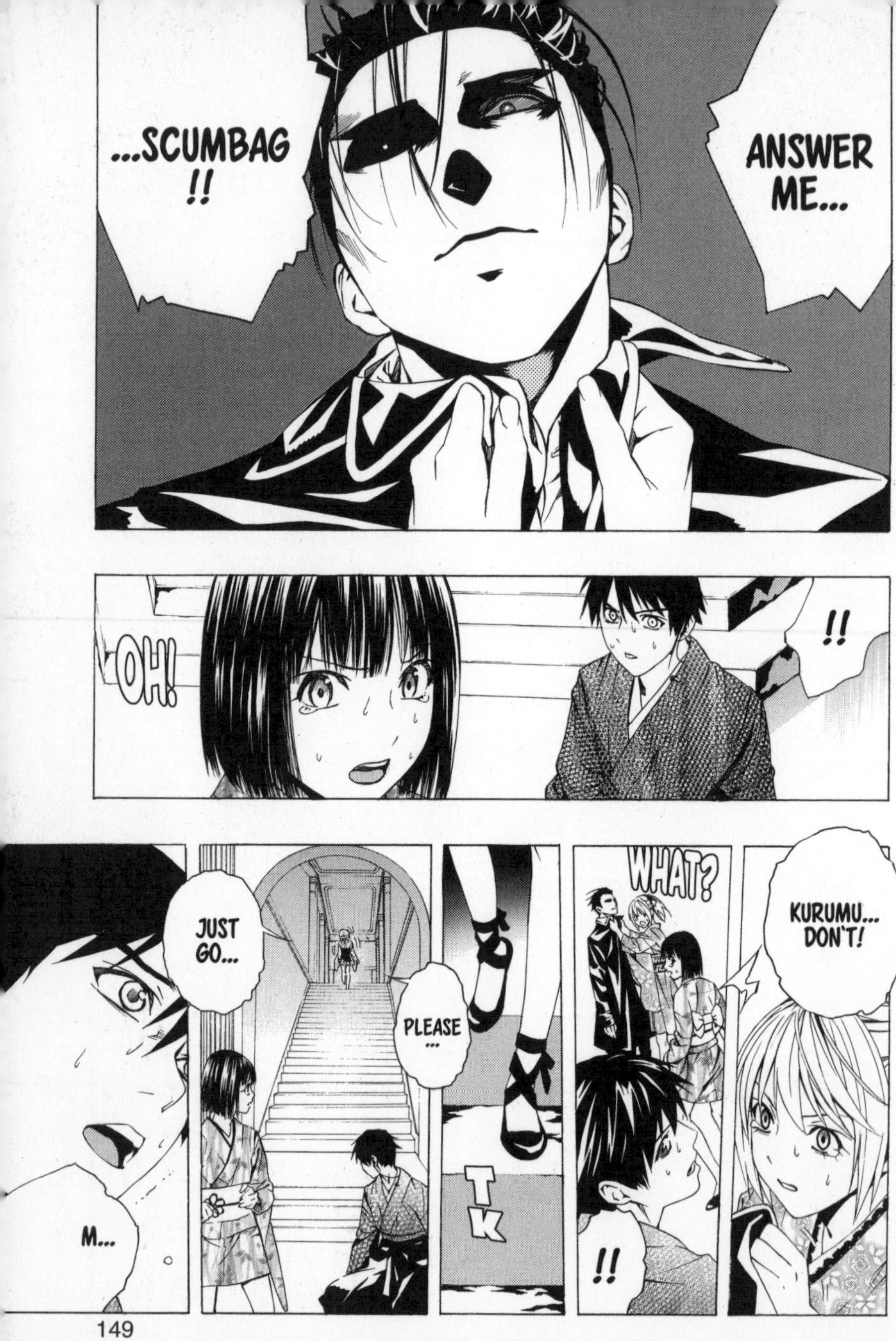
ANSWER ME...
...SCUMBAG !!
!!
OH!
KURUMU... DON'T!
WHAT?
!!
TK
JUST GO...
PLEASE ...
M...

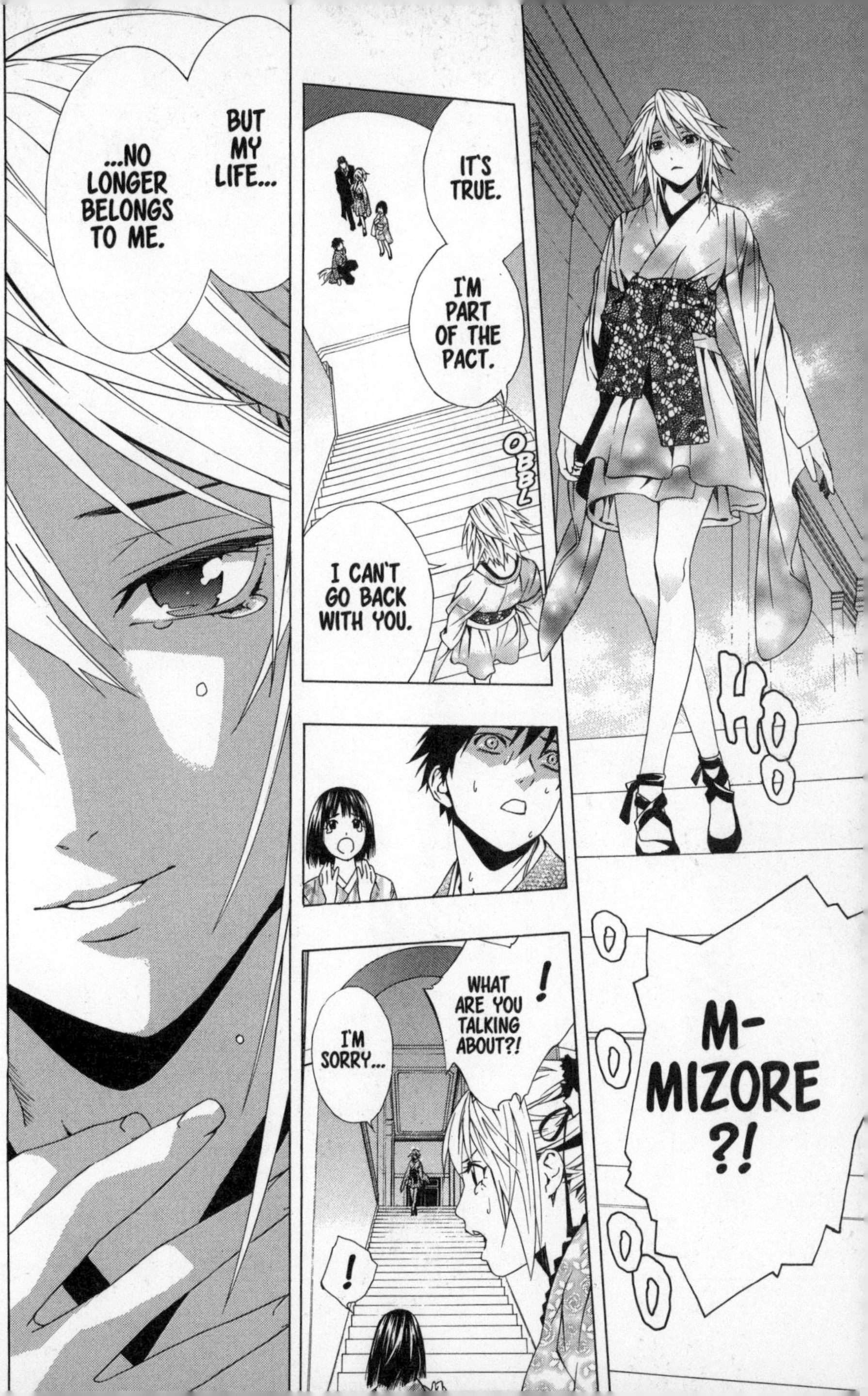
HOOOOOOO
M-MIZORE?!
IT'S TRUE.
I'M PART OF THE PACT.
OBBL
I CAN'T GO BACK WITH YOU.
WHAT ARE YOU TALKING ABOUT?!
!
I'M SORRY...
!
BUT MY LIFE...
...NO LONGER BELONGS TO ME.

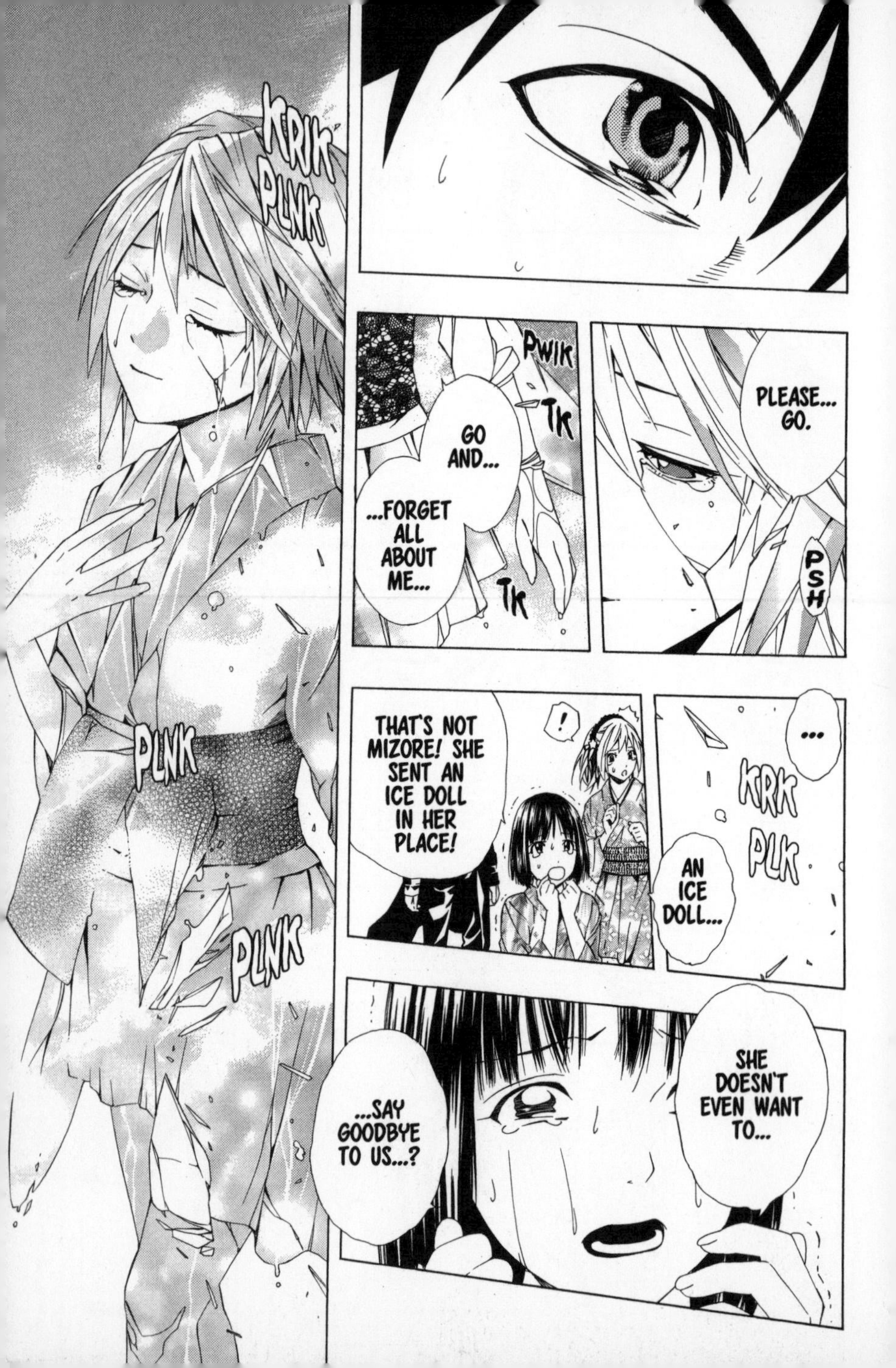
PLEASE... GO.
PSH
PWIK
GO AND...
TK
...FORGET ALL ABOUT ME...
TK
...
KRK
PLK
AN ICE DOLL...
!
THAT'S NOT MIZORE! SHE SENT AN ICE DOLL IN HER PLACE!
SHE DOESN'T EVEN WANT TO...
...SAY GOODBYE TO US...?
KRIK
PLNK
PLNK
PLNK

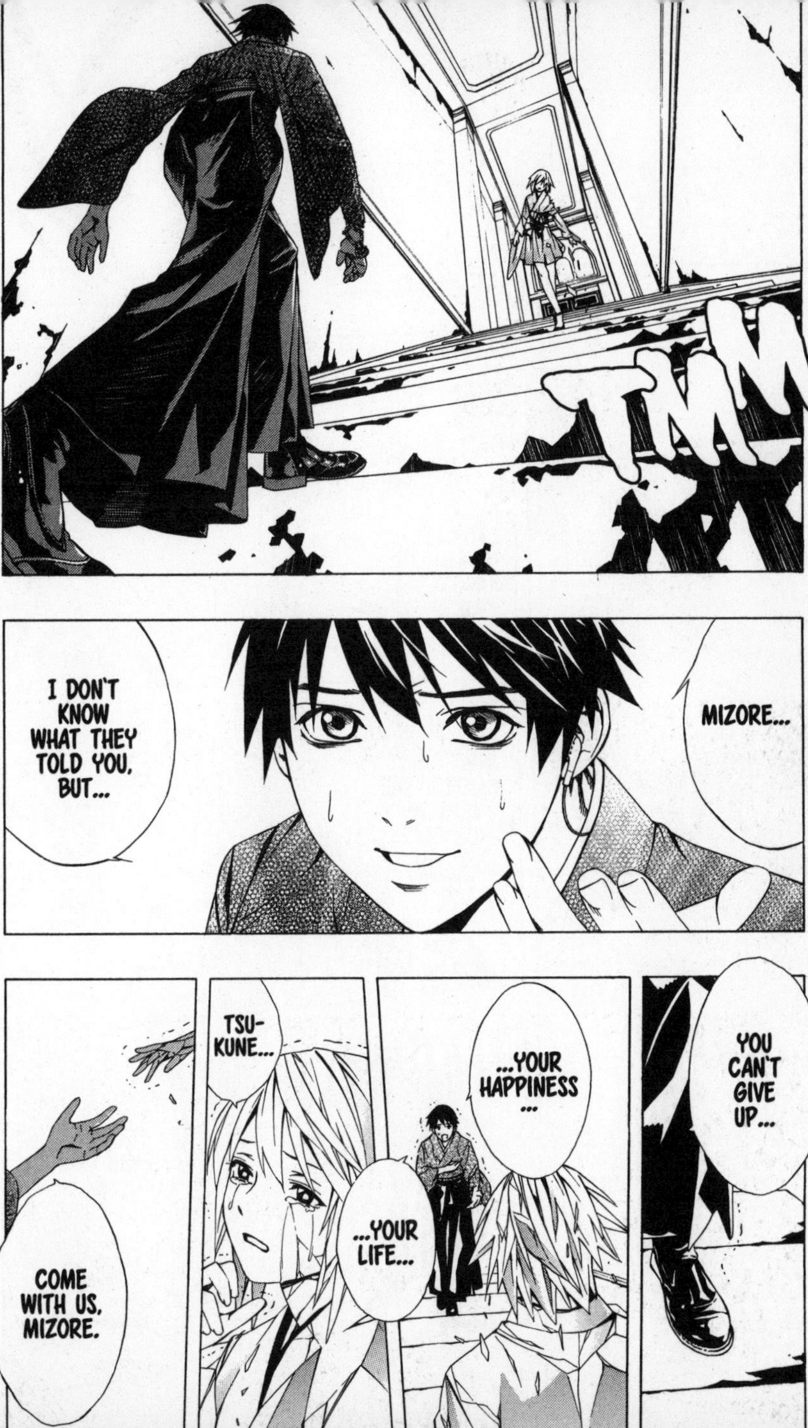
TMM
MIZORE...
I DON'T KNOW WHAT THEY TOLD YOU, BUT...
YOU CAN'T GIVE UP...
...YOUR HAPPINESS ...
...YOUR LIFE...
TSU-KUNE...
COME WITH US, MIZORE.

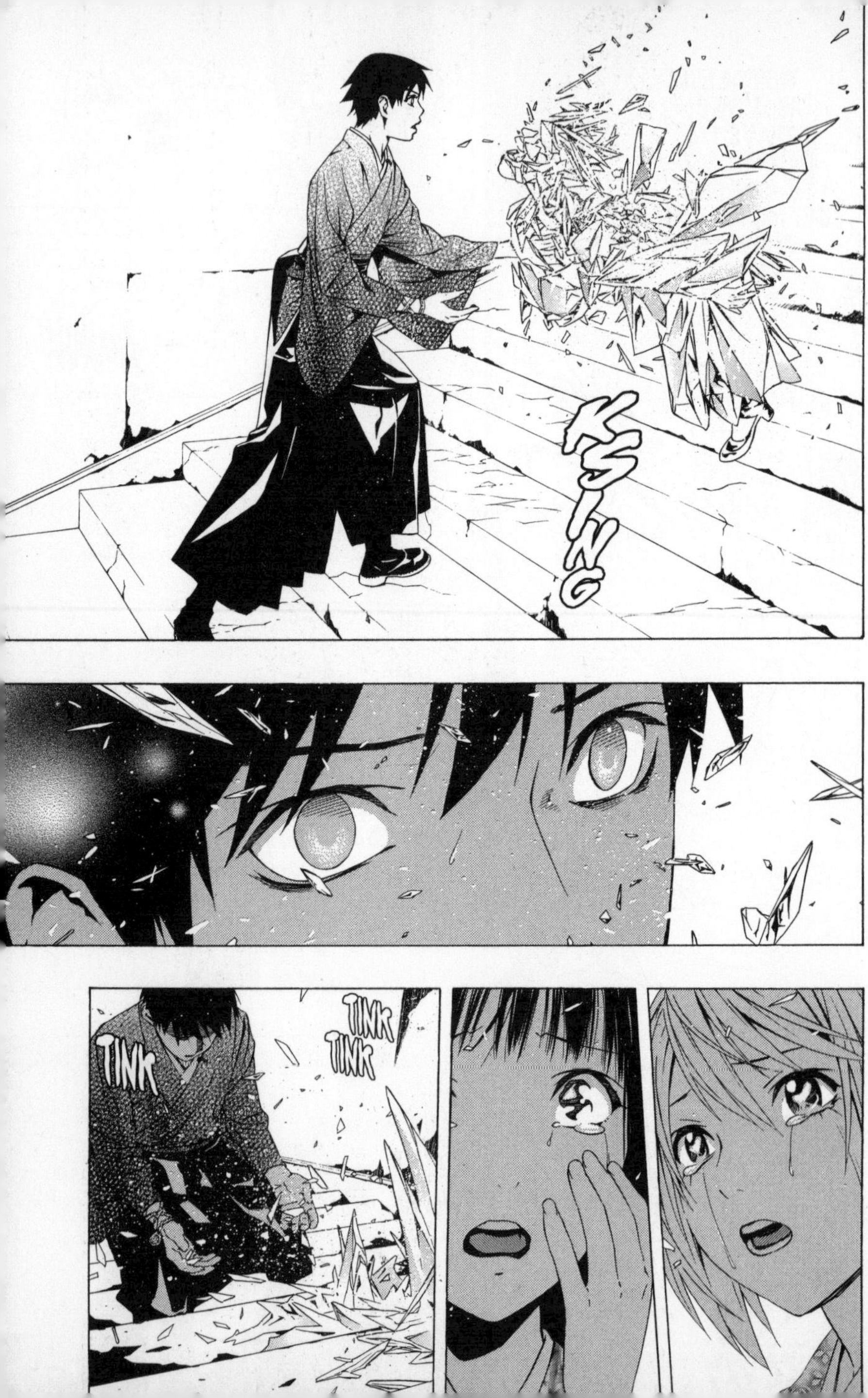
KSING
TINK
TINK
TINK

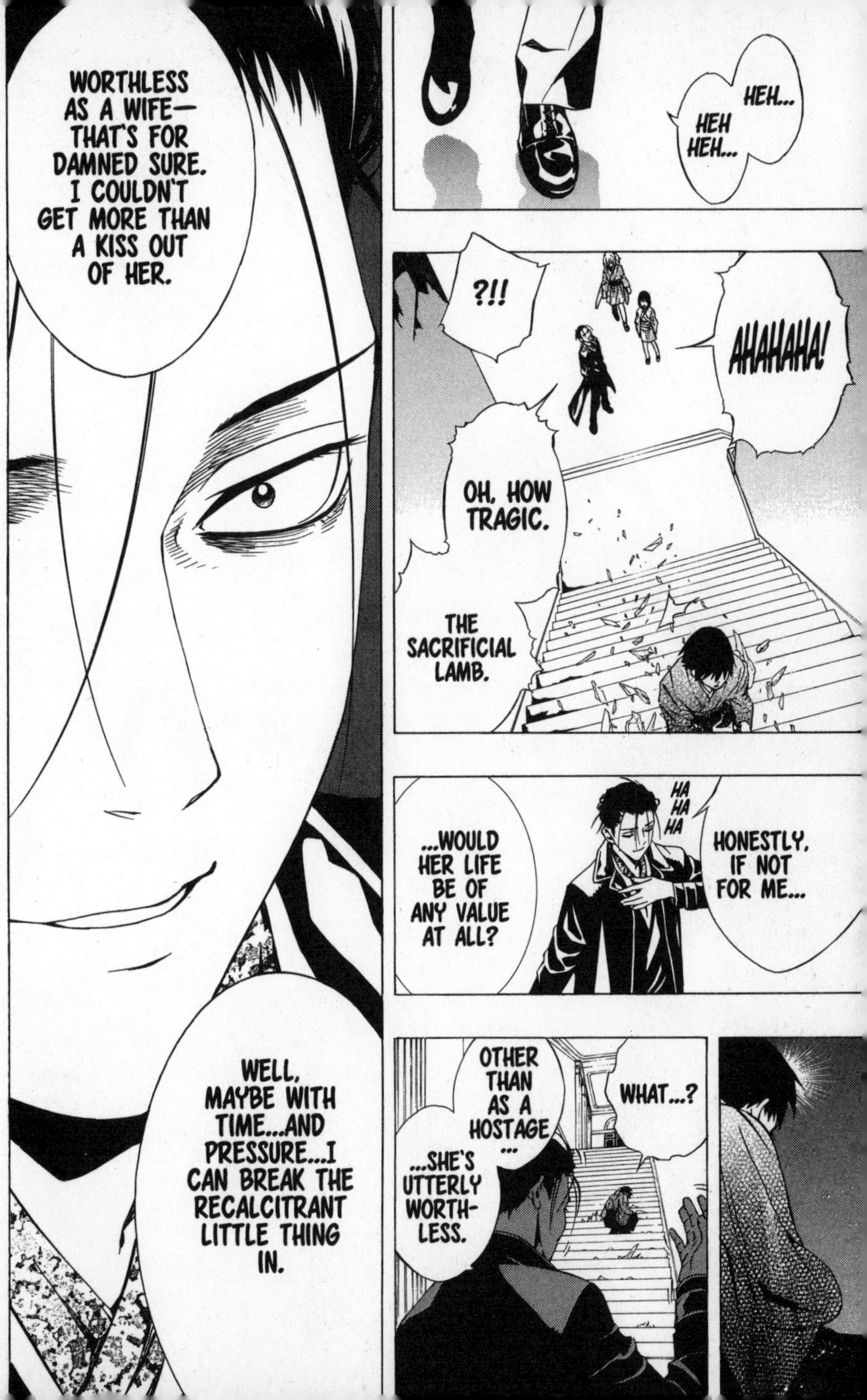
HEH... HEH HEH...
?!!
AHAHAHA!
OH, HOW TRAGIC.
THE SACRIFICIAL LAMB.
HA HA HA
HONESTLY, IF NOT FOR ME...
...WOULD HER LIFE BE OF ANY VALUE AT ALL?
WHAT...?
OTHER THAN AS A HOSTAGE...
...SHE'S UTTERLY WORTH-LESS.
WORTHLESS AS A WIFE— THAT'S FOR DAMNED SURE. I COULDN'T GET MORE THAN A KISS OUT OF HER.
WELL, MAYBE WITH TIME...AND PRESSURE...I CAN BREAK THE RECALCITRANT LITTLE THING IN.

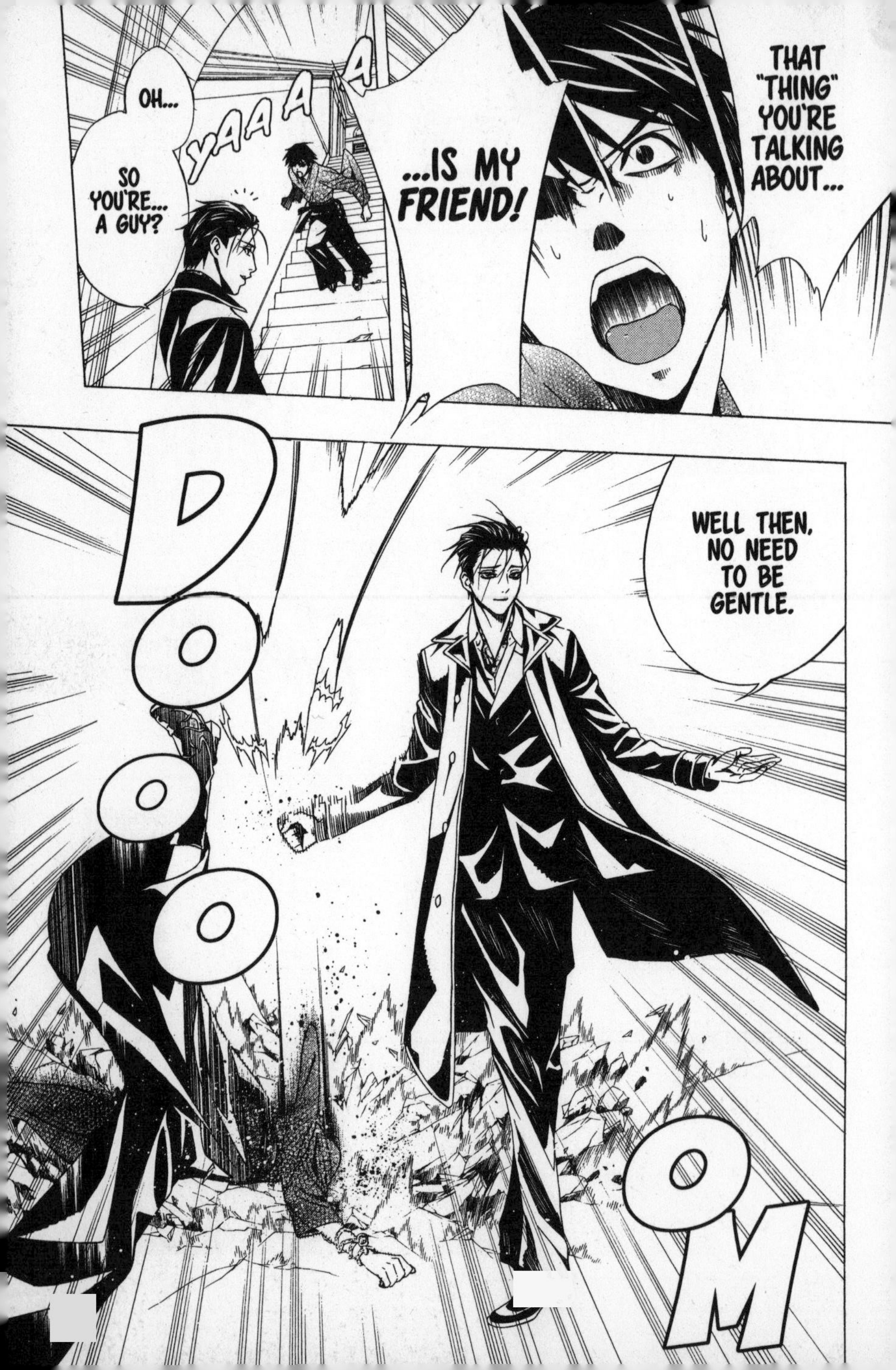

THAT "THING" YOU'RE TALKING ABOUT...
...IS MY FRIEND!
YAAAAA
OH...
SO YOU'RE... A GUY?
WELL THEN, NO NEED TO BE GENTLE.
DOOOOOM

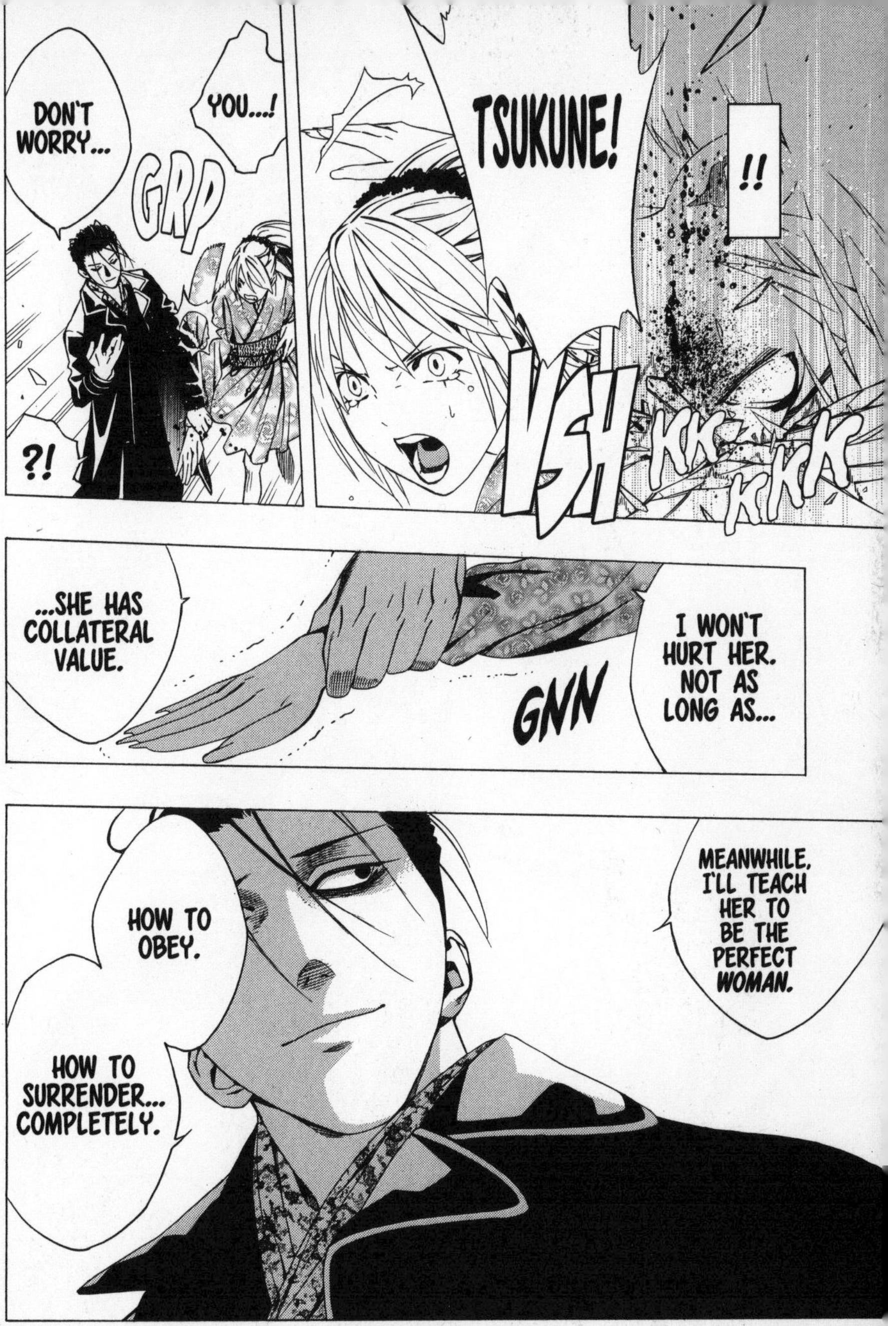
!!
VSH
KKK KKK
TSUKUNE!
YOU...!
DON'T WORRY...
GRP
?!
I WON'T HURT HER. NOT AS LONG AS...
GNN
...SHE HAS COLLATERAL VALUE.
MEANWHILE, I'LL TEACH HER TO BE THE PERFECT WOMAN.
HOW TO OBEY.
HOW TO SURRENDER... COMPLETELY.

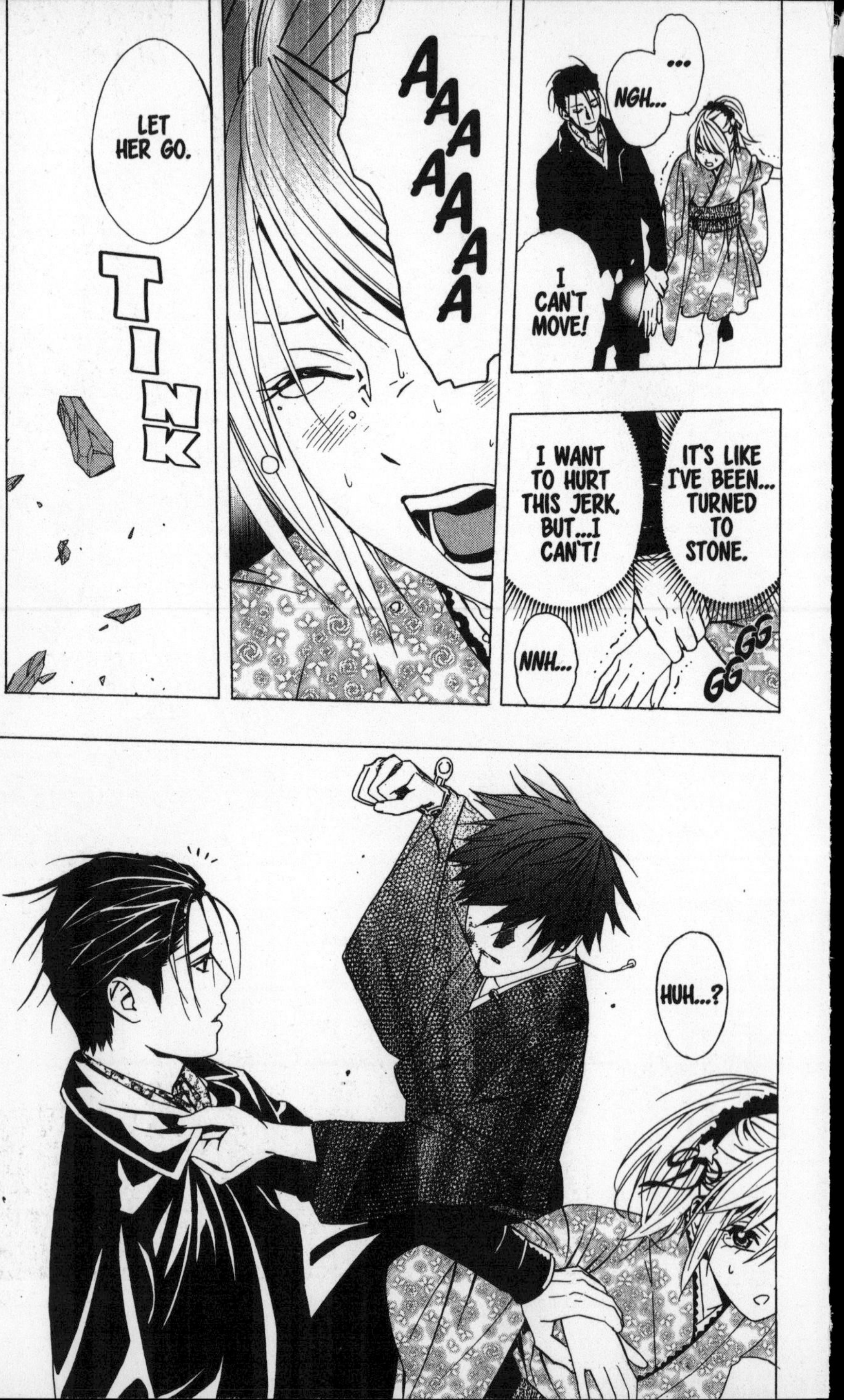
...
NGH...
I CAN'T MOVE!
IT'S LIKE I'VE BEEN... TURNED TO STONE.
I WANT TO HURT THIS JERK, BUT...I CAN'T!
NNH...
GGGG
AAAAAAAAA
LET HER GO.
TINK
HUH...?

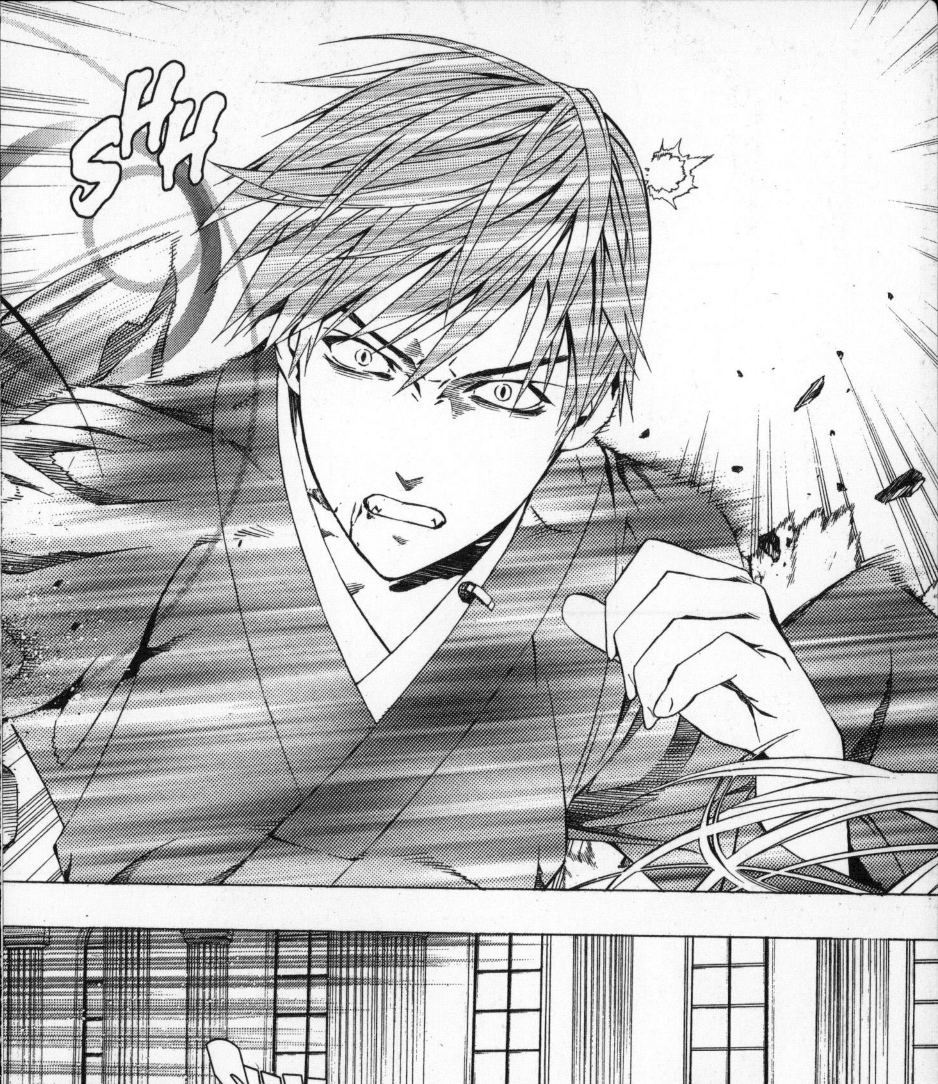
SHH
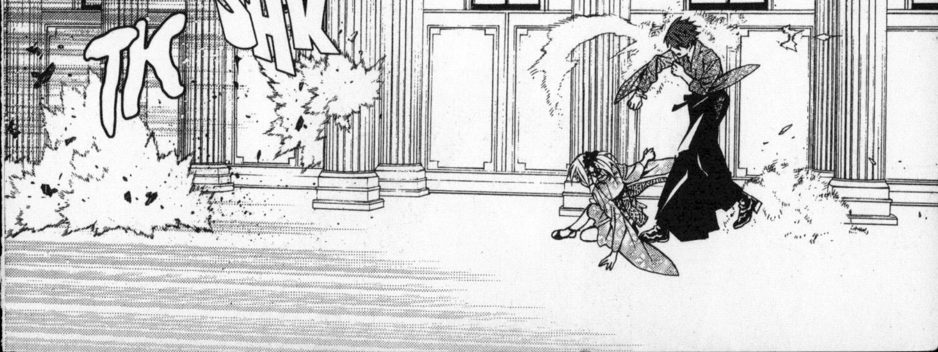
SHK
TK

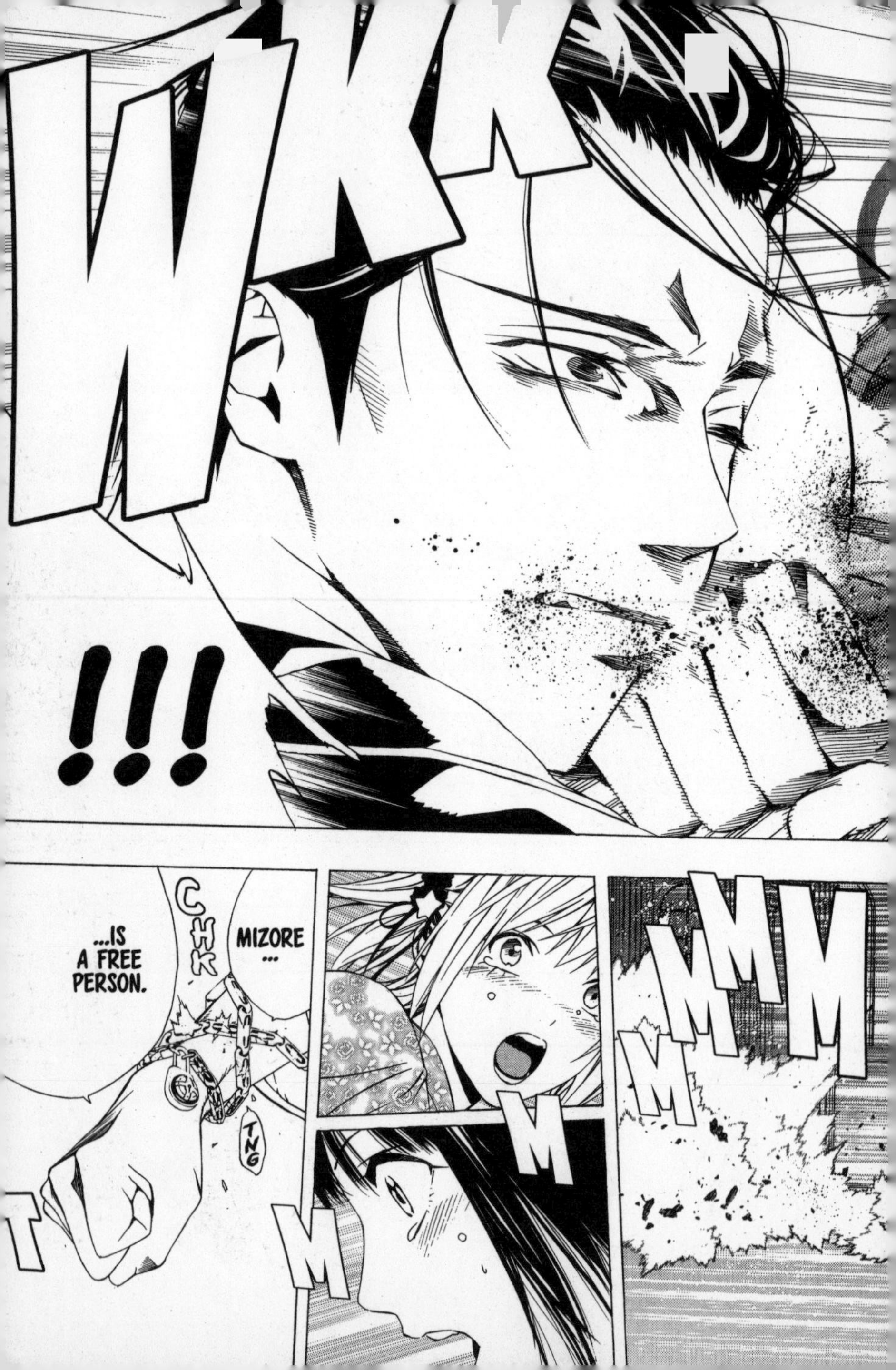

WKK
!!!
MMMMMMMM
MIZORE ...
CHK
...IS A FREE PERSON.
TNG
T

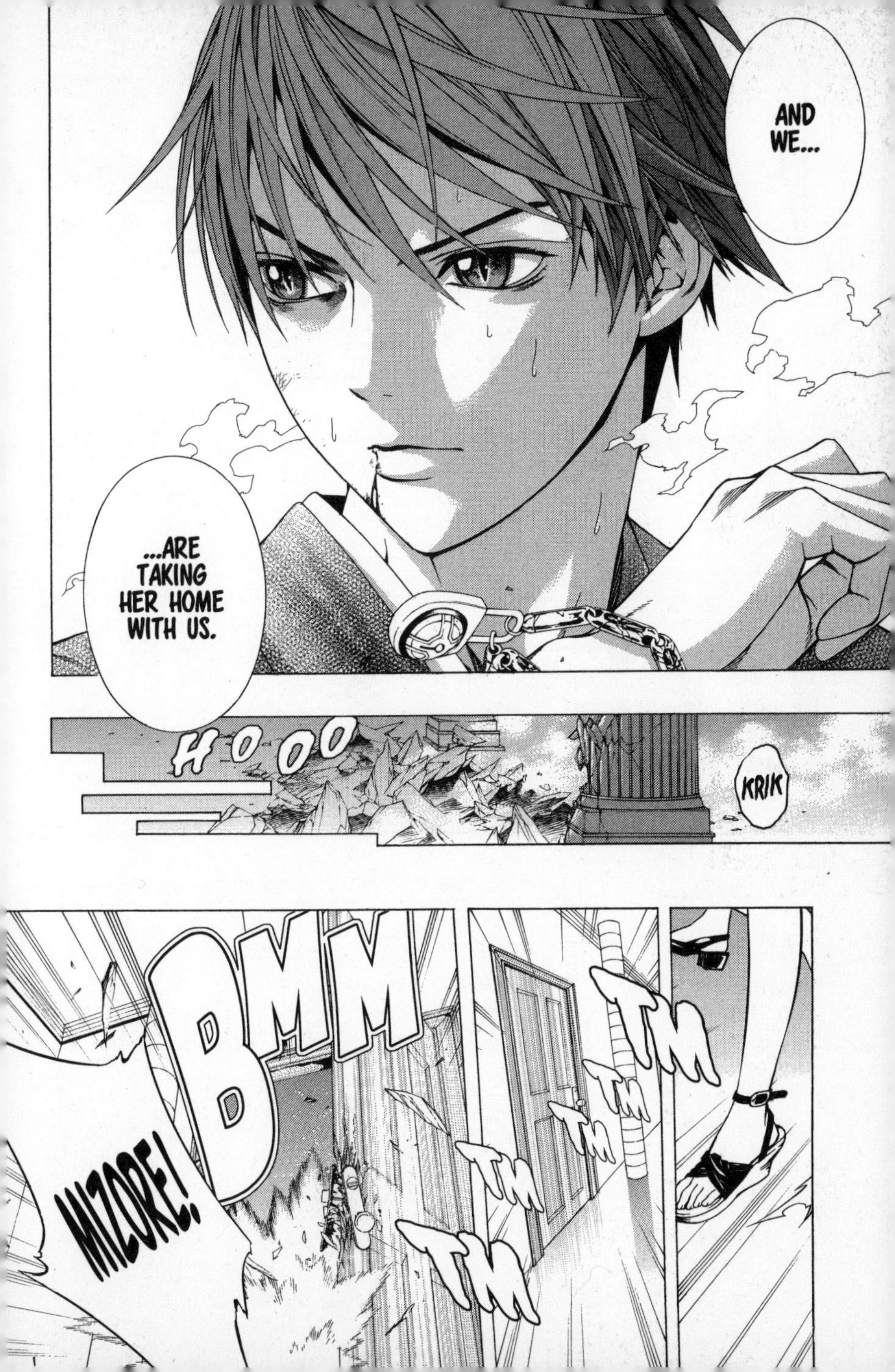
AND WE...
...ARE TAKING HER HOME WITH US.
KRIK
HOOO
TM
TM
TM
TM
TM
BMM
MIZORE!

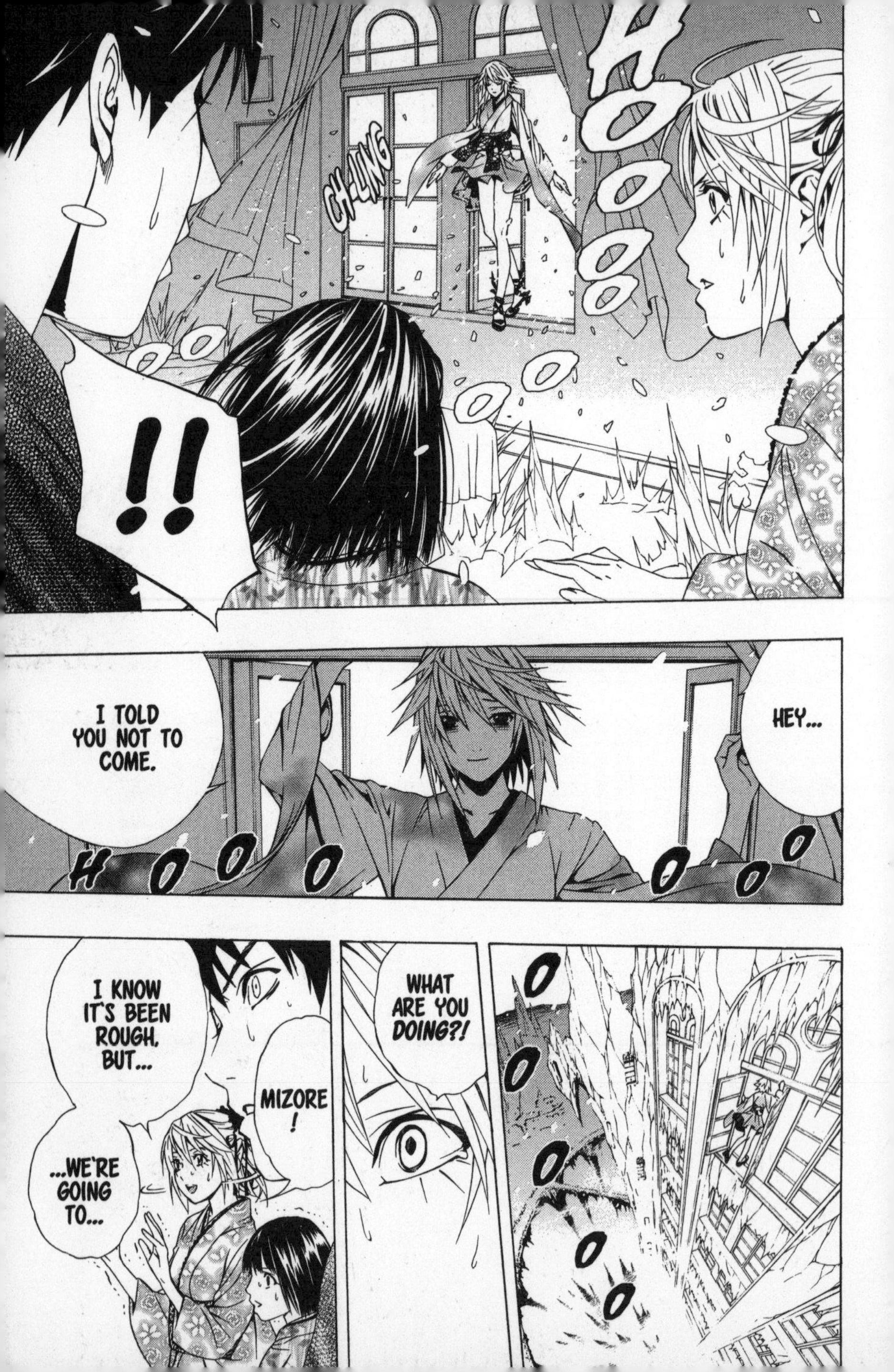
HOOOOOO
CHI-LING
!!
HEY...
I TOLD YOU NOT TO COME.
HOOOOOOO
OOOOOOO
WHAT ARE YOU DOING?!
I KNOW IT'S BEEN ROUGH, BUT...
MIZORE!
...WE'RE GOING TO...

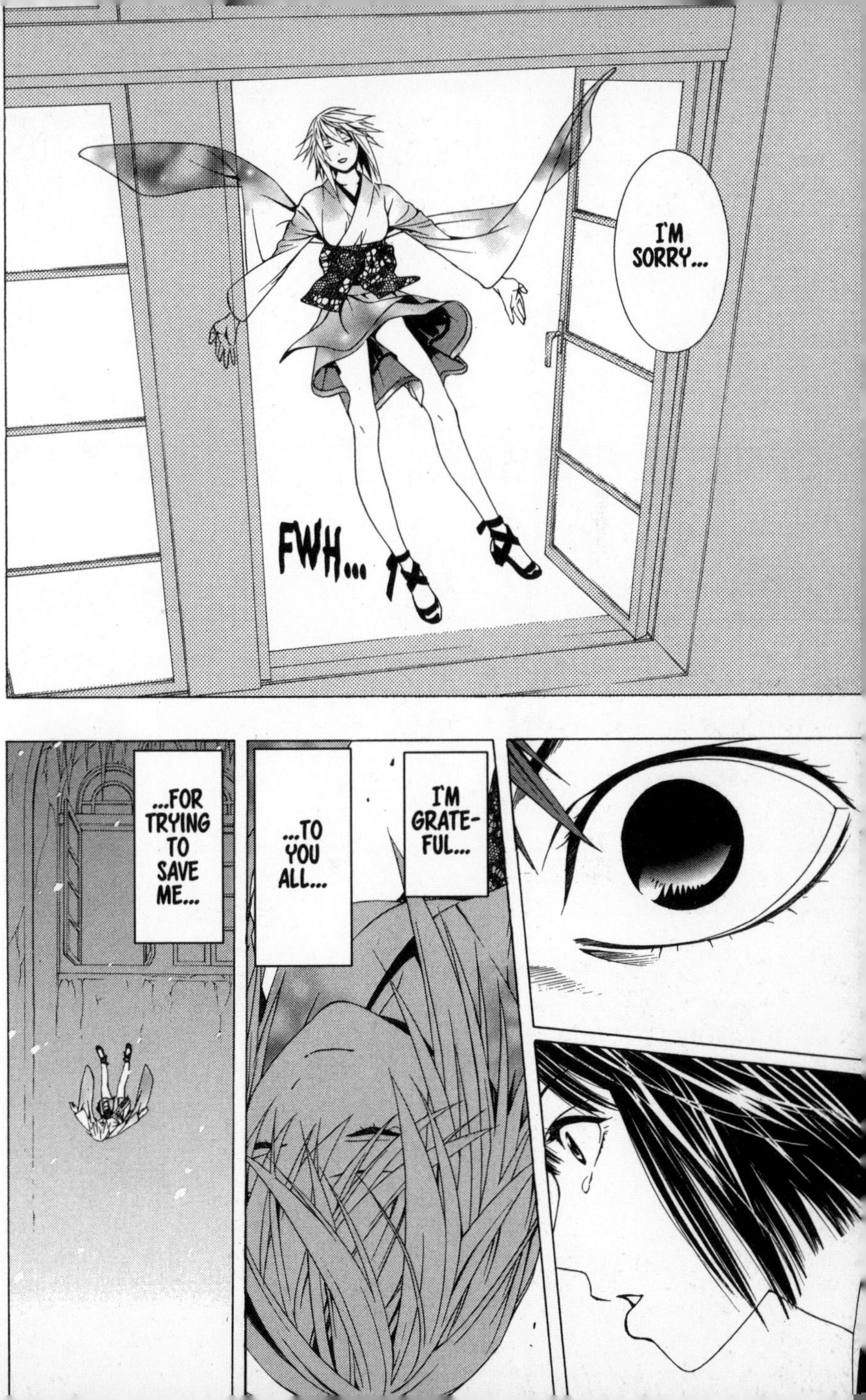
I'M SORRY...
FWH...
I'M GRATE-FUL...
...TO YOU ALL...
...FOR TRYING TO SAVE ME...

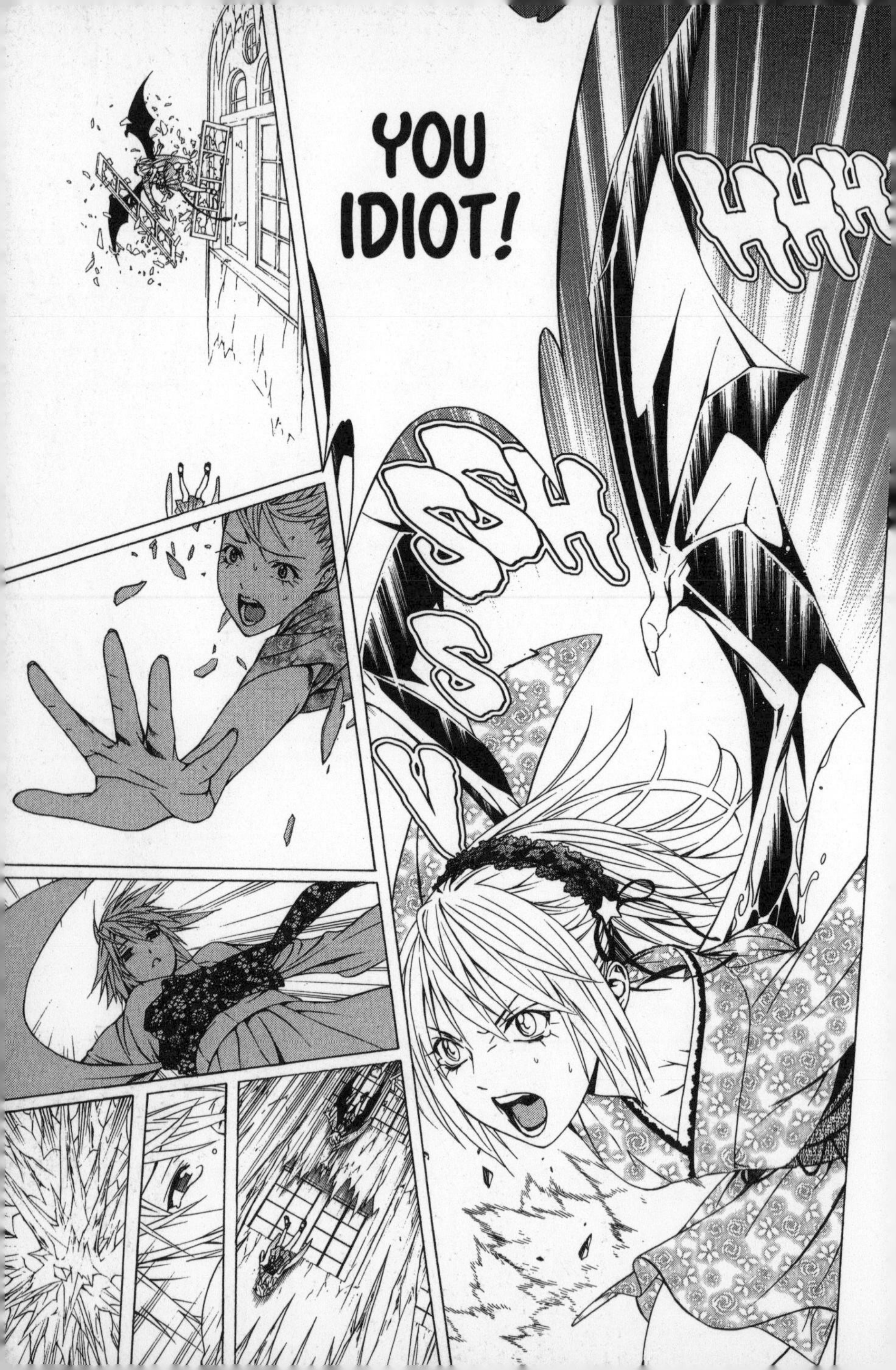
YOU IDIOT!

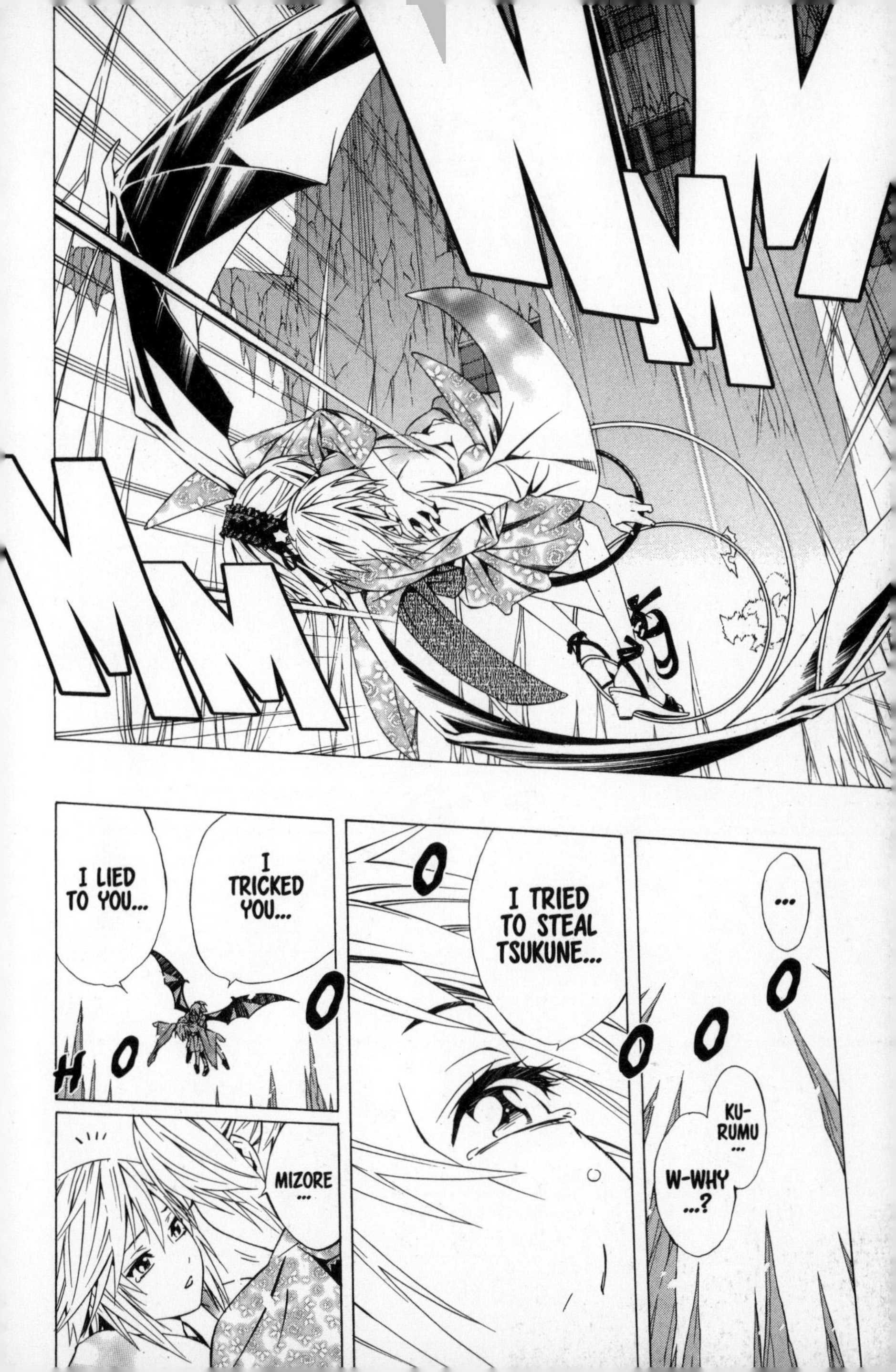
...
KU-RUMU ...
W-WHY ...?
I TRIED TO STEAL TSUKUNE...
I TRICKED YOU...
I LIED TO YOU...
MIZORE ...

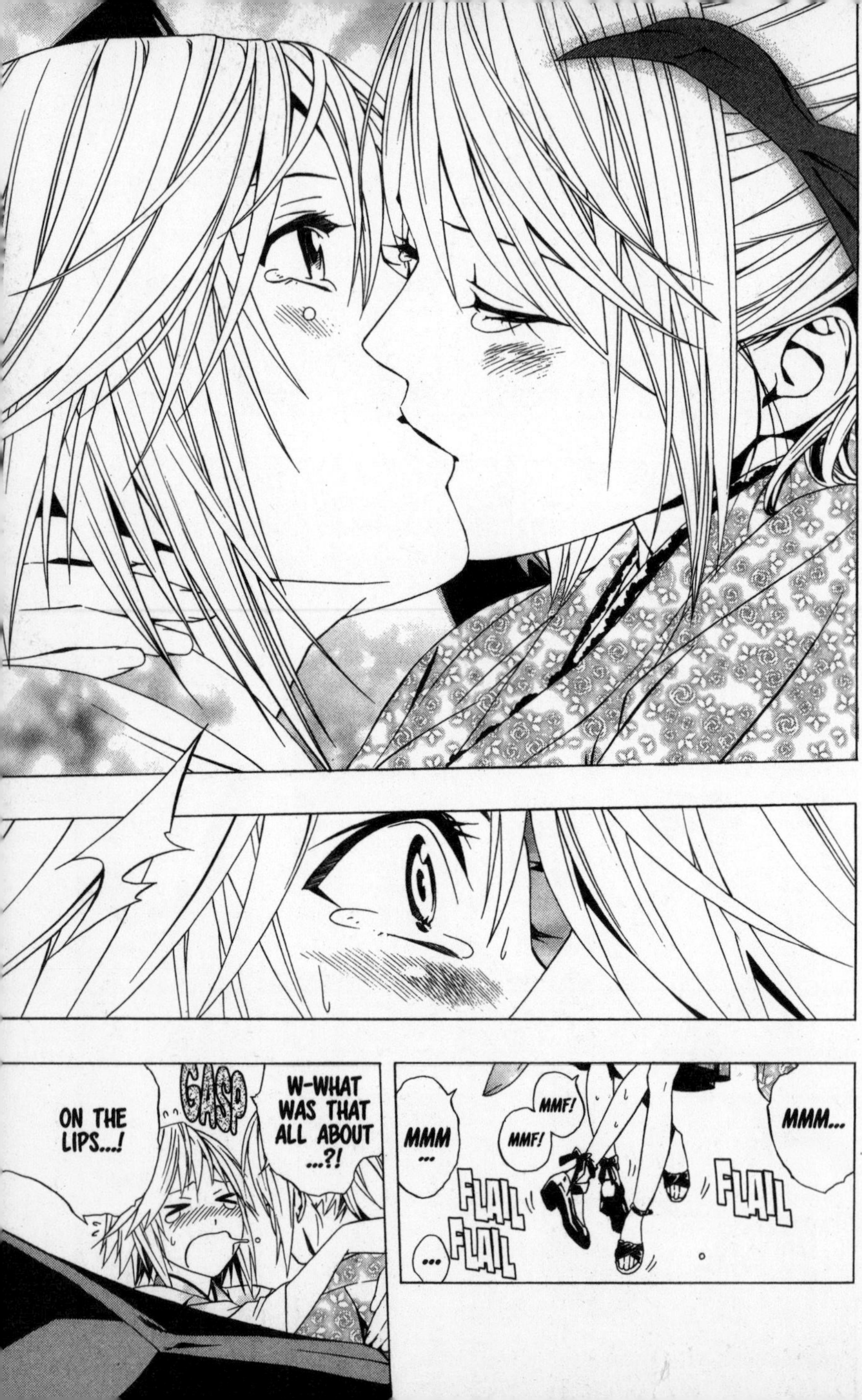
MMM...
FLAIL
MMF!
MMF!
MMM ...
FLAIL FLAIL
...
W-WHAT WAS THAT ALL ABOUT ...?!
GASP
ON THE LIPS...!

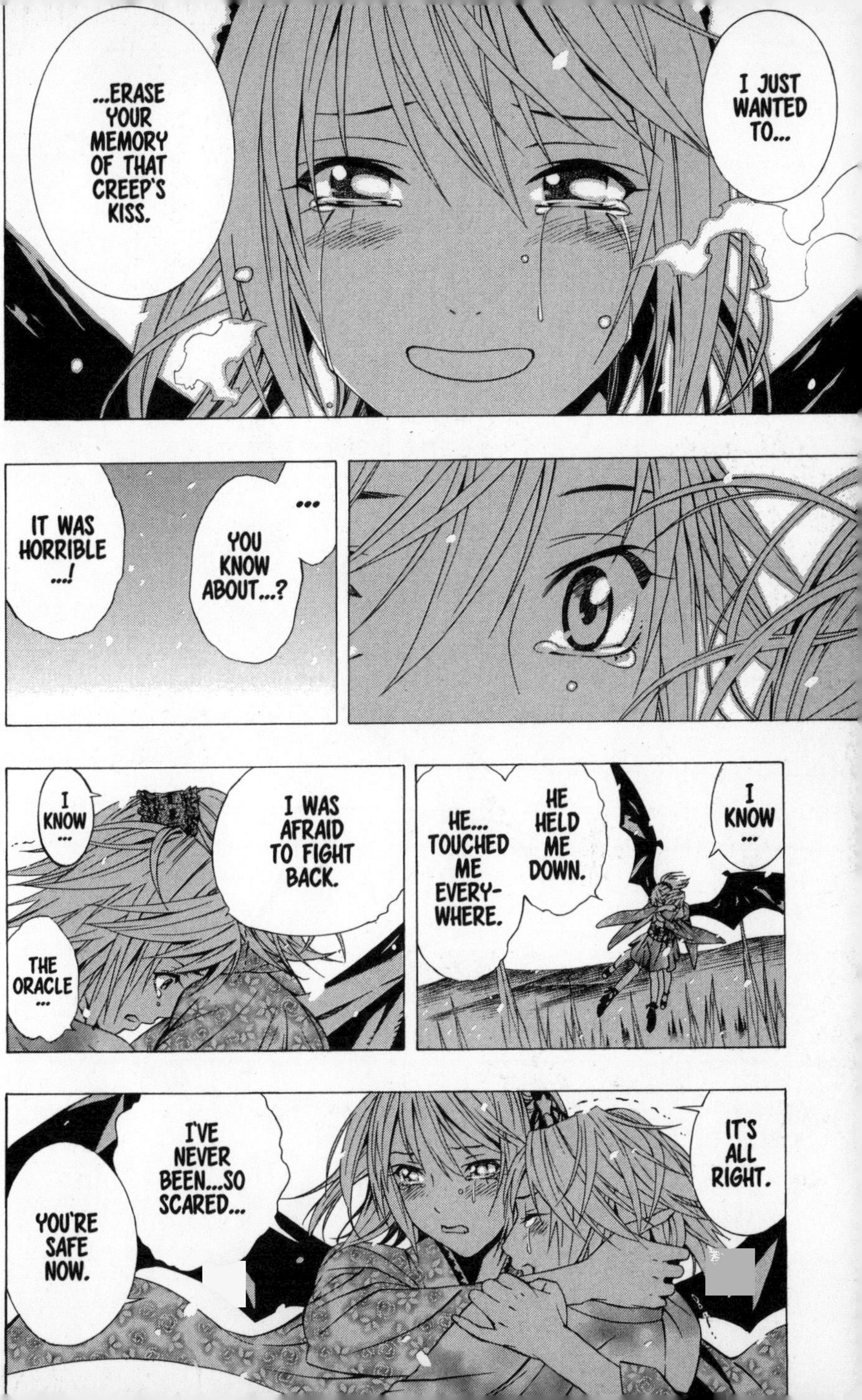
I JUST WANTED TO...
...ERASE YOUR MEMORY OF THAT CREEP'S KISS.
... YOU KNOW ABOUT...?
IT WAS HORRIBLE ...!
I KNOW ...
HE HELD ME DOWN.
HE... TOUCHED ME EVERY-WHERE.
I WAS AFRAID TO FIGHT BACK.
I KNOW ...
THE ORACLE ...
IT'S ALL RIGHT.
I'VE NEVER BEEN...SO SCARED...
YOU'RE SAFE NOW.

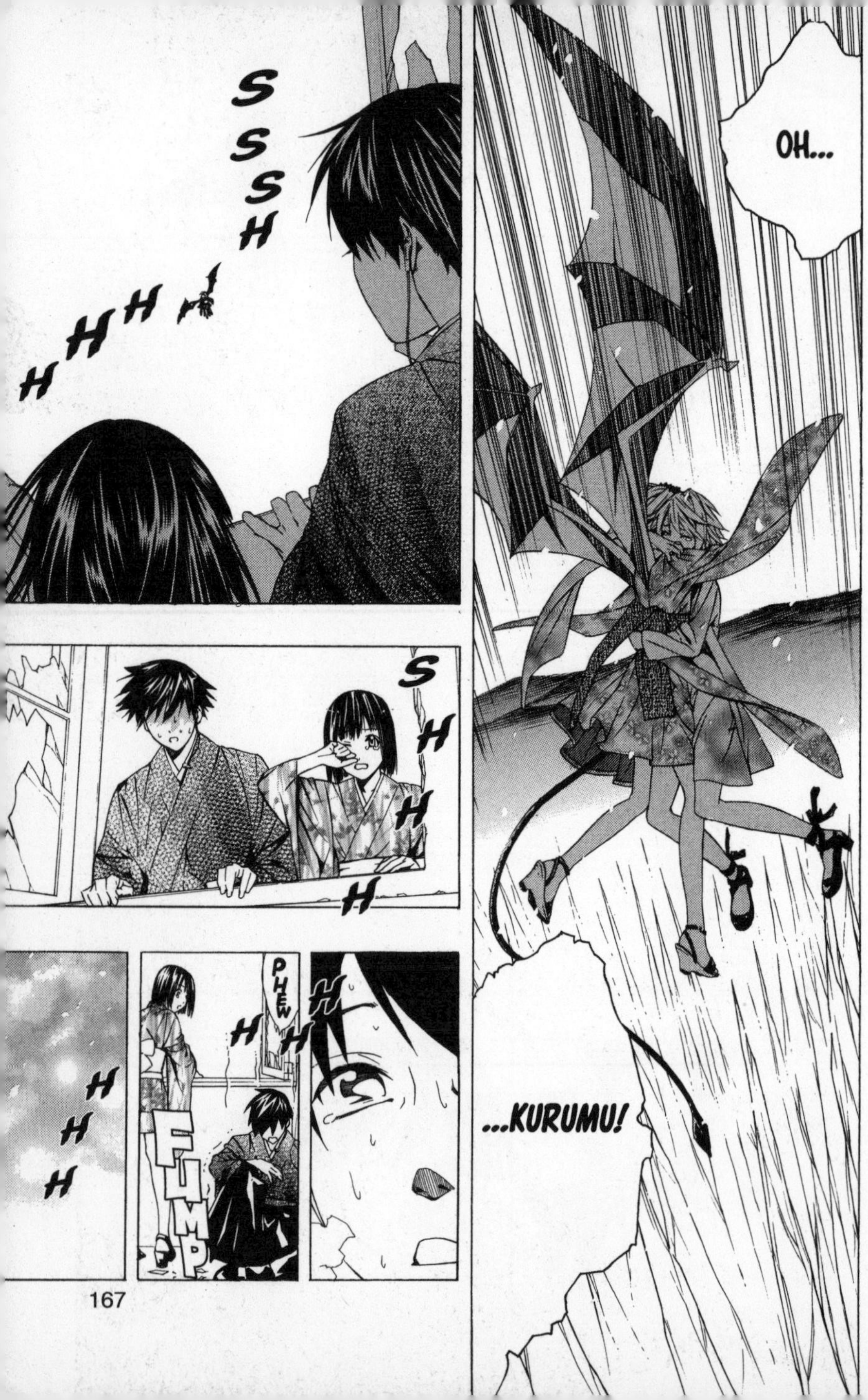
OH...
...KURUMU!
SSSH
HHHH
SHHHH
HH
PHEW
H
FUMP
HHH

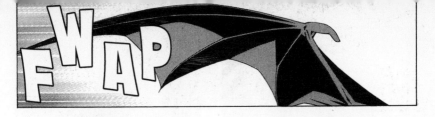

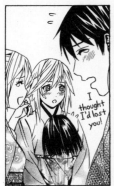

I thought I'd lost you!

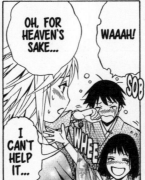

OH, FOR HEAVEN'S SAKE...

WAAAH!

I CAN'T HELP IT...

WHEE

SOB

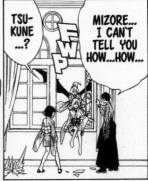

TSU-KUNE ...?

MIZORE... I CAN'T TELL YOU HOW...HOW...

F W P

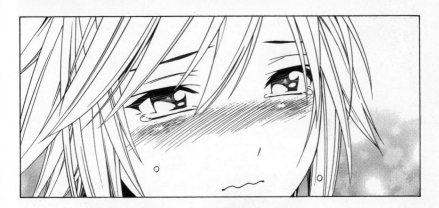

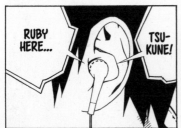

RUBY HERE...

TSU-KUNE!

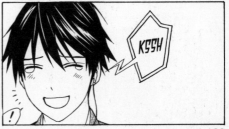

KSSH

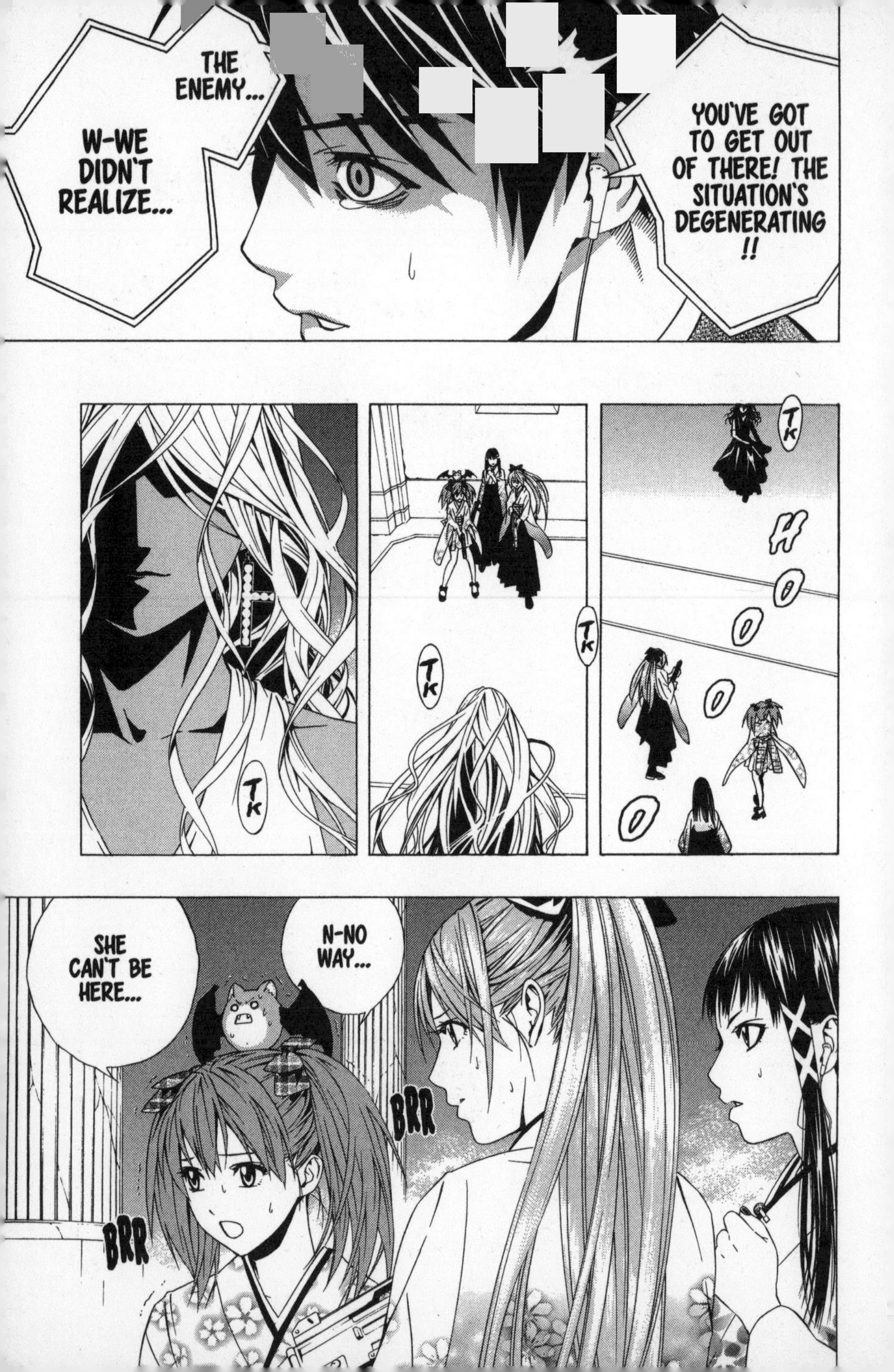
YOU'VE GOT TO GET OUT OF THERE! THE SITUATION'S DEGENERATING!!
THE ENEMY... W-WE DIDN'T REALIZE...
TK
HOOOOOO
TK
TK
TK
N-NO WAY...
SHE CAN'T BE HERE...
BRR
BRR

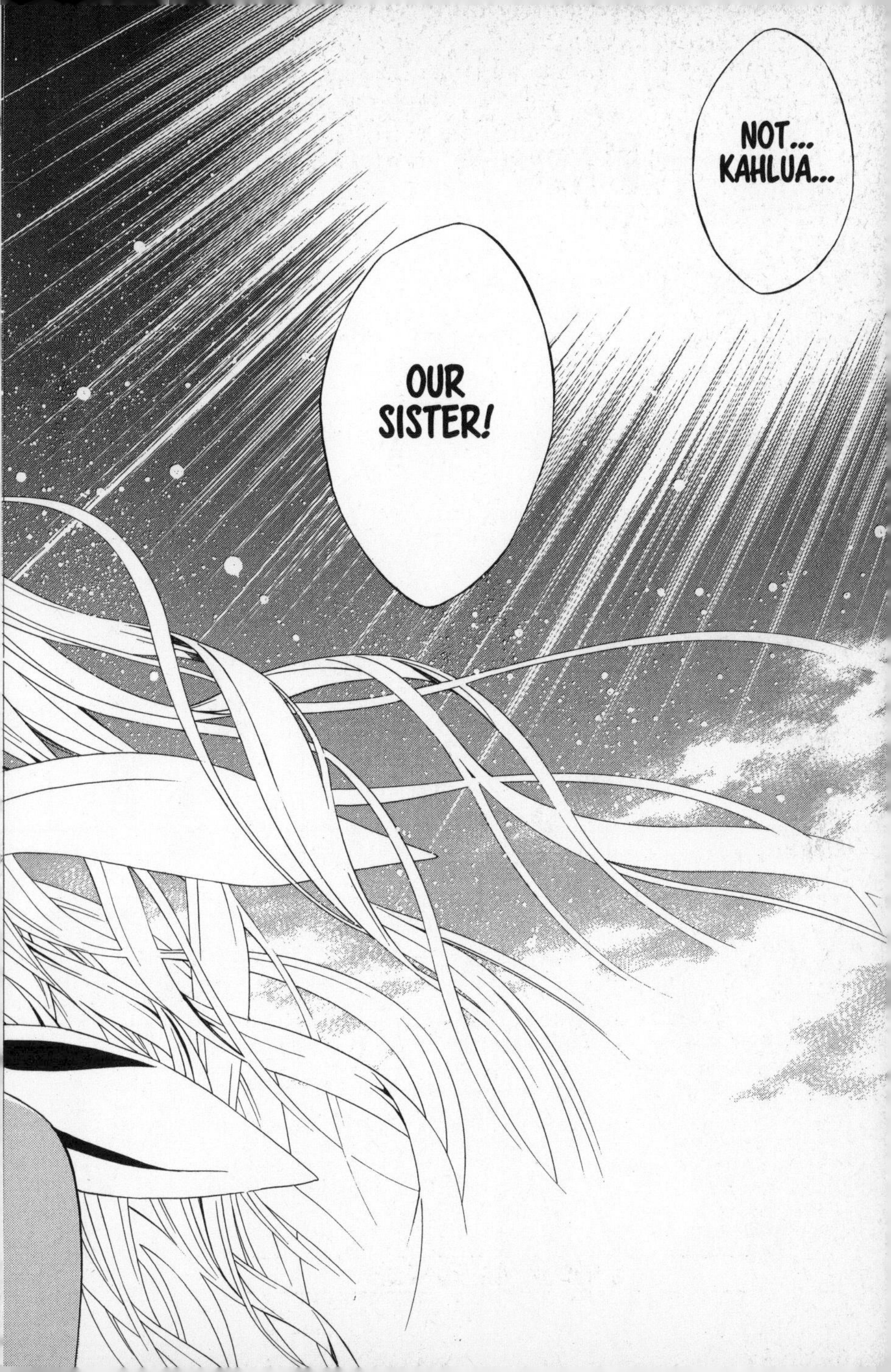
NOT... KAHLUA...
OUR SISTER!

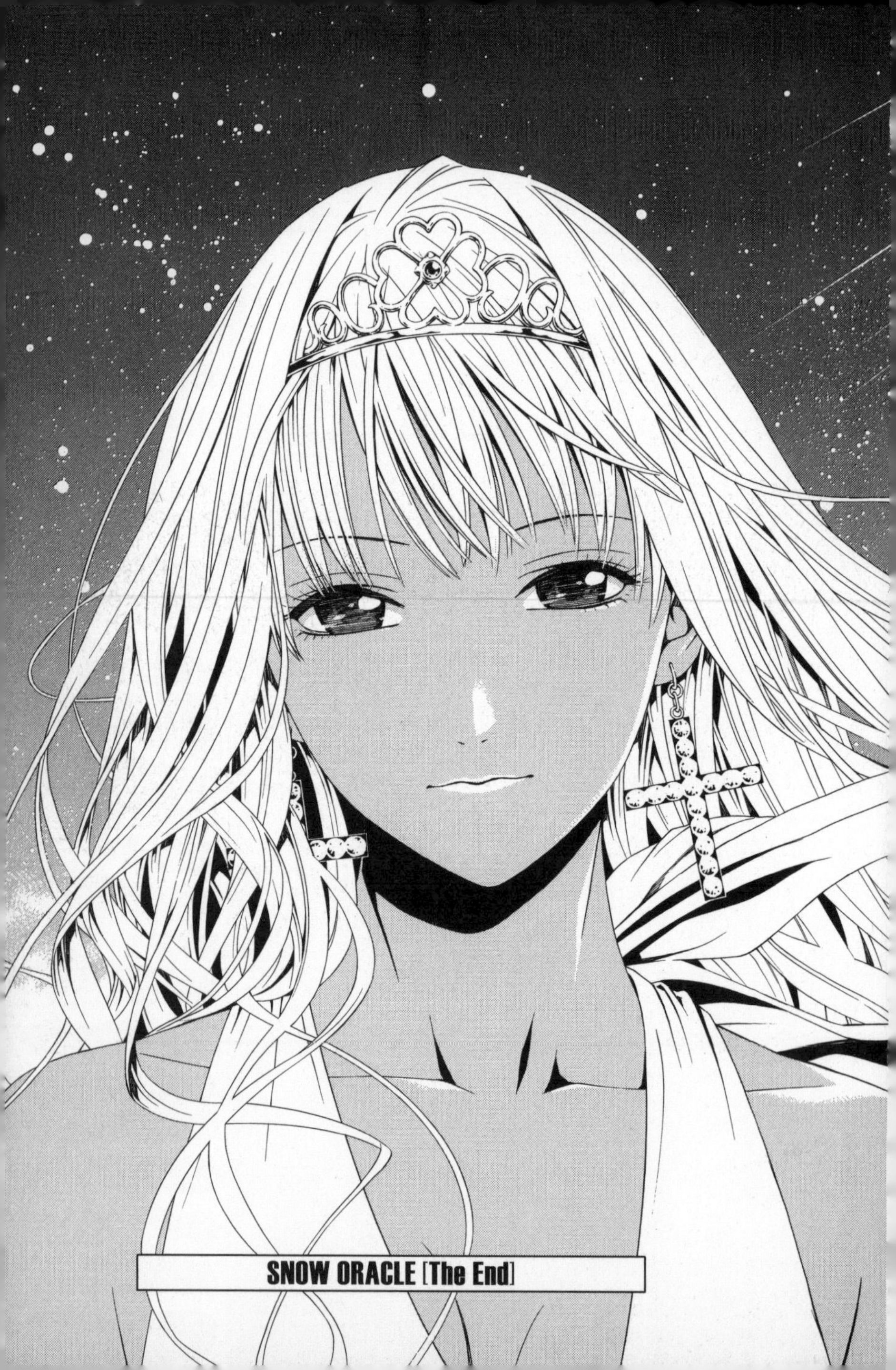
SNOW ORACLE [The End]

ROSARIO+VAMPIRE

Season II

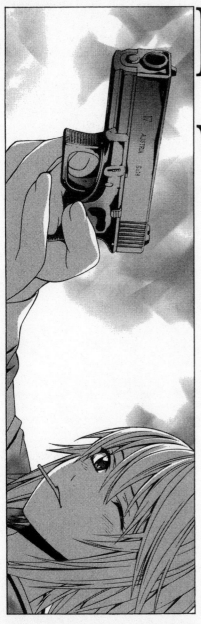

ROSARIO + VAMPIRE

Season II

Meaningless End-of-Volume Theater

III

• Kurumu Gets Prickly •

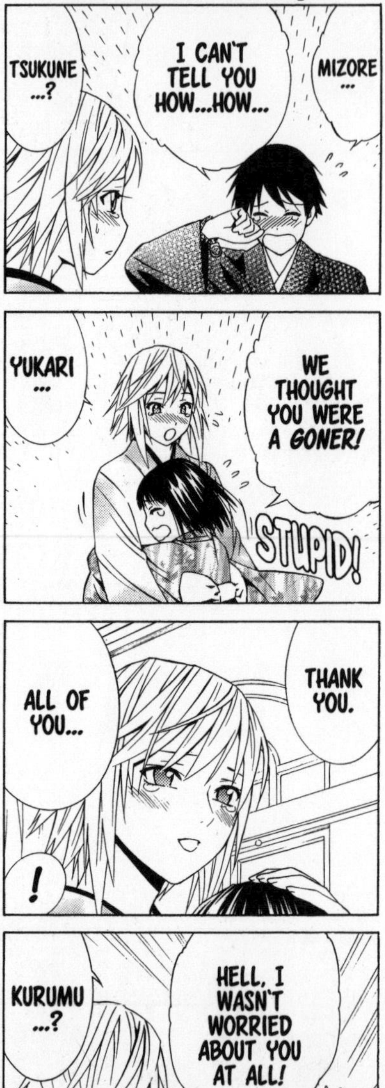
MIZORE ...
I CAN'T TELL YOU HOW...HOW...
TSUKUNE ...?
WE THOUGHT YOU WERE A GONER!
YUKARI ...
STUPID!
THANK YOU.
ALL OF YOU...
!
HELL, I WASN'T WORRIED ABOUT YOU AT ALL!
KURUMU ...?
?

• Kurumu Gets Dreamy •

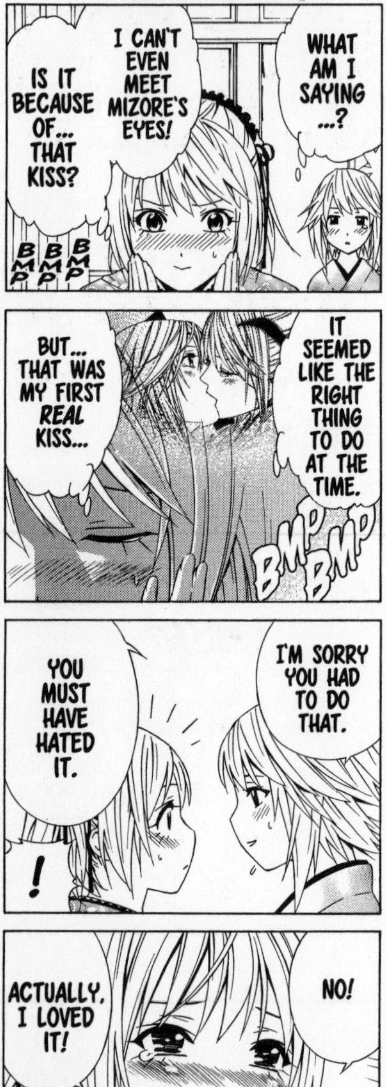
WHAT AM I SAYING ...?
I CAN'T EVEN MEET MIZORE'S EYES!
IS IT BECAUSE OF... THAT KISS?
BMP BMP BMP
IT SEEMED LIKE THE RIGHT THING TO DO AT THE TIME.
BUT... THAT WAS MY FIRST REAL KISS...
BMP BMP
I'M SORRY YOU HAD TO DO THAT.
YOU MUST HAVE HATED IT.
!
NO!
ACTUALLY, I LOVED IT!

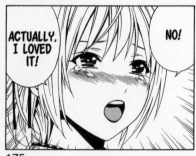

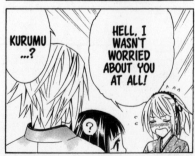

•Happy Ending?•

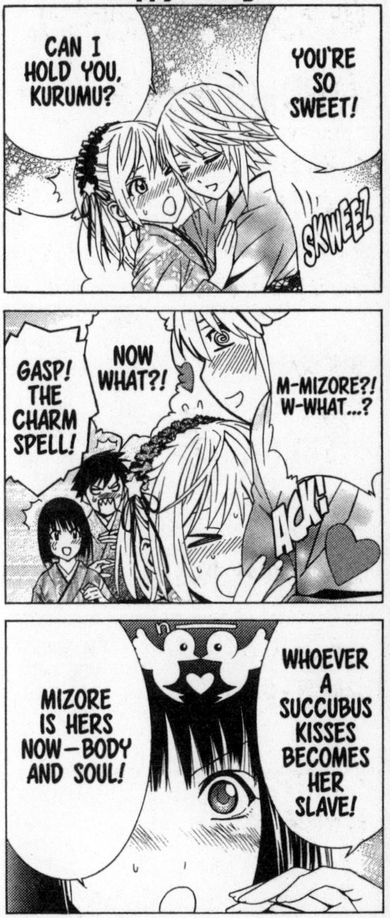
YOU'RE SO SWEET!
CAN I HOLD YOU, KURUMU?
SKWEEZ
M-MIZORE?! W-WHAT...?
NOW WHAT?!
GASP! THE CHARM SPELL!
ACK!
WHOEVER A SUCCUBUS KISSES BECOMES HER SLAVE!
MIZORE IS HERS NOW—BODY AND SOUL!
AND OOOH, HOW I WISH IT WERE ME!
HF
HF
WE CAN'T LEAVE THEM LIKE THIS!
SOME-BODY, STOP THEM!
OHHHH
BLUSH

•Meanwhile, Ms. Tsurara...•

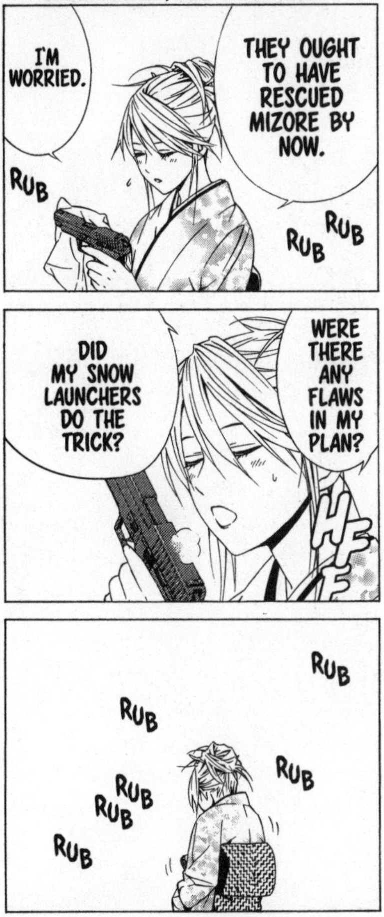
THEY OUGHT TO HAVE RESCUED MIZORE BY NOW.
I'M WORRIED.
RUB
RUB
RUB
WERE THERE ANY FLAWS IN MY PLAN?
DID MY SNOW LAUNCHERS DO THE TRICK?
HFF
RUB
RUB
RUB
RUB
RUB
RUB
OR SHOULD I HAVE DEPLOYED...
...MY SNOW-MACHINE GUN?!
KATATAT
TEE HEE
KATAT

Please send questions and fan letters to ➡ Rosario+Vampire Fan Mail, VIZ Media, P.O. Box 77010, San Francisco, CA 94107

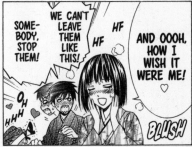

...
Ask me to come too...

Rosario+Vampire

Akihisa Ikeda

• Staff •

Makoto Saito
Kenji Tashiro
Nobuyuki Hayashi

• Help •

Hajime Maeda
Shinichi Miyashita

• 3DCG •

Takaharu Yoshizawa

• Editing •

Makoto Watanabe

• Comic •

Kenju Noro

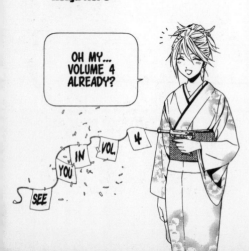

OH MY... VOLUME 4 ALREADY?
SEE YOU IN VOL. 4

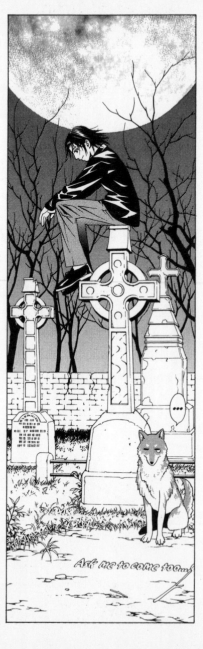

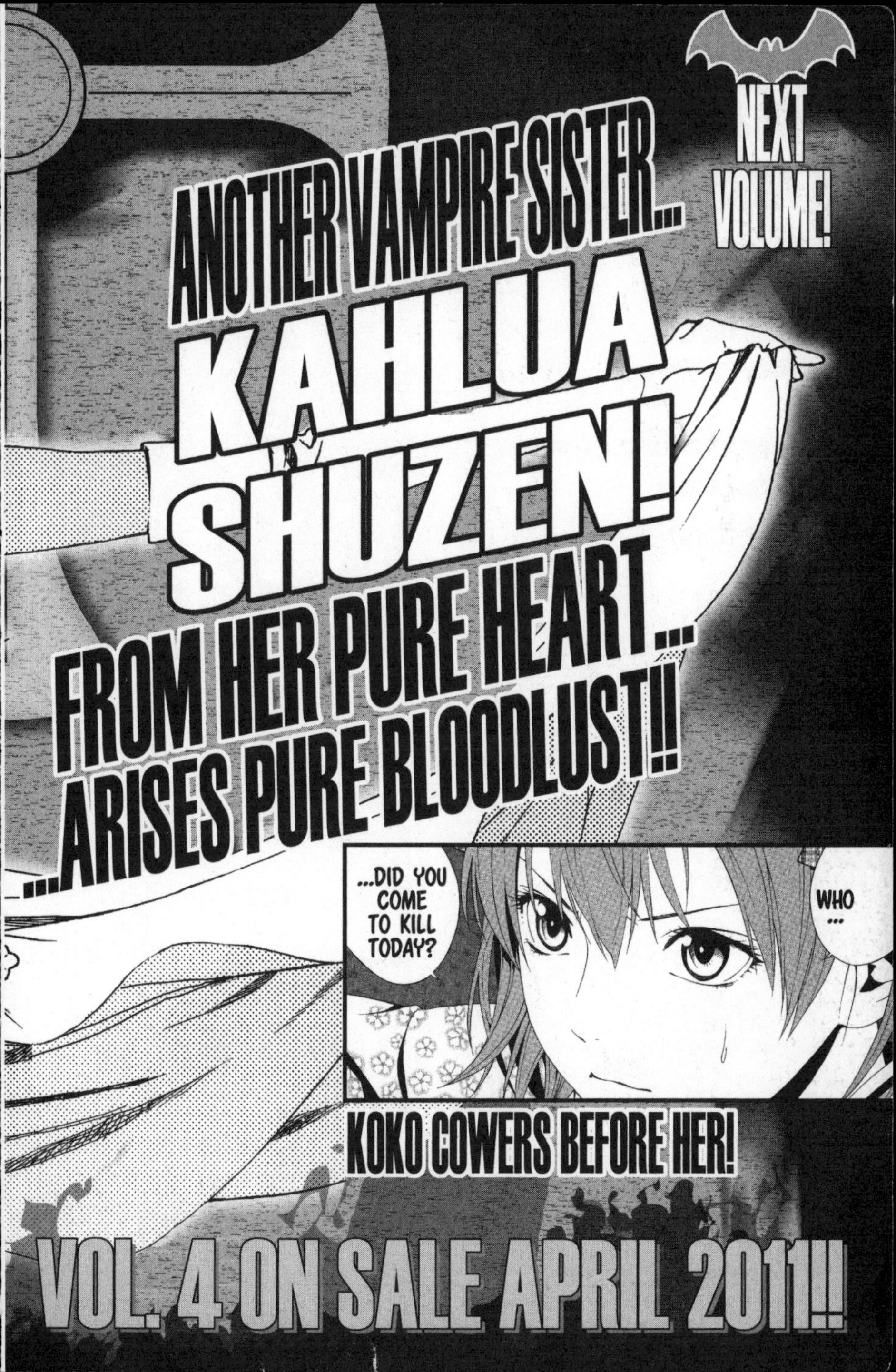
NEXT VOLUME!
ANOTHER VAMPIRE SISTER...
KAHLUA SHUZEN!
FROM HER PURE HEART...
...ARISES PURE BLOODLUST!!
WHO...
...DID YOU COME TO KILL TODAY?
KOKO COWERS BEFORE HER!
VOL. 4 ON SALE APRIL 2011!!

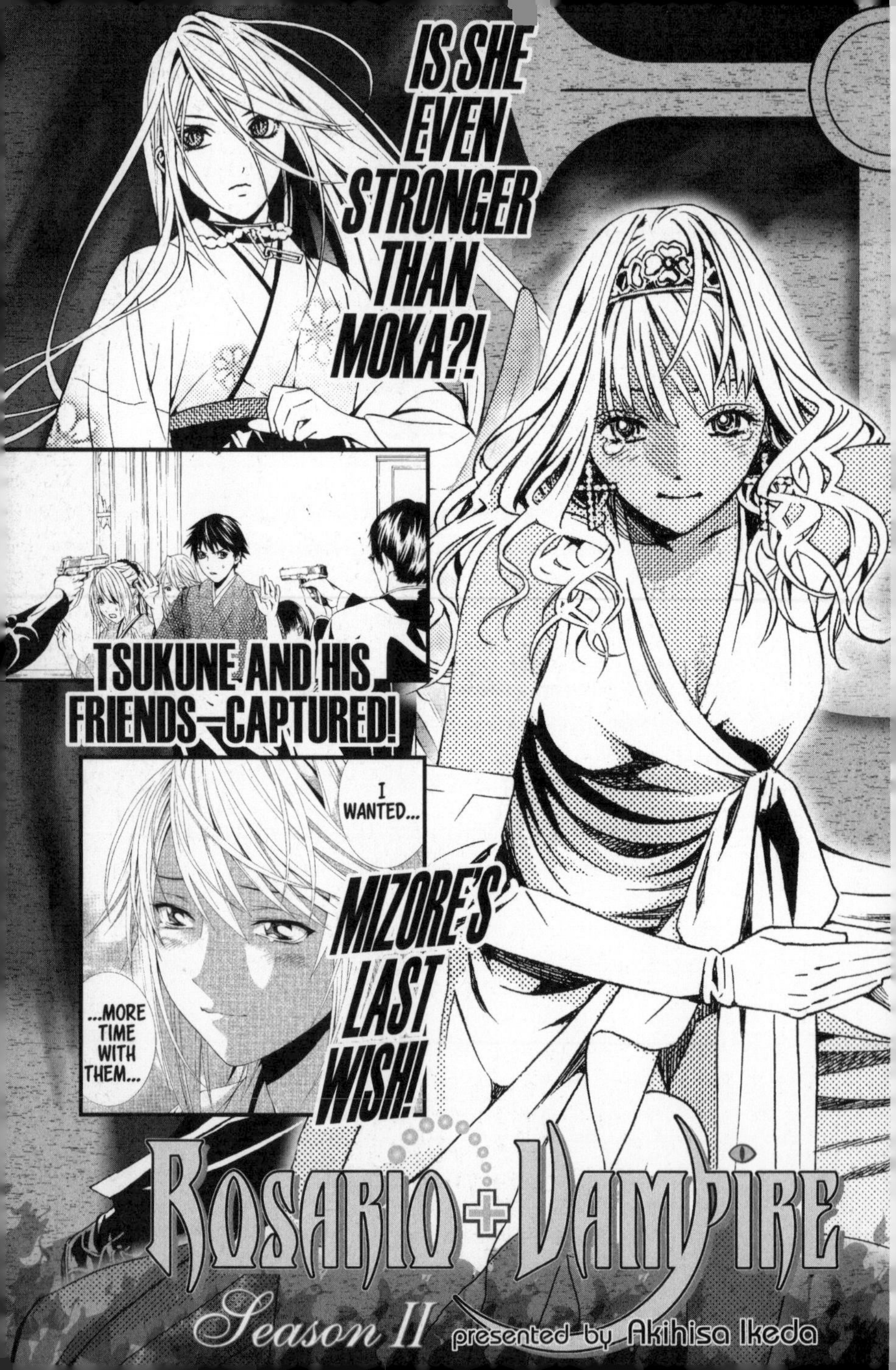
IS SHE EVEN STRONGER THAN MOKA?!
TSUKUNE AND HIS FRIENDS—CAPTURED!
MIZORE'S LAST WISH!
I WANTED...
...MORE TIME WITH THEM...
ROSARIO+VAMPIRE
Season II
presented by Akihisa Ikeda

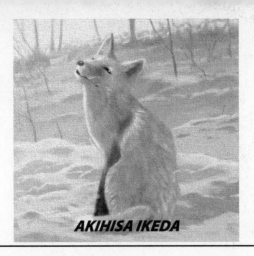

AKIHISA IKEDA

"What kind of story will bring out the best in this character...?" When writing manga, I build from the character. For Miss Nice Girl Moka, I might write a story about acting innocent, or about not being completely honest about the love at the heart of a friendship.

Hmm... What if the story were about Mizore? What would make her shine? From that question was born this volume's saga "Home of the Snow Fairy."

Mizore's unique awkwardness and innocence... I'll be happy if I've been able to capture those qualities...and convey them to you.

Akihisa Ikeda was born in 1976 in Miyazaki. He debuted as a mangaka with the four-volume magical warrior fantasy series *Kiruto* in 2002, which was serialized in *Monthly Shonen Jump*. *Rosario+Vampire* debuted in *Monthly Shonen Jump* in March of 2004 and is continuing in the magazine *Jump Square (Jump SQ)* as *Rosario+Vampire: Season II*. In Japan, *Rosario+Vampire* is also available as a drama CD. In 2008, the story was released as an anime. Season II is also available as an anime now. And in Japan, there is a Nintendo DS game based on the series.

Ikeda has been a huge fan of vampires and monsters since he was a little kid. He says one of the perks of being a manga artist is being able to go for walks during the day when everybody else is stuck in the office.

ROSARIO+VAMPIRE: Season II
3
SHONEN JUMP ADVANCED Manga Edition

STORY & ART BY **AKIHISA IKEDA**

Translation/Kaori Inoue
English Adaptation/Gerard Jones
Touch-up Art & Lettering/Stephen Dutro
Cover Design/Hidemi Sahara
Interior Design/Ronnie Casson
Editor/Annette Roman

Printed in the U.S.A.

Published by VIZ Media, LLC
P.O. Box 77010
San Francisco, CA 94107

10 9 8 7 6 5 4 3 2 1
First printing, December 2010

www.viz.com

www.shonenjump.com

CRYPT SHEET FOR

ROSARIO+VAMPIRE: SEASON II, VOL. 4
INNER GHOUL

TEST 4

TO GET IN TOUCH WITH YOUR INNER GHOUL...

a. go shopping

b. cuddle a teddy bear

c. brains...brains...

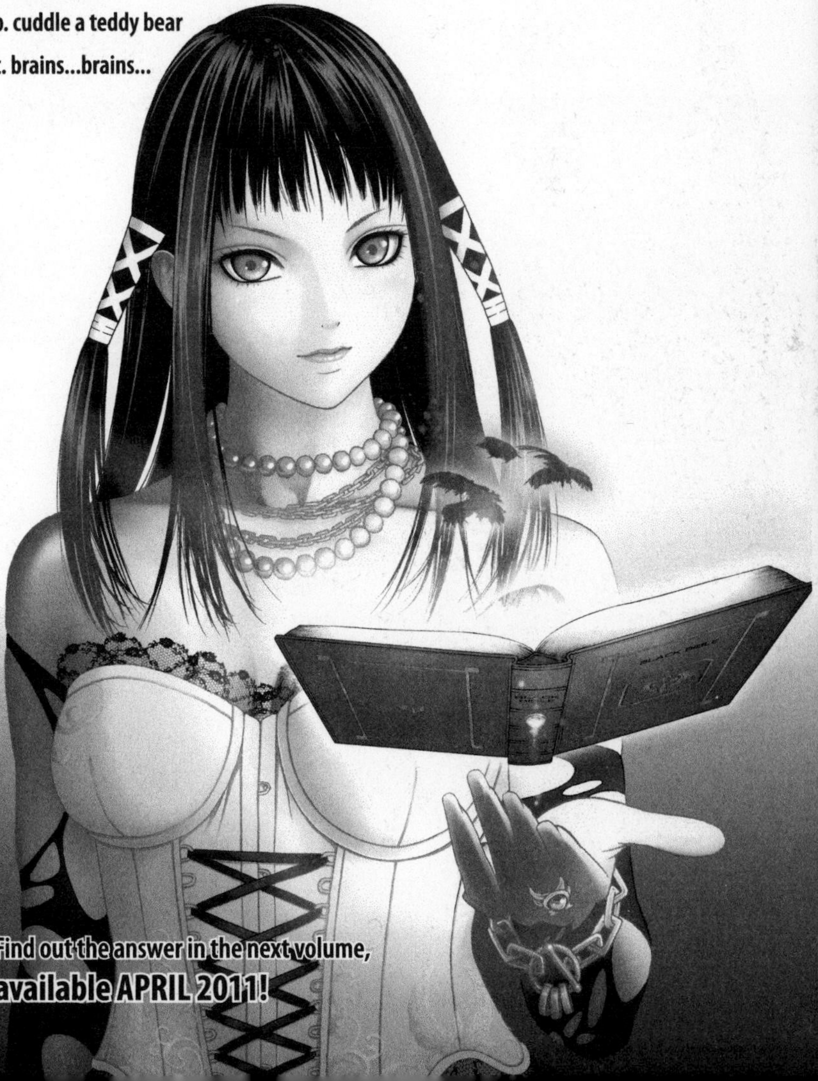

Find out the answer in the next volume,
available APRIL 2011!

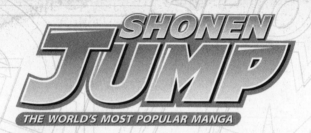
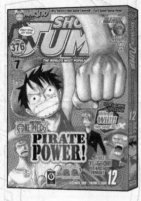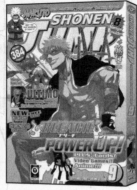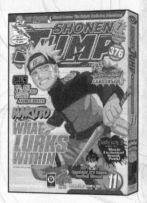

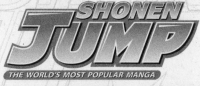

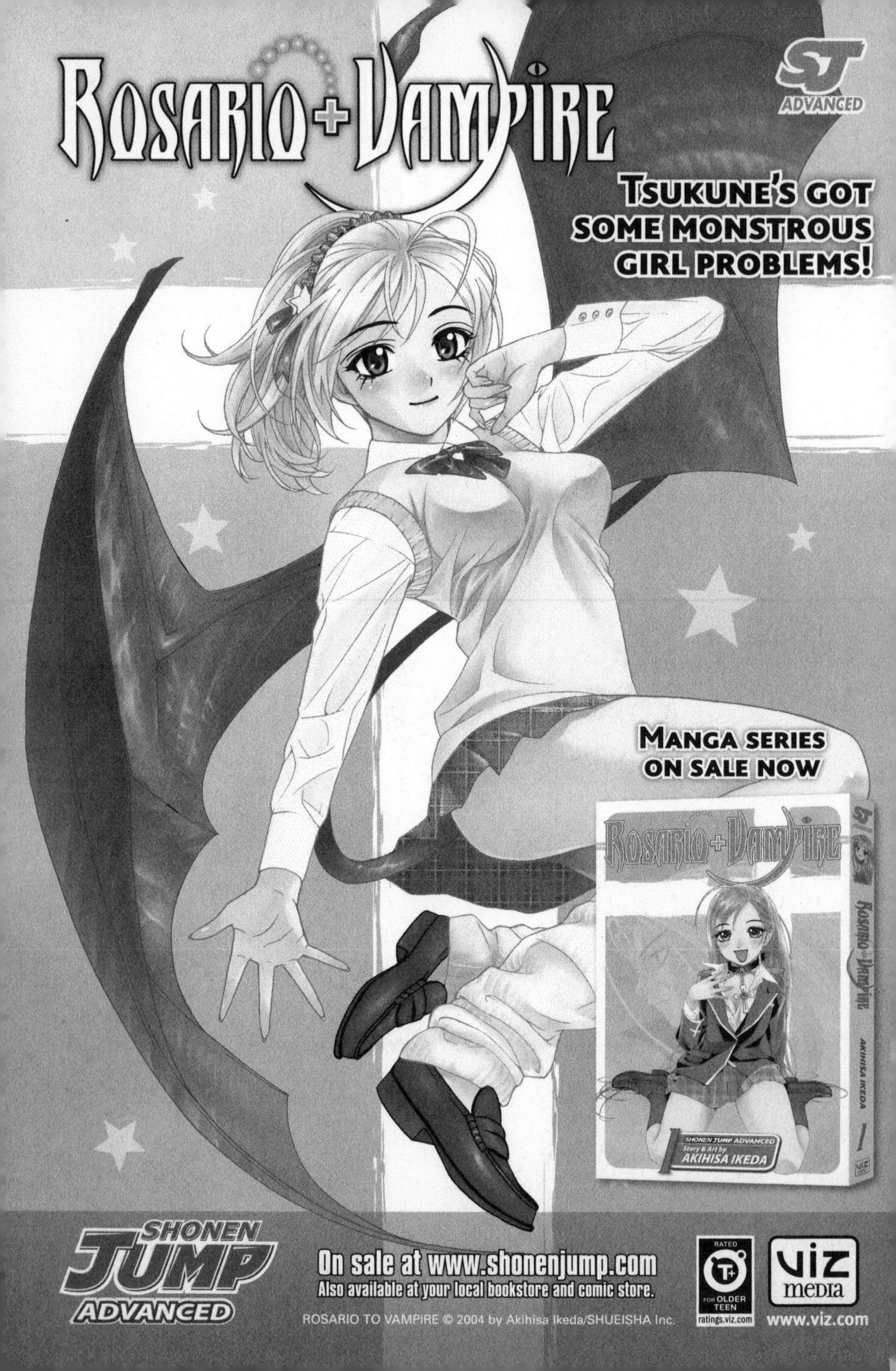

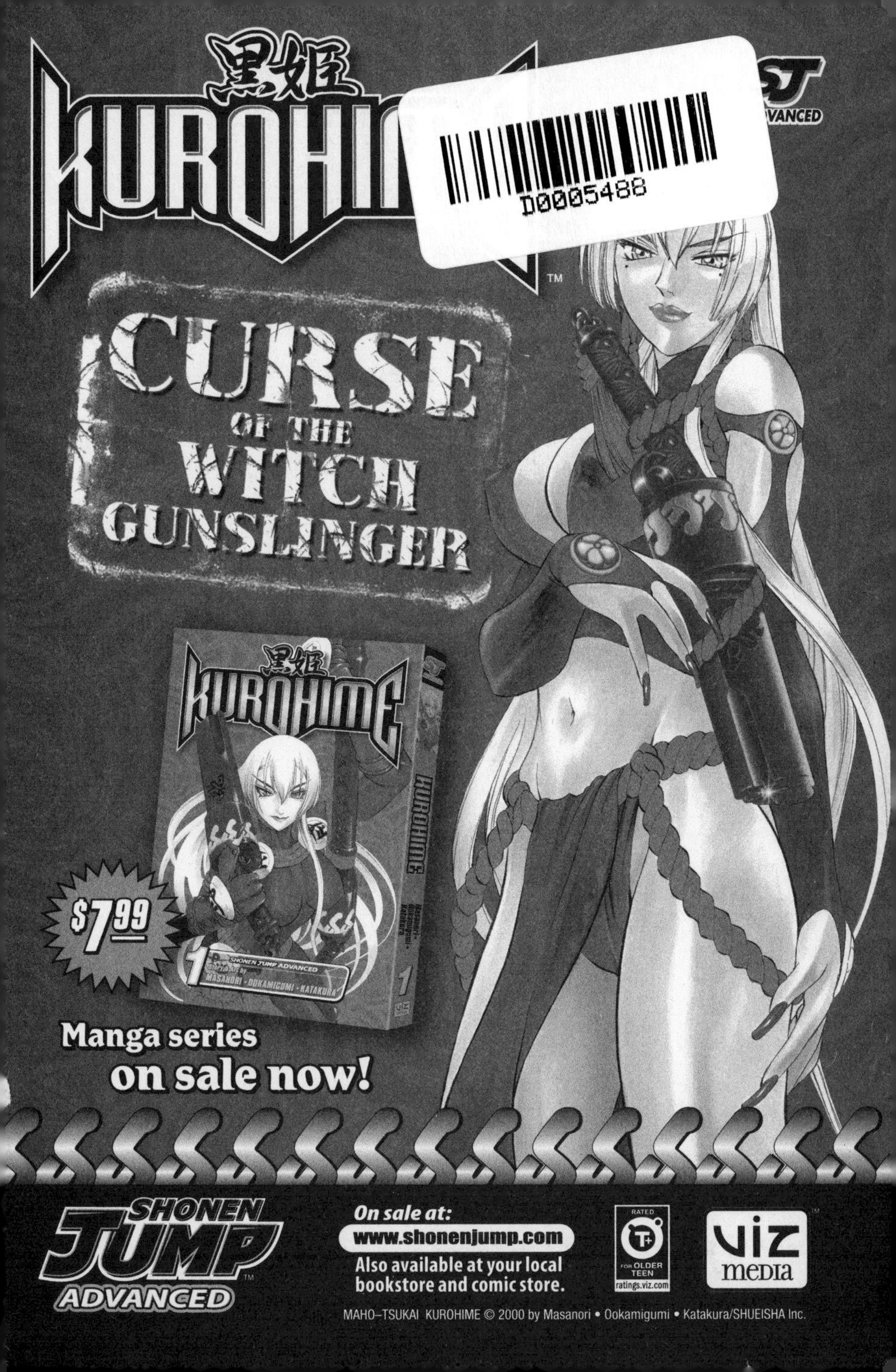
黒姫
KUROHIME™
SJ ADVANCED
CURSE OF THE WITCH GUNSLINGER
KUROHIME
$7.99
Manga series
on sale now!
SHONEN JUMP ADVANCED
On sale at:
www.shonenjump.com
Also available at your local bookstore and comic store.
RATED T+ FOR OLDER TEEN ratings.viz.com
viz media
MAHO–TSUKAI KUROHIME © 2000 by Masanori • Ookamigumi • Katakura/SHUEISHA Inc.